FUNDAMENTALS OF HUMAN COMMUNICATION

ROBERT G. KING

City University of New York

ILLUSTRATED BY PAIGE THOMPSON

FUNDAMENTALS OF HUMAN COMMUNICATION

MACMILLAN PUBLISHING CO., INC.

New York

COLLIER MACMILLAN PUBLISHERS

London

For
Hazel Embry King

P90
K47

Copyright © 1979, Robert G. King

Printed in the United States of America

All rights reserved. No part of this book may be reproduced or transmitted in any form or by any means, electronic or mechanical, including photocopying, recording, or any information storage and retrieval system, without permission in writing from the Publisher.

Macmillan Publishing Co., Inc.
866 Third Avenue, New York, New York 10022

Collier Macmillan Canada, Ltd.

Library of Congress Cataloging in Publication Data

King, Robert G.
  Fundamentals of human communication.

  Includes bibliographies and index.
  1. Communication.   I. Title.
P90.K47   001.5   78-15523
ISBN 0-02-364270-X

Printing: 1 2 3 4 5 6 7 8   Year: 9 0 1 2 3 4 5

PREFACE

SO YOU ARE TAKING a course in communication! Maybe it is a required course at your college or in your curriculum, or maybe you are taking it because you chose to do so. Either way, here you are. What have you gotten into?

Well, for starters, everybody communicates. Indeed, everybody *has* to communicate with other human beings. And surely we all agree that communication is basic and essential. But can it be studied, and can it be improved? This course is based on the belief that it can.

We are going to try to learn how the process of human communication works, what barriers it must overcome, and why breakdowns occur. How can human beings understand themselves and other people, and what prevents them from doing so? How can we influence each other and adapt to each other? How do we see the world, and why do we see it that way? How can we communicate with people who see the world differently from the way we do? These are the kinds of questions this course tries to explore.

What could be more important for each of us than the study—the systematic study—of what is involved in human communication? What could be more practical or relevant to our lives than such a study? No matter what job you get, you must communicate with other human beings. So this course should be useful and valuable to everyone.

I think the basic course in human communication (whatever it is called at your college or university) should provide solid information, and I think the textbook for that course should contain the necessary content—presented as clearly, concretely, and interestingly as possible. The material I have included had to pass this test: What does *every* educated human being need to know about the process of communication? The information, then, applies to a wide variety of communication situations. You should be able to see direct applications of the principles to your everyday life.

Although I have taken research findings into account in writing this book, the book is not a summary of research studies. Such works are helpful for the advanced student or the student majoring in communication. But this book was written for the beginning student. I assume this is the first course you have had in communication. It is an *introductory* text.

I believe every chapter in the text is important to a clear understanding of the fundamentals of human communication, but your instructor may decide to omit a chapter or two or some portion of a chapter. The instructor may also decide to assign the chapters in a different order from the one I have chosen. The order of the chapters makes sense to me, and it is the progression I use in teaching the course, but each instructor organizes material his or her own way. That is as it should be.

I have already said that I think the material we cover in this course is important and practical. I also think it should be enjoyable and stimulating. Let us actively and enthusiastically work together this term. Let's try together to learn how we can understand ourselves and other people better through communication.

I did not write this book, of course, in a vacuum. From my students and colleagues over the years, I have learned much, and I want to acknowledge that debt. I am especially grateful to Professor Jo-Ann Graham of Bronx Community College of the City University of New York for invaluable insights and suggestions. Special thanks are also due Mrs. Norma Polakoff, who generously gave her own time to assist me in this project. To Bill Gibson and Hazel King, who gave needed encouragement, goes my deep appreciation. I am sure you understand my deep gratitude to Paige Thompson, whose charming and fitting illustrations contribute so much to the book. I am indebted to Claire Counihan, the talented designer who provided the logo, layout, and design for the book, and to Susan Greenberg, the production supervisor whose patience, thoroughness, and expertise led and sustained me through the production process; both are dedicated professionals on whom I relied heavily. And I am fortunate to have been assisted in the preparation of this manuscript by Lloyd Chilton, the efficient and empathic executive editor at Macmillan who guided the project to its completion.

R. G. K.

TABLE OF CONTENTS

chapter 3
perception
59

chapter 4
perceiving your self
99

chapter 5
perceiving other selves
139

chapter 6
transmission:
sending oral messages
173

chapter 10
nonspeech communication
253

chapter 11
verbal messages:
purposes, types, and delivery systems
273

chapter 12
verbal messages:
structure and content
297

chapter 13
receiving messages:
observing and listening

1
OVERVIEW OF HUMAN COMMUNICATION

general goal:

To learn some basic terms related to the study of communication.

specific objectives:

After completing this unit, you should understand:

What communication, human communication, and speech communication are.

What the five levels of human communication are.

The concepts of commonality and individuality as related to human communication.

The three functions that human communication performs.

The difference between efficiency and effectiveness in human communication.

The vocal, verbal, and visual components of human speech communication.

The different ways in which we use the term *messages* in human communication.

The difference between primary and metacommunication.

What feedback is and how it works.

The difference between signal and symbol responses.

Barriers and breakdowns in human communication.

As you probably noticed, this book is not called *Fundamentals of Speech* or *Fundamentals of Public Speaking* or *Fundamentals of Speech Improvement.* Most colleges have courses to help you work on the way you speak every day; they also have courses to help you learn how to speak in front of an audience. But this book is not designed for such courses. Some people need to learn to speak a different way from the way they first learned; some people will need to learn the techniques of public speaking because they will have to talk in front of groups of people. But this book is designed for courses about something that *all people*—not just *some* people—need to know about: human communication.

Not everybody will have to talk in front of groups of people; not everyone will have to take part in discussions and committee decisions; not everybody will have to speak the Status Dialect of American English. But everybody *will* have to communicate. No matter what job you get, no matter what position in life you hold, you *will* have to communicate with other human beings, won't you? Then this course is practical and useful for you. It is about communication—everyday, real-life communication.

But what is *communication*? We use the word all the time, but what does it mean? You've heard people say, "We get along because we are able to communicate." Or "That professor talks a lot, but he doesn't seem to communicate." And Cool Hand Luke said, "What we have here is a failure to communicate!" So the word *communication* is a common word. But what does it mean?

In its broadest sense, the word *communication* refers to a process in which a response is evoked (or elicited or induced) by a message sent and received. There are three necessary elements, then, according to that definition: sending a message, receiving a message, and responding to the message. If that is our definition, it is certainly very broad. In that sense of the word *communication,* flipping a switch to turn on a light, pushing a button to ring a bell, the thermostat turning on a furnace, or a computer starting another machine are all examples of communication. Think about each of those examples. Was a message sent? How? Was a message received? How? Was there a response to the message received? In each case, a message *was* sent, a message *was* received, and the receiver *did* react to the message. So communication occurred.

That is communication in the broadest sense of the word. Then, in that sense, machines can communicate with other machines, can't they? Of course. And animals—the lower animals—can communicate, too, can't they? Of course. There are many examples of animal communication. Bees do a kind of dance, and the other bees find out where the food supply is. Mama pigs can tell the difference between baby pigs' squeals for "I'm hurt" and "I'm hungry." Some ants can organize themselves into an army quickly by communicating through touch. The messages may be simple, but there are messages sent and received, and the receivers respond to those messages. Clearly, these animals are communicating, as we have defined the word.

Human communication is communication in which a human being is involved, either as a sender or a receiver (or both). There are writers who have commented that human beings are really *transceivers*—combination transmitters and receivers all built into one unit. And we are transceivers, aren't we? We can transmit and receive at the same time. But more about that later.

Back to human communication—in which a human being is involved either as a sender or receiver. If you yell at your cat Anathema, and the cat runs and hides, there is human communication (there is a human sender). If you see a painting and react to it, there is human communication; or if you listen to a song and respond, there too is human communication. If you grip my hand or slap my face and I understand your feelings, there is human communication. In all of these instances, a human being is involved in the communication process; in the gripping and slapping examples, there are two human beings involved in the communication process.

In this course, we will be concerned only with communication within and between human beings. Communication between people and animals or objects—though it too is human communication—is not at the center of our focus. There are five levels on which human communication takes place.

five levels of human communication

Intrapersonal

At this level, communication takes place inside a human being. *Intra* means *within* or *inside*. Can communication happen *inside* one human being? Can a person be both the sender and receiver of the message—and the responder also? Yes, if you think about it. As a matter of fact, when you think, you are communicating inside yourself, aren't you? You are sending messages to yourself—not that you are talking or making noises, but you are sending and receiving messages. So the same human being is on both ends of the communication process! Actually, intrapersonal communication is very complicated, because the brain sends messages to parts of the body all the time, and there are messages coming in to the brain from all over the body as well.

Interpersonal

If communication takes place *between* human beings, then the interaction level is interpersonal. *Inter* means *between*. (*Inter*collegiate sports, you remember, are sports played between colleges, while *intra*mural sports are those played inside the same college.) Interpersonal communication is person-to-person communication; two people are involved in the process.

I do not want to give you the impression that person-to-person communication means that one person only sends messages and another person only receives messages. We are, as I mentioned earlier, transceivers. Each person involved in an interpersonal communication situation is both a transmitter *and* a receiver of messages. "But," you say, "what if only one of the two people talks? Then we have only one sender and only one receiver, don't we?" No. Think about it a moment. Even if only one of the two people speaks, doesn't that person get messages from the other person, even without words from that person? There are physical stimuli coming back to the speaker from that person (certainly visible and possibly vocal ones). The speaker picks up those cues and interprets them, so the speaker is not only a transmitter but a receiver of messages. By the same token, the "listener," without saying a word, did transmit messages, so that person also is both a receiver and a transmitter.

In interpersonal communication, when there are two people communicating, there are two transmitters of messages and two receivers of messages. One person is not the actor and the other the reactor; the two people are interacting. That is what interpersonal communication is all about.

Another level of human communication occurs when a person sends a message to a group of receivers at the same time. If you talk to your class, then you are communicating on this level; when the teacher talks to the class, person-to-group communication is taking place. You can think of many other examples, I am sure.

Person-to-Group

Can a group of people send a message to a single person? Yes. Indeed, if the class reacts as a group to your speech or the class reacts as a group to the teacher's lecture, then group-to-person communication has taken place. Can you think of other examples? What if you become ill and the class sends you a get-well card? Or what if a committee of the student government summons you to testify before them? Better, what if the officers of the student government notify you that they have selected you for the year's top honor? All are examples of group-to-person communication, but you can doubtless think of better ones.

Group-to-Person

Communication can occur at this level also. A country can send a message to another country. My union sends messages to the Board of Higher Education all the time, and the board sends the union messages in return. What other groups can you think of that communicate with each other?

Those are the five levels on which human communication takes place. Let us turn to the *two bases* of human communication.

Group-to-Group

bases of human communication

Commonality

If you look at the word *communication*, what word do you almost see in the first six letters? That's right: *common*. The word communication is related to other words with the same root: commune, communal, community, for example. Communication has to do with finding something in common. Human communication involves sharing—sharing meanings, sharing ideas, sharing understandings, sharing experiences—finding something in common! That is the basis of all communication: two human beings (or more) finding something in common—as human beings.

When two individuals communicate, they each bring to the communication situation their own accumulated experience, and each sends and receives messages out of that field of experience. To the extent that their fields of experience overlap, at least to the extent that their accumulated experiences are similar, they have a solid basis for communicating. If they had no common experience at all, then they would have nothing in common at all, and they could not communicate.

Of course, all human beings have some experiences in common. We all share some basic drives and needs. We are all mortal; we are all in the process of living and dying. Shakespeare gave his character Shylock words to remind us that all human beings, including members of a persecuted minority, have many things in common.

> I am a Jew. Hath not a Jew eyes? Hath not a Jew hands, organs, dimensions, senses, affections, passions? Fed with the same food, hurt with the same weapons, subject to the same diseases, healed by the same means, warmed and cooled by the same winter and summer, as a Christian is? If you prick us, do we not bleed? If you tickle us, do we not laugh? If you poison us, do we not die?
>
> *The Merchant of Venice*, Act III, Scene 1

It is clearly true that all human beings have some things in common. It is equally clear that some human beings have more in common than others do. The more in tune the communicators are, the more their fields of experience are in essential harmony, the more easily they can communicate effectively.

We tend to communicate most with people whom we perceive to be similar to ourselves. Partly for that reason, those people (who are most similar to us) will have the greatest influence on us, and they are the ones we will have the greatest chance to influence as well. If the communicators share a common background, common beliefs, common values, common attitudes, a common language, and common meanings, they have a basis for successful communication.

Individuality

Just as we must find something in common if we are to communicate, so also we must take into account the fact that all human beings are different.

We must allow for and accept differences, and we must face the nature of the other person (or persons) involved in the process of communication with us. And we must face our own nature as well. We each come to the communication event as human beings, having some commonalities with all other human beings and having many commonalities with some human beings. But we also come to that communication event as individuals with unique backgrounds and experiences and outlooks. Though it is more difficult to communicate with people who are quite different from ourselves, it is often necessary (and useful) to do so. If we are to succeed, we must develop *empathy*—the ability to look at the world from the other person's point of view, to see things as the other person sees them. We must try to develop insights into fields of experience very different from our own. Those insights also are an essential basis for successful communication.

Tony and Allen grew up in the same neighborhood in the same Southern town, attended the same elementary school, were members of the same Baptist church, sang together in the same choir for years, attended the same public high school and the same Baptist college, worked at the same supermarket in the summers, and majored in the same subject (business) at college. Both sets of parents were active in the church and in the local Democratic party organization; both sets of parents were college-educated and would be considered middle-class. When, during his sophomore year at college, Tony began having doubts about his religious faith, he decided to discuss the matter with Allen. How well would they have been able to communicate on the subject?

On the other hand, Allen met a young lady from Philadelphia the summer after his sophomore year at college. She was in town visiting a relative. Allen found her very attractive, but she was from a large city—a large Northern city, at that; she was a devout Roman Catholic and had only attended church-related schools; her family was relatively wealthy and staunchly Republican. Allen asked her for a date, and she accepted. How well do you think they might have communicated on that first date? How could they have used both common ground and individual differences as the bases of their interaction?

functions of human communication

We are ready now to turn our attention to the three *functions* (or uses) of human communication. Here we are concerned with what human communication does, what it is used for. (Do not confuse function with *purpose*. Something's *function* is what it, by its very nature, does; *purpose* has to do with the intention or goal of the user. The function of a typewriter is to type symbols on paper; I may use my typewriter to accomplish a wide variety of purposes.) There are three broad functions that human communication performs:

Development of Mental Processes

If you isolate a normal baby from human contact and communication and provide that baby only with necessary life support (feeding, clothing, bathing, and so on), will the child's mind develop? Will the child learn much? Will the child develop speech and language? Not much. To develop your mind, you need speech communication with and from other human beings. That is one of the basic uses of communication for us human beings—to help us develop our own minds. Communication with other people is necessary for intellectual growth. Just think how much you know from first-hand experience and how much of what you know you learned from other people. That should stagger your imagination, to think how dependent we are on communication for our learning, for our mental development.

Adjustment to Environment

Your environment, of course, is everything that is around you—including people. Adjustment means adaptation, fitting yourself in. Everybody works to fit into the world, to adapt, to adjust, to get along, to survive. And communication—message-sending and message-receiving—helps us in that process. I send messages to other people that help me get along with them, reduce tensions between us, and fit myself into their expectations and desires. And you doubtless send messages to the rest of us that help you get along with us. You and I also receive messages from other human beings that assist us in surviving and in accommodating to the world around us. It is through interaction (communication) with other human beings that we are assimilated; through interaction, we are changed, molded, modified so we will fit in with the people around us; we are thus, in the terms of psychology, *socialized*.

Of course, this process of adaptation continues from the time one is born until one dies. Throughout our lives, we are being modified through interaction, so it is probably more accurate to say that we are becoming socialized than to say we have become socialized. That is one of the basic functions of human communication—to help us adjust to the world we find ourselves living in.

Manipulation of Environment

Manipulation is not a bad word; it just means *trying to influence.* And everybody tries to influence the world and the people in it; isn't that true? Don't you say to someone if you find the room too warm, "Why don't you open the window a little?" You are using speech communication to adjust the world around you to fit you a bit more.

In the second function of communication that we listed, adjustment to environment, it was the other way around: communication helped fit you into the world. Here communication is helping you make the environment adjust to you! Or, put another way, the major difference between the second function and this one is the direction of modification or change. In the second function, the adjustment function, *we* change; we are modified; we are influenced. In the manipulation function, we communicate in order to change, modify, or influence the world (including other human beings) around us. In the manipulation function, communication is used as a means of controlling and regulating the environment.

Recently, some friends brought their fifteen-day-old baby to my house for a visit. Bill put the baby down on the couch for a while, but it was not long before the baby whimpered. Bill rushed over, picked up the child, and held her. Nichole hushed her complaining cry instantly. At fifteen days, she did not have language, but she could communicate. And she could already use communication to control her environment and make it adjust to her! That is the third function of human communication.

goals of human communication

We have looked at the uses, or functions, of human communication. Now we should look at the *two goals* of human communication. What are our targets? How do we judge whether our communication was successful? There are two aims or goals we strive for in communication, and therefore there are two tests by which we can evaluate the success of any interaction. These I have labeled *efficiency* and *effectiveness*.

Efficiency

The first goal in human communication is to be understood, to stir up a meaning in the receiver that is as close as possible to the meaning the sender intended when he or she sent the message in the first place. Here the question is: Did the listener *understand* the message? Did the message convey the ideas to the receiver that the sender wanted conveyed? If so, the communication was *efficient*. It was understood.

We do not send ideas through the air to other people. (I will explain the process in much more detail in the next chapter.) Instead, we send messages that stand for the ideas. Those messages represent our ideas, but they are not ideas themselves. We must stimulate ideas in the heads of other people. We induce ideas, but we do not transmit them. Receivers, then, take the incoming physical stimuli (the transmitted message) and attach meaning to them. Meanings do not come packaged in the messages. Meanings are attached, meanings are assigned, meanings are attributed by the communicators. The question we are addressing here is: Did the receiver attach, assign, or attribute a meaning similar to that of the sender? If the receiver understood the message essentially as the sender understood the message, then the communication was efficient.

If you ask the idol of your eye to marry you and that person says, "Not in a million years would I marry you!" the message was understood, though rejected. The communication was efficient, because the listener certainly had a correct and clear idea of what the sender wanted. Just because the person refused what you may have considered a very gracious offer doesn't mean the message was not understood! And understanding is the test of efficiency in communication.

Effectiveness

Of course, if you send a message in hopes of a particular response, you want that message to work. You not only want the message to be understood; you want the message to elicit the desired reaction. You hope to achieve your purpose, to get the response you want.

In the example I gave you before, the listener understood the message (the proposal of marriage), but the listener said no. The receiver did not respond as the sender had wished. The communication was efficient, but not effective. To be effective, the receiver of the message must give the response that the sender desired. That desired response is the test of effectiveness in communication.

So far, we have talked about human communication in general. Much of this course is about human *speech communication*—which, as you can tell, is a narrower term. But before discussing speech communication, we should note a few things about our approach to human communication in general.

There is one important characteristic of our definition of communication: our definition of communication is *receiver*-oriented. We have placed the receiver, rather than the sender, at the center of our focus on communication. That is no accident. I consider the receiver central. For communication to take place, as we have defined it, something or someone must receive a message and respond to it. Transmission alone does not make communication. No matter how much transmitting goes on, no matter how great the sender and the message may be, no matter how magnificent the techniques used in transmitting the message—if the message is not received and responded to, communication does not occur.

Let us put this concept on the human level. No matter how much talking or shouting or gesticulating you do, if there is no other person to receive the message and respond to it, there is no *inter*personal communication. There must, in interpersonal communication, be another person to hear and/or see your message in order to react to it.

Look at this example. Your plane has crashed on a desert island in the Pacific Ocean. You are the sole survivor of the crash. You are trying to attract the attention of passing aircraft and ships in order to get help. No one hears your calls or sees your signals. There was no interpersonal communication. No other person received your message and responded in any way. Was there any human communication at all? Well, there was doubtless intrapersonal communication. You monitored the message, and you would doubtless respond to the frustrating, ineffectual efforts. So there would be reception and response (and therefore communication), but it would not be interpersonal.

There is another implication of this receiver-oriented definition of communication. If two human beings are aware of each other, communication will occur. Think about it. If two people are in each other's presence, each will be aware of the other and the other's behavior, right? Then both will react to the behavior they perceive. Some reaction is inevitable, isn't it? Then communication is taking place. In that sense, any time two people are together, it is impossible for communication *not* to take place! Any time a human being attaches significance (meaning) to incoming physical stimuli and reacts, communication has occurred. Again, however, note that the emphasis is on the receiver/reactor in the communication process.

Let's look at an example. Suppose I meet my class in fundamentals of human communication and give what I consider one of my greatest lectures. The students are inattentive and restless. Most of them (perhaps all of them) do not understand the point of the lecture. An objective test would show that they did not master the material I thought I was presenting. Is communication taking place? Yes, it is. The students are reacting—even if they are not responding as I might have hoped. They are taking in some physical stimuli, interpreting them in some way, and responding. I certainly cannot claim that *no* communication is taking place, just because I am not accomplishing my objectives. From my point of view, the communication was not effective, but there has been communication! Also, I am bound to be aware of the class's negative reaction to the lecture. I will see them squirming in their seats, shuffling their papers, and tapping their pencils and pens on the desks. I may also note the blank stares and the furrowed brows. I will interpret those stimuli and react to them in some way. Communication—two-way communication, interaction—is clearly going on.

A third implication of the receiver-oriented definition of communication is that communication can occur quite apart from the intention of the sender. Even if a message-sender has a conscious purpose in mind (a goal he or she wants to accomplish in the communication situation), the sender may send unintended messages and reach unintended receivers. Actually, a better way of stating this idea might be that intended receivers may get unintended messages and that unintended receivers may also get messages.

Again, let us look at an illustration. Professor O. Y. Knott plans to go on a picnic with some friends immediately after teaching his afternoon class. To save time, he dresses in old clothes for the outing, and he wears them to class without giving any explanation. Several members of the class get a message from the professor's appearance. Some think him disrespectful to the class; some think he has "flipped out"; some think he has come upon particularly hard times. Professor Knott did not intend to send any of these "messages" to his students. Indeed, he is not aware that any of the students are getting these messages. He does intend to send messages to his students, but these are not the messages he intends to convey or thinks he is conveying.

In that lecture, Professor Knott uses a hypothetical example to illustrate some point. He says to the class, "How would you react if I were suddenly to start shouting, 'Professor Gadd is crazy! E. E. Gadd is totally insane! Gadd is crazy as a loon!'?" The door of the classroom is open, and a student walking down the hall hears Professor Knott shouting, "E. E. Gadd is totally insane! Gadd is crazy as a loon!" The message was not intended for that student, but he heard it anyway. Of course, he heard only part of the lecture, but he *did* get a message. Can you imagine how he reacted—especially in view of his devotion to Professor Gadd?

We need to keep in mind that the sender may be unaware of what message the receiver really got; that the message the receiver received may not be the message intended by the sender at all; that an unintended receiver may pick up the message without the sender's knowledge; and that the receiver's response may be entirely different from the one the sender wanted to get.

These reminders apply to all human communication. But what of speech communication? What is *speech*?

speech

Speech is the *act* of producing audible, visible, and verbal symbols. Speech is something you *do*. It is an action; it is an activity. That action involves something that our bodies do (so there is a physiological factor); something produced that can be heard (so there is an acoustic factor); and something produced that can be seen (so there is an ocular factor). In a very real sense, speech is a series of bodily movements made audible and visible.

elements of speech

There are three elements in *human speech communication:* the vocal element, the visible element, and the verbal element. Let us look at each of these components or elements one at a time.

Vocal

The vocal element of speech has to do with the use of the human voice. The voice *itself* (apart from the words used by the sender) sends us messages. There are four aspects of voice that can be varied: pitch (highness or lowness), volume (loudness or softness), rate (fastness or slowness), and quality (tone color or character or texture). You can change these aspects of voice and the changes will send messages to the listener. You know that you get messages not only from what a speaker says (the words) but from the way the speaker says it (the voice—the vocal element). You can probably say the single word *yes* a dozen different ways, varying the vocal element and thus changing the meaning. Try it and see.

From the point of view of the sender, this element is physical activity—the use of the body to convey meanings. From the point of view of the receiver, it is visible stimuli. These cues are taken in through the eyes of the receiver. How the speaker stands or sits (posture or stance), what gestures are used, the expressions on the face—the entire body really transmits impressions (messages) to the receiver.

Visible

Verbal symbols are words. Words are spoken symbols that stand for ideas. The verbal element of speech communication is that element that uses spoken symbols to represent concepts. It is the word component of the transmission.

Verbal

These, then, are the three elements that make up speech communication. All three are important components of speech. Whenever you speak, you are transmitting messages in three ways at the same time: with your voice (the way it sounds), with your body (the way it looks to the receiver), and with your words (the spoken symbols that represent your ideas). We will examine these components of speech communication in much greater detail in later chapters of this book.

messages

At this point, we should probably agree on a meaning or some meanings for a word already used often in this chapter: *message.* Communication, after all, involves the sending and receiving of messages. But what do we mean by the word *message*? A message is any sign or group of signs capable of being interpreted meaningfully. In other words, a message is something that stands for or represents ideas. A message is something that has significance for us; that is, we attach or attribute meaning to it. I said that messages are made up of *signs,* which are things that stand for something else. Things that *sign*ify point to something beyond themselves; they represent things or ideas or events other than themselves. Signs could be objects or sounds or marks on a page—anything that stands for something else. And it is signs that messages are made of.

In human speech communication, we use the word *message* in three different senses. In fact, there may be, in any human speech communication event, three distinct messages involved: the message in the mind of the sender, the message transmitted by the sender, and the message received and interpreted by the receiver. Can you see how different these three might be?

Let's say I decide to describe some object to a friend of mine. I want to convey the idea that the object was not very heavy, so I choose the words for my message: "It was very light." My brain gives the proper commands, and my body transmits noises to make the English words "it-was-very-

MESSAGE IN
MIND OF SENDER

MESSAGE
TRANSMITTED

MESSAGE
RECEIVED

The three messages involved in a speech communication event

light," with my voice making the chosen variations in pitch, volume, rate (including duration of sounds), and quality, and my body assuming the dictated stance and muscular tension, making the selected gestures, and controlling my facial expression. My friend hears the noises, recognizes the sounds (since we share the English code), reconstructs the words "it was very light," and interprets those words to mean that the object had a light, as opposed to a dark, color. Note the three messages: the one I formulated in my (the sender's) mind; the one I transmitted using the three components of speech; and the one the friend received and reacted to.

primary communication and metacommunication

We should probably distinguish between *primary communication* (main messages transmitted by the sender) and *metacommunication* (extra messages transmitted by the sender). The word *metacommunication* comes from the Greek word *meta,* which can mean *next to* or *along with* something else. *Meta* implies that there is a message communicated in addition to the main message; it implies that, as the main message is sent out, another message is sent along with it.

Metacommunication can be either *verbal* (in words) or *nonverbal* (not in words). The added message tells the receiver how to interpret the original message (or the main, principal message).

Let's look at an example of verbal metacommunication. If a mother says, "Don't you touch that vase! I'm not kidding this time. Don't you touch it!" the main message is quite clearly: "Don't touch the vase." The verbal metacommunication added (and the words of the metacommunication, the extra message, are quite clear too!) tells the child to interpret this (main) message as meaning business. The primary message conveys the principal idea; the metacommunication conveys information about how to interpret that main idea.

Another example: Mary always wears a fancy new hat on Easter. When her boyfriend arrived on Easter morning, she asked him how he liked the new hat. He laughingly (nonverbal metacommunication) replied that he thought it was the ugliest hat he had ever seen. But he quickly added the words: "You know I'm kidding, don't you?" The added words were verbal metacommunication, telling Mary that the main message was irony (the opposite words of what he meant).

Nonverbal metacommunication performs the same function as verbal metacommunication—giving clues on how to interpret the principal message. But, of course, the clues are given without words. They are the two elements of speech communication other than the verbal element: vocal and visual.

When discussed as nonverbal metacommunication, vocal clues have been called *paralanguage* or *paralinguistic features.* This term is based on the Greek word *para,* meaning beside or around. The nonverbal features of the voice are transmitted right alongside and around the primary message, which is packaged in words.

Paralanguage tells the listener how to interpret the main message—as all metacommunication does. The changes in pitch, rate, volume, and quality of the voice all help the listener interpret the main (primary) message, the main message given in words. Do not get confused. These features are the same features I discussed when listing the three components of speech communication. Writers who have discussed them in terms of paralanguage (a subdivision of metacommunication) are viewing these vocal features in terms of what they *do,* rather than what they *are.* It seems wise to me to present the information to you in both ways.

The other nonverbal kind of metacommunication is the speaker's physical activity—the visible component of speech communication. The technical term that has been applied to these visible clues to the meaning of the main message is *kinesics;* the more popular term is *body language.*

There are, then, two kinds of nonverbal metacommunication: *paralanguage,* taken in by the receiver with his or her ears, and *body language,* or *kinesics,* taken in by the receiver with his or her eyes. We will deal with both in greater detail in Chapter 6.

Metacommunication, whether verbal or nonverbal, provides the receiver with important and useful information. It should serve to underscore, reinforce, and clarify the primary message. If these secondary messages seem contrary to or contradictory to the primary message, the listener must try to decide which is more accurate and truthful—no easy task.

responses

In our definition of the word *communication* itself, we have focused on the receiver of the message. And we have said that no communication occurs unless there is a response—a reaction. Now we want to look at three important kinds of responses: feedback, signal responses, and symbol responses.

Feedback

Feedback, of course, is a term familiar to most of us. We have heard it used in electronics; in fact, we have heard the loud, unpleasant noise of feedback when microphones have picked up sound from the loudspeakers. We have all read, doubtless, about biofeedback, the conscious monitoring of parts of our bodies so we can send messages from the brain to better control them.

As used in communication theory, feedback means much the same thing as in the two examples just mentioned. Feedback is a response from the receiver of the message that affects the transmission of the sender. You can see, I believe, that there is a parallel with the first two examples. The loudspeaker was the receiver of the signal going out from the microphone/sender. When a response from the loudspeaker was fed into the microphone, the sending was affected. In that case, the result was a loud, unpleasant noise. In the instance of biofeedback, the brain in the person's body is the sender of messages, but responses come back to the brain from the organs being controlled. The brain then adjusts its transmission, depending on what responses come back.

In communication, feedback is a response from the receiver (or receivers) that affects the outgoing message of the sender. The sender monitors those responses and adapts the message he or she is sending, adjusting the outgoing message because of those responses. Unless the sender changes the message-sending to accommodate those responses, the responses are not feedback. For the receiver's response to be feedback, that response must in some way be picked up and used by the sender in the sender's transmission.

Perhaps we can understand feedback better if we look at a couple of examples. Dr. Dustin Rhodes is giving his favorite lecture on the sex life of the amoeba when he notices that several students are frowning. Dr. Rhodes concludes that the students must not understand the last point he has just made, so he repeats it in simpler terms. The students' response (frowning) was feedback for the professor, who used the information gained from seeing the signs of confusion to adjust his lecture.

Another example: Father O'Neel, the local parish priest, had been sent to the scene of a riot to try to calm the enraged mob. He had hardly begun to speak to the crowd when he noted that the more he spoke, the more unruly they became. He decided to cut his message short and flee for his life. The increased noise and activity of the group of people constituted feedback—because those responses from the priest's listeners were perceived by the speaker and affected his speech.

Feedback can be either nonverbal (like the frowns and the activity of the mob) or verbal. Feedback *can* be in words. Here's one example of verbal feedback: The Mize's fifteen-year-old daughter, Minnie, wanted to go to a movie with her friends on a school night. She asked her father, Max I. Mize, if she could go. He said "no," rather emphatically. The daughter then changed her approach and, in a super-sweet tone, began again, "Daddy, please can't I go? Everyone else in the crowd is getting to go!" In this case, Max's word "no" was feedback for Minnie; it affected the rest of the message she sent to her father. She changed her approach in terms of his response to her opening request.

Feedback, then, is the means by which a sender detects the effects of the message he or she is transmitting. The sender's feedback mechanism performs two related functions: (1) monitoring and (2) adjusting. As monitor, the feedback mechanism *evaluates* the output and the outcome of the transmission. It assesses the effort expended and the results achieved. As adjustor, the feedback mechanism *compares* the actual output and outcome with the intended output and outcome. If there is a difference between the intended results and the actual (monitored) results, then the feedback mechanism moves to *correct* the transmission. It permits the sender to adapt the transmission in order to more nearly reach the intended goal.

Feedback—the receiver's response monitored and utilized by the sender—may be either positive or negative. Positive feedback indicates that the message being transmitted is efficient and effective. It also indicates to what extent the message is being understood (efficiency) and is garnering the desired reaction (effectiveness). By confirming the efficacy of the transmission, positive feedback reinforces the sender during that transmission. Negative feedback, on the other hand, indicates that the sender's goals are not being achieved, that the message is inefficient (not understood adequately) or ineffective (not eliciting from the receiver the desired reaction). Although both positive and negative feedback are important to a message-producer, negative feedback is probably more important. It provides crucial information that the sender uses to modify and control the message being transmitted.

Signal and Symbol Responses

In addition to feedback, there are two other kinds of responses we should understand: signal responses and symbol responses. To do that, we must clarify three terms—sign, signal, and symbol.

A *sign* is something that stands for something else. Signs may be objects or sounds or marks on a page—anything that stands for something else. Things that *sign*ify point to something beyond themselves; they represent things or ideas or events other than themselves.

Signs are usually divided into two classes: signals and symbols. Both stand for something other than themselves, but they each have a different relationship to the thing signified. And we react to signals and to symbols differently. At least, we should.

Signals stand in a one-to-one relationship, a direct relationship, with whatever they represent. A traffic signal is a good example. The green light means *go*. It does not mean *go* sometimes and *slow* another time; when used as a signal, the green light means *go*! Period. The octagon shape of a road sign means *stop.* That shape is not employed to signal any other traffic instruction. Signals are not ambiguous!

We learn to recognize signs used as signals, and because of their one-to-one relationship with the thing represented, we do not have to think much about what they mean. Our reaction becomes almost reflexive. The red traffic light comes on, and we hit the brake. Signal responses, then, are reactions to signs that are almost instantaneous, nonthinking reactions. The recognition of the signal triggers the response.

Symbols, unlike signals, do not stand in a one-to-one relationship with whatever they represent. We use the same symbol to represent many different things, and we must interpret the meaning of the symbol, based on the context in which it is used and on the entire situation. We cannot sensibly respond to symbols with *reflex* action; we must *reflect,* "What does it mean this time?" That means that symbol responses take more time than signal responses do. Symbol responses are, necessarily, slightly delayed while we think things through.

Words, of course, are symbols, not signals. The same word (an arbitrary sign) can be used to mean many different things. How many different definitions (meanings) can you think of for the word *pot,* for example? Are some of the meanings nouns and some verbs? The range is rather wide, isn't it?

There are nonverbal symbols, too. What does an outstretched arm with the hand open, palm forward mean? Well, you say it might mean hello—or goodbye—or stop, depending on the situation. It means different things in different contexts. If the traffic police officer uses that hand sign (a gesture with symbolic meaning) at an intersection, it is unlikely that he or she is just greeting you in a friendly way or waving goodbye. What does it mean if someone puts his or her hands on the hips (his or her own hips, that is)? If my mother does it, I will probably interpret the symbol as irritation and impatience. If the official at a football game does it, I will interpret the sign as a symbol that someone was offsides on the preceding play. The point is that nonverbal symbols require us to reflect before assigning them a meaning, just as verbal symbols do.

In sum, there are two kinds of signs—signals and symbols. With signals, we always react the same way to the same signal. We are so conditioned that we react almost instantly. That is an appropriate response. With symbols, whether verbal or nonverbal, we do not always react the same way to the same symbol. Our response will be determined by the context of the symbol, so we must delay the response long enough to consider the symbol in relation to the entire situation. If we react to a symbol the same way no matter what the situation, reacting almost instantly and reflexively (the popular term is *gut reaction*), then we are using a signal kind of response to a symbol kind of sign. Signal reactions to symbols are often inappropriate and irrational responses. Cerebral reactions are more appropriate to symbols than are gut reactions!

barriers and breakdowns

There are two other important terms we must clarify at the very beginning of our study of communication. They are *barriers* and *breakdowns.* They are related, but different. Barriers exist; breakdowns occur. Barriers are obstacles to be overcome; they are things that get in the way and hinder or prevent successful communication. Barriers do not prevent communication from occurring. (Remember that communication is almost inevitable when two people get together.) But barriers can make communication more difficult. They can interfere with mutual understanding and accomplishment of the communicators' goals.

There may be barriers in the sender, in the receiver, in the message, or in the physical, social, or cultural environment. I am sure you can think of examples of barriers that might exist in all of them.

If the barriers are not overcome, then breakdowns may occur. Actually, the word *breakdown* is a poor one to describe what happens. Communication does not "break down," if you mean by those words that communication stops. Barriers cannot prevent interaction; rather, they distort the interaction, at least from the point of view of the sender.

If we are going to use the term *breakdown* at all, we must be very careful to label what kind of malfunction we are talking about, since the term is used to describe two very different situations. One kind of breakdown occurs when the communication is not efficient. That, you remember, is the situation in which the receiver did not understand the message in the same way the sender understood the message. The receiver's meanings were different from the sender's meanings. The problem is not that the receiver got no message at all, but that the receiver got a different message from that intended by the sender.

The other kind of breakdown occurs when the communication is not effective. Again, you will remember that this is the situation in which the receiver did not react to the message as the sender intended him or her to react. In this case, the receiver may very well understand the message and the sender's intent, but the receiver refuses to be influenced by the sender and the sender's message. From the point of view of the sender, the communication did not work (to effect the desired change or elicit the desired response); from the point of view of the receiver, however, the communication has worked very well. The answer just happens to be no! Or the answer is "I disagree." Those are valid and may be quite appropriate responses. I feel very uncomfortable calling this situation a breakdown, but most of the literature on the subject does so.

Because the term *breakdown* is used for the two different communication situations, I think it is extremely important to note the distinction between efficiency and effectiveness and label every breakdown accordingly.

Communication is a complicated process, perhaps the most complicated activity in which we human beings participate. We are now ready to turn our attention to what goes on in that complicated process and to the elements that are part of the process of human communication.

SUGGESTIONS FOR FURTHER READING

BERLO, DAVID K., *The Process of Communication* (New York: Holt, 1960).

BROWN, CHARLES T., and CHARLES VAN RIPER, *Communication in Human Relationships* (Skokie, Ill.: National Text Book Co., 1973).

DANCE, FRANK E. X., ed., *Human Communication Theory* (New York: Holt, 1967).

DANCE, FRANK E. X., and CARL E. LARSON, *The Functions of Human Communication* (New York: Holt, 1976).

McCROSKEY, JAMES C., and LAWRENCE R. WHEELESS, *Introduction to Human Communication* (Boston: Allyn and Bacon, 1976).

MILLER, GERALD, *An Introduction to Speech Communication,* 2nd ed. (Indianapolis: Bobbs-Merrill, 1973).

MORTENSEN, C. DAVID, *Basic Readings in Communication Theory* (New York: Harper & Row, 1973).

SCHRAMM, WILBUR, *Men, Messages and Media: A Look at Human Communication* (New York: Harper & Row, 1973).

SWANSON, DAVID L., and JESSE G. DELIA, *The Nature of Human Communication* (Palo Alto, Calif.: Science Research Associates, 1976).

WENBURG, JOHN R., and WILLIAM W. WILMOT, *The Personal Communication Process* (New York: Wiley, 1973).

2
HUMAN COMMUNICATION: THE PROCESS AND ITS ELEMENTS

general goal:

To learn how human communication works.

specific objectives:

After completing this unit, you should understand:
- Why some common myths about communication are mistaken.
- The difference between speech and nonspeech communication.
- The difference between intentional and nonintentional communication.
- The difference between efficient and inefficient communication.
- The difference between effective and ineffective communication.
- The difference between concord and conflict and the relationships between communication and conflict.
- What is meant by the process view of human communication.
- The five elements of the human communication process and how they are related and integrated.

BEFORE ANALYZING the process of human communication and examining the elements in that process, I think it would be wise to dispose of some mistaken myths about communication and to take note of a few reminders.

Communication, I think you will agree, is something *everybody* is talking about. Listen to what people are saying about communication, and you will probably discover several underlying assumptions. Three of these assumptions are quite mistaken. They are misconceptions about what the process of human communication is and what it can do. Because these mistaken myths are so pervasive, they are pernicious. Let's take a critical look at these myths.

three myths about communication

MYTH 1: Communication is inherently beneficial.

Communication is being hawked as the cureall for all our ills. It is widely revered as a magic potion, a sure-fire remedy for all our problems. According to this naive myth, a dose of communication will heal your family's troubles, your school's troubles, your company's troubles, your nation's troubles.

The line of reasoning seems to say that the lack (or absence) of communication is a bad thing, so the presence of communication must be a good thing. Always. Or: The failure to communicate can cause problems. Hence, if you have a problem, it can be solved by communicating.

Have you ever been given advice that was based on this mistaken myth about communication? Maybe, when you were having disagreements with your parents, you were told, "Just talk to them and tell them how you feel. That will solve it." Or perhaps, when you were dissatisfied with a course you were taking at college, you were advised to communicate your feelings to your professor so he or she would change the course to suit you better. (One of my friends *did* communicate with a professor, informing the professor that he was greatly disappointed in the course and in his teaching. Unfortunately, the professor did not change his methods, but he did change his attitude toward my friend and prevented him from getting his Ph.D. degree. I *told* you the myth was mistaken!) And haven't you heard someone say, "If we could just get them together and let them talk it out. . . . ?"

The belief that communication is, of itself, always beneficial is widespread. The flaw in this belief is the assumption that communication must (or can) always be good. Or bad. Communication is a tool; it is an instrument we human beings use. Of themselves, tools are neither good nor bad. They just are. The results of their use may be good or bad; the outcomes may be beneficial or harmful, but that depends on what they are used for and how they are used, not on what they are themselves. A knife is a tool, an instrument that can be used to wound or heal. So is communication! Sometimes human communication does make things better; sometimes it makes things worse. Sometimes communication helps solve problems; sometimes it creates problems or aggravates them. It certainly is not a panacea for all the world's ills.

MYTH 2: Increasing communication will necessarily decrease conflict.

This second myth is built on the first one. If communication is a good thing, and you can't overdo a good thing, then the more communication the better! If communication is a sure-fire problem-solver, then increasing the amount of communication will increase the likelihood of solving the problem.

No one doubts that communication *can* sometimes be used to reduce or to help manage conflict. But believers in this myth go much further. They believe that communication *always* reduces conflict. They further believe that the *more* the parties to a dispute communicate, the *less* conflict they will have.

Common sense should tell us that just increasing the amount of communication will not necessarily reduce conflict. If what I am transmitting is verbal abuse, will transmitting more of it reduce conflict? If what I am communicating is hostile and venomous, will communicating more lessen tensions and promote reconciliation? Hardly. The key to conflict resolution and reduction is not the amount of communication but the content of the communication.

MYTH 3: Communication skills are innate; either you have them or you don't.

This is an old myth, and it refuses to die. It takes various forms, but they all add up to the same mistaken notion. Have you heard people say, "Everybody can communicate. Why study it?"; or "Ability to communicate well depends on natural talent"; or even "Some people are just born with the ability to communicate better than others" and "The way I communicate is natural to me, and there is nothing I can do about it"?

Communication skills are learned. All of us learned to communicate; it did not just happen naturally. True, we were born with capacities, but we had to develop those capacities, and that development involved a learning process. Our communication skills may seem natural to us because we are used to them. We acquired them a long time ago, and we have forgotten how it was done—if indeed we paid much attention to the process while it was happening.

The ways you communicate were learned as you interacted with your environment. Your environment—everything, including the people around you—influenced the ways you learned to use the natural capacities your heredity gave you. Communication skills are acquired. The influences of your environment, your sensitivity to those influences, and the ways you received and reacted to those influences largely determined what communication patterns you learned.

Unfortunately, elementary and secondary schools have not provided students with a systematic study of the process of human communication. They too have taken it for granted, and students have had to manage on their own. Now, of course, you are studying how human communication works, and if you apply the principles you are learning to everyday communication situations, you should improve your communication skills.

five important reminders

After disposing of those three myths, and before analyzing the process of communication in some detail, let us take note of a few important reminders. Human communication includes: (1) speech and nonspeech communication; (2) intentional and nonintentional communication; (3) efficient and inefficient communication; (4) effective and ineffective communication; (5) concord and conflict.

Speech and Nonspeech Communication

1. Human communication includes both speech and nonspeech communication. Speech communication, as we have already seen (see pp. 12–13), involves the transmission and reception of three-component messages. These messages have a verbal, vocal, and visible element. Although most of the literature at present only distinguishes between verbal and nonverbal communication, I believe that distinction to be of somewhat limited usefulness. Speech communication involves *both* verbal and nonverbal elements. Our messages transmitted and received by speech communication contain both verbal and nonverbal elements, transmitted simultaneously and received simultaneously as a unified package. Indeed, two of the three components of speech communication are nonverbal: the vocal (or paralinguistic) element and the visible (or kinesic) element. Speech is made up of all three, and they are indivisible.

We human beings do communicate in ways other than with speech. Many of these ways have been examined in the literature, and they are usually discussed under the label of *nonverbal communication*. Without speech, we send and receive messages by touching, tasting, smelling, hearing (both sounds and silence), seeing (objects, action, or space), and perceiving time. These ways of communicating are discussed more fully in Chapter 10.

Intentional and Nonintentional Communication

2. Human communication includes both intentional and nonintentional communication. We have already noted this fact (pp. 11–12). Most of the books on human communication concentrate on intentional communication, especially on the intention (purpose) of the person producing the message. We human beings can deliberately transmit messages, intending

to evoke responses in another human being. Purposes are often classified according to the type of response one wants to elicit. (See Chapter 11.) But we must remember that both human beings in an interpersonal communication situation have purposes. The receiver has a purpose just as surely as the message-sender has a purpose. We shall look at the subject of purposes more closely a bit later in this chapter. It is enough for now to note three possible relationships between the intentions of the message-producer and the message-receiver:

1. The sender intends to send the message, and the receiver intends to receive the message.
2. The sender intends to send the message, but the receiver does not intend to receive the message.
3. The sender does not intend to send the message, but the receiver intends to receive the message.

In the first relationship, the intentions (purposes) of the sender and receiver are compatible; the communication may be both efficient and effective. In the second relationship, the receiver's intention is not compatible with that of the sender. In the third relationship, the sender has no intention of producing a message and is not aware that a message is being received. In this case, either (from the point of view of the sender) there is an unintended receiver or an unintended message received. (See pp. 11–12.)

Nonintentional communication of the third type of relationship is important, especially since the response was not deliberately evoked by the message-producer. If the sender is not aware of that response, he or she cannot adjust or reply to it. Ignorance is not bliss!

Efficient and Inefficient Communication

3. Human communication includes both efficient and inefficient communication. (See pp. 9–10.) Whether the receiver understands the message as conceived by the message-producer or misunderstands that message, communication takes place. Even if I say, "An ice age is coming," and you think I said, "A nice age is coming," human communication did take place. You reacted to what you thought I said; the communication was complete, if faulty.

Effective and Ineffective Communication

4. Human communication includes both effective and ineffective communication. (See p. 10.) As I mentioned in the preceding chapter, if there is a response from the receiver, communication has occurred— whether that response is the one the sender wanted or not. If you ask someone to come live with you and be your love, he or she may say yes or

no. If the answer is yes, the communication was effective; if the answer is no, the communication was ineffective. But there was communication, in either case.

5. Human communication includes both concord and conflict. A great deal of my time is spent in dealing with conflict of some kind. I doubt that I am atypical. How much of your speech communication involves conflict? That much? Then we had better examine concord and conflict a bit more closely.

Concord and Conflict

ELEMENTS OF CONFLICT

Concord and conflict are both sides of the same coin. Conflict includes either or both of the following: (1) disagreement over some issue, or (2) personal antagonism. Conflict involving disagreement on substantive issues results in *debate*. Conflict involving personal antipathy results in *dislike*. Conflict involving both results in a *dispute*. A debate is an intellectual struggle; dislike is personal and emotional; disputes contain both elements, involving conflict over both substance and personalities.

I am sure you can think of examples of all three types of conflict. A few years ago at a college I know well, there was a decision to be made: should the small group communication course be offered in the Department of Communication Arts or in the Psychology Department? Each department thought itself the logical home for the course; there was considerable disagreement, and an extensive debate resulted. The debate centered on the issues—the logical questions; the participants in that debate prided themselves for handling the conflict "professionally" and not "personally."

One of my friends was, in my judgment, an excellent department chairperson. He was an able administrator who "got things done." True, he did not consult his department on many decisions, but the decisions he made were usually astute. Some of his department members resented his style of leadership and openly called him "Machiavelli." With some contempt, he dismissed their complaints and noted that they probably had never even read *The Prince*! This conflict was less over substance than style; it was personality conflict.

The luxury apartment of one of my friends recently suffered severe water damage, as did many other apartments in the building. When the other apartments were repaired and hers was not, she confronted the building's board chairperson. That was the person, she was told, who had given the order not to repair her apartment. My friend presented her case on both an intellectual and an emotional level. She demanded equal treatment as a matter of justice. In addition, she made it clear what she thought of bigots who tried to discriminate on the basis of race. The dispute was quite heated.

ELEMENTS OF CONCORD

Concord is the reverse of conflict. Concord also is composed of two elements: (1) agreement on substantive issues, and (2) affinity—personal attraction. Actually, of course, the two elements are closely related. If two people are in agreement on many basic issues, if they share the same general view of the world, if their beliefs, values, and attitudes are parallel, then they will interact more often with each other. Also, when they do interact, their communication is more likely to be efficient (they share more common meanings) and effective (their responses are influenced by the same beliefs, values, and attitudes). When two communicators understand each other easily (their communication is efficient) and they often get the response desired from the other (their communication is effective), it is likely they will feel an affinity (a personal attraction) for each other. Agreement, then, contributes to affinity.

A number of writers on communication have used the word *homophily* to refer to the degree of similarity between communicators. Homophily refers to similarity in all areas, not just in intellectual ones; hence, it is a broader term than *agreement*. It would include similarity in appearance, background, and status, as well as similarity in viewpoints (agreement). Studies indicate that we tend to communicate more with people we perceive to be similar to ourselves. If we really are similar to the other person, our communication is more likely to be efficient and effective. And when we interact efficiently and effectively with another person, we are more likely to influence that person and be influenced by that person. This mutual interaction and reciprocal influence enhances the feelings of personal attraction (affinity).

THREE DEGREES OF CONFLICT (AND CONCORD)

All conflict is not equally intense; there are at least three different degrees of conflict. Note these three concord/conflict contrasts:

Concord:		Conflict:	Relationship:
Concurrence	/	Controversy..........	Dissenter
Cooperation	/	Competition.........	Rival or Opponent
Conciliation	/	Confrontation.......	Enemy or Combat

Controversy arises when there are decisions to be made. The necessity of choosing among alternatives makes controversy likely if not inevitable. Indeed, controversy is healthy in any organization or social system; it permits the exploration of various possibilities, broadens horizons, and fosters progress. Controversy occurs when advocates of different positions state and defend the options that they think are best. Your relationship with those advocating positions different from your own is that of dissenter. If they think their solution superior, they view you as the dissenter, and since you think yours is best, you view them as dissenters. In any case, the struggle is not a life-and-death matter. Eventually, a decision will be made, and you will all move on to examining other problems and making other decisions. If the decision reached is a wise one, everyone (no matter what side they took in the controversy) may share in the rewards and profit from the decision.

Concurrence is the opposite of controversy. When a decision is made, when there is unanimity on the choice to be made, then you have concurrence. The parties are of a single mind. When such agreement is reached after a controversy, consensus is said to have developed.

A second degree of conflict occurs when the outcome of the struggle is winning or losing. In this case, opponents will not share equally in the rewards. Competition results from two or more persons going after the same prize. Competition is not inherently evil or unhealthy, and competitors often respect each other if the "game" is played well. In this type of struggle, those in conflict are rivals or opponents. If two of us males are entreating the same young lady to go with us to the same dance, we are rivals. It is highly unlikely that she will allow both of us to take her to the dance! If my university tries to promote our leading football star U. R. Gross for the Heisman Trophy, we will find that we have many opponents—other schools and other football stars competing for the same award and recognition. Although competition is more intense conflict than is controversy, the struggle is still not a matter of life and death; the loser is not completely destroyed. One can, after all, enter another "game" and compete again. There will be other dances, for example, and there are other years to vie for the trophy.

Cooperation is the reverse of competition. The effort of the participants is expended *with* each other toward the same goal, not *against* each other for the same prize. To cooperate is to work together on equal terms; it implies coordinated effort. The other is not a rival or opponent (as in competition) but a colleague.

The third degree of conflict is combat or confrontation. In combat, the stakes are higher than in competition: there is a winner and loser, but this time the winner vanquishes the loser. The loser is harmed, eliminated, or absorbed. The very object of the fight is to destroy the other, to conquer or cut him or her down. The relationship is not merely that of opponents for the same prize (as in competition), but of enemies. In combat, enemies are intent on injuring each other.

Opponents in competition are often useful and sometimes necessary; they make us look better as we struggle to outdo them. Enemies in combat are, at the very least, aggravating nuisances. They are not only unnecessary; they are unwanted obstacles.

Conciliation is the antithesis of combat. Whereas confrontation and combat drive people apart, conciliation brings people together. Whereas combat and confrontation polarize people, conciliation unites people. In combat, one tries to destroy enemies; in conciliation, one tries to make friends and allies. Conciliation is an effort to reconcile people—not eliminate them.

FOUR LEVELS OF CONFLICT

Having looked at the three degrees of conflict (and concord), let us turn our attention to the four levels of conflict. Conflict occurs (1) within human beings—intrapersonal conflict; (2) between human beings—interpersonal conflict; (3) within groups—intragroup conflict; and (4) between groups—intergroup conflict. We will examine each of these levels briefly.

Intrapersonal Conflict. Conflict can occur within a person. We face intrapersonal conflict when we must choose among incompatible desirable alternatives. Alternatives are incompatible if selecting one means we cannot select the others. Our choices are not usually simple ones between right and wrong, good and bad, worthy and unworthy. What if we must choose among rights or select one among a number of goods? Then we have to deal with internal conflicts.

I am sure you can think of many examples from your own experience. Haven't you been pulled in opposing directions at the same time? Haven't you faced conflicts in desires (wants), needs (drives), beliefs, values, and attitudes?

Here are a few examples that come to my mind. NBC-TV is broadcasting the NCAA basketball finals at the same time PBS is telecasting Baryshnikov's newest ballet live from Lincoln Center. I want to watch both of them, but I can't. Which will I choose? My best friend and I are stranded in the desert with only one canteen of water. I feel that I'm dying of thirst, but I doubt there is enough water for both of us. Which need will guide my behavior—survival or social? In my biology classes, the professors taught me that human beings evolved from other creatures; in my Sunday School classes, I was taught that the human race was created *as is* by God. Which will I choose to believe? I value both freedom of the press and the right of a defendant to a fair trial. Am I in favor of newspapers printing information about murders and suspects before the trial begins? I love Greece and the Greek people; I also despise prejudice and intolerance. How will I react when my Greek friends speak contemptuously of all Turks?

Each of those examples poses an intrapersonal problem, because the choice presented is between two positively valued possibilities. How can you choose between two mutually exclusive alternatives, when you really want to hold on to both? Neurotic people cannot deal well with such dilemmas. They feel trapped, and they try to avoid choosing. Indeed, the situation may cause them great anxiety!

What about the rest of us? We try to resolve the conflict by making a choice. One method of dealing with such conflicts is to establish priorities—ranking the alternatives in order of importance to us. (Is making money more important to you than honesty?) Another method is to compartmentalize one's life, making one choice in one area of one's life and a different choice for another area. (My cousin was trained in science but was devoutly religious. I asked him how he managed that, and he told me, "I leave my mind in the vestibule of the church. In scientific matters, of course, I use my reason; in matters of faith and morals, I accept the Church's teaching without any question.") Another method, of course, is to rationalize away the conflict. ("I believe that God created mankind, but He used the evolutionary process to do it.")

The subject of rationalization leads us to the theory of *cognitive dissonance,* a theory closely related to intrapersonal conflict. If a person believes or knows two contradictory concepts, that person experiences cognitive (knowing) dissonance (clashing, disharmony). Everyone tries to keep his or her belief system in harmony; we try to keep it consistent. So, somehow or other, we have to fit the clashing information into our system. Rationalization is the use of self-deceptive reasoning to explain away the contradiction. Here's an example: A few years ago a dreadful pedant was telling me that smoking marijuana *must* be prohibited by law, because, he said, it clearly harmed the human body. I did not argue with him about the question of whether marijuana was harmful or not, but I did observe that I thought it ironic for him to be making the argument while he puffed away on a Marlboro. He flushed, stamped out the cigarette, and snapped, "But I don't inhale!" Sure. Now, he knows that cigarette smoking is harmful, but he also knows he smokes and he likes smoking. How can he reconcile the two? He rationalizes and thus reduces the cognitive dissonance.

Interpersonal Conflict. Interpersonal conflicts are struggles between individuals. The conflict may be of any one of the degrees of intensity we have discussed before: controversy, in which there is disagreement over beliefs, values, or attitudes; competition, in which the persons have incompatible goals; or combat, in which each seeks victory over the perceived enemy.

Intragroup Conflict. I confess I find this category difficult to deal with, because the conflicts within a group will clearly be between persons. And we have discussed interpersonal conflicts already. Why the separate category at all, then? Well, it *is* true that there are some aspects that seem distinctive about conflicts inside a group. After all, the group has a common history, a common sense of identity and belonging, a set of common values and norms, and probably a set of common objectives and tasks. With that much in common, with that much homophily, conflict within the group is especially difficult to manage. Such conflict may threaten the smooth functioning of the group itself if it gets out of hand. And conflict with others in the same group may produce more personal tension and even anxiety than conflict with "outsiders." It does not differ in its essential nature from other interpersonal conflict; it may differ somewhat in its effects and the way it is perceived by others in the group.

My brother told me recently about a basketball team composed of especially talented players. Unfortunately, the players were competing against each other for attention and reward, and the team was not doing as well as it should. This intragroup conflict was undermining the effectiveness of the group.

The Democrats in my local Democratic club display every form of intragroup conflict. There is an abundance of controversy, incessant competition, and, all too often, out-and-out combat!

Perhaps, though, none of us needs to go farther from home than our own families to examine intragroup conflict. Do the children dissent from their parents' values or beliefs? Do the brothers and sisters compete for the parents' affection and approval? Does the conflict ever go beyond controversy and competition?

Intergroup Conflict.   Groups, unorganized and organized, vie with each other. Right now, the "pro-abortionists," who advocate women's freedom to choose, and "anti-abortionists," who advocate the fetus's right to live, are embroiled in a controversy. On one side are such organizations as Planned Parenthood, and on the other are such organizations as the Right to Life Committee. At the international level, the United States of America and the Union of Soviet Socialist Republics are engaged in intense competition—for status, for influence, for economic and military superiority. We can be thankful that the conflict is noncombative. Most of us remember too well when our nation was engaged in combat with other nations.

You can doubtless think of many examples of intergroup conflict involving such groups as families, unions, corporations, churches, fraternities and sororities, lodges, social clubs, political parties, professional associations, civic organizations, charities, nations.

FIVE RELATIONSHIPS BETWEEN COMMUNICATION AND CONFLICT

But, you say, what is the relationship of communication to conflict? What role(s) does communication play in these conflicts we have discussed? It seems to me that there are five roles or relationships: (1) communication can cause conflict; (2) communication can exacerbate conflict; (3) communication can prevent conflict; (4) communication can reduce conflict; and (5) communication can alleviate conflict. Let us look at each of these relationships briefly.

1. *Communication can cause conflict.* As I noted earlier, the important thing is not *whether* there is communication, but *what* is communicated. To cause conflict, accent the negative! Begin by zeroing in on points of difference in your world view. Point out major differences in what you believe and what the other communicators believe; make clear that you do not share their values and attitudes. Emphasize the differences in your respective backgrounds, the groups you belong to, and the loyalties you hold dear. Disagree with every viewpoint expressed as often as you can. That may not generate competition or combat, but it certainly ought to stimulate controversy and get conflict off to a good start.

Another way to cause conflict with communication is to stress the incompatibility of your respective goals. Make it clear that your purpose(s) is quite different from that of your receivers' purpose. In addition, refuse to cooperate. Let them know that, since you have conflicting aims, you certainly can't work with them in achieving their goals.

Communication is also likely to cause conflict if you disclose aspects of yourself that the receivers will view negatively. They will react to your messages, in part at least, on the basis of what they think of *you*. If you tell them things about yourself that they disapprove of, the likelihood of conflict is greatly increased.

An excellent way to cause conflict is to give vent to your negative feelings about the people you are communicating with. Display your antipathy; manifest your hostility; flaunt your contempt. Get those feelings out in the open! Put your receivers on the defensive with strong verbal and nonverbal attacks. You will maneuver them into conflict rather quickly.

A final hint for conflict caused by communication: Undercut the other people's self-esteem at every opportunity. Put them down! Cut them down to size! Sarcasm works wonders. A little belittling goes a long way. And ridicule is effective too. Point out the other people's weaknesses, flaws, foibles, faults, mistakes, inconsistencies, misconceptions, miscalculations, ignorance, defects, unattractiveness (or repulsiveness, if possible), inexperience, oversights, blunders, delusions, illusions, inexperience, indiscretions, ineptitude, folly. If you can think of other inadequacies, throw them in also. Humiliating the other people, undermining their self-esteem (their feeling of self-worth), should provoke a healthy antagonism and generate a good conflict!

2. *Communication can exacerbate conflict.* Of course, any of the helpful hints I gave about causing conflict with communication would also work in increasing or intensifying conflict. In general, to exacerbate conflict, concentrate on the points of disagreement you have with the other persons, and emphasize your personal dislike of the other persons. Focus on the issues on which you take opposing stands and make transparently clear the personal antagonism you feel.

3. *Communication can prevent conflict.* Just as communication can contribute to causing conflict or making it worse, so communication can contribute to preventing conflict.

One way to help prevent conflict is to communicate your desire to concentrate on the task at hand. Focus on the problem to be solved, and demonstrate your willingness to work with the others in finding a solution. Indicate to your receivers that you have no preset plan or idea that you are going to try to put over on them. Make it clear that you have not already decided on a solution or course of action, but rather that the decision is yet to be made—together.

Another way to help prevent conflict is to be open-minded and to communicate this open-mindedness to your receivers. A person who is open-minded is willing to examine new and different ideas, to participate in new and different experiences, and to consider the possibility of change. A person who is open-minded willingly exposes himself or herself to people, outlooks, and experiences quite different from his or her own. Such a person is always searching for new information, even if it is contrary or contradictory to the store of information and beliefs that that person already has. Open-minded people are willing to consider what other people say—no matter what it is. (See pp. 80–82 for more information on open- and closed-mindedness.)

A third method of conflict-prevention is empathy. Empathy is the ability to see things from the other person's viewpoint—to put oneself into the other person's shoes. It involves understanding the other person's beliefs, values, and attitudes; it means seeing the situation as the other person sees it. Carl Rogers has offered an excellent suggestion for testing and improving empathy. In a discussion with someone, state your answer to what has just been said *only* after you have restated accurately the other person's ideas and feelings. The other person will be the judge of whether you restated his or her position accurately. That would mean you cannot reply to someone's message until you make it clear that you understand the message as that person understood it. It may sound easy, but it is extremely difficult. Still, we must learn to develop that kind of empathy if we are to use it to prevent conflict.

The fourth suggestion builds upon the first three. To help prevent conflict, establish an accepting, cooperative, participative, nonthreatening, supportive climate. You will notice a great deal of redundancy in the adjectives I used; I think the idea so important that I have said it in several different ways. Set up an atmosphere of mutual trust and shared rewards. If trust exists, and that trust is justified, then the communicators can take risks. They can disclose themselves rather freely without fear, and they can speak candidly on the issues without psychologically threatening the other people. In this atmosphere, negative judgments are held in abeyance, and new ideas are examined and explored. In addition, when the climate is supportive (encourages free, open, and honest communication), people are not forced into a win-or-lose situation. With shared rewards, everyone can win. In such a climate, conflict is greatly reduced or prevented.

4. *Communication can reduce conflict.* The discussion on communication that causes and intensifies conflict probably gave you some insights on how to use communication to reduce interpersonal struggles. Here, briefly, are a few hints:

Focus on the points of agreement rather than on the points of disagreement. There will be issues on which you agree. Start with those. Then, emphasize the goals you share with the other communicators. Make clear the possibility of shared rewards, and demonstrate your willingness to cooperate in achieving the shared goals. Disclose those aspects of yourself that your receivers will view positively. Establish common bonds with your receivers. Work to develop trust and a nonthreatening communication climate. And, finally, give positive feedback to your receivers; be sensitive to their needs and feelings. Give both verbal and nonverbal responses that will encourage the other people and reduce their defensiveness.

5. *Communication can be used to alleviate conflict.* Let us look briefly at three methods employed to resolve conflict: negotiation, mediation, and arbitration.

Negotiation is the process involving joint deliberation—direct interaction, discussion by the parties to a dispute of their differences on matters of mutual interest and concern. It is aimed at settling the differences and resolving the problem in some way acceptable to both. Its result, if successful, is compromise—an agreement that all parties can live with.

In negotiation, the parties to a dispute reveal the range of solutions acceptable and unacceptable to each of them. If the solutions that the parties consider acceptable overlap, compromise is possible and settlement should result. Of course, these mutually acceptable solutions may not be (probably will not be) the preferred solutions for either party, but they can form the basis of an agreement. If there is no overlap of acceptable solutions, each party must modify its range of proposed solutions and match them up again. Until there is an area of overlap on acceptable solutions, no compromise can be reached.

Mediation is a process in which someone who is not a party to the dispute is brought into the bargaining to assist in resolving the conflict. The person who is brought in (the mediator) must be acceptable to all parties to the conflict and is brought in by mutul consent. The mediator does not make a decision, but does convene and chair the meetings. The mediator's role is to help the parties make a decision. The mediator is a catalyst who helps clarify the issues and the various positions on the issues, facilitates cooperative communication and inhibits destructive communication, serves as messenger for the various parties, and tries to stimulate the parties to view solutions they may not have considered before. The mediator is there to recognize and remove the obstacles that are preventing the parties from coming to a mutually satisfactory agreement.

Arbitration is the process by which a decision in a dispute is made by an outside person. When the parties are unable to come to some acceptable compromise through direct negotiation or to reach a satisfactory solution with the aid of a mediator, they may turn to an arbitrator to settle the dispute for them.

The arbitrator has to be acceptable to all sides. Waiving their rights to decide for themselves, the parties give the power to make a binding decision to the arbitrator. The arbitrator listens to the case that each side presents, weighs all the evidence and the arguments presented, and reaches a decision. All the parties must then abide by whatever decision the arbitrator renders. Arbitration is used when all other means of resolving conflict have failed.

Having disposed of some myths about communication and having taken note of a few reminders, let us turn our attention to the process of human communication and the elements in that process.

human communication as a process

David K. Berlo published his great book *The Process of Communication* in 1960. Almost every book on communication published since has noted that human communication is a *process,* not something static. That concept is an important one, and we should look at it a bit more closely. There are, I think, five implications of the process approach to human communication.

The word *process* comes from a Latin word meaning *going forward* or *proceeding.* A process, then, involves a progression; it has to do with ongoing movement. A process is a series of actions that proceed. They go somewhere. There is linearity over time. A communication event, if communication is a process, progresses; it moves forward in time.

Another implication of the word *process* for students of communication is this: a process is a dynamic phenomenon. *Dynamic* is the opposite of *static,* or *at rest.* A process is constantly changing as time goes by; there is continuous motion. And the actions and functions are not so much one after another as simultaneous. Anything in process is changing all the time, and the inherent activity is going on all at the same time.

One definition of *process* is: operations that produce something. This definition of process focuses less on what process is than on what it does. A process consists of actions, changes, or functions that produce a result. A process has an outcome; a process has a product; a process effects change.

One important aspect of any process is mutual interaction. The elements or variables affect each other. The concept of process reminds us that the ingredients are not just added up or even mixed together. They act on each other—each affecting the others, each changing the others. Perhaps the best illustration is from chemistry. Think of the difference between a mixture and a compound. In a mixture, the ingredients are mixed up together, but they retain their own identities. In a compound, the elements interact; they affect each other when they come together; they lose their separate identities and produce something else. A process involves more than the sum of its parts.

The final implication in the word *process* is to be found in this definition: a process is an integrated system involving interdependent variables (or elements). A process has order; it is a *system.* There is a structure, a pattern, to the process. This organized system involves elements that work together in some orderly or methodical way. The elements work together as a whole (the system is integrated) and thus achieve (or produce) an outcome.

How do these aspects of the meaning of the word *process* contribute to our understanding of human communication? Let us review: a human communication event (1) takes place in time and moves forward in time; (2) is dynamic—constantly changing; (3) produces a change or achieves an outcome; (4) involves mutual interaction, each communicator affecting the other(s); (5) involves a group of interrelated elements working together as a whole system.

A process is difficult to study. If it is constantly moving, continuously changing, always progressing, how can it be examined? You have to stop something to get a good look at it. But if you stop something dynamic, you change its essential nature. Then what you look at is a distortion of the thing itself.

The problem of trying to analyze the process of human communication can be compared to trying to analyze a ballet. A ballet is an event that has all five of the aspects I just mentioned. Look back and see if they do not apply. If I am going to try to show you what happens in a ballet, Gerald Arpino's *Trinity,* for example, I can show you a photograph taken during the ballet. That photo stops the action; it freezes the motion. We can study the photograph closely, and from that photo we can learn many useful things about the ballet. But the ballet itself is much more than we can capture with a still photograph. As we look at that photo, we must remember that it represents that ballet in a very limited way. Its static representation fails to capture the dynamics that are the very essence of the ballet experience itself.

So too, any time we analyze the process of human communication, we must stop the action to examine it. But we must remember as we do so that we are failing to capture the dynamics that are the very essence of the human communication experience.

I need to point out another limitation of our study of the process of human communication. Although we will look at basic elements involved in the process, we will not be looking at *all* of the elements that are at work. The process is far too complex to admit of a complete treatment of all the elements. At least, to this point, not all the variables have been determined. We will be looking at the most important factors—or at what we now believe to be the most important factors—in that process. We must also look at these factors or elements in some kind of order. We cannot discuss them all at the same time, even though in real life they *operate* at the same time. We are forced to examine the elements one at a time. Since there is no beginning and no end in this process, where do we start, and how do we arrange the sequence of elements for analysis? The order is arbitrary. Do not get the impression that the human communication process itself functions in the order that the elements are presented here. Our list of elements, then, is incomplete, and we will be studying that list of elements in an artificially imposed order. As inadequate as it is, I hope our discussion of this complex process will be stimulating and enlightening.

the five elements of the human communication process

These five elements, I believe, constitute an irreducible minimum: context, sender, message, delivery system, and receiver. The context is the environment *in which* the communication event takes place. The sender is the person *who* produces a message. The message is *what* the sender produces, to which the receiver attaches significance (meaning). The delivery system is *how* the message is conveyed from the sender to the receiver. And the receiver is the person *by whom* a message is taken in, assigned meaning, and reacted to. We will look at each of these elements in more detail.

Context

Communication does not take place in a vacuum. It always occurs within a context, and that environment affects the communication process. Other words for context might be *situation* or *setting*. We all communicate in a wide variety of situations each day, and we must adapt to those different communication settings.

Each communication context has three aspects or dimensions: the physical context, the social context, and the cultural context.

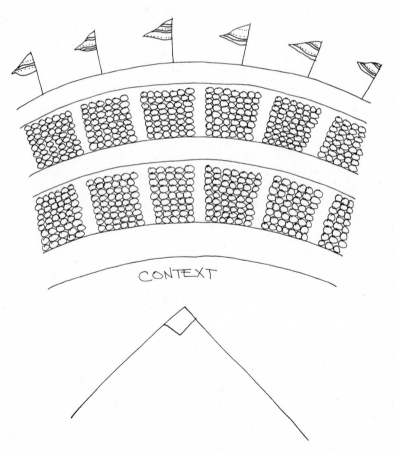

One of the five elements of the communication process:
Context

The *physical context* has to do with when and where the communication event takes place. We human beings exist in time and space, and the communication in which we are engaged occurs within the boundaries of time and space. Put another way, we human beings are, at least in part, physical beings; we live in the material world, and we are part of that material world. Our physical environment influences us and affects our communications.

You may not have considered *time* as part of your physical surroundings before. But, if you think about it a bit, I think you will agree that we do live within time boundaries. Time imposes limitations on us; it is a kind of framework for our existence—and our communications. And that time framework affects the outcomes of our communications.

Just think about it. Even if the human communicators (transceivers) are the same people, and the message is the same message, and the other aspects of the physical surroundings are the same, can the factor of time affect the receiver's response? Indeed. I do not like to teach a class right after lunch. Or at 8:00 A.M., for that matter. My experience is that class-room communication is more efficient and effective at other times of the day. The classroom may be the same; the teacher and students may be the same; the lecture may be on the same subject. But that difference in *time* matters!

I am sure you can think of many examples from your own life of instances when someone wanted to talk with you, and you had to say (or wanted to say), "I'd love to discuss that with you, but I haven't *time* right now." Or: "I'm sorry, but—much as I want to discuss that with you—we'll have to do it some other *time*." Each person has his or her own priorities for the use of time, so we must be sensitive to others and try to send our messages at appropriate times. Don't we all appreciate the person who says, "I want to talk to you about . . . Is this a convenient time?" Or: "When would it be convenient for me to talk with you about . . . ?"

"There is a time and place for everything." So the old saying goes. The physical context of communication includes not only when, but where. The material, or tangible, setting also affects the communication that takes place within it. Even if the other elements of the communication event remain relatively the same (they cannot remain completely the same, since the environment will affect them), is a change in the *place*—the physical surroundings—likely to change receivers' responses?

On warm days, when the air conditioning was not working well in our windowless classroom, students have requested that we move the entire class outdoors under the trees on campus. I have been faced with a dilemma! The physical setting of the classroom is certainly not conducive to positive responses and increased learning. The room is too small; it is crowded; it is too hot; the air is stale; the paint color is unattractive; the students' chairs are hard and uncomfortable; and there are cigarette butts scattered about the floor. The lack of windows admits no natural light, and the electric lights in the room are not very illuminating (thanks to an energy-saving drive on campus). Still, I hesitate to take the class outdoors. True, there would be fresh air and light. We could sit on the grass instead of those wooden chairs. We would be less crowded, and the setting would be far less formal. But there would be countless distractions. The setting would not be as regimented and controlled. The passing cars, the strolling students, and the scampering squirrels might be far more interesting than my lecture. Some students might be more concerned about avoiding grass stains than about taking adequate notes. What would you decide if you were in my place?

Think about the classroom as a physical context for a moment. Are there different arrangements of the furniture in your various classrooms? Does it make a difference as far as communication is concerned? Does the arrangement of desks affect you as a communicator? How?

There may not be *a* time and *a* place for everything, but certainly some times and some places are more appropriate for particular interactions than others are. I would be delighted to discuss Reinhold Niebuhr's theories on the nature of mankind or Martin Buber's concept of the "Wholly Other" with you, but *not* during a basketball game at the Rupp Arena when Jerry Jones is about to attempt a free throw that would win the game and clinch the Southeastern Conference championship! Please! I'd be flattered and interested if you whispered, "Let's get together some time," though I might be put off if you said it at the funeral home during the wake for my best friend. And generally, I have found crowded subway platforms are not the best places to make proposals—either in business or romance.

SOCIAL CONTEXT: RELATIONSHIPS

The *social context* is determined by the relationship between (or among) the communicators. Just as there is a physical environment, there is also a social climate or social setting for the communication event. That social context sets certain boundaries or perceived limits on the interaction; it establishes certain expectations. Thus, the social context markedly affects the communications, because it limits the communicators' choices (if the perceived limitations are observed). It also affects the outcomes of the communications if the limitations are not adhered to, because the receivers will probably respond on the basis of their shattered expectations. They will perceive the message sent as "out of bounds," and they will react accordingly. The point is that receivers react to messages, based in part on the perceived relationship between the sender and the receiver. Isn't it true that some people can say something to you without offending you, while other people can say the same thing and offend you greatly? And isn't the difference in your reaction probably the result of a different *relationship* between you and the two sets of folks?

There are probably three aspects of social relationships: role, status, and attraction. Let us look at each of these briefly.

Role. *Role* is a term related to the communicators' relative functions. Professional or business relationships, friendship, or kinship are examples.

Such relationships might be: teacher-student, professor-dean, sales-person-client, employer-employee, supervisor-worker, friend-friend, brother-sister, husband-wife, parent-child. These roles occur as you take part in a larger social structure or organization, it is true, but they are personal relationships. And these role relationships carry with them, in each culture, certain limitations, boundaries, or expectations. Those limits affect human communication.

Will a professor accept suggestions about his or her teaching methods more readily from a student, a colleague, or a dean? The message may be exactly the same, and the physical setting may be the same. But will the difference in source and the receiver's relationship with that source make an important difference in the response?

The walls in my apartment house are thin, and I cannot avoid over-hearing my neighbors sometimes—especially if they are shouting. Recently I heard the voice of the thirteen-year-old son, in a heated exchange with his mother, yelling: "Dammit, shut up! I'm a person too!" How would you react to that message if you were the mother? Do you consider it out of bounds for a son to talk that way to his mother?

More recently, an acquaintance called me while he was on the job. I could hear his supervisor saying, in the background, "You are not supposed to use the company phone for personal calls. We have a pay phone for that purpose." I was nearly deafened by the response, shouted at the supervisor: "That's right, O flunky of Management! Bust the chops of the poor workers! Work us like dogs, enforce the rules to the letter, tighten the screws on our shackles, and look the other way when managers do what they damned well please!" Was the worker staying within the expected boundaries imposed by the social context? In this particular communication event, was Walter playing his culturally prescribed role? Well, you are likely to say, it depends on the climate. Was the atmosphere serious or trivial (or comical)? Was it formal or informal? The worker could have been clowning, satirizing his role, and the supervisor may have understood and appreciated the joke. Maybe!

Status.   The second aspect (or component) of social relationships is *status.* Here we are dealing with prestige, power, or influence. In the relationship between (or among) the communicators, where does the status lie? Are the communicators of equal or unequal status? Perceived differences in status affect the communication event. For one thing, people of similar social status are more likely to have contact with each other. There are studies that indicate people tend to choose friends (and initiate communication) with persons of the same or higher social status. Receivers' responses may be based on whether the communication transaction was appropriate for the respective statuses of the communicators.

I was reminded of this principle on a visit to Greece last year. A Greek friend and I were entering his apartment building. He is an M.D. and owns a condominium in the building—the penthouse, as a matter of fact. When we came into the lobby, the superintendent of the building was mopping the lobby floor. He stopped, looked up, and said, "Καλημέρασου." My friend was incensed, and he began to fume in English—a language unknown to the super. "Did you hear that?" he said to me. "Impudence, disrespect, vulgar rudeness!" He raged on. Now I know only a little Greek, but I did understand that the super had simply said, "Good morning to you." Of course, he had used the familiar *you* pronoun rather than the polite form for *you*. The familiar form is used (speakers of Spanish will recognize the same distinction in Spanish) for children, people below you in rank, and close friends and family. I frankly thought the super was just trying to be friendly and cordial with his greeting. My friend (social status is even more important to the Greeks than to us Americans) felt insulted that one of low social status would presume to be friendly. It was all right for the super to greet him with a "good morning," provided he noted, syntactically, the difference in their status!

Attraction. The third component of the social context is personal *attraction* (or lack thereof). This element of social relationships derives from the communicators' attitudes toward each other. Do they regard each other with affection or hostility? Do they feel friendly or unfriendly toward each other? What are the personal "vibes" in their relationship? Just how highly do they regard each other, or do they hold the other person(s) in low esteem?

The social context will be determined by the communicators' relationships, and those relationships will be determined by their respective roles, their perceptions about status, and how well they like each other.

CULTURAL CONTEXT

The third aspect or dimension of communication context is *cultural context*. When we human beings come to a communication situation, we do not come alone. We bring with us the influences of the groups to which we belong. And all of us belong to *many* groups—not just one. The cultural context has to do with the respective cultures of the communicators.

As I am using the term, *culture* refers to a group's customary ways of looking at the world and judging behavior. Culture is the sum total of the customs of a group of people. It is the standardized ways of thinking, feeling, and acting acquired in a group and enforced by group pressure. It involves common perspectives and common practices; it involves common beliefs, values, and attitudes; it involves standards used in evaluating behavior. It provides blueprints for living, guides for daily life, maps for making choices.

Does every group develop its own culture? Yes, indeed. The group has a sense of identity. "We" belong, and "they" don't; that makes us a group. Members of the group have a sense of identification; they feel included. Members of the group have a sense of loyalty to the group, too. It is "our" group; it is "my" group. The group will develop customary ways of looking at things and customary ways of doing things. That is culture.

Culture, of course, is learned. We learn what the group believes to be true and false, what the group regards as valuable and worthless, and what the group is for and against. Those are the group's beliefs, values, and attitudes. We learn them through communication with other members of the group, and they are passed down in the group from generation to generation. We also internalize the group's *norms,* standards used in judging behavior. Norms are guidelines that specify appropriate or inappropriate behavior, approvable or unapprovable behavior.

If you abide by the group's norms, then your behavior is—that's right—*normal.* If, on the other hand, you do not conform to the norms of your group, then your behavior is—hold on to your hats—*abnormal.* That means, of course, that the concepts of normal and abnormal are directly related to some specific group's standards of conduct and that normal behavior in one group may be abnormal in another.

Now back to cultural context: each of us brings to every communication event the beliefs, values, attitudes, and norms we have internalized from the groups we belong to. They surround us like a huge, invisible bubble. We never escape them completely. When we communicate, they are there—in us and around us—our portable world view, our cultural conditioning.

Think of all the groups you belong to and have belonged to over your lifetime. I am not talking about formal organizations necessarily, just identifiable groups that you have felt a part of. Can you make a list? Start with your family. That was the first one, wasn't it? Then your childhood friends. What groups came next? As an exercise, I just sat down and listed some of the groups I have been a member of, groups that mattered to me and that exercised some influence on my life. My list is far from complete, but it comes to one hundred groups! How many can you think of yourself?

Fine, you say. I have belonged to many groups. I now belong to many groups. And each of these groups has beliefs, values, attitudes, norms, and practices that have affected my view of the world. I bring those cultural influences with me whenever I communicate with another human being. But just how does the cultural context affect the communication event?

Well, many of your group memberships will be irrelevant to a particular communication event, but some of them will matter. Which ones matter vary from communication event to communication event. It depends on what you and the others are talking about and with whom you are talking and listening. "Well," said one of my friends recently, "tell me when my being a Black female would not be an important factor in the cultural context of a communication event!" I told her of a conversation I had with a Black American couple and some Turkish nationals in Istanbul. In that conversation, the cultural differences that mattered were the differences between Americans and Turks—not between Blacks and whites! She conceded the point, and she reminded me of James Baldwin's essay about going to France and discovering he was an American.

One may communicate with another person who is perceived as a member of the same reference group, and one may communicate with someone perceived as a member of a different reference group. The subject matter may make the difference. For example, I come from a Christian tradition, a Protestant Christian tradition, a Free Church Protestant Christian tradition. If I am talking with someone who comes from a Roman Catholic Christian tradition about Jesus' Sermon on the Mount, we will probably find ourselves functioning as members of the same relevant reference group (Christians), and the context will be intracultural (within the same culture). On the other hand, if we are discussing the doctrine of the infallibility of the Pope, we will probably find ourselves functioning as members of different relevant reference groups (Protestants and Roman Catholics), and the context will be intercultural or cross-cultural (between or across cultures). Now, if I am discussing the doctrine of the infallibility of the Pope with a member of the Protestant Episcopal Church, we two will likely function as members of the same relevant reference group (Protestants) and the context will be intracultural. But if I discuss with that same Episcopalian the program for the joint sunrise Easter service, we will likely *not* function as members of the same relevant reference group. My Free Church background is quite different from the liturgical background of Anglicans. The context, though we are both Protestants, will be intercultural!

There is another complicating factor we must face, however. People who are members of a group and who are, therefore, immersed in its culture may conform or not conform to the prevailing culture. One may be within the culture and rebel against it. Whether one is a conformist or nonconformist is also an ingredient of the cultural context.

If, in relation to the message and the communication situation, the communicators are members of the same relevant reference group and bring to the communication event the same cultural heritage, they may: (1) both conform to the culture, (2) both not conform to the culture, or (3) one conform and the other not conform to the culture. In a very real sense, the third possibility presents an intercultural context!

If the communicators are not members of the same relevant reference groups, but rather are members of significantly different reference groups, they may clash on beliefs, values, attitudes, norms, or practices. These, of course, are the crucial points of difference among cultures. Since so many people take their culture for granted and associate primarily with those who share the same perspectives and practices, they may be shocked by cultural differences. Indeed, they may be very intolerant of cultural differences. They may well assume that their culture (beliefs, values, attitudes, norms, and behaviors) is absolute instead of relative. Right, period, instead of right for us (or me). And superior to all other systems. A good example is this incident witnessed by a friend of mine. An American Roman Catholic male working in Japan discovered that his Japanese secretary saw nothing wrong in having a pregnancy terminated by a physician. He exploded, "These Japanese have no morals!"

We have looked at three aspects or dimensions of the communication context: the physical context, the social context, and the cultural context. Let us turn our attention to the message-sender.

Sender

The sender is the source of a message. The sender is the person or persons who produce(s) behavior that stimulates ideas in a person or persons. The sender is the message-producer, the message-transmitter. Remember that human beings are transceivers; they both send and receive messages, and they can do both at the same time. Also remember that a human being can send messages to and receive messages from other people (interpersonal communication) *and* send and receive messages within himself or herself—inside his or her own body (intrapersonal communication). We are pulling out the single function of sending, of message-production, in order to be able to analyze it more easily. Do not get the idea however, that "the sender" is one discreet entity, one separate *person,* and "the receiver" is another discreet entity, another separate person. When two people are communicating together (a two-person group is called a *dyad*), both are performing the sending and receiving functions simultaneously, even if one does all the talking and the other never says a word! For clarity, however, we must look at the two functions (sending and receiving) separately. That procedure makes sense. The person performing the two functions may be the same person, but the functions themselves are different.

What happens in the sending element of the communication process? (We will focus on intentional speech communication, although we have

SENDER

**One of the five elements of the communica-
tion process: Sender**

already noted that human communication includes more than just intentional speech communication.) Briefly stated, the sender responds to some stimulus (either internal or external) in terms of his or her conditioned perceptions, fixes on some goal or purpose, has an idea for a message that will (perhaps) accomplish that purpose, chooses symbols for the message, encodes the message, and transmits the message in code.

RESPONSE

When we look at any communication event, we always pick up the story in the middle. Something has always gone before—no matter where we start. We have chosen to start by looking at the sender's response to some stimulus. That makes sense to me, but clearly the stimulus preceded the response. The sender is reacting to something. The stimulus may be something he or she sees, hears, tastes, smells, touches, or feels. The stimulus may be what someone else says or does. Or the stimulus may be some internal state; the person might feel hungry or sad or lonely or in pain. In any case, something stimulates the sender to respond. The person's response will be determined in part, of course, by the nature of the stimulus. But it will also be determined by that person's way of looking at the world, which, for want of a better metaphor, we will call *filters*.

FILTERS

We all look at the world, other people and ourselves through a kind of mental eyeglasses. Think of the metaphor for a moment and see how it applies to our perceptions. Filters are devices that screen out some things and let others through. You photographers probably put filters over your camera lenses to keep out some light rays and let others in. The filter in your coffee-making machine at home lets the coffee-flavored water pass through, but it holds back the coffee grounds. Maybe your eyeglasses (speaking literally now) are tinted. If so, you chose the tint to color (and thus distort somewhat) what you look at. My sunglasses ("shades") protect me from looking at the sunny world as it is; they keep out the bright, painful glare and let through light rays I can deal with more easily. Our mental filters work much the same way.

As we will see in much more detail in Chapter 3, we learn how to look at the world. Our perceptions, what we think we see and how we interpret what we think we see, greatly influence our responses to the incoming stimuli.

When little Nichole was born, she had no set of beliefs, values, or attitudes. She had no sentiments or loyalties. She had no standards by which to judge beliefs or behavior; she was not *ab*normal, but she was *a*normal—without norms at all. She had no categories into which to lump people, and she had no prejudices—ethnic, national, or religious. She was neither biased (leaning) toward or against the Baptists or the Buddhists, theists or atheists, Democrats or Republicans, capitalists or communists. She had not learned anything about shame or guilt or blame or sex roles.

Nothing embarrassed her; she did not think anything was "dirty" or "disgusting." As Oscar Hammerstein rightly observed, "You've got to be carefully taught." And those we come in contact with from the day we are born are busy teaching us! They put the filters on us through which we look at the world. "Stop that, Nichole. Nice girls don't do things like that!" "You should be ashamed of yourself. God saw what you did!" And "Mother doesn't want you associating with that sort of people. They're not our kind." Or "How are you going to get ahead if you don't . . . ?" Or "Look out for number one. No one else will." Or "You don't want to be a tomboy; it's not feminine!"

Our parents get the first chance to put filters over our mental eyes, but others soon join in—clergy, teachers, friends, TV personalities. And we are carefully taught till the layer of filters is thick! The filters are our perceptual screen, and they help determine what stimuli we respond to and how we respond. The response leads us to aim toward a goal or *purpose.*

PURPOSE

The purpose or goal is what the sender is trying to accomplish. The sender must decide what effect he or she is trying to produce. We settle on a target: What do I want to happen as a result of my message-producing? What response am I trying to elicit? Intentional communication always has the aim of inducing a specific response from some human being(s). The specific purpose, then, is the specific reaction the sender wants from the receiver(s). The question is: What belief or behavior does the sender want (intend) his or her message to produce (or effect)? In order to accomplish that purpose, the sender must stir up ideas in the mind of the receiver(s), and to do that we construct and transmit messages. The sender, therefore, must determine the meanings he or she wants stirred up in the receiver(s). That leads us to the *ideas.*

IDEA(S)

At this step, one has a thought or feeling that he or she would like to share. What occurs is not completely clear. We formulate an idea; we are "thinking." Psychologists have called this process *cognition.* This state involves electrical impulses and chemical changes inside our bodies, particularly within our brains. Thinking is really physiological; it is electrochemical happenings within one's body.

There is a debate about the relationship between language and thought. Do we think in words? If so, the words are tools of thought, and language would be *necessary* for cognition. Do we *always* think in words? Here the answer is *no.* Admittedly, we do not know much about the neurophysiology involved, but we can think without the use (or manipulation) of words. Mathematicians, I am told, can think in mathematical symbols. Ah, but you say, they are still *symbols*! True, and musicians can think in musical symbols as well. But, musicians, you know that you can also think a tune! You can look at a piece of music that you have never seen before and think the melody in your head. You may also be able to think the harmonic progressions in your head. Now we are not thinking in symbols—musical or otherwise; we are certainly not thinking in words. But we are thinking!

Some writers call this idea step a *preverbal state.* And it *may* be. But I do not think we can totally rule out the possibility that developing most ideas and the use of verbal symbols (words) are interrelated. Certainly, if we are going to transmit a message to another human being, we must select symbols through which to do so. The next intrapersonal communication step (within the sender), then, is selecting the *symbols.*

SYMBOLS

Thinking is, in part at least, reviewing alternatives and making choices. Although we may not be able to separate them completely, the preceding step involved deciding on the thoughts or feelings to be shared with another human being. The question there was: What *meaning(s)* do I want to stir up in the mind of my receiver? At this step, the question is somewhat different (though it is related). The question now is: What symbols will I choose to represent my ideas? What words do I have to choose from (that I know) that will also be known to my listener? What symbols are likely to stimulate in him or her meanings similar to my own? The sender may examine many possible verbal symbols before selecting the most appropriate symbols for the sender, the receiver, and the situation.

Thus far, the process is all internal. The happenings are inside one's skin. But we are getting ready to transmit the message we have chosen. We cannot transmit the ideas (the thoughts and feelings) themselves. They are electrical impulses and chemical reactions that remain locked up inside our bodies. The words we have thought of are also abstractions; after all, they were *thought* of and are therefore untransmittable. We must code the message in some form that is capable of being sent outside our bodies and retrieved by other persons. We therefore turn these symbols into *code.*

CODING

A code is a system of signs, things that can stand for something other than themselves. Signs represent something else. The code we use for our most complicated and important messages is language. A language, as we shall see in much more detail in Chapter 6, is a conventionalized system of arbitrary vocal signs. A language code, then, is a spoken code. Writing is an attempt to represent that spoken code and thus preserve it.

When we transmit messages through speech communication, we use verbal symbols—the code of language. There are other codes that have been used, of course. $\cdots$ $---$ $\cdots$ is a representation of a message in Morse Code. In class I can tap out the dits and dahs so my students can hear the code as it is actually used. I have never tried demonstrating smoke signals in class, but that is a form of coded message also. So too are the drum signals that were used in Africa. Languages use sounds in their codes—sounds made by the human beings themselves. Every language has its own system of sounds. English uses about forty-two; Spanish uses thirty-two. If we are going to use a particular language code, we must learn the sounds. We must learn to recognize the sounds, differentiate among them, and produce those sounds with our own bodies.

My little niece Jenny is now learning which sounds matter in the code we call the American English language. She is learning to tell an $\bar{e}$ from an $\bar{a}$ and a t from a d. If she did not learn this, she would not be able to hear or transmit the difference between *meet* and *mate* or between *do* and *two*.

At this step of the process of message-producing, the sender must turn the words into sounds of the code. Of course, the sender must first choose what code to send the message in, if the sender is fortunate enough to know more than one. (I envy my friend Dimitri Manouskos, because he can shift from Greek to French to German to English as easily as I shift from formal to informal Standard American English!)

Let us suppose that I am responding to noises coming from my teenage son that he thinks are music and I think are unbearable. My musical background provides my filters and shapes my perception of his wailing. My purpose is to reduce irreversible damage to my ears and to increase my sense of comfort and well being. I have the idea that a message asking him to desist will accomplish this purpose, and I intend to share my thoughts and feelings about his vocal production. I have a number of options about how to word that message. I could say, "Would you please reduce the decibel level to zero?" Or: "Your poor old dad would appreciate a little peace and quiet." Or: "I'm sure you could find a better place for your serenade." Or countless variations on this theme. I decide on a short two-word message: "Stop it!" To send that message, I will need to produce six speech sounds: s, t, $\ddot{a}$, p, i, and t. The two t's will not be exactly alike, but let us not worry about that right now. I know the forty-two sounds of American English and their usual variations; I have picked out the ones for the words I have chosen. My task is now *transmission*.

We transmit the selected elements of the code (the sights and sounds). We make noises and movements with our bodies, and the coded message goes out via sound and light waves. The brain has ordered the body to make the necessary adjustments, and the sounds and the movements are produced. Sometimes, it is true, one gets his or her tang tongueled; there may be a slipup between the orders given by the brain and the various parts of the transmitting system. In general though, we are able to produce the coded messages that we intend to. We are now ready to look at the third element (or component) in the speech communication process: the transmitted message itself.

In interpersonal communication, the transmitted message (as distinguished from the intended message and from the received message) is audible and

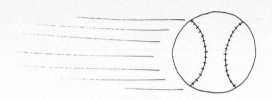

MESSAGE

**One of the five elements of the communi-
cation process: Message**

visible physical behavior. It is something that is heard and seen by a receiver; it is something that has been done by a sender.

What can we say about the sights and sounds of transmitted messages? A great deal—as you will see in Chapters 6, 10, 11, and 12. For now, it is enough to note that there are three components in any transmitted message. Any message in human communication will have these three elements: a code, a content, and a structure.

CODE

Messages come to us in the form of some kind of system of signs. They come mediated through signs—either signals or symbols. (See pp. 17–18.) We send and receive messages in code. (A code, you remember, is a system made up of signs—things that represent or stand for other things.) If we are to receive and understand any message, we must know the system of signs used in sending that message. Even if the message is unintentional, the receiver will interpret the message based on some signal or symbol system. If messages are to be interpreted as a sender intends, the sender and receiver must share the same code.

Most writers have divided codes into verbal and nonverbal codes. This division (word codes and nonword codes), though common, has some major disadvantages. I think it is more useful to divide messages in human communication into speech and nonspeech messages than into the usual categories of verbal and nonverbal messages. True, most of the literature on communication employs the verbal/nonverbal distinction, although many writers mention the problems associated with such a division. I confess to using those terms also, but the more relevant distinction, I believe, has to do with speech and nonspeech messages.

Each spoken language is a code. If one doesn't know the language, it is a secret code. But each linguistic code contains both verbal and nonverbal elements. When a person learns American English, for example, that person learns not only the sounds, grammar, and words of the language, he or she also learns the intonation patterns (speech melodies) and other paralinguistic features of the language. (See pp. 15 and 178–181.)

As I have noted earlier, when we speak we send three concurrent (simultaneous) and inextricably interwoven elements: the verbal, vocal, and visible elements of the speech communication message. When we speak, we transmit speech sounds that, combined, make words; we transmit variations in our voices that suggest our feelings and attitudes; and we transmit visible bodily activity. All three elements, taken as a whole, are the speech message. Two of these elements are nonverbal, and one is verbal (word-making). But they form an impression as a whole. We receivers do not get separate verbal and nonverbal impressions. The speech communication message is all tied up together—transmitted together and received together.

But there are messages we send and receive that are not speech communication messages. It is important that we study them as well. These unspoken codes are, for the most part, what writers are discussing when they analyze "nonverbal communication." (Remember, the two exceptions are the nonverbal elements in speech communication: paralinguistic features, the vocal element of spoken messages, and kinesics, the bodily activity or visible element of the spoken message. We will look at those in more detail in Chapter 10.) There are different kinds of codes. Spoken languages are only one. But all messages in human communication are sent and received in code. Receivers decode the messages and interpret them (assign them meaning).

CONTENT

Messages will come in code, but they will carry *content*. There is information in messages. If I transmit the sequence of noises (sounds) to form the word *shut*, then I have certainly not transmitted the code to be translated *open*. The bits of information in messages cut down ambiguity; indeed, each bit cuts it in half. If I transmit the sequence of sounds for the words *shut it*, we have excluded the possibility of *open*, but *it* is ambiguous. If I choose to transmit sound sequences for *shut the door* or *shut your mouth*, however, I have included another bit of information in the message as transmitted.

STRUCTURE

The third component of messages is *structure*. Any message will have some form. Indeed, it is impossible for anything that exists not to exist in some form! The difference between "He shut the door" and "The door was shut by him" is a difference in form—not in content. Another example: "That class is boring" and "How boring that class is!" differ in structure, not in content. We will analyze structure of messages in more detail in Chapter 12.

A transmitted message, in summary, is behavior of a sender, to which a receiver attaches significance. That message will be sent (and received) in code; it will have content; and it will be structured. We are now ready to

The Delivery System

look at the fourth component of the speech communication process—the means by which we get the message from the sender to the receiver.

Writers on communication have called the delivery system either *channel* or *medium*, and they have used the terms interchangeably. The plural of channel is channels, of course, and the plural of medium is media. As we will see in a little more detail in Chapter 11, not only have these two terms been used as synonyms, both have been used to refer to two separate and distinct features of the delivery system. No wonder students get confused!

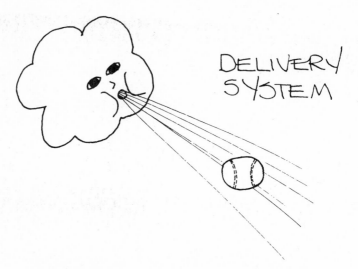

One of the five elements of the communication process: Delivery system

We can distinguish at least two features of the delivery system, the system through which a message is delivered (conveyed or transmitted) from a sender to a receiver. Without a message, there will be no reception and no response—and no communication. The message must be delivered, so a means for conveying the message is necessary for communication as well. But that means (delivery system—usually called channel) often has at least two features (or aspects).

MESSAGE VEHICLES: CHANNELS

There must be a means for conveying the message itself. Usually our messages are carried to other people by means of the senses. Messages are coded, after all, into physical stimuli; those physical stimuli reach us receivers through the senses. Our senses are our "windows to the world."

When one person speaks to another, the transmitted message is encoded in sound and light waves. That message comes to the receiver through two channels: hearing (auditory) and seeing (visual)—two of our five senses. When you greet a long-absent friend, you may not send your message through speech; instead, you may express your thoughts and feelings in an embrace. The channel—the vehicle that carries your message—is the sense of touch (tactile). Can you think of an instance when the senses of taste and smell are used as channels (vehicles) for conveying a message?

VEHICLE CARRIERS: MEDIA

There often is, in the delivery system, a vehicle carrier as well as the message vehicle. As I have indicated, the message vehicle (channel) is usually one of the five senses. But we ingenious human beings have devised many ways of getting those message vehicles to our intended (and sometimes unintended) receivers. Confused? Maybe I can make it a little clearer with an illustration.

If you are watching a program on television, through what channels (I don't mean 11 or 13) are you receiving messages? Through what channels are you getting the messages delivered? Both seeing and hearing, you say, and that is right. So the channels (message vehicles) are visual and auditory senses. But what is the TV? What part did it play in getting the message to you? It was the means by which the sights and sounds came; it was the method of delivering the images and noises to you. The TV carried (or conveyed) the message vehicles (the two message channels) to you; the TV, then, is a vehicle carrier. And to make things clearer, I prefer to call vehicle carriers *media*. One vehicle carrier is a *medium*.

Consider one other illustration. When you talk on the telephone with a friend, what channel is being used to convey your messages? The auditory channel, right? The messages come back and forth from person to person through the hearing channel. That is the same channel that is used when we talk with a friend in face-to-face conversation. But this time we have another feature in the delivery system. We have the telephone; it is the medium used to transport your message vehicle (channel).

This distinction between two aspects of the message-delivery system is not, at present, in general use, but I believe it solves a terminology problem. If we use the term *channel* to designate what carries the message and the term *medium* to designate what carries the channel(s), the two aspects of the delivery system can be kept in a little clearer focus. We are now ready to consider the fifth element (or component) in the process of human communication: the receiver.

Receiver

The receiver is the one who acquires and consumes the message. The receiver is the person or persons who attend(s) to and react(s) to the sender's communicating behavior. Again, we must remember that we human beings are transceivers; we are both senders and receivers of messages. What we are analyzing now is the receiving function of human communication. Receiving is one component of the human communication process. We now focus on what occurs in that component.

Briefly stated, the receiver receives the coded message, decodes that message into code elements, combines those code elements into symbols, attaches meanings to those symbols, and, under the influence of the receiver's own purpose(s) and filters, responds to the reconstructed message. We will consider each of these steps in the receiving component.

RECEPTION

At this step, the receiver picks up signs. The receiver takes in physical stimuli. He or she sees something, hears something, feels, tastes, or smells something. In speech communication, the receiver hears and usually sees the behavior of the sender.

RECEIVER

One of the five elements of the communication process: Receiver

But what do we hear and see? At the reception step, we take in sound waves and light waves. The sound waves strike our eardrums and set up vibrations there; the light rays enter through the pupil of the eyeball and strike the retina. We do not *hear* speech sounds such as *s* or *k*; we hear vibrations. We do not *see* images; we see light rays reflected off images. That is what we receive. We must be able to recognize those physical stimuli as elements of a symbol system; at that point we are involved with *decoding*.

DECODING

I remember listening to broadcasts as a child that challenged me to break the secret codes being used on the broadcasts. It was very exciting—at the time. Any code that one doesn't know is a secret code. Traveling abroad, I long to be able to break the codes of languages unknown to me. It is frustrating to be able to hear the speakers and see the speakers but not be able to decode their messages! There is nothing wrong with my reception (hearing); the problem comes at the decoding step and gets compounded thereafter.

If there is nothing major wrong with my hearing, I can hear particular frequencies. My hearing mechanism can pick up the vibrations. To be able to decode, I must be able to recognize certain frequencies as particular sounds of a language. At the decoding stage, the receiver identifies the perceived frequencies (vibrations) as discreet speech sounds. "That noise I hear is a *g* or a *y*," for example. There is very little difference between *ē* and *ĭ*, but in English that little difference matters a lot. That little difference separates *neat* from *knit, reed* from *rid,* and *scene* from *sin.* The receiver must be able to discriminate the forty-two phonemes (significant sounds) in American English. In addition, the receiver must be able to recognize all the variations of a particular sound and disregard the differences that are insignificant. We have five variations of /t/ in American English, for example. We must be able to identify correctly all those allophones (varieties) as *t*. That, too, is part of decoding. The *t* in *matter* sounds a great deal like a *d*, but the receiver must correctly identify the sound as *t*. Otherwise, *matter* will be translated *madder*!

In the decoding process, we break the code by recognizing the parts of the code when we receive them. It is not enough to recognize the segments of a code, however. In speech communication, we must do more than just identify the specific sounds of a language when we hear various frequencies. The receiver(s) must put those speech sounds (those code segments) together into *symbols.*

SYMBOLS

We must, in our heads, string those individual sounds together and thus create words. In a very real sense, the receiver constructs the words—or at least, reconstructs the words—inside his or her brain. I am sure some doubter is thinking, "But the sender sends *words,* and the receiver receives *words.* The message comes to the receiver packaged in words already. There is no need for the receiver to *construct* words." Sorry. The sender in speech communication sends out (transmits) noises; those noises set up vibrations, or sound waves; those sound waves start the eardrums of a receiver vibrating; the receiver notes the vibrations and categorizes them as speech sounds. The receiver then figures out what words those speech sounds make.

I am sure some of my readers are not yet convinced. Try this: Say the words *stop it* out loud, just as you would if you were talking in regular conversation to someone else. Now say the sentence again, and listen carefully to the way the sentence is transmitted. How many syllables does that sentence contain? That's right: two. Where do the syllables divide as you say the sentence out loud? Say it again and check it out. That's right again: sto-pit! Did you transmit one word and then another word, separating the syllables between the two words? No. You did not send *stop/it* but *sto/pit*. The receiver must put the sounds and pauses (junctures) back together and out of *sto/pit* reconstruct *stop/it*. If you are not yet convinced that the receiver must create words out of the sounds perceived, try the same experiment with *hold on*. You will find that the sender will send the sentence *hol/don*, and it is up to the receiver to figure out the words *hold/on*.

Once the receiver turns the sounds into words, the receiver searches his or her mental file of meanings and assigns *ideas* to those words.

IDEAS

The receiver attaches meaning to the reconstructed words. If the receiver has no experience with a particular word and has never learned a meaning for that word, then the receiver cannot assign meaning to that word—unless he or she can guess it from the surrounding words (the verbal context).

Some books on communication have discussed "the transfer of meaning" from one person to another. Meanings are not transferred, however. Instead, they are stirred up; they are called forth; they are induced. Meanings do not reside in the words, and words do not carry meanings. We human beings have the meanings in our heads, and we attribute meanings to words. Another way of saying the same thing is this: we associate meanings (thoughts and feelings) with words. So, while words do not carry meaning, they do conjure up meaning in the receiver's mind.

The receiver will react to the meanings attached to the words that are perceived, but the receiver will also react, in part at least, on the basis of his or her own *purpose*.

PURPOSE

Obviously, the receiver will respond partly in terms of what the message is understood to mean. But, just as the sender has a purpose to fulfill in the communication situation, so too the receiver has a purpose (an aim or goal) to be accomplished. The receiver's purpose will also affect the outcome—the receiver's response.

The purposes of the sender and the receiver may be either compatible or incompatible. They need not be identical, but for communication to be effective (for the sender to accomplish his or her purpose), the two purposes must be at least complementary.

Let us take a hypothetical instance. I feel hungry (stimulus) and respond, based on my filters (conditioning). Since I grew up in my mother's home, where she always said, "Eat. You have to eat to live!," my filters incline me to a favorable view of good, nourishing food. My purpose is to satisfy my hunger, to alleviate my felt need for food. So, since I am sitting at the dinner table with my family, I get the idea for a message that will help accomplish my goal of filling my tummy. I decide on the words that I think will produce the desired effect: "Please pass me the mashed potatoes." I note the sounds needed to transmit that coded message (the code required is English in this case), and I transmit the coded message with my speech mechanism. My family hears the noises produced; actually, they receive the sound waves that resulted from my produced noises. They decode the message, turning the noises into speech sounds of the English language in their minds. They then group those sound sequences into words (symbols), also in their heads. They attach meanings to the words, so they get an idea of what my message was intended to mean. They know the words *please* and *pass* and *me* and *mashed potatoes*. They share with me very similar meanings for those words. They understand what I want, so the communication was efficient. But do they respond as I want them to? Probably not. *My* purpose, you will remember, was to get food and enjoy it and alleviate my nagging hunger. *Their* purpose is to assist the physician in keeping sugars and starches *from* me—and *for* themselves, I bitterly add. Our purposes are not complementary; instead, our purposes are contradictory. And the communication, judged on the basis of the sender's intent, is not effective. Someone will doubtless send me back a message suggesting I take another helping of green beans.

Receivers not only react to the reconstructed message on the basis of their purposes; they also react on the basis of their *filters*.

FILTERS

All human beings have on mental eyeglasses, through which we look out at the world. Whether we are, at the moment, looking at a transceiver's sending or receiving, the person's filters will affect the communication. Our filters affect our sending and our receiving. We respond through our view of the world. We cannot see things as they are. Many writers say, therefore, that we create our own "reality." Our general view (our filters) obviously affects our response to a particular stimulus.

Finally, we receivers—based on the idea that we attributed to the symbols that we put together from the sounds that we interpreted from the vibrations we received *and* based on the purpose(s) we have in the communication situation *and* based on the filters through which we screen everything—make a *response*.

RESPONSE

We react. Now I can hear some of you saying, "But that is where we came in. You started with *response* when you began discussing the sender." And you are quite right. Communication is a continuous cycle; it is a circular process. And this *is* where we started in considering the elements of the process of human communication.

We have, therefore, looked at the five elements of the communication process—the context, the sender, the message, the delivery system, and the receiver. These components are interrelated and interdependent; they each affect all the others, and they all must work together as a whole for the process to succeed.

SUGGESTIONS FOR FURTHER READING

APPLBAUM, RONALD L., OWEN O. JENSON, and RICHARD CARROLL, *Speech Communication: A Basic Anthology* (New York: Macmillan, 1975).

BACH, GEORGE R., and PETER WYDEN, *The Intimate Enemy* (New York: Avon, 1968).

BERLO, DAVID K., *The Process of Communication* (New York: Holt, 1960).

CIVIKLY, JEAN M., ed., *Messages: A Reader in Human Communication*, 2nd ed. (New York: Random House, 1977).

CONDON, JOHN C., JR., *Interpersonal Communication* (New York: Macmillan, 1977).

DANCE, FRANK E. X., ed., *Human Communication Theory* (New York: Holt, 1967).

DEVITO, JOSEPH A., "Some Intercultural Communication Conflicts," *Communicology: An Introduction to the Study of Communication* (New York: Harper & Row, 1978).

DEVITO, JOSEPH A., ed., *Communication: Concepts and Processes* (Englewood Cliffs, N.J.: Prentice-Hall, 1971).

FILLEY, ALAN C., *Interpersonal Conflict Resolution* (Glenview, Ill.: Scott, Foresman, 1975).

KONSKY, CATHERINE, and DAVID LARSEN, *Interpersonal Communication* (Dubuque, Iowa: Kendall/Hunt, 1975).

LIN, NAN, *The Study of Human Communication* (Indianapolis: Bobbs-Merrill, 1973).

MILLER, GERALD R., and HERBERT W. SIMONS, eds., *Perspectives on Communication in Social Conflict* (Englewood Cliffs, N.J.: Prentice-Hall, 1974).

MORTENSEN, DAVID, *Communication: The Study of Human Interaction* (New York: McGraw-Hill, 1972).

STEWART, JOHN, ed., *Bridges Not Walls*, 2nd ed. (Reading, Mass.: Addison-Wesley, 1977).

ZIMMERMAN, GORDON, JAMES L. OWEN, and DAVID R. SEIBERT, *Speech Communication: A Contemporary Introduction* (St. Paul, Minn.: West Publishing Co., 1977).

3
PERCEPTION

general goal:

To learn what the process of perception is and how it is related to human communication.

specific objectives:

After completing this unit, you should understand:
What the process of perception is.
What the steps in the perception process are.
Some factors that impose limits on our perceptions.
Some variations in stimuli that affect our perceptions.
How we can check (verify) our perceptions.
Some basic principles of perception.

the process of perception

YOU AND I LIVE IN TWO WORLDS—the world inside-my-skin and the world outside-my-skin—and we are constantly collecting information about both worlds. Hunger pangs tell me I have worked past the dinner hour; pains in my side tell me I have run too far or too fast for my age and condition; my stopped-up nose and watery eyes tell me it is hay fever season again; my sweating palms and dry mouth tell me I am more nervous than I thought I was. This information was collected from the world inside-my-skin. But, through the senses, I get information about the world outside-my-skin. The five senses are my windows on the world around me. I see a patch of poison ivy and recognize a dangerous enemy; I hear Anathema meowing and guess the poor cat's in trouble again; I smell great aromas as I approach the front door and I know the evening's menu; I taste one sip of milk from the new carton and discover the milk is sour; I touch the Charmin to find out if it is as soft as the commercials say it is.

The brain is the message center and control center, where messages about our two worlds are received and, sometimes, stored. But will everyone looking at the same scene *see* the same thing(s)? Or will everyone listening to the same concert *hear* the same thing(s)? No, people's *perceptions* vary. Perceptions?

Perceptions is not a new word to you. You have probably said to a friend, "Well, we just don't have the same perceptions about that," or "I think I perceive that a little differently than you do." Haven't you had some friend tell you about a person that was "striking and attractive" only to find, when you met the person thus described, that you thought the person ordinary and *un*attractive? Or have you been told about some "beautiful" painting or piece of music, only to be disappointed when you saw or heard it? There is an old saying that refers to perception: "Beauty is in the eye of the beholder!"

But what is perception? It is a process by which we try to make sense out of reality. My perception is my image of something; my perception is my awareness of something and how I see the thing I am aware of. Nobody sees things exactly as they (the things) are; our perceptions are imperfect and always somewhat distorted. When we talk about how things are (whether things outside our skins or inside our skins), we are talking about how we *think* they are—about our perceptions of them. That is why some writers say that whenever we talk about anything, we are talking about something that has gone on inside us (rather than purely external "reality") because we are talking about our perceptions. Perception is a process that goes on inside us.

Perception is the process of *gathering* information, *selecting* what to notice from that information, *mixing* that selected information with previously gathered information and beliefs, *organizing* the mixture into some pattern, and *interpreting* the organized mixture as meaning something. There are, then, five steps in the perception process. Let us look at that process step by step.

the five steps in the perception process

There are five steps in the process of perceiving: (1) gathering, (2) selecting, (3) mixing, (4) organizing, and (5) interpreting.

Gathering

The process of perception starts when we take in some information. From the world outside our skins, we collect data through the senses—seeing, hearing, tasting, smelling, touching. This data-collection step is not as simple as one might think.

One of the steps in the perception process: Gathering

Of course, we know that we take in information by seeing. But *what* is it we see? And *how* do we see? What is it we actually gather in, visually? We take in light rays! When we look at some object out in the world around us, we do not see the object itself; rather, we pick up light reflected from the surface of the object. Just as we do not see stars themselves, but the light reflected from the surfaces of the stars—just so, we pick up light reflected from the objects we "look at" here on earth.

But some objects, you will say, do not just reflect light rays from their surfaces (the light coming from the sun or moon or some artificial source); they *emit* light. Flashbulbs and flashlights and auto headlights and incandescent bulbs, and so on. Yes, that is true. The light rays that reach our eyes are either emissions or reflections of light. But the important thing to remember is that seeing begins with radiation hitting our eyeballs.

Some objects reflect more light than others, and the light rays vary in wavelengths. Because of those differences, differences in brightness and color are apparent to us. Physically, light waves are not colored; in fact, they are not even visible!

Light enters the eye through a transparent window called the *cornea*, passes through a hole in the thin, pigmented layer (the colored *iris*) called the *pupil*, then passes through the *lens*, which focuses it on the *retina* (the light-sensitive tissue at the back of the inside of the eyeball). The *retina* (which contains hundreds of thousands of nerve endings) converts the light energy that strikes it into nerve energy. The rays of focused light that fall (upside down, by the way) on the retina stimulate nerve impulses in the nerve endings of the retina (called *rods* and *cones*); these nerve impulses are carried by the large bundle of fibers called the *optic nerve* to the midbrain area; then they travel over fibers to the *occipital lobe* at the back of the brain. There the nerve impulses are interpreted, and we "see."

We have looked at one of the five methods of gathering data from the world outside our skins: seeing. As I said before, the gathering, or collecting of data (which is but the first step in the process of perception), is not simple; rather, it is very complex. Each of the five senses involves a complex reception, transmission, and interpretation system. The brain receives nerve impulses that we "hear" as sound; it receives nerve impulses that we taste as flavors; it receives nerve impulses that we feel as hard or soft or sharp; it receives nerve impulses that we smell as odors. And when we feel pain, the brain is receiving nerve impulses. All involve reception of nerve impulses, but each has its own different receptor tissues.

The process of perception begins with step 1: gathering. We take in information—light waves, sound waves, tastes, odors, tactile sensations. In this complex step, the external stimuli are converted into nerve impulses inside our bodies, and the brain interprets those nerve impulses. Thus, we see, hear, taste, smell, and touch. We get impressions (Our information is really guesses, isn't it?) about the world outside our skins.

Selecting

We human beings experience hundreds of different sensations every instant of our lives. We are constantly being bombarded with all sorts of stimuli! Human beings are walking receiving sets, and our receivers are always open—always "on." A person receives through all five channels (the five senses) all the time unless he or she has a physical handicap. The physical reception of the stimuli from the environment—the experiencing of sensation—is only the first step in the process of perception.

One of the steps in the perception process: Selecting

We gather in far more information than we can possibly process. We cannot possibly give attention to and deal with all the different bits of information that our five senses gather for us. At any given second, we cannot be aware of, or pay attention to, everything in our environment; we cannot notice everything that is happening around us. We cannot concentrate on everything at once. We must make choices. We must *select* what we will focus our attention on, which means that there are some things that will get less attention and some things that will get no attention at all.

Look at this picture. What do you see? What is it a picture of?

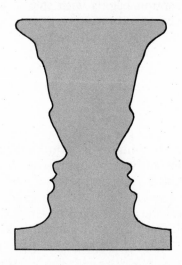

If you said it is a vase, then what part of the space did you give attention to and what part did you ignore? If, on the other hand, you said it is two people facing each other, which parts were you selecting to notice and which parts were you not selecting for attention? In either case, your eyes took in the entire picture, but you *selected* part of it to focus on.

In step 2 of the perception process, we pick out some stimuli (of all those taken in at step 1). Step 2, selection, is the subtraction step in the process, because we leave out many of the things we have gathered in (in step 1). It is very important that we understand this concept; the implications are tremendous. If everyone omits many of the details taken in (or put another way, ignores much of the information collected), then *all perception is partial!* Everyone's perceptions are necessarily incomplete and imperfect. It is true that "we know in part." Shouldn't that make us more tolerant of others who have differing perceptions?

A little later, I will discuss specific factors that limit our perceptions. These factors help determine what each of us will select to notice and choose to ignore. Of course, some selection is done *for* us; sometimes I am unable to gather the information. In that case, my perception is still partial, but the selection was not purely a matter of my choice. In general, however, most selection *is* a matter of choice—though the choices may not be made on the conscious level!

What do we tend to choose to notice? Generally, we select those stimuli that fit our past experience, our present concerns and needs, and our future hopes and expectations. We pay attention to what is comfortable to us, what is pleasant to us, what is important to us, what is believable to us, and what is understandable to us. In other words, we tend to select (or focus on) those stimuli that conform to and confirm our own view of the world.

Our five senses take in vast amounts of data and send a barrage of nerve impulses to the brain. We cannot handle all this incoming information, so we select some of it for special attention. Out of the multitudes of stimuli bombarding us each instant, we choose some to notice and deal with. For that reason, our perception is selective and partial. And our perceptions of "reality" are imperfect and incomplete.

Mixing

If step 2, selection, is the subtraction step in the process of perception, then step 3, mixing, is the addition step. It is at this point that we add in what we already know and believe. We never perceive anything in a vacuum. We bring to the experience of the present stimulus our previous experiences and our world view.

Here are some marks on the printed page. How would you identify them? What would you call them?

5

One of the steps in the perception process: Mixing

If you identified these marks as the number five, you did so because you *added* to the present visual stimulus information garnered a number of years ago. Doubtless, there is some proud parent or dedicated teacher who first introduced you to your numbers and taught you what a five looked like. You have amassed quite a file of information by this time in your life, and you bring that file with you to the perception process.

You bring not only information to the perception process; you also bring your values, attitudes, and beliefs. These, too, you have learned. They have been shaped by your experiences and interactions with other human beings. Call that general mind-set your world view. True, it was shaped by your experience; it is equally true, however, that it now *shapes* your experience because it affects your perception of all incoming stimuli.

What you already know and believe is an important added factor in the perception process. Your knowledge and beliefs are mixed in with the stimuli you have selected to notice. So the stimuli are changed, not only by leaving some parts out, but by adding other things in.

A great minister once observed to me that all of us, when reading the Bible (or any other book), read more *in* than we read *out*! He understood the third step in the perception process.

Many writers have noted that we do not *discover* reality but instead *create* reality. Perception is a mental process—and therefore a very personal process. Each of us has his or her own distinctive world view, based on our previous experiences, and that world view is utilized (added in) whenever we respond to a new stimulus. What we see is not what we get! What we see (perceive) is that part of what we see (gather) that we choose to see (select) *plus* the accumulation of all our previous choices (mixed in). Choice among options is at the heart of creating; since present and previous choices play so important a role in the perception process, you can see why writers say we *create* the reality we perceive.

Does it really make a difference what kind of world view we mix in during the perception process? Granted that we do bring in (add) our previously acquired knowledge and beliefs, is that collection so different from person to person? Will this addition step radically affect what we think we see? Yes, indeed!

Think for a moment of two nurses who work in the operating room of a great metropolitan hospital. Both come in one morning and look at the list of operations scheduled for that day. As they look at the list, they *gather* information about the nature of the procedures to be performed by the operating team. Depending on their interests, specializations, and prejudices, they notice some operations on the list more than others; they *select* what they will notice most on the list. If one of the operations on the list is an abortion, and if one of the nurses is a devout Roman Catholic, while the other is a nominal Protestant, each nurse will probably *mix in* a very different set of religious and moral principles. The world view of the devout Roman Catholic nurse is likely to be absolutist; the world view of the nominal Protestant nurse is likely to be relativist. That is, the first nurse probably believes that there are absolute moral principles of right and wrong that are universal and unchanging; the second nurse probably believes that what is right and wrong varies from situation to situation and that what is "moral" depends on (or is relative to) the choices available in each instance. Each nurse would create a different mixture for his or her "reality" when he or she mixed the information on the list with his or her (previously chosen) outlook. They both mix in what they already subscribe to, but if what they subscribe to is radically different, the "realities" they perceive (think they see) are also radically different.

Let us review the steps in the perception process so far. Step 1: gathering—we take some information in. Step 2: selecting—we pay attention to part of that information. Step 3: mixing—we change that incomplete information by adding to it other information and beliefs. If step 2 reminds us that the perception process is partial, then step 3 reminds us that the perception process is creative!

Organizing

When we ended step 3, you remember, we had a mixture, made up of that part of the original information left after step 2 and the addition of material from our brain storehouse. Now we come to step 4, and we try to organize that mixture into some manageable form. We impose some kind of order on the mixture. We give it structure. Here, again, we are *creating*. Note the words *we try, we impose, we give*. We do not discover or find patterns so much as we make them or fashion them.

One of the steps in the perception process: Organizing

We feel uncomfortable with what is random and disordered. We can grasp (understand and remember) something that has sensible structure better than something that does not. We can cope with information more easily if it has a coherent form. Hence, we organize the mixture we have created and further perfect (change) our creation of perceived reality.

Some psychologists believe that all human beings have a need for order and consistency; this need, they believe, is innate. Other psychologists believe that the search for order is learned; human beings who prefer order, they believe, have been thus conditioned by their environment. Whichever school of psychology is right, it is quite likely that *you* prefer order to chaos and that this preference will have an important effect on your perceptions.

Let us check to see if, indeed, you *do* search for order and attempt to organize in the perception process. Look at these dots on the page:

Did you perceive the dots as groups of dots or as random, individual dots? Did you "see" arrangements of dots? If so, you organized the dots into patterns so you could deal with them more easily. Were they all various kinds of triangles? What did you have to *add* in your mind to make the triangle arrangements? Or, did you think the dots made up just one figure? What kind of figure was that? Why did you see it as a whole? What did you have to supply to create its unity?

Let's look again at those "marks on the printed page." When you were asked what you saw there or how you would identify the marks, what did you answer?

$$5$$

Did you answer "five" or "two straight lines and a curved line"? If you said "five," what did you have to *do* in your mind to organize the lines *into* a five? Clearly, the five is not on the paper; it is not complete. You must close or connect the lines in your mind to turn the lines into the number five. That structure or pattern was not on the paper but *in your mind!*

Let's try again. What would you say this is?

$$13$$

Did you say the lines were the number thirteen or the letter *B*? Or are you now so suspicious that you said it was only lines on the page? Or did you see something besides thirteen or *B*? Note that the context exerts an influence on how we organize stimuli in our minds. Here are the same lines again, put into two different contexts. Do you "see" (organize) the same thing both times?

$$13\ 15\ 17 \qquad BDF$$

I said earlier that making choices lies at the heart of the creative act. I hope I have proved to you that you have a number of choices you can make when you decide on an organization or structure in the perception process. You are being creative, then, when you construct a form in your mind, when you make an order for your perception of reality. Of course, you recognize that your previous learning greatly influences the forms you choose. What forms you already know, what categories you already think in, what ways you have of looking at things—these affect (perhaps *effect*) the structures you make in your mind.

Perhaps you know about or have taken the famous Rorschach test. Hermann Rorschach, a Swiss psychiatrist, devised the test by making some ink blots on pieces of paper. The ink made shapes on the paper, and subjects were asked what they "saw." Each person organized the shapes in his or her own mind; when each told what he or she "saw," the subject was telling much more about how he or she organized reality than about the blots of ink on the paper!

What generalizations can we make about the organizing step in the perception process? I think we can safely conclude that: (1) we tend to group together things that we think are similar; (2) we tend to group together things that are located near each other or that can be made into a unit of some kind; (3) we try to organize things into some unified whole; (4) if necessary, we fill in blanks or gaps to complete a form; (5) we will use the context to help determine what form to impose; (6) we will use forms, structures, and categories that we already know or that are consistent without previous experience.

Interpreting

We now come to the last step in the process of perception. We have taken something in, discarded part of it, added to it, and organized the mixture we have thus created into some orderly form. Now we come to the last step and ask the question: what does it *mean*? And we *attach* meaning—our own meanings—in our minds.

One of the steps in the perception process: Interpreting

At the beginning of this chapter, I said that perception is a mental process by which we make sense out of reality. It is at the last step that we really try to make sense of something: we interpret it as having some significance, some meaning. Only if this incoming information means something does it make any sense!

We feel uncomfortable with uncertainty and ambiguity. The random, the absurd, the meaningless make us uneasy. So at the end of the process of perception we have to make inferences (conclusions or guesses) about what the organized mixture we have created (that began with an incoming stimulus) *means* and *how it relates* to the rest of our perceptions.

We try, at this point in the perception process, to answer the question: what does this represent? We attach meaning to it; we associate meaning with it; we impose meaning on it. We infer (guess) its significance. Thus we complete the shakily unreliable (but the best we have) process of perception!

Can you interpret these figures? Do you perceive a message in each one?

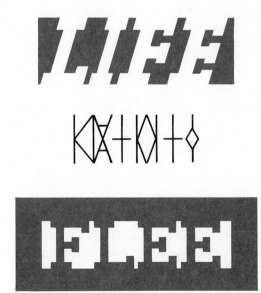

limitations that affect perception

The ability of human beings to sense stimuli staggers the imagination. Our brains receive stimuli from both internal (inside the body) and external (outside the body) sources. From external sources, our five senses gather impressive amounts of data. We can distinguish thousands of different hues. We can hear sound vibrations from 20 to at least 13,000 cycles per second and we can sense the presence or absence of higher and lower frequencies as well. We can recognize several thousand different smells, and, if we do not smoke, can differentiate some ten thousand variations of sweet, sour, bitter, and salty tastes. Although some parts of our body are more sensitive than others, our sense of touch all over the body is phenomenal.

Great as our ability to receive stimuli is, we do have limitations, and those limitations affect the perception process. Earlier we noted that we are not aware of all the incoming stimuli. If we did not select out, screen out, much of the incoming stimulation, we would not be able to function at all. There are just too many stimuli at any given moment of our lives to deal with them all; there are literally thousands of incoming bits of information vying for our attention every instant, and we cannot possibly process and respond to all of them. The question rises, however: what determines which stimuli get processed and dealt with? Which stimuli *are* perceived (complete the process all the way to Step 5, interpretation)? Generally, we perceive: (1) what we are *able* to, (2) what we *want* to, (3) what we *need* to, (4) what we *expect* to, and (5) what we are *trained* to perceive. We will consider each of these limitations, because they are so important to an understanding of perception. (And a person's perceptions are basic to all of his or her communications!)

Ability

It would seem obvious, on the face of it, that a person cannot perceive what that person is not *able* to perceive. Indeed, it sounds circular, but it is not. There are physical, physiological, and psychological limits on our abilities. These limits prevent us from gathering stimuli from our environment.

PHYSICAL LIMITS

By physical limits, I mean those factors outside our bodies that prevent the gathering of stimuli. The limitations are imposed by the environment.

One such limitation is imposed at times by one's position in space. Where I am determines (and limits) what I can see and hear, for example. I recently went to an Off-Broadway play. Unfortunately, I did not see much of it. My seat was directly behind a large pillar; the pillar was directly between me and the stage; my view of the proceedings was quite limited!

This year at the national NCAA basketball tournament, I observed what I thought was a very questionable foul call by an official. The official could not possibly have seen the contact (had there been any) from his position on the court. Sadly for one of the teams, the official's physical limits on his ability to perceive did not prevent his calling a foul!

There can be physical limits placed on any of your senses and their ability to gather information for you. If you have tried to hold a conversation on a New York City subway platform while a train is approaching or departing, you know that there can be limits imposed on your ability to hear. The title of the play *You Know I Can't Hear You when the Water's*

Physical limits on one's perception

Running reminds us of another such situation where there are physical limits on hearing. Try to play the piano with gloves on; you'll detect some limits to your sense of touch. Try to smell the fragrance of a rose while someone cooks fish in the same room; you may discover some physical limits on your sense of smell. Wine-tasters rinse out their mouths with water between sips of different wines to try to counteract physical limits on their sense of taste.

In sum, we take in what we are able to get at physically. We do not gather (and therefore do not perceive) a stimulus if something else gets in the way.

Now we come to limits on our ability to perceive that are caused by our own bodies. There are physiological (bodily) limits on our ability to sense stimuli.

Usually at this point in a class in human communication, I turn to a student and ask, "What song are they playing on WABC right now?" Sometimes my students say, "How should I know?" or "Are you crazy? Nobody's playing WABC here." and I reply, "You mean you can't hear it. The radio waves are going through your body at this very instant!" Of course they are, but our bodies are not equipped to pick up the radio waves. We have to have special equipment for that.

It is no news to you that there are sounds our human ears cannot detect. Those of you who have dogs may have whistles that emit high frequencies that your dog can pick up but that sound like silence to us human beings. I

PHYSIOLOGICAL LIMITS

confess I am still amazed when Dammit comes running in response to that silent whistle!

Our eyes have their limitations also. We can see only a tiny fraction of the complete light spectrum. Our unassisted eyes cannot see X-rays, ultraviolet rays, or infrared rays. These physiological limitations certainly affect our perceptions. How differently we would perceive the world around us if, like Superman, we had X-ray vision!

So far, I have talked about physiological limitations on our perception ability that are common to all human beings. But some of us have other bodily limitations in addition to those common to us all. I, for one, do not have 20/20 vision; I am blessed with myopia (nearsightedness) and astigmatism. Without the corrective lenses of eyeglasses, my ability to perceive is certainly limited. Several of my friends are color blind. They have inherited a defect in the cones of the retina, and they tell me they see the world as many of us watch TV—in black and white rather than in living color! They perceive shapes, but the shapes are in various shades of grey.

Some of us have hearing problems that limit our ability to gather (and thus perceive) stimuli. I recently had an audiologist friend test my hearing, and I discovered that I have lost the ability to pick up some frequencies that I once could detect. Several recent studies have indicated that many American young people have rather severe hearing losses; extensive exposure to highly amplified rock music may account for the damage. Another (rather uncommon) problem is that of tone-deafness. In this case, the

**Physiological limits on one's
perception**

person has difficulty distinguishing among pitches (the highness or lowness of frequencies of sound waves). Such a physiological limitation would certainly affect the person's perceptions of both music and speech, since pitch variation is an important element of both.

There are many things in our environment that do not register on our sensory receiving sets; our nervous system is a marvel, but there are many possible stimuli it does not have the ability to collect. Because of the limits imposed by our bodies, we miss many of the things going on around us. In addition to the physiological limitations common to all human beings, some of us have additional limitations on one or more of our senses. All of these limitations restrict the stimuli we can gather and therefore reduce the extent of our perceptions.

Thus far I have discussed two types of limitations on what we *are able* to perceive: external limitations in the physical environment and limitations in the human body itself. Some of you may believe those two categories cover all the factors limiting our *ability* to perceive. If so, you believe that psychological factors can be explained in terms of physiology (the way the body functions). Others, however, may insist that there are purely psychological limits on some people's ability to perceive. They would point out that a person with extreme neurosis (a functional mental disorder that hinders the person's functioning but is not as severe as psychosis) or with a psychosis (a severe mental disorder characterized by some degree of personality disintegration and an inability to relate to one's environment and to other people) *cannot* perceive as the rest of us do. Indeed, neurosis and psychosis *do* limit what stimuli a person can gather, and they further limit a person's ability to process the incoming stimuli through the entire perception process.

PSYCHOLOGICAL LIMITS

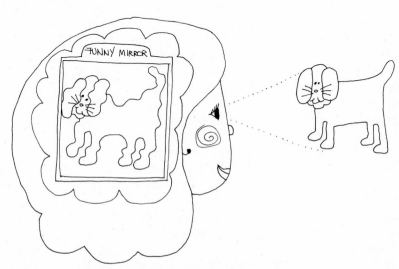

Psychological limits on one's perception

To make the concept of neurosis clearer, just think of someone who is hysterical, or someone who has a driving obsession, or someone who has some variety of phobia, or someone who is plagued with extreme anxiety. Any one of these people might be limited in their *ability* to take in certain stimuli that came their way. They certainly would be limited in their ability to handle certain incoming stimuli and to interpret them correctly.

In the case of psychosis, just think of the limitations on the perceptions of one who is paranoid (having delusions either of grandeur or of persecution) or of someone who has one of the many forms of schizophrenia (a group of mental disorders marked by fundamental disturbances in reality relationships). Psychotics certainly have some limitations in their ability to take in and process information.

Clearly, psychological disorders—both extreme neuroses and psychoses—can limit the ability of a human being to perceive incoming stimuli.

Wants

Not only are we limited to perceiving what we are *able* to perceive; what we *want* to perceive also affects (and limits) our perceptions. Since perception is a mental process, when we talk about what we see, we are really talking about what we think we see (and hear, and smell, and taste, and touch). And what we think we see is determined in part by what we want to see.

You have heard of wishful thinking. It really exists; in a sense, that is what we are discussing here: perceiving what we wish or desire rather than what is. Our central nervous system can hinder or block out stimuli that upset us or make us uncomfortable (that *threaten* us, in psychological jargon). It can also facilitate the input of stimuli that we agree with (or perhaps more accurately, that agree with *us*). Selective perception is a means of defense against unwanted stimuli, and it works so well that we may not even be aware we were exposed to the unwelcome stimuli!

What kinds of things are so threatening that we are likely to shut them out? Primarily, those things that challenge our world view—our composite picture of the world. That world view is based on and made up of beliefs, values, and attitudes. We tend to perceive whatever will support, strengthen, and confirm our beliefs, values, and attitudes, and we tend to block out (and thus not perceive) whatever violates, attacks, or is inconsistent with our beliefs, values, and attitudes.

Some definitions are necessary if we are to understand this principle. *Beliefs* are propositions or statements of principle that one holds to be true or valid; they are opinions or convictions or doctrines. Beliefs are the conclusions one has reached based on his or her perceptions. We like to think we have arrived at these conclusions logically, but that may or may not be the case. Instead, we develop our beliefs through first-hand experience (perception) and through interaction with other people, especially

Perceptual defenses

those whom we regard as especially significant in our lives or whom we respect as authorities.

When we speak of a person's *values,* we are referring to the criteria that person uses in judging (or rating or e*valu*ating—determining the value) ideas, behaviors, events, people, or things. Our values are our guidelines to what is of worth and what is not and what is worthy and what is not. Our values are our concepts of good and bad, right and wrong, desirable and undesirable, valuable and worthless. Each of us learns his or her value system early in life, and those value concepts we learn early have a rather sturdy, lasting power to them; it is not impossible to change them, but it is certainly very difficult to do so.

So far we have defined beliefs and values. But what are attitudes, and how are they different from the other two? *Attitudes* are inclinations, biases, leanings toward or away from something. Now notice those synonyms for attitudes; they all have the same picture built into them. Inclination comes from the word *incline;* you know what an incline is. It veers in one direction or the other. Those of you who sew know what a bias is also;

a bias is a slant—a diagonal. As for leaning, one can lean to one side or the other. Attitudes are related to something specific; we do not have attitudes in general, but rather we have an attitude toward something in particular. Another way of saying it: An attitude is a tendency or predisposition to react favorably or unfavorably toward something. Because each attitude does relate to a specific thing, it is easier to change a person's attitude about that specific thing than it is to change a person's values—which are more general, more basic, and more enduring.

How are beliefs, values, and attitudes related? Beliefs are concerned with what is possible, probable, or certain. Values are concerned with what is valuable or worthless. Attitudes are orientations for or against something. I can have a belief *in* or *about* something; I can value something (or not value it); I can have an attitude *toward* something. To be more specific: I *value* (cherish) the principle of free speech. I *believe* anyone should be allowed to advocate any position without government interference or censorship. I have a positive, or favorable, *attitude* toward the American Civil Liberties Union, an organization dedicated to defending the Bill of Rights.

Can you list some of the things that you value highly, that you think are of great worth? Can you list some of your basic beliefs, the propositions that you think are certainly (or at least probably) true? Now think of some specific people or groups or organizations. Are your attitudes toward them positive (or favorable) or negative (or unfavorable) or neutral?

Beliefs, values, and attitudes vary in three basic ways: (1) position on a continuum, (2) strength or intensity, and (3) importance. Beliefs vary on a continuum from *impossible* to *certain*. Values vary on a continuum from *no worth* to *much worth*. Attitudes vary on a continuum from *against* to *for*. The strength of intensity with which a person holds a belief, value, or attitude can also vary. The degree of strength with which you hold a judgment can vary from weak to very strong. The last factor that can vary is importance. How critical is this belief or value or attitude? How high is it on the person's scale of priorities? All of these variables affect the influence that a particular belief, value, or attitude will have on a person—and therefore on that person's perceptions.

	Belief	Value	Attitude
Position on Its Continuum:	impossible/possible/ probable/certain	no/little/some/much *worth*	against/neutral/for
Strength or Intensity:	weak/moderate/ very strong	weak/moderate/strong	weak/moderate/strong
Importance:	little/some/much *importance*	little/some/much *importance*	little/some/much *importance*

I have said that we human beings perceive what we *want* to perceive and that we tend to perceive whatever will support, strengthen, and confirm our beliefs, values, and attitudes. Clearly, the more strongly a person holds a belief, value, or attitude and the more importance that person attaches to a belief, value, or attitude, the more likely perception is to be affected.

A few years ago, I was having dinner at a restaurant with a teacher friend in a small Southern city when a couple and their twelve-year-old son entered. The boy had been a student of my friend in the nearby public school. "He's mentally retarded," my friend told me, "but his parents won't admit it." I, of course, asked if the school authorities and others had discussed the boy's abilities with the parents. "We talked to them as directly, honestly, and clearly as we could. After all, they live with the child and have observed him first-hand from birth. But they just can't see it," he said. "They just don't want to!" My friend went on to explain that the parents, both of whom were well educated, placed great *value* on intelligence and formal education. That value was quite important to them, and it was intensely felt. They *believed* that intelligent, educated parents would produce intelligent, if not gifted, children. Their *attitude* toward their child was quite favorable, naturally, and they viewed him in a positive light. The appearance, behavior, and academic record (plus the testimony of school authorities) of the child were in conflict with their value system, belief system, and attitude. They *wanted* to see their son as having at least average intelligence and ability, and indeed that is what they *did* perceive.

There have been some interesting scientific studies of perceptual defenses. In some studies, investigators have flashed words on a screen, one after another, very quickly. Most of the words were neutral, nonemotional words—certainly nonthreatening words. Interspersed in the sequence, however, were taboo words (obscene words—not "acceptable" in "polite society"). The investigators were interested in the subjects' responses to these taboo words, since many people seem to be threatened by profanity or obscenity in language, even when the words are not directed against them personally. If a person values highly the middle-class language norms (standards), believes that taboo words should not be spoken or written by "respectable" people, and has a negative attitude toward speaking and writing "such words" and against the people who do say or write those words, then that person is likely to feel threatened by the use of such words and to build perceptual defenses against such incoming stimulation. Indeed, the results of the studies confirm this theory. Some people were not even aware of having been exposed to the words; they claimed they did not see them! What they did not *want* to see, selective perception defended them from seeing (perceiving).

Other studies have followed the same procedures, except that researchers have used pictures rather than words. Scattered among the simple, pleasant, noncontroversial pictures were pornographic pictures. The results have been the same as in the experiments with words: many people did not perceive the pornographic pictures to which they had been exposed. Presumably, these people found the "obscene" pictures too hot to handle—too threatening to deal with—so they eliminated them at the selection step of the perception process. Evidently, some stimuli are *too* stimulating, and people do not want to deal with them. Selective perception defends us (or protects us) from such threatening stimuli.

To some extent, all of us (human beings) demonstrate perceptual defenses (blocking out stimuli that threaten our values, beliefs, and attitudes) and perceptual facilitation (giving attention to those stimuli that support our values, beliefs, and attitudes). Indeed, there is a principle not only of selective perception; there is a principle of selective *exposure*. Most of us tend to expose ourselves (if we have a choice in the matter) only to those stimuli that are consistent with our world view and to those sources of information that are similar to us and agree with our world view.

My mother, for example, would turn off the television set rather than listen to a speech by President Nixon. She refused to expose herself to anything he had to say. Encouraged by the ecumenical spirit and Vatican II, I recently invited a devout Roman Catholic friend of mine to attend a program at Judson Memorial Church, a liberal Baptist church in New York's Greenwich Village. He quickly declined; he does not attend anything in Protestant churches except weddings and funerals. He too had definite limits on the stimuli to which he will expose himself.

Selective exposure, then, is another protective, screening device we use. It preceeds the perception process, because perception begins with the exposure to (or gathering in of) some stimulus. By selective exposure, we try to avoid even coming in contact with stimuli that we think we will not agree with, or that might be threatening to, our world view. If by chance we *are* exposed to stimuli we do not want to deal with, then selective perception (or perceptual defense) works to "protect" us.

As I said, *all* of us practice selective exposure to some extent, and all of us utilize the same process of perception (including perceptual defenses). But some of us are extremely selective, both in terms of exposure and perception. Such people are called *dogmatic* or *closed-minded*. The dogmatic person is rigid in ideology, simplistic in thinking, illogical in evaluating messages, easily influenced by authority figures, closed to information contrary to his or her viewpoint, and intolerant of those with differing views. This inflexible mind-set, of course, seriously affects a person's ability to process information. The closed-minded person is absolutely certain that what he or she believes is absolutely true and that the final word on all subjects is already in. Such an orientation would inevitably distort that person's perception of incoming stimuli by avoiding and excluding some stimuli and twisting many others.

Note the major contrasts between open-minded and closed-minded people:

The closed-minded person:

1. Usually (almost always) practices selective perception.
2. Is "other-directed," getting beliefs from other people and from groups he or she is identified with; needs the reinforcement of other people's similar views; relies on authorities to evaluate information for him or her.
3. Views the source of information and the information itself as inseparable.
4. Is unlikely to differentiate among messages coming from contrary world views, believing them all bad and therefore all the same.
5. Evaluates messages emotionally, based on his or her personal drives.
6. Is ideologically rigid (closed to different or new ideas or information).
7. Prefers second-hand sources that share his or her viewpoint.
8. Has a bipolar orientation, thinking in simplistic either-or categories.

9. Ignores, distorts, rejects, and attacks messages that are at variance with his or her own world view.
10. Judges other people in terms of the similarity or dissimilarity of their world view to his or her own and is intolerant of those with differing views.

The open-minded person:

1. Sometimes practices selective perception.
2. Is rather "inner-directed," evaluating information for himself or herself.

3. Separates the source of information from the information itself.

4. Differentiates among messages coming from contrary world views.

5. Evaluates messages logically, checking support and reasoning.
6. Is ideologically flexible (open to new ideas and information and willing to modify beliefs).
7. Seeks best sources of information, preferably first-hand sources.
8. Has a multifaceted orientation, seeing complexities and examining many alternatives.
9. Seeks to understand messages that are at variance with his or her own values, beliefs, and attitudes.
10. Judges people on many bases, not merely in terms of similar or dissimilar world views and is tolerant of (accepts) those with differing views.

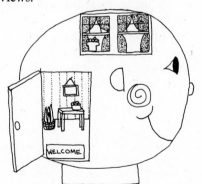 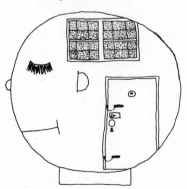

An open mind and a closed mind

Closed-minded people are very insecure. Their system of values, beliefs, and attitudes is quite fragile. They are completely committed to the entire structure, as if changing one single belief or attitude would cause the entire system to collapse. Dogmatic people are an extreme example of the principle that what we think we see is determined in part by what we want to see. They illustrate the principle—carried to its extreme—that, in the perception process, we can block out incoming stimuli that threaten us and we can facilitate incoming stimuli that reinforce our world views.[1]

Needs

Just as what we want to perceive helps determine what we indeed do perceive, so what we *need* to perceive also affects what we do perceive. *Wants* are desires or preferences; *needs* are more basic drives.

Various psychologists have used different classification systems to categorize the basic human needs (or drives). Although the categories, or labels, differ somewhat, there is no great disagreement about the nature of our drives. Perhaps the most widely circulated classification system is that of Abraham Maslow. He listed five categories of needs: (1) physiological, (2) safety, (3) social, (4) self-esteem, and (5) self-actualization. Maslow maintained that the five classes of needs formed a kind of hierarchy, or ranking system, the lowest having the highest priority and number five having the least priority. He argued that human beings will attend to their most pressing, vital needs before they will attend to the less basic ones. We seek to fulfill several drives at the same time, but we will give more urgent precedence to some drives than to others.

When we talk about needs or drives, we are talking about forces that motivate all human beings. I frankly am not convinced that Maslow's fifth "need" is universal: the need for self-actualization, the need to attain one's greatest potential, to develop to the fullness of one's ability, to become what one can be. Instead, I submit for your consideration this list of five basic human needs, also arranged with the most basic (or vital) coming first: (1) survival, (2) sex, (3) security, (4) social relationships, (5) self-esteem.

Remember that we are talking now about inner drives common to all human beings; we are not talking about *values*. The drives will be present, but one can learn a value system that negates or places low worth on some of the drives and their satisfaction. Let us look at each of these kinds of needs briefly.

---

[1] The "true believer," as Eric Hoffer labeled the dogmatic person, can be of any race, any religion, any political persuasion, and any nationality. What all dogmatic people have in common is not *what* they believe but *how* they believe it. One can be as closed-minded a liberal as a conservative or as dogmatic a Protestant Christian as a Roman Catholic Christian or as rigidly closed-minded a Muslim as a Christian. No one group has a monopoly on dogmatism! For a scientific study of dogmatism, see Milton Rokeach's book, *The Open and Closed Mind* (New York: Basic Books, 1960).

Pyramid of needs (drives)

The *survival* needs are those required for preservation of the body's life and health. If we are to sustain life, each of us must have sufficient food, water, and sleep. These physiological (body) needs are primary if we are to continue our earthly existence.

After meeting those needs that insure one's survival, the person's next most basic need, I think, is *sexual*. Sexual orientations may vary, but sexual drives are universal. I can offer no proof that this drive takes precedence over the need for security and comfort, but I am convinced that that is the case. The sex drive is deep and powerful, and once a person's thirst has been quenched, that person's hunger has been alleviated, and that person's exhaustion has been relieved by sleep, the next unsatisfied yearning will be for sexual fullfillment.

The third basic need is for *security*. We need to be safe and comfortable. We need to be protected from the environment; we need clothing and shelter.

The first three needs I have listed are all physical. Survival needs help insure the continued existence of the body; sexual needs help perpetuate the species; security needs are concerned with the body's health and safety. The fourth need turns outward; we human beings need *social relationships* with other human beings. Homo sapiens is not naturally a solitary animal. We need other people. We need ties—relationships—with people. We need to feel accepted by others; we need to feel included, that we belong. We need the affection of others; we need friends, and we need love.

Finally, we have some inward needs as well. We have needs related to our selfhood. We need *self-esteem*, self-respect. This need is different from the one I just discussed. We need to have a sense of identity, of being "somebody," somebody worthwhile—somebody that we ourselves can like! Every person will meet this need in different ways, depending on that person's value system, but all people have this need. Some people may fulfill this need by trying to become all they are capable of achieving—self-actualization. Others may achieve their ego needs in different ways. But the need, or drive, to be a person you yourself can like is there in all of us.

I began this section by stating that we tend to perceive what we *need* to perceive. In other words, our basic needs influence our process of perception. Let us look at just a few examples of this principle.

If you are hungry, are you likely to notice physical cues related to food more quickly than you would if you were not hungry? Right you are—you would. There have been some interesting studies to substantiate this finding. Maybe you have passed a water fountain in the hallway of some building countless times without noticing, only to "discover" it suddenly one day when you were particularly thirsty.

Do our sex drives play any part in our perceptions—especially of other people? Do you tend to like people (of either sex) better—especially on first meeting—if they are good-looking? Now, be honest! If you are sexually attracted to someone, are you tempted to overlook many of that person's faults and to exaggerate such traits as their intelligence? Yes, sex does influence our perceptions.

One of the most interesting studies of the influence of what we need on what we perceive was done with children. Rich children and poor children were shown pictures of coins and later asked to guess their size. Would you have expected the children's differences in affluence to have affected their estimates? It did. The poor children thought the coins were much larger than the rich children did!

Here is a hypothetical example. Suppose you are on your way to work or to school, and you are running late. You do not have your watch on, so you do not know exactly how late you are, but you know you are pressed for time. You are standing at the bus stop—the same place you stand every morning to wait for your bus. Across the street is a bank with a large clock attached to its sign. Is it more likely that you will notice the clock today than on other days when you have stood in the same spot looking in the same direction? Yes, probably you will be aware of the clock today—perhaps for the first time. Because you *need* it!

Expectations

It should come as no surprise to you that what we *expect* to perceive exerts an influence on what we do perceive. Our expectations can color and distort our perceptions. It is not that what you see is what you get; it is that what you expect is what you see!

Of course, fraternities and sororities at colleges do not have the silly kind of hazing of initiates that they used to have. But in the old days, these groups capitalized on this principle of perception for many of their hazing techniques. One group I know of kept telling their pledges that they were going to have to drink a glass of blood—real cow's blood obtained from a slaughterhouse not too far away. Members would say how awful it looked and smelled and tasted when they had to drink the glass of blood for their initiation. For some time before the fateful event, pledges were reminded of what was coming. At the time of the "ordeal," the pledges were given a glass of tomato juice to drink, but many were convinced they had drunk real blood!

One of my acquaintances, a New Yorker whose knowledge of the United States stopped at the Hudson River, was cast in a road show of a play and had to join the group in Louisville, Kentucky. He was met in a late-model automobile by someone I know after he had landed at the modern airport in a jet plane. They drove over well-paved six- and four-lane expressways past middle-class suburban housing developments. He looked at everything. When he returned to New York City, he was asked what Kentucky was like. "Interesting," he said. "So quaint. So primitive. So old-fashioned. Out of another century!" He had gone to Kentucky expecting to see barefoot hillbillies living in cabins, and that is almost what he perceived.

In one of the most interesting studies of the influence of expectations on perception, some school teachers were given classes of students as nearly alike in ability as possible. The students in the respective paired classes were equally well prepared academically and equal in terms of intelligence. The individual teachers were told something different, however. Some teachers were told that they were getting the bright students in that grade, and other teachers were told that they were getting the slower students. Remember, there was no real difference in the paired classes, although the teachers had been informed that students had been grouped into classes by ability. At the end of the term, the teachers were asked to rate their classes and their experience in teaching that term. The grades achieved by the students in the paired classes were also compared. What do you think the outcome was? The teachers who had been told that they had the bright students reported that they had never had such fine, able students and were delighted to report that their teaching experience that term had been an unusual joy. On the other hand, the teachers who had been told that they were getting the poorer students reported that their students were dumb, unmotivated, and difficult to work with. In terms of grades achieved, there was also a significant difference in the paired classes. The "bright" sections got much higher marks (and evidently actually achieved more learning) than did the students in the "slow" sections. The difference in the classes was not in the student's abilities, but in the teachers' expectations. They perceived what they had been led to expect to perceive!

Why do expectations affect our perceptions so profoundly? Because perception is our way of looking at something. And expectation is a special way of looking at something beforehand. When you expect something, you look at it as much more than probable. Looking ahead, you consider it almost certain, almost inevitable. You have almost no reservations about whether it is likely. Expectation, then, is a kind of preperception. You have looked at something ahead of time, and you see it as reasonably sure. When you actually encounter the thing itself (whatever the stimulus is), you are apt to perceive (again) the "sure thing" you anticipated.

Training

In a very real sense, we all learn to perceive. We learn what to perceive, and we learn how to perceive. We also learn the categories, classifications, or meanings that we use in the final interpretation step of the perception process. Our category systems result from our past experience and our language (which we learned). True, our physiology (body) plays a large part in the gathering of stimuli, though there is strong evidence that conditioning greatly affects our neurobiology. But clearly, the recognition, labeling, and interpreting of the stimuli are *learned*.

In the room where I am writing this material, the temperature is ninety degrees Fahrenheit. My body is experiencing physical sensations. I learned long ago to label those kinds of sensations hot! *Hot* is a concept, a category, a label. That label brings with it certain associations or meanings. Those associations or meanings are based on previous experiences that have also been placed into the same category. I learned what the concept *hot* meant, and I learned to interpret certain sensations as hot. My perceptions are certainly affected by my past experiences and by language, which gives me the labels to classify and interpret experiences.

The process of perception is a mental process. Like all mental processes, it is developed; it is learned. We are born with the bodily machinery needed to perceive, but we are not born with perception or the process of perception. Granted, we begin learning the process very early in our lives, but we cannot say exactly at what point. Maybe from that first rude stimulus (the slap on our little bottoms), we begin trying to make sense of reality, to gather, select, mix, organize, and interpret incoming stimuli.

Recent studies have made some revolutionary discoveries about the way we learn to perceive reality, the world around us. Those studies indicate that we not only learn to perceive; we actually learn to *see*. That is, our visual machinery is strongly affected by our early experiences. Our ability to see the world later on in our life is drastically affected by that conditioning.

David Hubel and Torsten Wiesel, two biologists at Harvard, pioneered vision research with experiments on cats. External forces, they discovered, exert great influence on the way the brain develops. For their experiments, the two scientists used normal baby kittens. They were interested in the effect of early environment on the development of certain nerve cells that can function as *feature detectors*. These cells respond to the specific shapes seen by the eye. In one experiment, they kept a kitten in complete darkness until it was grown and then examined the feature detectors of the brain. The feature detectors had remained very immature and undeveloped. They were present, as they had been all along, but they were still as immature as a baby kitten's are and did not show the development one finds in a normal adult cat. In a later experiment, the two researchers tried covering one of a kitten's eyes to see what influence it would have. The results were interesting. The feature detector nerve cells are connected to both eyes in normal kittens and adult cats. But in *this* cat, the connections had all gone to the one eye that could see during its developmental stage of life. The feature detectors were normal! One of the other important discoveries of this team was that there was a sensitive period in the kitten's development when the visual acuity of the brain could be influenced; in the case of kittens, it was from age three weeks to the age of three months.

Other research based on these early studies is even more startling. Colin Blakemore and Graham Cooper, of Cambridge University, used two sets of kittens to see if the feature detector brain cells could be manipulated by putting the kittens into particular controlled environments. Both sets of kittens were normal and intelligent. One set was put into (and reared) in an environment consisting only of vertical stripes; the other, in an environment consisting only of horizontal stripes. After the age of three months, when they had finished the developmental stage, the cats were put into an environment in the real world. Their behavior was amazing. The "vertical cats" never tried to jump up on a chair or table; the "horizonal cats" jumped onto tables and chairs with no difficulty, but they kept bumping into the legs of chairs and tables—a problem the vertical cats did not have. When the brains of the cats were studied, the vertical cats had no horizontal feature detectors, and the horizontal cats had no vertical feature detectors. The poor cats were really blind to things that cats raised in a normal environment can see. The two sets of cats faced the same world as other cats, but they did not see the same world. Indeed, the two sets of cats did not see the same distorted view of reality; each set was blind to a different aspect of the world.

Most researchers now agree that the period crucial to a kitten's visual development is three weeks to three months; the age of five weeks seems to be especially important. Blakemore says the visual-sensitive period in human beings is probably the years two to four. There is evidence that our conditioning in those crucial years affects what (and how) we humans see and therefore perceive.

Formal training also affects our perceptions. We cannot all perceive the same things, because we have not all been taught the same things. Just think of a few examples.

What do you perceive as you look at this:

What did it mean to you? Could you hear it as well as see it (mentally, I mean)? If you have not had training in music, the chances are that those lines and flecks and specks and dots meant nothing to you. You could see them all right, but you could not interpret them—as a musician could.

Not too long ago, the former First Lady of the United States had an operation for tumor of the breast. While she was on the operating table under anesthesia, the surgeon took a sliver of tissue for a frozen section. The tissue was put on a slide and examined under a microscope. A technician, looking at the tissue, would tell the surgical team whether the tumor was benign or malignant. Now, what if they had asked *me* to look through the microscope and tell them what kind of tumor it was? I could have looked. No question about that. I could probably have adjusted the microscope so I could see the cells. But, looking right at the cells, I would not have perceived the cells as malignant (as the technician did); I do not have the necessary training.

An artist, a medical doctor, and a clothing designer may all look at the same body, but will they perceive that body the same way? Will they see the same things? Probably not; each will see something the others may be blind to, because each is trained to look for something different.

A friend of mine recently bought a beautiful new home. Actually, the house is over two hundred years old. He looked the property over very carefully before deciding to buy it. He covered every nook and cranny of the house himself, poking here and peering there. But before he signed a contract, he hired a civil engineer to inspect the property. The engineer looked at the same things my friend had examined, but he could perceive things that the prospective owner could not; he was *trained*.

stimulus attributes that affect perception

The factors that limit our perceptions (which I just discussed with you) are all *internal limits*, with the possible exception of the physical limits on our ability to perceive, and even those result in internal limits, because they limit our ability to perceive. Now we turn our attention to factors related to the stimuli themselves—factors that also affect our perceptions. Certain characteristics of the stimuli themselves will have an influence on what we pay attention to or are aware of, how much attention we give, and how long we attend to (or focus on) that particular stimulus. There are, I think, five such attributes of stimuli: (1) strength of the stimulus, (2) size or duration of the stimulus, (3) vitality of the stimulus, (4) form of the stimulus, and (5) context of the stimulus. We will look briefly at each of these properties of stimuli.

Strength of the Stimulus

The more *intense* (or *strong*) the stimulus, the more likely we are to notice it and let it hold our attention. We are more likely to perceive (be aware of) a loud noise than a quiet one, a bright color than a subdued one, a high-pitched sound than a low-pitched one. If you hear a loud bang or a loud cracking noise, are you not likely to pay attention to it? Is it not probable that it will grab your attention? Intense stimuli grab the person's perception and then grip it.

Not only do we tend to notice strong or intense stimuli; we also tend to notice big or long stimuli. The larger the *size* of a stimulus, the greater the *amount* of a stimulus, the longer in *duration* a stimulus is—the more likely it is to be perceived. When you glance at the front page of a newspaper, do you not perceive the headlines and the boldfaced type first? If there are two ads on a page for competing companies, are you not likely to perceive the larger of the two first? When you first enter a room, you will probably perceive the bigger objects in the room first, won't you? And which commercial is more likely to get through to you—a ten-second commercial, a thirty-second commercial, or a one-minute commercial? I think the longer one has the best chance of your perceiving it. The dimensions (size, amount, length) of a stimulus affect its chances of being perceived.

Size or Duration of the Stimulus

We are more likely to perceive *vital* stimuli than static ones. Dynamic, vivid stimuli are more arresting than less lively ones are. Are you more inclined to notice a new, unfamiliar stimulus than an old, familiar one? Well, think about it for a minute. You probably pay little attention to the dishes from which you eat your meals, but if suddenly, at one meal, the dishes were completely different, would the change affect your perception of the dishes? Probably. Changes in stimuli are more likely to be perceived; we find newness and novelty striking. It is now May, and the temperature has been in the low 70s for several weeks. Today, in a matter of hours, the temperature dropped to 38 degrees Fahrenheit. Do you think people paid much attention to the temperature as long as it was relatively steady? Do you think they noticed it when it dropped? Of course, we tend to notice changes in stimuli, and we tend to take special note of sudden changes or differences. If someone is playing the piano, and all the piano-playing has been within a relatively low-volume range, wouldn't you be apt to notice a sudden crashingly loud chord? The contrast helps grab at our perception process. We tend also to notice movement and speed. Would an audience be more aware of still pictures flashed on a screen (slides, perhaps) or movies? The animation, the movement, the liveliness of the movies would make them more perceptible. A few years ago, I went to see a dance program presented by a major European ballet company; the program was heralded as a "great new breakthrough in dance." I watched the company sit or stand almost motionless for over two hours. There were a few movements, but they were slow, undramatic, ordinary locomotion to get

Vitality of the Stimulus

from one place to another. I had great difficulty concentrating on the work; to be honest, I found it a crashing bore. The lack of vitality—of dynamism—of the stimuli I was attempting to pay attention to made attention and perception much more difficult and much less likely!

Form of the Stimulus

The form of the stimulus affects perception. What forms are we more likely to perceive? Simple, rather than complex ones. Coherent, rather than amorphous ones. Those that are easy to recognize, rather than those that are difficult to recognize. Part of the process of perception, you remember, is organizing—seeing a structure. The easier it is for us to create a sensible structure out of the stimuli, the more likely we are to do it. Suppose your organization is planning some kind of advertising campaign and is going to put posters in the city's buses. Would you advise them to put as much printing on the poster as possible, so they could get more information to the public? Not if you really understand this principle related to perception! If you make the poster too complicated, too complex, too crowded with bits of information, viewers may perceive nothing at all. The simple stimulus, which receivers can grasp easily, is more likely to be perceived.

Context of the Stimulus

The background, the setting, the environment of any stimulus will affect the way that stimulus is perceived. We do not perceive stimuli in isolation, but rather in relation to the context in which they are found. There are multitudes of stimuli competing for our attention all the time in any situation, and the nature of the other stimuli will necessarily influence how we perceive the stimulus in question. The other elements in the setting may affect any of the steps of the perception process. If the other stimuli are too strong, we may not select a particular stimulus at all. The situation will certainly affect what previous experiences, information, and beliefs we mix into the perception of the given stimulus. Other stimuli present in the situation may also affect how we will organize and interpret a stimulus. For example, would you interpret a student's closed eyes in the same way if the student were sitting in a chair in the student lounge instead of in a classroom during a class? The stimulus may be the same (the closed eyes), but the context is quite different, and the interpretation will be based not just on the stimulus but on the environment as well.

checking our perceptions

Whenever we talk about something (whether that something is in the outside world or in our inside worlds), we are not talking about the way it *is,* but about the way we *think* it is. In all our perceptions there is an element of distortion. About all our perceptions there should be an element of doubt.

How can I be sure that the way I think something is resembles the way it really is? Or can I be sure at all? Are there ways of checking our perceptions? Can we verify them and thus reduce a bit of the uncertainty about them? Yes, we can reduce uncertainty—though we cannot eliminate it completely. There are four methods of checking on, or attempting to validate, our perceptions:

1. Compare your perception with other people's perceptions.
2. Compare your present perception with your previous perceptions.
3. Compare your perception (based on a stimulus gathered through one of the senses) with perceptions based on other senses.
4. Check your perception experientially—by comparing your perception with experience based on that perception.

Let us look briefly at each of these methods of validating perceptions.

Comparing with Other People's Perceptions

A perception is a theory about reality; it is a guess about the way things are. One way to test such a theory (a perception) is to find out what other people's perceptions of the same thing are. We try to determine whether other people see it—whatever *it* is—the same way we do. Do their perceptions, their theories, their guesses match ours? We report on the results of our perception process—on how we interpret the information our senses have gathered—and we ask other people if they have sensed the same things and interpreted the sensations the same way we have.

In a real sense, what we think of as reality is based on consensus. If enough other people make the same guesses (interpretations) we do, if their perceptions match ours, then we conclude that our perception has passed the first test. Since we tend to trust perceptions that pass this test, some writers have said that, for most of us, ordinary reality is reality by consensus—*consensual reality.*

There are dangers built into this first test of our perceptions. As you know, the answers you get are determined in part by whom you ask. If you check with others who have the same background, cultural ties and conditioning, and world view that you do, how likely are you to discover perceptions that vary from your own? Depending for perception validation on other people has a built-in flaw, unless you check with many other people *and* you are sure to check with people who might see things differently from the way you do. If our "validators'" biases are the same as ours, their perceptions may very well contain the same distortions that ours have. And those distortions then go undetected and uncorrected.

Comparing with One's Previous Perceptions

Earlier I noted that from our perceptions we form categories, classifications, or concepts. These concepts we can store away and thus accumulate systems of concepts. When we need to, we can recall or retrieve this data about our previous experiences. The ability to form concepts, to classify previously learned information, to store that classified information away, and to retrieve that material when we need it makes it possible for us to compare present perceptions with previous ones. We can therefore check the present by the past and test new observations by comparing them with old ones.

Here again, we face a danger. Since all perceptions are somewhat distorted, checking a present imperfect perception against past imperfect perceptions will not yield absolute certainty on the accuracy of the perception. Still, it is another means of testing one's perceptions.

Comparing with Perceptions Based on Other Senses

All perception begins with the collection of sense data. Sometimes we get information about an object or event from several senses at the same time. Checking the resulting perceptions against each other can be helpful in determining what "reality" is.

Recently I heard a noise from another room. I could not tell if the person I heard was laughing or crying. I ran into the room to see; I had inferred from the sound that she was crying. When I saw her, I knew I had been mistaken. She was convulsed with laughter.

Another case: In New York City recently, someone I know opened a briefcase, and inside I *saw* a gun. No mistaking it. It was a revolver. A real one. My friend saw my facial expression and perceived it rightly to express confusion, shock, and concern. *"No sirve,"* he said. ("It doesn't work.") Evidently my expression did not change; I was not convinced. He then took out the gun, and he pulled the trigger six times. I saw him pull the trigger, and I *heard* the harmless clicks. The second sense served as a test of the perception formed on the basis of the first one, and it proved to me my first perception had been wrong.

Sometimes the information provided by the other senses will confirm a perception; sometimes the information provided by those senses will contradict or disprove a perception. In either case, when possible, it is useful to check perceptions by comparing them with perceptions based on other senses.

Checking Perceptions Experientially

Perceptions, I have said several times, are guesses about reality. The last way to test those theories is to put them into practice, to act on them, and see if they work. This is a pragmatic approach. Act as if the perception is valid and find out what happens!

For example: You see a little dog leashed to a parking meter outside a grocery store. You perceive the dog as friendly. You approach the little Yorkie and pet him. If he bites you, your inference was incorrect. But you were clearly using the fourth test for validating perceptions: act on your perception, and then compare the experience with the perception.

basic principles of perception

We have been discussing perception for a long time, and I hope we understand the complicated process a little better now. An understanding of perception is essential to an understanding of human communication.

Through the process of perception, you and I form our impressions of reality—of ourselves, of other people, and of the world. Through the process of perception (and our ability to group perceptions into categories or classes and to store information for later retrieval), we develop the ideas and feelings that are the substance of the messages we communicate.

Our perceptions of ourselves will affect our communication. (More on that in the next chapter.) Our perceptions of other people will certainly affect our communication with them. (We will have a chapter on that as well.) And our perceptions of the world (our values, beliefs, and attitudes) will be a major factor in our communication; indeed, they are much of the stuff we communicate about. (Granted, what we perceive and how we perceive determines what we understand and believe. It is equally true, however, that what we understand and believe determines what we perceive. Put another way, our understandings and beliefs are the results of previous perceptions categorized, classified, and stored; our present perceptions are influenced by these understandings and beliefs. It is a circle!)

What generalizations can we make about the process of perception? There seem to be five basic principles related to perception:

1. Perception is subjective and limited.
2. Perception is learned.
3. Perception involves attaching meanings.
4. We attempt to keep perceptions stable.
5. We attempt to establish consistency among our perceptions.

Let us look at each of these principles as a kind of review.

Subjectivity

You would not know what someone's perception of something was by merely analyzing the stimulus. The perception process starts with the reception of a stimulus, but that is only the beginning. Perception is a mental process, and it is therefore a creative process. The perceiver is not a passive receiver, but an active participant in the process. Out of the five steps in the process, four are clearly active (requiring choices on the part of the receiver). Even the gathering step is active, in the sense that the perceiver has exercised selective exposure prior to sensing the stimulus. To a great extent, our perceptions are creations of our own minds. Our perceptions are not objective descriptions of things as they really are, but subjective interpretations of things as we think them to be.

The principle of *subjectivity* reminds us that when we talk about what something is or how something is, we are really talking about what (or how) it seems to us. And we must remember that other people can observe exactly the same things and arrive at very different perceptions. Surely, the principle of subjectivity ought to make us a little more tolerant of those whose perceptions do not agree with ours—those who see the world a little differently from the way we do.

This principle also reminds us that our perceptions are limited. Our perceptions are imperfect. "Seeing is believing," we are told. But can you always rely on your senses to tell you what to believe? People believed the earth was flat because that was what they saw! And would you not believe, from looking, that the night sky is a black roof over the earth and that stars are tiny, stationary lights hung in that roof? Just by looking, you would believe that a fallen tree (or a stone lying on the earth) was a solid, motionless mass of matter, wouldn't you? Relying on your ears alone, would you believe that there are sounds with frequencies about 20,000 cycles per second? No, since we cannot hear them!

Of course, we have to use our sense perception. But we also have to remember the limitations that sense perception has. And we have to leave room in our belief system for the possibility that our senses may fool us!

Conditioning

There is no point in belaboring this principle again. Perception is learned. We learn how to perceive and we learn what to perceive. We probably do not realize (perceive) how much of our reality has been programmed into us by our cultural *conditioning*.

This conditioning takes place during the time we are most plastic or flexible—when we are least aware of what is occurring and when we have the least power over our own destinies. (Remember the kittens!)

We are probably taught to perceive things that are not there at all, and doubtless we are also taught to ignore important things that are there. Like the deprived kittens, we may miss many useful things that surround us and we may encounter obstacles unnecessarily—all because of our learned perceptions.

Meaningfulness

Perception involves attaching meanings to physical sensations. We associate meanings with the sensations; we impose meaning in the perception process. The end result of the perception process is an idea, an interpretation. That is why some have defined perception as making sense out of sensations.

There are many factors (some related to the perceiver and some related to the stimulus) that exert an influence on the imposition of meaning.

Stability

The principle of *stability* reminds us that we attempt to keep our perceptions stable (or constant). We make mental adjustments to keep our impression of something from changing—even though the raw, incoming data about that thing is changing. In other words, the principle of stability refers to our attempts (based on previous knowledge and experience) to keep from varying a perception of something just because the information about it gathered by one of the senses is changing.

Is it still not clear? Maybe an illustration would help. If you are standing on a street corner watching a car come toward you down the street, what happens? Is the *image* of the approaching car (what you see) the same size the entire time? No. The image of the car (which you see) is smaller when the car is farther away, and it (the image) gets larger as the car gets closer to you. Indeed, the image projected on our retina increases in size as the car approaches us. The physical stimulus changes; the image gets larger. But do we perceive the *car* as getting larger as it approaches us? Of course not, you say. That is ridiculous. But is it? Are the physical stimuli not indicating increased size? Yes, but we do not interpret the image's increase in size to mean that the car itself is increasing in size. We perceive the car as remaining the same size; we perceive the size of the car to be stable or constant or unchanging—in spite of the evidence to the contrary! We have learned that objects stay the same size whether they are near or far away, and we have also learned that they appear to increase in size, but that this is an optical illusion. We are not fooled by the illusion, because we impose stability on our perceptions of moving objects. Just as we stabilize many other perceptions. Doesn't this principle also apply to shapes and sounds as well as to size? Isn't that what the artist's principle of *perspective* is all about?

The principle of stability refers to the mental adjustments that we make to keep our perception of something from changing just because the stimuli we are receiving give the illusion of change.

Consistency

We organize our perceptions into categories by grouping similar perceptions together. In this way, we simplify our total picture of the world and make responding to it easier. Because we have a symbol system (language), we can label the categories in our classification system. We thus construct concepts or ideas. Earlier in this chapter, I referred to the concept of *hot.*

Many different perceptions are covered by that concept; the stimuli on which each of those perceptions is based vary considerably, but—seeing common attributes in all of them—I have grouped them together.

You can see, then, that we try to structure the sensations we receive. Based on our past experience and our language system, we organize our perceptions into a system of categories that makes sense to us. We ourselves create this structure in our minds. The classes into which we pigeonhole things do not exist in nature, but in us; we develop the categories. The meaningful groups are the products of our sensing, our perceiving, and our labeling.

How is this *categorizing* accomplished? By *abstracting* and *generalizing*. In abstracting, we think of particular qualities or characteristics, without thinking of specific instances, cases, or things. When abstracting, we pull out and focus on the attributes we think are essential or important. And we ignore all the other differentiating attributes. In the process of abstraction, we separate the essential, inherent qualities of something from the actual thing of which those qualities are a part.

By deciding on what we think are the essential characteristics of something, we can form categories. We can put all the things with the same essential characteristics together into one category. Note that *we* decided on what characteristics were important, so the categories are our own creations.

On the basis of these categories (grouped according to abstracted essential properties), we generalize. The generalizations we make are about the *categories*—not about individual instances or individual perceptions. Generalizations are conclusions we reach about the entire category.

Using abstraction and generalization, we categorize our multitudes of separate perceptions; we sort out our perceptions into simple, coherent, meaningful groups. Then we must construct a structure of those categories. We must determine the relationships among the categories of perceptions and organize the categories into some orderly pattern.

The principle of *consistency* reminds us that we attempt to establish consistency, congruency, or harmony among our many perceptions and among our categories (or concepts). These categories or concepts are our structure for viewing the world, and we try to keep that view in balance and harmony. Contradictions in our world view create tensions in us, and we try to resolve the contradictions and restore consistency.

The need for consistency has been given several different names. Leon Festinger first presented the concept in his *A Theory of Cognitive Dissonance*. He said that relationships between categories or concepts (*cognitions*) could be consonant (in agreement or balance) or dissonant (in disagreement or imbalance). Charles E. Osgood and Percy H. Tannenbaum refer to this principle as *congruity theory*, and Fritz Heider, in his book *The Psychology of Interpersonal Relations*, calls it *balance theory*.

Festinger's terminology is now common. If a person takes in a piece of information that does not fit into the world view the person has already

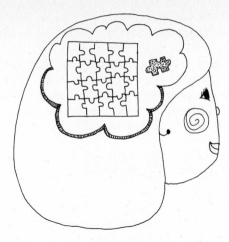

Cognitive dissonance

constructed, he or she experiences *cognitive dissonance.* You have probably heard a friend comment, about someone who is facing the problem of inconsistency in his or her belief system, that the person is experiencing cognitive dissonance. There are several ways we can reduce dissonance, but I will not discuss them at this point. It is enough now to know that we do attempt to keep our perceptions consistent with each other; we try to keep our world view (structure of categories) in harmony and balance.

SUGGESTIONS FOR FURTHER READING

ALLPORT, FLOYD N., *Theories of Perception* (New York: Wiley, 1955).

DEMPSEY, DAVID, "Eye Openers," *The New York Times Magazine,* July 20, 1975, pp. 10, 41–48.

FERGUS, R. H., *Perception* (New York: McGraw-Hill, 1966).

FESTINGER, LEON, *A Theory of Cognitive Dissonance* (Evanston, Ill.: Row, Peterson, 1957).

GERARD, RALPH W., "What Is Memory?," *Contemporary Reading in General Psychology,* Robert S. Daniel, ed. (Boston: Houghton Mifflin, 1959).

HANEY, WILLIAM V., "Perception in Communication," *Basic Readings in Interpersonal Communication,* Kim Giffin and Bobby R. Patton, eds. (New York: Harper & Row, 1971).

HEIDER, FRITZ, *The Psychology of Interpersonal Relations* (New York: Wiley, 1958).

LEWIN, ROGER, "Observing the Brain Through a Cat's Eyes," *Saturday Review/World,* October 5, 1974, pp. 54–56.

MASLOW, ABRAHAM, *Motivation and Personality* (New York: Harper & Row, 1970).

MASLOW, ABRAHAM, *Toward a Psychology of Being* (New York: Van Nostrand, 1968).

PINES, MAYA, "Speak, Memory: The Riddle of Recall and Forgetfulness," *Saturday Review,* August 9, 1975, pp. 16–20.

ROCK, IRVING, *An Introduction to Perception* (New York: Macmillan, 1975).

ROKEACH, MILTON, *The Open and Closed Mind* (New York: Basic Books, 1960).

ROSENFELD, ALBERT, "How Real Is Our Reality?," *Saturday Review/World,* October 5, 1974, p. 51.

ROSENFELD, ALBERT, and KENNETH KLIVINGTON, "Inside the Brain: The Last Great Frontier," *Saturday Review,* August 9, 1975, pp. 12–15.

VERNON, M. D., *The Psychology of Perception* (Baltimore: Penguin, 1962).

VERNON, M. D., "Perception, Attention, and Consciousness," *Foundations of Communication Theory,* K. K. Soreno and C. D. Mortensen, eds. (New York: Harper & Row, 1970).

WHEELESS, L. R., "The Relationship of Attitude and Credibility to Comprehension and Selective Exposure," *Western Speech,* vol. 38 (1974), pp. 88–97.

4
PERCEIVING YOUR SELF

general goal:

To learn how your self-perceptions affect your communication.

specific objectives:

After completing this unit, you should understand:
What self-image, ego ideal, and self-esteem are.
What the component parts of self-image are.
How your self-perceptions developed.
How your self-perceptions influence your com-
munication.

IN THE PRECEDING CHAPTER, I discussed with you the process of perception. Anything a person is aware of, that person has a perception of. Another word for perception might be *impression*. Anything a person knows about or thinks about or is aware of the existence of—that thing exists in the person's mind in the form of some impression.

When we arrive in this world as babies, we have no preconceived (sorry!) notions about what anything is like—the world, abstractions, other people, ourselves—anything. Indeed, when we arrive as babies, we are not able at first to differentiate between our environment and ourselves. We have to *learn* to think of ourselves as separate from the world around us. We have to learn how to think of ourselves; more accurately put, we have to learn *what* to think of ourselves.

We human beings have to learn who we are. Each of us develops a perception, an impression, of what kind of person he or she is. We call that mental picture a *self-image*. But where does that composite picture come from? We develop it (it evolves) out of our sensory experiences and our interactions with other human beings. More about that later.

We human beings also have to learn who we ought to be. We learn standards by which to judge or evaluate ourselves. We develop a mental picture of an ideal person; we call that impression an *ego ideal*. We will come back to that concept too.

We apply the standards we have learned (from other people, of course). We judge ourselves as we think we are (our self-image) against the standards set by the self we think we ought to be (our ego ideal), and that evaluation results in a judgment about our own worth. We decide how we measure up to the goals we have learned to set for ourselves; we develop some degree of *self-esteem*. We must return to that concept also.

Now I can almost hear some of you saying, "Why are you trying to make this so complicated? I know who I am; I know what I am like; I know what kind of person I am. What more is there to it than that?" Ah, but do you *really* know yourself as you *really* are? Remember what we discussed about perception. Our impressions, including those about our own selves, are partial, imperfect, selective, necessarily distorted. Our perceptions of our selves go through the same process of perception as any other impressions or awarenesses do. Those perceptions are just as faulty as the rest of our perceptions. I can tell you what I think I am like; I can tell you my perceptions about myself. But I cannot accurately tell you what I am really like. That is known, if at all, only to God.

What is the *self* anyway? What do we mean by that word? We human beings are able to contemplate, to look at, our own existence. We are able to be the object of our own enquiry and examination. We are not just the subjects (the *I*), then, but the objects (the *me*). I can think about me, and I can talk about me; I can judge me, and I can praise or blame me. That whole being I can treat as an object is the self—my self.

Some writers think it worthwhile to distinguish among these selves:

Me as I am
Me as I think I am
Me as others think I am
Me as I think others think I am
Me as I think I ought to be
Me as I think I measure up to what I think I ought to be

The *me as I am* is the real, complete me. But that me is known, as I said earlier, only to God. I cannot know myself completely; I cannot know everything there is to know about myself. Other human beings cannot know me completely or objectively either. "For we know in part. . . . "

The *me as I think I am* is my self-image. We will look at the various aspects of that mental picture, but it is a whole picture—consistent and organized. (The cityscape on the facing page [side-turn] represents one student's self-image.) Just as I am a person in the process of becoming, so my self-image is in process—constantly developing and evolving with me.

The *me as others think I am* exists in the minds of those who know me. It is their individual perceptions about what kind of person I am. Each friend and acquaintance of mine, I assume, has a different impression of me; each has his or her own mental picture (like my self-image, it is a composite made up of different elements blended together) of who I am. I can know the me as others think I am only secondhand. And I never know the complete picture that exists of me in anyone's mind. I do get information, of course, about those perceptions, but I get only fragmentary reports as my friends, family, and acquaintances communicate with me.

The *me as I think others think I am* exists in my own mind. I have put that impression together from reports from and interactions with other human beings. "I know what you think of me, and you are dead wrong!" Have you ever said that to somebody, or have you ever wanted to say that to someone? Well, you have a perception, an impression, about how that person sees you. You have a perception of what that person's perception of you is. Remember how imperfect perceptions are. Just as that person's impression of you may be quite mistaken, so your impression of what the other person's view of you is may also be quite mistaken! We will look at this matter again when we look at the social aspect of one's self-image.

The *me as I think I ought to be* is what I referred to earlier as the ego ideal. It is the picture in one's mind of what one ought to be and what one ought to do. Call it conscience if you like; it is the collection of standards that have been internalized by an individual through interacting with other human beings and participating in reference groups.

The *me as I think I measure up to what I think I ought to be* is my self-esteem. It is my rating of how I meet the standards I have set for myself. This particular way of saying it focuses on the fact that my judgments about my success or failure to meet my goals are perceptions (what I think), as are the goals themselves. This phrasing reminds us that

both my ego ideal (what I think I ought to be) and my self-esteem (how I think I measure up) are mental impressions; they exist in my head.

Let us look at self-image, ego ideal, and self-esteem in a little more detail.

self-image

What kind of person do you think you are? When you think about yourself (and we all think about ourselves quite a bit), how do you see yourself? If someone asked you, "Who are you?," what would you answer?

Emily Dickinson wrote,

> *I'm nobody. Who are you?*
> *Are you nobody, too?*

Well, everybody is *somebody*. The question is who—or what. The composite picture we call self-image consists of the beliefs you have about your being and functioning, about *who* that somebody is.

SELF IMAGE

Self-image

There are, I think, at least six aspects or components of a person's self-image: (1) a physical self, (2) an intellectual (thinking) self, (3) an emotional self, (4) a philosophical self, (5) a social (relating) self, and (6) a communicating self. Let us look at each of these aspects or components of one's self-image.

Physical Self

We human beings exist as part of the physical world, and we each have some picture in our minds of ourselves as *physical* beings. We have some idea of what kinds of bodies we have; we have some notions about what we look like. Now, those ideas may or may not match reality (as others perceive it), but they form an important component of our mental image of our selves.

**One of the aspects of one's
self-image: Physical self**

I am told that one of the greatest problems overweight people may have is related to this component of self-image. Since one's self-image is developed rather early in life, and since many presently obese people started out in life thin, many large people may not see themselves as too large or overweight. Their self-images did not change when the physical realities changed! I can almost hear you doubters saying, "But they have mirrors! They can *see*!" Remember that we are dealing with perceptions and that we see what we need to and what we want to. In this case, one may still see what he or she used to!

There is a physical me, and I have some impressions about that physical me, but those impressions may be somewhat out of whack. I will never forget Celia, one of my best and brightest debaters. On every debate trip, she spent a great deal of time putting on her makeup and changing clothes. After each new application of makeup and change of apparel, she would appear and ask how she looked. I would tell her what I believed to be the truth: she looked fine. No, the makeup was not too much; like Baby Bear's soup, it was just right. The dress was quite stylish and becoming. She should wow debaters and judges alike! But she would respond, "You're just saying that. I know I still look awful." Celia thought of her physical self as unattractive. She believed herself too tall and too heavy. She considered her features harsh and her skin just plain ugly. I thought she was wrong and told her so, but I never really modified her concept of her physical self.

How do you see *your* physical self? These questions might help you focus on the answers to that question, but you are certainly not obligated to share the answers with anyone unless you choose to do so.

I would describe my body as _____.
My most attractive physical feature is _____.
My most unattractive physical feature is _____.
My face is _____.
I look best in _____.
I look worst in _____.
My general appearance is _____.
The clothes I usually wear are _____.
I am sexiest when _____.
I am ugliest when _____.
I am most attractive when _____.
The aspect of my looks I am most ashamed of is _____.
The aspect of my looks I am most proud of is _____.
If I could change my looks, I would _____.
A well-known person I resemble is _____.
My coordination is _____.
My athletic ability in general is _____.
I use my body _____.
My gestures and body movements are _____.

That is hardly an exhaustive list of questions, but it should get you started thinking about your physical self. You can probably make a much better list of questions than this one. If you do, I would be delighted if you sent it to me!

Intellectual Self

The second aspect of self-image is the mental me, the *intellectual self.* We each have an impression of how much brain power we have, do we not? We have an idea about our intellectual capabilities and aptitudes. Just as we have a set of notions about the nature of our bodies (our physical selves), so we have a set of notions about the nature of our minds (our intellectual selves).

How do you classify yourself in terms of brain power? How smart are you? Are you a fast or slow learner? Can you master some kinds of material more easily than others? Do you have some natural intellectual gifts and talents? How good are you at reasoning? Can you analyze problems and find solutions? What kind of thinking can and does (they may not be the same) your thinking self do? How well do you gather, assimilate, and store information? How good is your memory?

Again, we must remember that we are dealing with perceptions. My concept of my intellectual powers and my actual intellectual powers may or may not match. I am sure you have known people whose self-image did not coincide with your estimate of their intellectual prowess. I remember

**One of the aspects of one's
self-image: Intellectual self**

one young man rather vividly who, though I thought him rather dull and slow-witted, believed he had the mental capacities to be a neurosurgeon. On the other hand, I will never forget a young fellow who said the same thing every time he turned in an exam paper to me: "Well, here is another *F* paper. I just can't take tests!" I thought the student to be of at least average intelligence, believed he could take and pass exams, and noted that he maintained a *C* average on the exams in the course. In my judgment (which is not, of course, infallible), both of these students pictured their intellectual selves inaccurately.

How do you see your intellectual self? Here are some questions to stimulate your thinking. Remember, the answers are for your enlightenment and need not be shared with others.

I would describe my mind as _____.
My greatest intellectual gift is _____.
My greatest intellectual handicap is _____.
My greatest talent is _____.
My memory is _____.
I learn quickly in _____.
I learn slowly in _____.
In analyzing problems, I _____.
My best subject in school is _____.
My worst subject in school is _____.
I have a natural aptitude in _____.
I have no natural aptitude in _____.
I concentrate best when _____.
My attention span is _____.
I can gather and assimilate information when _____.
I consider my reasoning power to be _____.

This is not meant to be an exhaustive, but a suggestive, list of questions. It should serve to get you started examining your impression of your intellectual self.

Emotional Self

The third aspect of self-image is related to the *emotional self.* We are not just physical beings or thinking beings; we are emotional beings. We have drives, motives, and feelings. And each of us has an inner picture of how we respond to those drives, motives, and feelings.

One of the aspects of one's
self-image: Emotional self

I discussed needs (or drives) with you in the chapter on perception. (See pp. 82–84.) You will remember I suggested that all human beings have five basic needs: the need to survive, the need for sex, the need for security, the need for social relationships, and the need for self-esteem or self-respect. How driven are you? Or, more to the point, how driven do you think you are? What do you think you need most? How much do these needs that all of us have matter to you?

In addition to needs, we human beings have motives or motivations. These motivations are concerns. The basic needs or drives seem universal; all human beings share them; all human beings have them all the time. Motivations, on the other hand, are not universal; some people are concerned about some things more or less than other people. The motivations arise out of our needs; they are based on our needs. But they are secondary.

We all have a drive to survive; we have a need to live. Based on that drive or need, we have several concerns that motivate our behavior. I am concerned, for example, about having a place to live to protect me from the elements. As I write, the temperature outside is 32 degrees Fahrenheit (0 degrees Celcius), so I am particularly aware of my concern for a dwelling place. I am concerned, too, about having food to eat and liquids to drink. I am concerned about having clothes because they help satisfy my need to survive in this weather. I would be less concerned about clothes, I think, if I were lucky enough to live in the tropics.

What are your primary concerns? What motives influence your decisions and your behavior? How aware of those motivations are you? One more illustration: All human beings need social relationships; we need satisfying interactions with other people. That is a driving force in our lives. How does that force, that drive, generate motives or concerns in you? Are you concerned now about the health of some particular relationship? How concerned are you about having lots of friends or about being considered friendly? Doesn't that concern affect your behavior?

We not only have needs (or drives) and motives (or concerns); we also have feelings. Feelings are often called emotional states. They are more transitory than concerns. Sometimes I am happy; sometimes I feel sad. Occasionally I feel depressed, and at times I am positively elated. No, I do not consider myself manic-depressive, and it was unkind of you to think so. Though if I were, I think it would be a good thing to be aware of it and to face it (making it part of my self-image).

I am not a "scaredy cat," but I do feel fear from time to time. I also feel disgusted, angry, repelled, attracted, or delighted. I am capable of feeling affection and hate, joy and sorrow, concern and disinterest.

Each of us is some sort of emotional being, and each of us has an internal picture (impression) of what *kind* of emotional being he or she is. After all, one is an integrated personality—a whole being, and the self-image will be some kind of single, organized picture. So are you basically a happy person? Are you a stable person—not static and unchanging, but relatively steady in your emotional self? Are your emotional fluctuations within reasonable bounds (whatever they are)? Are you brave, fearful, or stoic? Do you give vent to your emotions or do you try to control them? Are your decisions and your behaviors more determined by your "heart" than by your "head"? Do you think your emotions control you more than you control your emotions? Do you have a chip on your shoulder—angry at the world? Would you describe yourself as an angry young man or young woman? What are your major concerns (motivations)?

How do you see your emotional self? Again, here are some questions to start you thinking.

I think of myself as:
    emotionally stable
    emotionally unstable
    manic-depressive
    usually happy
    usually unhappy
    unusually happy

unusually unhappy
flighty
angry at the world
generally contented
generally discontented
optimistic
pessimistic
brave
cowardly
in control of my emotions
controlled by my emotions
sentimental
unsentimental
feeling secure
feeling insecure
liberated
hung up
sexually mature
sexually immature
a can-do person
inadequate to many of the tasks I face
having a positive attitude toward life
having a negative attitude toward life
satisfied with my life
dissatisfied with my life
generally rational
generally irrational
mature
immature

These options certainly do not exhaust all the possibilities. I would be *happy* if you would send me suggestions for additions to the list. Don't suggest "all of the above" and "none of the above," please. In one of my more cynical moments, I thought of those too, and I decided against them. Here are the rest of the questions:

I feel happy when _____.
I feel sad when _____.
I feel most secure when _____.
I feel most insecure when _____.
My sex drives are _____.
I feel most competent when _____.
I feel least competent when _____.
I feel most angry when _____.
I am most disgusted by _____.
I feel most affection for (or when) _____.
I feel most hate for (or when) _____.
I am most concerned about _____.
My biggest worry is _____.
I am least concerned about _____.

The fourth aspect of self-image is related to the *philosophical self.* As we discussed in Chapter 3, every person has a world view—an organized set of beliefs, values, and attitudes. Call it a philosophy of life; call it a frame of reference. It is a package of rather consistent principles that the person holds. (See pp. 76–78.) Not only do I affirm these principles; I am aware of myself as a person who affirms these principles. The principles are part *of* me!

**One of the aspects of one's
self-image: Philosophical self**

I know what I believe about the way things are—what's so and what's not so. I know how I judge value—what I think is worth something and what I think is worthless. And I know my attitudes—which things I lean toward and which things I am against. I identify with those beliefs, values, and attitudes, and I identify those beliefs, values, and attitudes with myself.

Could you make a list of your basic beliefs? Could you identify the values (guidelines) you use in judging what is of worth and what is not and in deciding what is worthy and what is not? Could you make a list of the behaviors, traits, concepts, people, or organizations toward which you have favorable and unfavorable attitudes? It is an exercise worth trying.

How would you characterize your own philosophy of life? How do you see your philosophical self? Maybe these questions will help you focus this component of your self-image more sharply:

In terms of politics, I think of myself as:
Republican
Democratic
Conservative
Liberal
Socialist
Communist
_____

conservative
liberal
anarchist
indifferent
moderate
radical
activist
leftist
rightist
––––––––––––––––

In terms of religion, I think of myself as:
very religious
devout
nominally religious
indifferent
atheist
agnostic
believer
theist
hostile to organized religion
cynic
––––––––––––––––

Hindu
Buddhist
Zen Buddhist
Zoroastrian
Muslim
Jewish (Orthodox, Conservative, or Reformed?)
Christian (Roman Catholic, Orthodox, Protestant, or ?)
Mormon (organized or reorganized?)
Christian Scientist
Pentecostal
Evangelical
Fundamentalist
Unitarian
––––––––––––––––

It is impossible, of course, to give you an adequate checklist of questions
about your beliefs. The range of subjects is much too broad; we could not
even make a dent. Still, here are a few questions to get you started thinking
about your beliefs.

I believe:
democracy is _____.
capitalism is _____.
free enterprise is _____.
socialism is _____.
America is _____.
the United States of America is _____.
the President of the United States is _____.
sex is _____.

men are _____ .
men should _____ .
women are _____ .
women should _____ .
homosexuals are _____ .
bisexuals are _____ .
transsexuals are _____ .
the Pope is _____ .
the Pope should _____ .
parents should _____ .
the Constitution of the United States is _____ .
the United States Bill of Rights is _____ .
marijuana is _____ .
alcohol and other drugs are _____ .
war is _____ .
terminating a fetus is _____ .
the Equal Rights Amendment is _____ .
Prohibition was _____ .
outer space contains _____ .
organized crime is _____ .
the United Nations is _____ .
the United Nations should _____ .

It is just as difficult to prepare a list of provocative questions about values as to prepare one about beliefs. Indeed, it may be even more difficult. I would value your suggestions to improve this list.

I judge something good if it _____ .
I judge something bad if it _____ .
I judge something right when _____ .
I judge something wrong when _____ .
I judge something desirable provided _____ .
I judge something undesirable provided _____ .
I think something respectable if _____ .
I think something not respectable if _____ .
I count something valuable that _____ .
I rate something worthless (or at least worth less) if _____ .
I call something abnormal that _____ .
I call something normal that _____ .
I judge something unattractive if _____ .
I judge something attractive if _____ .
I give positive evaluations if _____ .
I give negative evaluations if _____ .

Beliefs are convictions; values are criteria—standards to judge by. Attitudes are inclinations—biases for or against something. Our attitudes are more specific, in one sense, because they are directed toward or away from something. Your attitudes, then, will be positive (favorable) or negative (unfavorable). The question is: Which way do you lean?

To check your attitudes, you must ask yourself, "Am I for it (whatever *it* is), against it, or neutral?" Here are a few topics. Note what your attitude is with regard to each. Then make up a better list of topics!

Am I against, neutral, or for:
absolute freedom of speech
Richard Nixon
the Equal Rights Amendment
an independent Palestinian homeland
Anita Bryant's stand on equal rights for gay Americans
premarital (or extramarital) sexual relations
cohabitation (without benefit of clergy)
Martin Luther King
nonviolence
the FBI
apartheid
monarchy
benevolent dictatorships
student involvement in curriculum decisions
tenure for college professors
social fraternities and sororities
Jimmy Carter
organized religion
affirmative action for minorities
censorship of pornographic materials
Karl Marx and his economic theories

The qualities I most admire in people are ————————.
The public figure I most admire is ————————.
The public figures who most nearly reflect my own views
are ————————.
The qualities I most detest in people are ————————.
The public figure I most dislike is ————————.
The public figures with whom I disagree most are ————————.
The organizations with which I identify most closely
(agree with most often) are ————————.
The organizations with which I disagree most strongly
or disapprove of most strongly are ————————.

Social (Relating) Self

The fifth aspect of self-image is related to the *social self*. The social self is me as I relate to other human beings. Each of us has a mental picture of how he or she relates to others. Perhaps you should go back and review quickly what we have already discussed about social relationships. (See pp. 40–42.) Here we are focusing not so much on the relationships themselves as on the individual communicator's *perception* (image) of the relationships and of his or her ability to relate. Part of one's self-image is: How do I view myself in relation to the other people in my life? How do I fit? How do I get along?

**One of the aspects of one's
self-image: Social self**

When talking about social relationships, we noted three aspects of those relationships: roles, status, and attraction. Our image of the social self will also take into account those three aspects of relating: roles, status, and attraction. Your picture of your social self will depend on what roles you see yourself fulfilling; what status, power, or prestige you see yourself accorded; and how attractive you think your personality is to other people.

How we view our relationships with others is extremely important. This component of self-image markedly affects whether we attempt to communicate with others, how we communicate with others, and ultimately how well we relate to others.

I have a set of relationships with the members of my family. How do I see those relationships? As far as roles go, I am a son, or I am a brother, or I am an uncle, or I am a father, or I am a husband. I have certain expectations about those roles, and I have certain perceptions about how I fulfill those functions. I will keep those perceptions to myself. What about status or prestige? Well, as I see it, the other family members do accord me some status. They respect the vocation I chose, the education I pursued, the books I wrote. And, in the family, my travels bring me a little prestige and maybe a little envy. I think I am also accorded a little honor for being older than most of my relatives. Finally, what about attraction or attractiveness? Do I think the other members of the family like me? Well, it varies from relationship to relationship, but most of them seem to tolerate me at least!

I have a set of relationships with the people I work with. I have impressions about all of those relationships also. I have a pattern of relationships with my acquaintances and friends, and I have an idea of what those relationships are like too.

How do you see yourself as a relating (social) person? Are you outgoing or introverted? Are you a people person? Do you make (and keep) friends easily? Do you trust other people? Do you like other people? Do you think other people like you? Do you accept other people who are different from yourself? Do you have a wide circle of friends and acquaintances? Would you call yourself popular? Are you influential in your relations with other people? Are you more likely to be influenced or to do the influencing? What kind of people do you relate to most easily? What kind of people do you have the most difficulty relating to? What kind of relationships do you have with your family? With your schoolmates? With those you work with? With those you are romantically involved with?

Communicating Self

The sixth aspect of self-image is related to the *communicating self.* Don't you have a conception of what kind of communicator you are? How do you see yourself in terms of your skills in communicating? How well do you speak? What kind of voice do you have? Do you speak the Status Dialect of American English? (Another way of asking that question is: "Do you speak properly—in proper talk?") Are you a confident speaker? Is your articulation clear and crisp without being pedantic and overly precise? Is your bodily movement natural, spontaneous, appropriate, and unobtrusive? Do you have a good vocabulary with a wide range of options for wording messages? Can you organize your thoughts as you speak? *And* are you a good listener? Do you let other people know you are interested in listening to what they say? Do you listen with an open, inquiring mind? Do you get messages right when you listen—that is, when you listen, is the message you get an accurate message? Do you think you are a sophisticated listener, or do you think you are naive and easily fooled?

So far we have discussed the six aspects or components of a person's self-image. Let us turn now to the subject of ego ideal.

ego ideal

The ego ideal, as I said earlier, is the *me as I think I should be.* Each of us has a picture in mind of what kind of person he or she wants to be or feels he or she ought to be. By interacting with other human beings (especially those who matter to us) and by participating in many reference groups (where the other members of the group exert pressure on us to accept and abide by their norms), we have internalized a set of standards. We know what (we think) an ideal person is like.

Note the self-image and ego ideal revealed in this statement: "*I* don't do it (self-image), but I know I should go to church every Sunday!" (ego ideal) Or this statement: "They say I should spend two hours of study for every hour spent in class (ego ideal), but I'm lucky to put in one for one."

Ego ideal

(self-image) Or this statement: "OK, maybe you shouldn't have sex with somebody unless you really love them (ego ideal), but the way I decide is this: if I like 'em, I let 'em, and if I love 'em, I help." (self-image) Or this statement: "No, I didn't vote this time. (self-image) Sure, voting is a part of good citizenship, but . . . " (ego ideal)

We have ideas about what we ought to do and what we ought to be. Some people call that *conscience*. It isn't a bad word, provided we all remember that conscience is not given, or inherited, or innate. It is learned. It is developed. It is learned from communicating with other human beings. *What* you learn and what standards you develop—what kind of picture of your ideal self you internalize—depends on the people you communicate with and the people who matter (are significant) to you.

Does that mean, then, that the ego ideal (conscience) is relative rather than absolute? Yes, it is relative, because it is *related* to the individuals and groups who have influenced your development as a person. What kind of ideal person do you see in your mind? It depends on (is related to) the beliefs, values, and attitudes of the people who influenced you. So my ego ideal and your ego ideal are likely to be quite different? Probably. The more nearly alike our backgrounds were, of course, the more nearly alike will be our ego ideals.

What kind of person do you think you *should* be? Or, put a different way, what kind of person do you *want* or *hope* to be? Perhaps we could even ask: What kind of person do you *struggle* to be?

I remember a good friend of mine whose sexual drives were directed toward members of his own sex. I was a little shocked when he told me he was going to get married. Several years later, I said to him, "Dick, are you happy?" And his reply clearly stated his ego ideal. He said, "We are not put here on earth to be happy; we are placed here to do right! Whether I am happy is irrelevant." Other people, of course, may have internalized a different ego ideal—one in which the ideal person is happy. For Dick, the ideal person was righteous—happy or not.

Have you ever analyzed your own ego ideal? It might be useful to do so. Think about what kind of person you think you should be. Here are some questions to help you focus on your ego ideal.

Physical aspects:
    I admire people who are physically _____.
    A physically attractive person is _____.
    A physically healthy person is _____.
    An ideal body is _____.
    Ideally, my physical appearance would be _____.
    Ideally, my clothes would be _____.
    To satisfy me perfectly, my voice would have to be _____.
    Ideal features would be _____.
    Ideally, I would be physically able to _____.
    Ideally, I would be able to move my body _____.
Intellectual aspects:
    I admire people who are intellectually _____.
    In terms of mental ability, I wish I were _____.
    Intellectual gifts I wish I had include _____.
    I ought to use my mind _____.
    I wish my education _____.
    I would like to have a talent for _____.
    I wish I could learn _____.
    Ideally, my memory would be _____.
    I ought to be able to concentrate _____.
    I wish my attention span _____.
    Ideally, I would be able to gather and assimilate information _____.
    Ideally, I would be able to reason _____.
Emotional aspects:
    I admire people who are emotionally _____.
    Emotionally, I wish I were _____.
    Emotionally, I ought to be _____.
    With regard to my feelings, I should _____.
    An emotionally stable person is _____.
    An admirable person _____ his or her drives (or needs).
    Ideally, a person _____ his or her motivations.
    Ideally, a person _____ his or her feelings (states).
Philosophical aspects:
    I admire people whose philosophy of life (viewpoint) is _____.
    I ought to believe _____.
    Everyone ought to believe _____.
    I ought to respect and value _____.
    Everyone ought to respect and value _____.
    I respect people if their attitudes _____.

I am sorry (or ashamed) I do not believe _____.
I am sorry (or ashamed) I do not value _____.
I am sorry (or ashamed) I do not lean toward (like) _____.
I am sorry (or ashamed) I do not belong to _____.
I am sorry (or ashamed) I do not agree with _____.

Social aspects:

I admire people who relate to other people _____.
Perfect interpersonal relationships are _____.
I admire people who fulfill the roles (functions) of _____.
The roles (functions) I should fulfill are _____.
I should fulfill those roles by _____.
I would be most respected by others _____.
People achieve status if (or by) _____.
I would be most influential if _____.
A most attractive personality is _____.
I would have a most attractive personality if _____.
I would get along with other people better if _____.
In relating to others, I should _____.
To improve my interpersonal relationships, I should _____.
An ideal relationship involves _____.
An ideal _____ (role such as father, wife, lover, friend) is _____.

Communication aspects:

The ideal human communicator is _____.
The type of speaker I admire most is _____.
The type of listener I admire most is _____.
To be a good conversationalist, one should _____.
Ideal communication skills are _____.
I think interpersonal communication is successful if _____.

I am sure you can add excellent items to all these lists. The questions here are meant just to get you started. Having discussed ego ideal, let us now turn to self-esteem.

self-esteem

Self-esteem is one's feeling of self-worth; another word for it, perhaps, is self-respect. To find one's self-image, one asks the question: what kind of person am I? To find one's ego ideal, one asks the question: what kind of person should I be? To determine one's self-esteem, one asks the question: how do I like the person I think I am?

We have talked about attitudes before. Attitudes are inclinations—positive or negative, favorable or unfavorable. Each of us has a set of attitudes toward his or her own self. That set of attitudes is self-esteem.

In a very real sense, self-esteem is the difference between one's ego ideal and one's self-image. If there is a great difference between the me-I-think-I-should-be and the me-I-think-I-am, then I will have low self-esteem. On the other hand, if there is not too much difference between those two, then I will have high self-esteem. No one, of course, reaches his

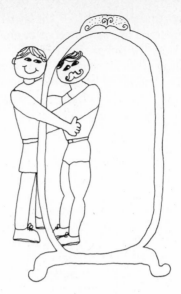

Self-esteem

or her ideal in every regard. As Robert Browning put it, "A man's reach should exceed his grasp/Or what's a heaven for?" There will be some tension in us, because we know we have not achieved all we could be or should be. If we come close enough to the ideal, we will be (relatively) satisfied with ourselves; we will have favorable attitudes toward ourselves; our self-esteem will be high. But if one falls far short of the ideal, then he or she will be very dissatisfied with himself or herself, the attitude toward the self will be unfavorable (or negative), and the self-esteem will be low.

Even people labeled saints have ego ideals, self-images, and self-esteem problems. Note the comments of Saint Paul: "I do not understand what I do, for I don't do what I would like to do, but instead I do what I hate!" (Romans 7:15, as translated in the Good News Bible.) It is of some comfort to me to know that others do not reach the standards of their ego ideals either!

What kind of attitudes do you have toward yourself? Do you genuinely like yourself? Is the person you think you are one you respect and can admire? Can you be proud of the person who lives in your skin? Are you the kind of person you look up to? Are you the kind of person you would want for a relative, a coworker, a friend? Do you honestly think you are an admirable human being? Do you approve of the person you have become and are becoming?

It might be worthwhile to list all the attributes you like about yourself. Note all the things about yourself you can be proud of. Note all the things that are positive and worthwhile. Include every "good" thing you can think of about yourself.

Then it might be worthwhile to list all the attributes you dislike about yourself. Note the things you are ashamed of or that you feel guilty about. Note your faults and your failings.

Now, after examining your strengths and your weaknesses (as you perceive them), do the strengths come out ahead? In general, do you believe yourself to be a person of character, competence, and charisma (interpersonal attractiveness)? Is your overall self-appraisal positive? Then your self-esteem should be high.

three questions

Before going on to examine our perceptions of other people, we should look at three questions related to self-perception and a few general reminders. The three questions are: (1) How did your ideas about your self (self-image, ego ideal, and self-esteem) develop? (2) Is there a *real* you? and (3) How do one's perceptions about oneself affect communication? We will examine each of the questions briefly.

How Did Your Ideas About Your Self (Self-image, Ego Ideal and Self-esteem) Develop?

Our impressions of who we are, what we should be, and how well we like ourselves are formed by our experiences—especially our interactions with other human beings. One's concepts about oneself, then, are *built*—constructed primarily out of materials gleaned in communication with other people.

A newborn baby has no ideas about himself or herself. That baby, like the rest of us, must *learn* who it is, what an ideal self would be, and what attitudes to direct toward itself. A person *achieves* selfhood. The self does not exist, waiting to be discovered. Instead, a self must be *developed*.

We develop our ideas about ourselves partly through our reactions to sense perceptions. We see images of our bodies in mirrors and pictures; we hear our own voices (imperfectly, I grant you) as we speak; our senses of taste, smell, and touch provide us with information about ourselves; and we have, through our nervous systems, the ability to monitor our internal states as well. We experience our internal states and our reactions to external stimuli, and those experiences help develop our ideas about our selves.

A more important source of materials for building one's self-image, ego ideal, and self-esteem, however, is the reference groups to which one belongs. Those groups play an important role in teaching us who we are, who to be, and what attitudes to take toward our selves.

The groups we belong to—from the family on—help us define who we are; they contribute to our evolving self-image. They help teach us the answers to these questions:

In what group of people am I included?
What roles do I perform?
What status (or rank or level of prestige) am I achieving?
What behaviors do I perform?

I think of the first primary group I was conscious of belonging to—my immediate family. That small group certainly had a great influence on my ideas about my self. Like the other members of that clan, I was reminded often that I was a King, that the Kings were an old and respected family with traditions and standards and loyalties, that membership in that family brought some privileges and many responsibilities. I was included in that worthy clan; I belonged! In that group, I learned what my functions (roles) were. I was a son, a grandson, a brother, a cousin, a nephew; later I became an uncle and even a great uncle. And, through interactions with family members—and sometimes, it seemed to me, with the family as a whole—I got impressions about my status. I discovered my place in the pecking order; or at least, I got an impression of my relatives' perceptions about my place in the family pecking order. I eventually perceived (whether correctly or not I shall never know) that scholarship brought less status than athletic ability. From that primary group, I learned names (or categories) for behaviors, and I learned to identify behaviors I performed and activities I engaged in. Thus my self-image grew.

The groups we belong to, from the family on, help us form some structured picture of who we ought to be; they contribute to our evolving ego ideal. They contribute to our learning the answers to these questions:

In which groups should I be included, or what should I be identified with?
How should one perform his or her roles (functions)?
How should status be achieved, or how is status achieved?
What standards are used in judging (evaluating) behavior?

My family certainly had an influence on my ego ideal. If I were a King, I would presumably be identified with certain groups and not with others. I would be a Baptist, for example. Did my great-grandfather not found several Baptist churches on his way west? And just to make sure, I was put into the Sunbeams as soon as possible! In the family, I learned what was expected of each of the roles I had been assigned—son, grandson, brother, and so on. "Honor thy father and thy mother." The family invoked the authority of God to back up that role expectation! And "a good brother looks after his little brother." Of course, I learned about status. I learned that grandparents get respect because of their age and experience. I learned that parents have more status and authority than children do. I learned lots of things about status! I learned about standards for deciding what is right and wrong, good and bad, approvable or unapprovable. "Nice boys don't do that." Or "How can Mother and Dad be proud of you if you behave that way?" Or "That's immoral!" And how about "Shame on you!" Norms were not always stated negatively. "Did you see how well the Graber children behaved at church today?" "Always remember the Golden Rule: Do unto others. . . . " The family was helping shape my ego ideal.

Just as the groups we belong to help us develop our individual self-images and ego ideals, they also contribute to the formation of our sense of self-worth, our self-esteem.

The groups we belong to exert pressures on us to conform to the standards they uphold. When we communicate with members of the group(s), we will discover what is expected of us. And we will soon sense that the group's expectations weigh heavily on us. Even when the group is not present, even when no member of the group is physically present with us, we feel the pressure to conform to the group's expectations. When we do fit the expectations and standards of the group, we will be rewarded; when we do not, we will be punished. Maybe the reward and punishment are only verbal, but they are real and important to us. "Great job, son." "Proud of you, boy." "That's the way!" Or "What a disappointment you have been!" "We couldn't be more disappointed in you!"

The family is just one group that helps us develop ideas about our selves. All the groups we belong to throughout our lives exert influence on our self-images, ego ideals, and self-esteem.

A third source of materials for building one's ideas about one's self is interaction with other individuals, especially those who matter to us. Those "significant others" in our lives are often friends, fellow employees, supervisors or other authority figures. These other people react to us, and we get a picture of ourselves from those reactions. We learn about ourselves from other people. Indeed, from almost every interpersonal communication transaction one gets some clues about how the other person(s) see(s) him or her. Our perceptions of how other people view us affect our perceptions of ourselves.

We do not find our identities ready-made; we form our identities slowly. Those ideas about ourselves continue to develop and evolve until we die. A person incorporates into his or her self-image, ego ideal, and self-esteem the impressions about the self that are received from other people. We absorb what other people think we are, what other people think we should be, and how well other people like us.

I must be careful not to say to little Nichole, "How's the little fat baby today?" I don't want her to incorporate *that* into her self-image! When I see Jenny has grabbed something she should not have, I am likely to stretch out my hand and say, "Thank you." When she gives me the forbidden item, I praise her by saying, "That's a good girl." So ego ideals are constructed. When Tony moved into a new neighborhood, he met a fellow teenager (a female) who lived in the same apartment house he did. He introduced himself, saying, "Hello. I'm Tony. I'd like to be your friend." Her response, "I don't want to be your friend," did not raise his self-esteem.

As we engage in interpersonal communication with other human beings, we note the categories in which they seem to place us. Other people do classify us, categorize us. They identify us with various groups (age groups, sex groups, religious groups, political groups, national groups, ethnic groups, socioeconomic groups, for example); they assign us various roles (lover, husband, wife, employer, employee, professor, student, dean, for example); and they place labels on our personalities (stable, unstable, neurotic, manic-depressive, shy, sensitive, abrasive, aggressive, humane, inhumane, freaky, flaky, serious, happy-go-lucky, for example). One puts these reactions of other people into some kind of configuration and arrives at a self-image. Put another way, we learn how other people categorize us, and we accept the classifications as valid.

Self-esteem depends, in large measure, on whether we think other people's responses to us are generally positive or negative. If a person senses general approval from other people he or she cares about (those "significant others" again), then the self-esteem will be high. The person will have self-respect. But if that person senses general disapproval from other people he or she cares about, the self-esteem will be low. If one is given praise rather than blame, respect rather than disrespect; is accorded status and prestige rather than being looked down on; and finds warmth and affection extended, rather than coldness or hostility—then one's self-esteem should be high.

I have said that self-image, ego ideal, and self esteem are ever evolving. We form those ideas early in life, but they continue to change as we grow as people. What about the continuing development of those ideas about our selves? If those ideas change, it is likely that the changes will result from interactions with other people who matter to us. As we communicate with other people, we will reveal our ideas about ourselves. We certainly will transmit messages in terms of who we think we are! There are, I think, three possible kinds of responses from other people to our ideas about our selves. The response will either accept the sender's ideas about himself or herself, reject the sender's ideas about himself or herself, or deny the sender's ideas about himself or herself.

As I send messages to you, I will give you impressions about what I think about myself. I will probably reveal a good deal about my self-image, ego ideal, and self-esteem. If you understand what my picture of my self is, and you accept that picture and are willing to deal with it on my terms, you will strengthen and support my ideas about myself. The acceptance of other people is extremely important to all of us. Each of us is committed to the me-I-think-I-am, and each of us seeks to maintain his or her self-esteem. Each of us wants to be *accepted*.

It is possible, however, that some person I talk to may reject my picture of me. That person will understand how I see myself, what I think I ought to be, and whether I like myself, *but* that person will not approve of me, not accord me status, and will not be friendly toward me. The other person has *rejected* my me. That person has looked at my me and turned thumbs down! Their loss, I hope you say. Well, at least I comfort myself with thinking, "At least they understood my me; at least they looked at me as a

Acceptance

real person." I *might* even try to look at the reasons for the rejection and see if there is any sound basis for it!

A third possible response to my self-revelation, embodied in some transmitted message either directly or indirectly, is denial. This reaction is different from rejection. The person who rejected my me examined it, understood it, and refused to accept it. That person looked at my me but withheld approval. Rejection may be painful, but denial is devastating!

Rejection

When someone rejects me, that person disagrees with my picture of myself, with my view of the world, with my value system and possibly disapproves of me, my view of the world, and my value system. But at least that person treated me like a person. In denial, the person is not rejected; the person is ignored. His or her existence is not even acknowledged; it is *denied.*

As Shakespeare's Hamlet said, "To be or not to be: that is the question." But the question about being or not being was a matter, Hamlet thought, of his own choice. He could make the decision of whether he existed or not. In the response of denial, someone else makes that choice. The receiver, not the sender, decides whether to permit you to exist—at least in his or her world! Denial turns you into a nonbeing. Personally, I would much rather you had contempt for me as a person than have no recognition of my person-ness at all.

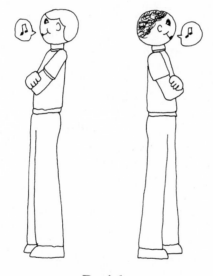

Denial

I can imagine you are saying, "I don't see how someone can be in conversation with another person and have his or her person-ness denied." But I can think of several instances that would make the idea clear. I recently tried to discuss with a colleague what I considered a gravely serious problem. After I had expounded on the problem as I saw it, I waited for the response. The person said nothing. Absolutely nothing. It was as if I had said nothing at all! A friend told me of a conversation he had with one of his acquaintances. He revealed what he thought was a very startling secret. There was a reply, but it had nothing whatever to do with what my friend had been talking about. The acquaintance said, "You have such a lovely set of teeth. Are they all yours?" In another instance, I was sharing with someone I thought was a friend a matter of great personal concern to me. Before I could finish the exposition of the momentous personal problem, I was interrupted with, "Do you think U.K. will win the NCAA in basketball this year?" In each of these instances, the receiver was not dealing with the sender, as the sender saw the sender, at all. They were neither being accepted nor rejected; they were being ignored—denied.

Surely, I have established that one's ideas about the self result from experiences with his or her own senses, with groups of which he or she is a member, and with other people who are significant in his or her life. Let us move on to the next question:

Is There a Real You?

Thus far we have been talking about one's perceptions of himself or herself. Those perceptions, like any others, may be relatively accurate—or not. We have also concentrated on the self that one is conscious of; we have not dealt with those parts of ourselves that we have buried, or forgotten, or repressed. That emphasis is justified, I think, because it is who I think I am, I think I should be, and whether I like myself that is critically important in human communication. After all, I behave and I communicate on these bases, rather than on the basis of what I really am.

But is there a more complete picture than the one I have in my mind? Well, let me suggest for your consideration my house of the self. It is an attempt to diagram the "real self."

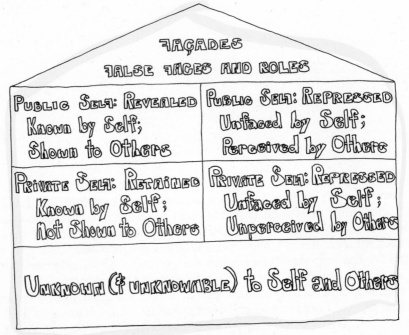

King's House of the Self

"What nonsense," I can hear you saying! "It looks like four rooms (arranged into a first and second floor), a basement, and an attic, with some words written in. Well, that's what it is, but at least examine it before you decide it is total nonsense.

Let's take the "basement" first. There are many things about myself I do not and cannot know. No one else can know them either. They are part of me; they affect me; they help make me who I really am. But I cannot apprehend them. I do not know everything I would like to know about my heredity; I do not know everything I would like to know about my genetic structure and how my body works. Indeed, the greatest scientists do not know many things about our bodies either. True, they are learning more all the time, but there are still many important secrets left to unravel. It is not that those things are not part of me; they are. It is that they are underground—thus far, at least, beyond our knowing.

On the "first floor," there are two rooms. What they have in common is that other people cannot see into them. They are what B. F. Skinner has called my "private self." The difference between the two rooms is that in one case I am aware of aspects about my self, but I do not choose to share them with others, and in the other case I have aspects of my self that I have not faced. The difference between the first-floor level and the basement is that first-floor matters are knowable. On the one hand, I can know these aspects, I do face these aspects, but I keep them to myself; I retain them. On the other hand, I can know these aspects, but I do not face them. I repress them. And other people do not detect them either.

The "second floor" is made up of two rooms that comprise my public self. This is what other people see. Part of that public self, the aspects about me that other people perceive, is public because I know it and choose to share it with others. I am aware of these parts of my self, and I reveal them. The other part of that public self is composed of aspects of the "real me" that other people see, although I do not see them myself. I could perhaps see them, but I do not perceive them; I repress them. Through my own perception processes, I avoid seeing them.

Finally, there is the "attic." Up to now, the house has been composed of realities—at least as they are perceived. The *self as I know it* and the *self as others know it* are honest selves. Even if I do not choose to show the self as I know it, direct deception is not necessarily involved. Isn't there a difference between not telling the whole truth and telling a lie? Besides, I have a right to privacy, don't I? And I have the right to decide to whom and under what circumstances I will reveal various aspects that I perceive about my self. The "attic" goes beyond the question of retaining or revealing how I see my self.

The attic is made up of façades—false masks we put on to hide our real selves. Deliberate deception is involved. We try to appear to be something we are not. We pretend to belong when we do not; we act as if we had certain roles (functions) when we do not; we feign feelings and attitudes we do not really have; we claim to hold certain beliefs when, in truth, we do not. We attempt to disguise our real selves—at least the selves we think we are—and present a dishonest, distorted image of ourselves to others. I hope you do not think I am using moralistic terms to describe this roof we use to cover our real selves. *We all* use façades; we all put on false faces to the world; we all cast ourselves in misleading roles. That is why I included it as an integral part of the house of the self. We use these covers to help protect ourselves. (That's what roofs are for, isn't it?) And self-protection may sometimes be necessary. We'll talk about self-disclosure a bit more later.

I do not know whether my diagram of the real self makes sense or not. I need some feedback on it. But I do believe all the parts of the building exist in all of us. I may not know or understand all the portions of that building, but—from basement to roof—I know they are there!

How Do One's Perceptions About One's Self Affect Communication?

SELF-PERPETUATION

Greatly. Let us look at four important phenomena: (1) self-perpetuation, (2) self-consciousness, (3) self-revelation, and (4) self-preservation.

Each of us thinks, acts, and communicates on the basis of his or her self-perceptions. Think of what you are doing right now, for instance. You are reading this textbook, probably for some course you are taking at college. Why are you doing that? Why read the textbook? "Because," you are probably thinking, "I am a student, and students read textbooks. Certainly good students read textbook material assigned by their instructors, and I want to be a good student. And finally, I take pride in doing things well; I give my best to every class; and the best student in the course certainly must read the text material!" Doesn't that answer contain indications about your self-image, ego ideal, and self-esteem? And are not all these indications related to what you are doing and why you are doing it?

Everybody acts like the kind of person he or she perceives himself or herself to be. Self-image affects behavior. So also human beings act like the kind of persons they think they ought to be. Ego ideal affects behavior. It is equally true that people act like the kind of persons they have positively or negatively labeled themselves. Self-esteem affects behavior.

That is why I called this phenomenon *self-perpetuation*. Once we get these pictures about ourselves in our minds, we tend to perpetuate them by adjusting our thoughts, acts, and interactions to match those pictures.

A friend of mine, Bob Beimdick, teaches junior high school. He was telling me recently about one of his students. At the beginning of the year, Paul told Bob that he was not a good student in math. When Bob saw Paul's report card for the first quarter, he noted Paul's *D* in math. Paul reminded him, "I told you I wasn't a good student in math!" Bob is convinced that Paul's problem is less one of ability than of self-image. He is a prisoner of the picture of his abilities that he has already internalized.

And, thinking he is a poor student in math, he doesn't try very much, he expects to fail, and the outcomes continue to confirm his expectations. It is a self-perpetuating self-image—a kind of self-fulfilling prophecy.

At a recent meeting of our college senate (made up of students, faculty, and administrators), a controversy erupted, pitting a group of students against a group of faculty members. When the dispute became bitter and personal, the group of students walked out of the meeting. The president of the student body was not a party to the dispute, but she walked out too. When asked why, she said, "The president of the student body, as leader of the student caucus, ought to stand with students." She was behaving in a way that was consistent with her image of a good student leader. By doing so, of course, she was perpetuating that image of how a student leader acts.

The following case is hypothetical, of course. Any resemblance to an actual person is mere chance. I've heard of a high school teacher who is convinced that nobody likes him, everybody is against him (especially his chairman and the administration), and students are out to destroy him. He cannot take any suggestions—to say nothing of criticism. Nothing suits him; everything, he thinks, is terrible and getting worse. To say he is pessimistic (about his future, the school, the city, the country, the world) is an understatement. He criticizes everybody and everything he comes in contact with. If his attitude toward himself is negative, his attitude toward everyone else in the world is negative minus! He is blunt, abrupt, and gratuitously insulting. He puts down everyone he meets. He is not happy, and he makes everyone else miserable too. His motto seems to be: complain, criticize, condemn, and commiserate. I am not a psychologist, but I suspect he has a negative attitude toward himself—low self-esteem. He seems to think he is a failure as a professional and as a person; I think he is right. But he is right, in large part, because he lives up to the labels he has attached to his self.

John Condon's comments are relevant:

> We have a tendency to live up to our labels, whether those labels have been applied by others (clown, party girl, brain, and so on) or those we have chosen for ourselves (clown, party girl, brain, and so on). . . . Responding to such labels gives us direction, even if the direction is backwards; responding to such labels helps us decide what to do and what not to do, even if the choices are not the wisest.[1]

SELF-CONSCIOUSNESS OR SELF-CONFIDENCE

What kind of person I think I am, what kind of person I wish I were, and how much I respect myself (in sum, my self-perceptions) will affect how much confidence I feel in the presence of other people. If I think I am a person of character, competence, and charisma, I am likely to feel at ease in social situations; I am likely to demonstrate poise and self-assurance. On

---

[1] John C. Condon, Jr., *Semantics and Communication*, 2nd ed. (New York: Macmillan, 1975), pp. 63–64.

the other hand, if my picture of myself contains major flaws and weaknesses, if there is a great gap perceived between my self and my ideal, and if my evaluation of my self is generally unfavorable, then I am likely to feel uncomfortable, ill at ease, self-conscious.

Most of us probably feel a bit apprehensive about new, unfamiliar social situations. Who does not have a little fear of the unknown? Real anxiety—disabling shyness, embarrassment, or terror—is self-consciousness carried to an extreme. That kind of self-consciousness may be the result of perceptions of oneself as inadequate, unattractive, unlikable.

SELF-REVELATION

One's self-perceptions affect his or her communication with other people by influencing one's willingness to show himself or herself openly and honestly to other people. Self-revelation, or self-disclosure, involves sharing with another person or persons personal information they are unlikely to know otherwise. In self-revelation, we communicate some aspects of our private store of information about ourselves; we let other people see what makes us individual. Through self-disclosure, I lift my masks and let you view the me I think I really am.

Self-revelation (or self-disclosure)

Self-perceptions affect self-revelation in a number of ways. They will help determine whether we reveal ourselves at all, when and where we do so, to whom we disclose personal information, and what we reveal.

It is obvious that the kind of person one thinks he or she is, the kind of person one respects, and whether one likes oneself or not will play a part in determining *whether* that person chooses to reveal the self to another. Many books on interpersonal communication urge students to be open and honest with other people; those books encourage increased self-disclosure. Frankly, I have serious reservations about that kind of blanket advice.

Trust

True, a deep and meaningful relationship with another person depends on the two people's mutual trust and mutual openness and honesty. It also depends on their mutual liking (maybe loving), acceptance, and good will. But you must decide whether to disclose personal aspects of yourself to another; and that decision, rationally, rests on whether the self-disclosure will enhance (deepen and strengthen) the relationship.

There have been many studies about self-disclosure, but the results are not completely clear. Sidney M. Jourard, who has done many of the studies, believes that too much (however much that is) or too little (however much that is) self-disclosure is a sign of poor mental health. If that is true, the belief that increasing the amount of self-disclosure will necessarily lead to personal growth and improved mental health is not true.

The point is this: The sender must decide whether to reveal his or her inner self. The sender will make that decision, in part, according to the sender's evaluation (perceptions) of the receiver(s) and, in part, according to the sender's perceptions of his or her own self.

Our self-perceptions will also influence the circumstances (the *where and when,* how often and how much) in which we will disclose our selves. Even if I decide that self-disclosure is going to enhance the relationship (that's the question of whether to reveal or not to reveal one's self), I must still decide the circumstances and the amount of that self-revelation. Here the question is: Is self-revelation appropriate now, here? And what is thought to be appropriate, of course, is related to who I think I am.

I shall never forget an incident of self-disclosure that occurred during my college years. One of my closest friends sought me out at the fraternity house; he said he had something very secret he wanted to share with me. The fraternity house was not the place to discuss it; neither was a restaurant or an empty classroom. We settled on the deserted campus chapel as the most private, quiet place we could find. We discussed the matter then at great length, but in the intervening years only one other time has either of us referred to it—even when there is no one else around.

Self-perception will influence our choice of the person(s) *to whom* we reveal our selves. I don't reveal my complete self, my inner self, to just anybody and certainly not to everybody! The studies indicate what common sense would lead you to expect: people tend to disclose more personal information about themselves to others whom they perceive to be like them than to those who are different from themselves. That means that I must match my perceptions about myself (especially my values) with my perceptions about you (especially your values). I will probably disclose myself more to a person who shares my values, because that person is more likely to evaluate the me I show in the same way that I do.

Self-perception will also affect *what* we disclose about our selves to others. The content of what I portray will depend on what I perceive when I look at my self. Assume I have decided to be open about some aspect of my self (whether?), that this is an appropriate time and place for such self-revelation (where and when?), and that you are a person with whom I want to share those aspects of my self (to whom?). Still, what I share with you depends on what or who I think I am, who I think I should be, and my attitudes toward my self. The self I present will be the self I perceive.

Of course, what I share with you will be tempered by some factors other than just what I see as my self. I have choices to make about just how honest I want to be with you (there are degrees of honesty, after all), about how intimate or deep or confidential the information I share will be (I can be honest about superficial matters or very private ones), and about how positive or negative the information will be (I can tell you good things or bad things, things I like or things I dislike, things I'm proud of or things I'm ashamed of).

The point is this: What I think about my self will certainly affect what I reveal to you about my self.

A final word about self-revelation: disclosing one's self is risky business. You can know me as I know myself only if I permit you to. I must invite you and usher you into my private world. By doing so, I make myself vulnerable to you. My self is naked, exposed, unprotected. As we noted earlier (see pp. 125–128), you may accept me, reject me, or deny me. Rejection is painful, and denial is crushing. If I decide to disclose my self to you, I am taking that risk, because without that self-revelation and the trust it implies, our relationship cannot grow. If I trust you (and you trust me) and I open my inner self to you, it is because I value the relationship more than I fear the danger of rejection or denial. I hope you will respond with good will, support, understanding, and acceptance and will open your self to me.

SELF-PRESERVATION

We human beings try to maintain our perceptions of our selves. We try to keep those perceptions consistent and whole; we are concerned with preserving our pictures of who we are. That is the sense in which I am using the term *self-preservation.* There is evidence that, for many people, preserving their self-perceptions is even more important than preserving life in the organism!

How do we attempt to preserve self-perceptions? Primarily by control of the outgoing and incoming messages. The messages we send out are usually consistent with our self-perceptions. What we say is a reflection of who we think we are. Even how I choose to say what I transmit is influenced by who I think I am.

We preserve our self-images, ego ideals, and self-esteem even more by control of incoming messages. In the last chapter we talked about selective exposure. (See p. 80.) We tend to avoid exposing ourselves to messages that do not fit our perceptions of our selves. If I see myself as a Democrat, am I likely to attend a Republican rally or tune in to a Republican campaign program on TV? If I believe nice people do not view pornography, am I likely to buy a copy of *Screw Magazine*? If I consider myself a poor public speaker, am I likely to get involved in a public debate on corruption in my labor union? Think of the kinds of programs you watch on television. Are they related to your ideas about your self? What kinds of programs do you avoid? Why?

We cannot always avoid receiving messages that are inconsistent with our self-perceptions. That is, we cannot always avoid being exposed to such messages. How do we preserve our self-perceptions then? Often by ignoring, misinterpreting, or twisting the incoming message. Review the chapter on selective perception; we use the perception process to defend and preserve our ideas about our selves.

We preserve our self-perceptions not only by selective exposure, selective attention, and selective perception, but also by selective retention. Yes, that is right. We tend to remember the messages that fit in with our perceptions about our selves. The messages that don't fit into that pattern of perceptions are more easily discarded and more quickly forgotten.

two reminders

Having attempted to answer the three questions related to self-perception, let us look at a couple of general reminders about self-perception before going on to examine the challenge of perceiving other people.

Reminder 1	One's perceptions about self are in process. Just as each person is constantly changing, evolving, developing, so each person's self-perceptions are also in process of becoming. Nothing in the world is static; everything is moving. I am not always sure everything is moving forward, but it is moving. Heraclitus was right: You can never step in the same river twice; both you and the river will be different the second time. You are both changing; you are both in process.

From the day we are born until the day we die, we are progressing in person-ness; we are developing as human beings. We are becoming persons, or, more accurately stated, we are persons becoming. We are never finished products until death. And some people believe that even then there is a Master Printer who writes at the bottom of *that* page "more."

Change is inevitable; we should not fear it. Denying change will not prevent it; ignoring change will not arrest it. We are continuously changing. So are our perceptions of our selves. Of course, those changes are gradual—so gradual they are almost imperceptible. Momentous changes in our self-perceptions cause us great difficulty; so do sudden changes in our ideas about our selves.

Still, it is important for us to remember that, when we talk about one's self-image, ego ideal, and self-esteem, we are not talking about something fixed, rigid, static, immutable; we are talking about some perceptions that are in process and that can be changed. Indeed, they *are* changing and developing continuously. And they will continue to change and evolve as long as an individual exists as a conscious being.

Reminder 2	A "healthy" person knows the self, accepts the self, and likes the self.

The Oracle at Delphi gave good advice: "Know thyself." Not easy advice to follow, but good advice nonetheless. And old Polonius, speaking the words Shakespeare gave him, was not far amiss:

> *This above all: to thine own self be true,*
> *And it must follow, as the night the day,*
> *Thou canst not then be false to any man.*[2]

Each of us must look at himself or herself as honestly and objectively as we can. We must keep our store of information about ourselves current—up to date. It is easy to picture oneself in terms of information that is no longer true or valid. One must keep checking the information, just as one must check all perceptions. (See pp. 90–93.) Of course, one way to do that is to check one's own perceptions against those of other people. That is one way of guarding against deceiving oneself about one's self. Robert Burns put the idea poetically:

> *O wad some Power the giftie gie us*
> *To see oursels as ithers see us!*

[2] William Shakespeare, *Hamlet,* Act I, scene 3.

It wad frae monie a blunder free us,
An' foolish notion;
What airs in dress an' gait wad lea'e us,
An' ev'n devotion![3]

You probably know many people who have self-perceptions that are out of whack with reality. At least, the way these people perceive themselves and the way other people see them are vastly different. You probably have also noticed that their unrealistic self-perceptions cause problems in interpersonal communication. Not to "know thyself" is a severe handicap.

Not only does the healthy person look at the self as objectively as possible, the healthy person accepts what he or she sees in the self. We have talked about acceptance as one possible response of others to one's self (see p. 125), but now I am focusing on one's own reaction to one's self. By *acceptance* I mean a recognition of the worth of the self, an appreciation of that self's right to exist. It does not necessarily involve approval of what the person does, but it does involve an acknowledgment of the person's right to be. Acceptance implies understanding, without necessarily judging, the self. A healthy person not only knows what kind of person he or she is, but also accepts that person's right to exist.

Acceptance also implies recognition of a whole, functioning person. If I accept my self, I see that self as able to function; I see that self as sufficient to cope—to perform the tasks life requires of me. I see that self as capable of responding to my environment, including the other people in the world. And if I am able to respond (response-able), I am responsible; I am accountable for my decisions and my behaviors. A person who accepts the self is able to take responsibility for the consequences of his or her actions.

If I accept my self, I accept my self's right (as well as ability) to make choices, and I am willing to state what I believe and act on what I believe. And I am willing to take the consequences if my beliefs or actions turn out to be wrong or mistaken. If I accept my self, I am willing to run the risk of making mistakes. As a human being subject to error, I am equal to, but not inferior or superior to, other human beings—who are also liable to error. I accept my fallibility as part of my person-ness.

Finally, the healthy person not only knows the self (so far as that is humanly possible) and accepts the self; the healthy person likes the self. Acceptance does not imply approval or affection. I can accept someone as a person whose actions I do not approve and for whom I have little personal affection. I do not have to like you or endorse what you do to accept you as a human being. But a healthy person goes beyond mere acceptance of self and *likes* the self.

The healthy person has high self-esteem—not unjustified conceit or insufferable arrogance—but a genuine regard for the self. Do you like the person you think you are? Or, put another way, are you the kind of person you would want for a friend? Do you see yourself as an admirable person? Do you feel genuine affection toward yourself?

---

[3] Robert Burns, "To a Louse: on Seeing One on a Lady's Bonnet at Church."

There is nothing wrong with self-liking. Indeed, it is necessary for a self that relates well to others. The Biblical injunction, "Thou shalt love thy neighbor as thyself," is rooted in sound psychology. It presumes that before you can love another person you must first love yourself. And if the Bible endorses loving yourself, it *must* be all right to do it!

Let us turn our attention now to the way we perceive other people. As we have already noted, there is a close relationship between our perceptions of our selves and our perceptions of other persons. An excellent comment on that relationship is in a poem by my cousin Julie Smith Beasy:

> *I need to find myself.*
> > *Where am I?*
> *I need to know my desires.*
> > *What are they?*
> *I have to find my life.*
> > *Where is it?*
> *I need to share a love.*
> > *Help me.*

SUGGESTIONS FOR FURTHER READING

ALLPORT, GORDON W., *The Nature of Prejudice* (Cambridge, Mass.: Addison-Wesley, 1954).

ALLPORT, GORDON W., *Pattern and Growth in Personality* (New York: Holt, 1961).

DERLEGA, VALERIAN J., and ALAN L. CHAIKIN, *Sharing Intimacy: What We Reveal to Others and Why* (Englewood Cliffs, N.J.: Prentice-Hall, 1975).

GORDON, CHAD, and KENNETH GERGEN, eds., *The Self in Social Interaction* (New York: Wiley, 1968).

HAMACHEK, D. E., *Encounters with the Self* (New York: Holt, 1971).

HORNEY, KAREN, *Our Inner Conflict* (New York: Norton, 1945).

HORNEY, KAREN, *Neurosis and Human Growth* (New York: Norton, 1950).

JOURARD, SIDNEY M., *Disclosing Man to Himself* (New York: Reinhold, 1968).

JOURARD, SIDNEY M., *The Transparent Self* (New York: Van Nostrand, 1971).

JOURARD, SIDNEY M., *Healthy Personality: An Approach from the Viewpoint of Humanistic Psychology,* (New York: Macmillan, 1974).

JOURARD, SIDNEY M., "Self-Disclosure: The Scientist's Portal to Man's Soul," in *Messages: A Reader in Human Communication,* 2nd ed., Jean M. Civikly, ed. (New York: Random House, 1977), pp. 162–167.

KELLEY, EARL C., "The Fully Functioning Self," in *Bridges Not Walls,* 2nd ed., John Stewart, ed. (Reading, Mass.: Addison-Wesley, 1977), pp. 106–117.

MIDDLEBROOK, PATRICIA NILES, *Social Psychology and Modern Life* (New York: Knopf, 1974).

ROGERS, CARL R., *On Becoming a Person* (Boston: Houghton Mifflin, 1961).

ROKEACH, MILTON, *Beliefs, Attitudes and Values* (San Francisco: Jossey-Bass, 1968).

SHERWOOD, JOHN J., "Self Identity and Referent Others," *Sociometry,* vol. 28 (1965), pp. 66–81.

SULLIVAN, HARRY STACK, *The Interpersonal Theory of Psychiatry* (New York: Norton, 1953).

VILLARD, KENNETH L., and LELAND J. WHIPPLE, *Beginnings in Relational Communication* (New York: Wiley, 1976).

5
PERCEIVING OTHER SELVES

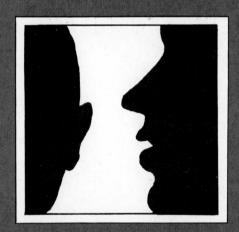

general goal:

To learn what is involved in perceiving other people and to develop skills in interpersonal perception.

specific objectives:

After completing this unit, you should understand:

The nature of the person perception process.

The goal of empathy and what is involved in empathizing.

Some factors that affect the person perception process.

Some common pitfalls and dangers in the person perception process.

the person perception process

FIRST WE LOOKED AT the process of perception in general. Then we considered the ways a person perceives the self. Now we examine perception of other people.

No matter what we are perceiving, the steps in the process are still there. (Review pp. 62–71.) When the object of our perception is another human being, however, we must keep in mind that the process is *quite* complicated. We do form impressions—total impressions—of a person, but we do so on the basis of many stimuli. How do we form those impressions?

Forming an impression of another person

Although there is not complete agreement on how the process of perceiving other persons works, it seems to me that we do six things in forming an impression of another person: (1) observe cues, (2) make inferences, (3) make judgments, (4) look for consistency, (5) categorize or generalize, and (6) make predictions. We will examine each of these.

The first part of forming a picture of another human being involves gathering and selecting information about that person. We collect data; we *observe cues*.

Observing Cues

When you meet someone for the first time, what do you notice first? As in any situation, you are exposed to lots of incoming stimuli, but you will select some to notice and ignore many other features. What do you note about a person first? That's right. Physical characteristics. You see the person as an object—with physical properties. I do not know which physical characteristics matter most to you and thus which you will focus on and which you will ignore. But you are certain to get some ideas about the person as a physical being.

Do your pay attention to the person's size, height, skin color, hair color, eye color, facial features? Do you guess the person's weight? Do you note the body type (physique)? Do you note various proportions? Do you notice how the ears are shaped or how far they stick out from the head? Do you notice how big the feet are and which way the toes point? Do you pay attention to wrinkles or skin blemishes? Do you detect tattoos? Do you check out how the person is dressed? The style, color, material of the clothing? The kind of shoes the person wears? What color the socks (if any) are? Are you aware of the hair style, the makeup (or lack of it), or the jewelry of the person? Are you sensitive to odors? Do you pay attention to the kinds of cologne, perfume, or aftershave lotion worn? Do you look for moles, scars, birthmarks, freckles, or age spots? Stretch marks maybe? What kinds of physical characteristics do *you* observe?

Not only do we observe a person's physical characteristics; we also observe the person's actions. We note behaviors. Again, of course, we are selective in our noticing. What I notice may escape you altogether, and what you pay attention to I may ignore. But all of us will notice behaviors. We will be aware of some things the other person does.

Do you pay attention to the way a person moves? Or how a person gestures? Do you note facial expressions—smiling, frowning, brow furrowing, teeth clenching, and so on? How about knuckle popping, nail biting, or scratching? Are you likely to notice if someone spits on the floor, coughs without covering the mouth, or throws something on the floor or sidewalk? If you are at dinner with someone, do you notice how that person uses eating utensils? If you are on a bus, do you notice whether a young person gives up a seat for an older passenger? Would you pay attention if some adult slapped a child in your presence? Do you take note if someone lights up a cigarette? The point, of course, is that, though each of us may notice different things, all of us observe and are aware of other people's actions, their behaviors.

A third kind of cue we observe is intentional communication on the part of some other human being. When someone else speaks, what do you notice? Are you keenly aware of voice differences? Do you note the pitch range (key) in which a person talks? In other words, does a high-pitched or low-pitched voice make some impression on you? Do you differentiate among different voice qualities (timbres)? Do you notice whether the voice quality is breathy, nasal, husky, mellow, strident? Are you sensitive to the volume a speaker uses? Do you notice if a voice is loud or soft—or how loud or how soft that voice is? What about rate? Do you pay any attention to how fast or slow a speaker talks?

Speakers must articulate (produce) sounds of a language. Do you notice a person's articulation patterns? Do you take into account whether a person speaks with clear, precise sounds or with slack production? Does mumbling bother you? If a person leaves out a lot of sounds or mispronounces many words, do you notice?

If a person "has an accent" (speaks in a particular dialect of the language), are you conscious of it? If a person speaks a different dialect from the one you use, that person may use different sounds in the same words from the sounds you use. The person may also use different words for things from the ones you are accustomed to. Do you pick up those differences? If the other person speaks a nonstandard dialect of the language (see pp. 206–208), that person may not only use different sounds and different words, but different grammatical patterns as well. Will you note them?

Will you be sensitive to what kind of vocabulary a person chooses for transmitting messages? Are you word-conscious? Will you take notice of whether I advise you to "be honest and forthright" or to "tell it like it is"? Or whether I inform you "I am very irritated with you" or suggest you "drop dead"? Are you especially sensitive to taboo words? (See pp. 225–226.)

And what about the visual component of speech? Do you note what gestures and other physical activity a speaker uses to accompany the spoken words? These, too, are apart of the other person's speech communication. And, just as we observe another person's physical characteristics and actions, so we also observe the person's communication efforts.

Making Inferences

We do not stop at observing, of course. We *make inferences* about what we have observed. Inferences are guesses—logical (?) leaps in which we draw conclusions from what we know or believe. (See Chapter 11.) So, based on the stimuli we are receiving (our observations), we make inferences about the other person's intentions (purposes) and internal states (especially feelings and attitudes).

These inferences are based on three assumptions. For one thing, we assume that what we observe is what the other person intends. We assume that the other person causes (and intends to cause) the physical characteristics, actions, and communicative behaviors that we receive through our senses. If we believe that "actions speak louder than words," we hold that belief because we assume that those actions reveal a person's intentions. Why do we believe those actions send messages? Because we believe those actions were consciously and deliberately chosen.

Of course, this assumption is not totally valid. All our physical characteristics, actions, and communicative behavior are not consciously and deliberately chosen. It is not always my conscious purpose to look the way

I look (far from it!), to do the things I do, or to say the things I say in the way I say them. But we operate (make inferences) on the basis of this assumption anyway, don't we?

People can make choices; they can cause their behavior; they can vary or change their behavior. Within limits, people have control over their physical appearance. I can choose to eat that piece of chocolate pie or not; I can forego that super-thick shake—or not. I decide whether to get a haircut and what style to tell the barber to give me, whether to wear a beard, and what kind of clothes to buy and wear. I have even more control over what my body does—my actions—than I do over how my body looks. If I walk to the grocery rather than drive the car there, it may be that I decided to walk instead of ride. (Of course, it may also be that the car is in the shop again.) And within the limits imposed on me by my background, I can control my message transmission. Maybe. Since we know that people *can* cause much of what we observe, we assume they *do* cause what we observe.

The second assumption underlying our inferences is that what we observe is an accurate indication of the other person's inner states. We assume that what we see and hear reflects what the other person thinks and feels. Maybe it does and maybe it doesn't, but that is what we assume anyway!

The third assumption on which we base our inferences is that other people are a great deal like ourselves. Our experiences and natures affect the inferences we make, because we assume that other people's characteristics, behaviors, and communications mean the same thing on and from them that they would on and from us. To the extent the other person has had a background similar to the person making the inferences, the assumption is valid. But no two people are exactly alike, and this assumption can sure lead us astray! (More about projection later.)

So much for the underlying assumptions. What kinds of inferences do we make? What kinds of conclusions do we draw from observing the other person? Two kinds at least: Those about their intentions and those about their internal states (what they think and feel).

We do not stop with observing what another person looks like or does or with recording the other person's message transmission. We ask ourselves, "Why?" And then we guess. That is what inferences are, after all. We guess the other person's purposes. We reach conclusions about what results the other person is trying to achieve. We infer: She (or he) intends to. . . .

Recently, a Hispanic friend and I were walking down the street in New York. It was a lovely spring day. We saw a young woman in her mid-twenties coming toward us. She was dressed in a tight-fitting skirt and an extremely tight-fitting knit sweater. My friend whistled loudly enough for her to hear and then made some other sounds with his lips. Instead of acknowledging his audible comments with a smile, she frowned and speeded up her gait. He did not understand her response at all. He said: "She must have wanted men to come on to her. Otherwise, she wouldn't have worn that outfit!" He observed how she looked—specifically, what she wore—and he inferred her intentions. Evidently, he guessed incorrectly.

Another instance comes to mind. A few years ago, I was talking with a professional wrestler after a match. He was furious. His anger was directed at the opponent he had faced in the wrestling show. He mentioned several things that the other wrestler had done in the course of the match and said, "That s.o.b. was really trying to *hurt* me!" This conclusion was an inference based on the behavior he had experienced in the ring. From his observations of actions, the wrestler inferred what the other person's purposes were.

Not only do we infer other people's purposes (intentions); we also reach conclusions about their internal states. From what we observe, we infer what the other person thinks and feels. We seem especially prone to conclude what the other person's attitudes are.

Can you think of instances in which you inferred someone's emotional state from his or her appearance? Frowns, smiles, tears, droopy lips, downcast eyes? Yes, but also perhaps clothing. Do you guess something about a person's mood from the color of the clothes he or she wears? One of my colleagues greeted me recently with the words, "You must be in a bad mood today. You're wearing your funeral suit!" Do you think posture is a mood indicator? Some of my friends do. One commented, "D. (David) Prest is a beaten man. Just look at the way his shoulders are slumping!"

We also get clues from someone's behavior about their internal states. We don't observe joy, sorrow, anger, hostility, or friendliness directly. We see behavior, and we may infer that the person has certain feelings. Haven't you heard someone say, "Boy, was he angry! He was mad as hops." Or even "I could see how angry he was; he was fuming." Now that speaker could not *see* anger, though if you were to ask, the speaker might insist he or she did see the anger in the other person. Pinned down, he or she should admit that what was seen had to do with clenched fists, gritted teeth, squinted eyes, furrowed brows, hunched shoulders, plus the pounding of the fists on the table and the kicking of various pieces of furniture. From those behaviors, one inferred what emotions were being experienced within the individual. But it was still an inference—a guess—and it could be mistaken.

Don't we make inferences about people's attitudes? Indeed we do. "Oh, he doesn't like me. I can *see* it!" You can see dislike? Well, not really. But we often say we can. And worse still, we think we can. We do not often remember that these conclusions are fallible guesses. We jump to our conclusions from our observations, but we must remember that conclusions and observations are not the same thing. We derive conclusions from observations; we do not observe the conclusions themselves. "I don't have to ask him what his attitude is. I can see it in his eyes." See an attitude? Impossible. Attitudes are internal and therefore invisible. Indeed, communication problems may result if I believe I can *see* or *hear* or *sense* attitudes, feelings, beliefs, values.

Making Judgments

A third factor in forming an impression (perception) of another person involves evaluating what one observes and infers. One starts with the known (imperfectly known, but known) observations; then one guesses about the unknown by making inferences. On top of that, we *make judgments*. We judge both the known and the unknown—both the data and the conclusions.

Think about it for a moment. We judge the physical characteristics we observe, don't we? Asked to describe a friend's eyes, an acquaintance gave this "description": "dark brown, sparkling, intelligent, honest, enquiring, warm, beautiful." Can you separate the (1) observations, (2) inferences, and (3) judgments? Judgments are ratings, evaluations, and they are extremely personal (subjective). (See Chapter 11.)

Note the judgment in this piece of "description":

> The bully (aged ten) threw the little victim (aged nine) on top of a parked car and began viciously punching him. He stopped beating the victim for a moment, but stayed poised—menacing all the while. His clenched fist was a threat; his cocked arm was a dangerous weapon ready to be used again. The greedy little monster began using his other hand to go through the terrified victim's pockets—searching, no doubt, for the lunch money he thought was there.

Again, can you separate the observations, inferences, and judgments? Did your list of judgments include: bully, victim, viciously, menacing, threat, dangerous, weapon, greedy, monster, terrified? We do judge the behavior we see, don't we?

Are there judgments in this "description" of another person's communication attempt?

> His voice is nasal; he always speaks in a whine. It grates on the ears, like the grinding of a poorly oiled motor. With his jaw immovable and his lips barely moving, he mumbles out his monosyllabic words. His sentences are syntactic disasters; they are verbal thickets, with an abundance of verbal weeds, such as "you know" and "like uh." It is a pain to have to listen to him.

Aha! You did notice the judgments scattered here and there. I am not completely certain the person I have quoted knew he was telling more about his own personal ratings of the communication effort than about the communicative behaviors themselves. In other words, there was more of the observer than observee in this "description."

We not only guess what people's intentions are; we then proceed to judge those guessed intentions. We infer what the other person's purpose(s) is (or are), and then we evaluate those inferred purposes. Before you say, "No, I don't" think about it for a moment. The wrestler who said, "That s.o.b. was really trying to hurt me," was not only guessing the opponent's motives; he was rating those motives—negatively. "He was trying to hurt me" is an inference about purpose; "he is an s.o.b." is a judgment about the person with such unworthy and unprofessional intentions.

My brother and I were discussing a particular basketball player. He said,

"That fellow has very limited natural ability, but he has lots of desire." We were both watching the player's behavior; we saw him in action. My brother made inferences about his native skill and his intentions: his drive, determination, and effort. Then my brother went on: "You have to admire a person like that." He judged the player on the basis of the intentions he guessed he had. I agreed with him.

We also evaluate the thoughts and feelings that we infer other people have. We guess what the other person is thinking and feeling, and then we judge those thoughts and feelings. I am sure you can think of more examples than I can, but here are a few for starters:

> Throughout the meeting, he was unbelievably arrogant—an attitude ill becoming one in his position!

> I know the loss hurt him deeply. He cried. And I think he was ashamed he cried, but I don't think he should feel that way. Men have a right to cry.

> Throughout the prayer, she kept her eyes open. She must be one of those damned atheists or agnostics!

Looking for Consistency

Let us consider a fourth factor in person perception: we *look for consistencies*. We try to form an impression of another person. *An* impression is *one* impression. We therefore look for patterns—patterns of behavior, patterns of intentions, and patterns of internal states.

True, a person's behavior is changing all the time; so too is the person's communication; even the person's physical characteristics vary from time to time. What one observes about another person, then, will be quite varied. But we do seek to find some common elements—some common thread—out of which to form a coherent picture of the other person.

We look for some common element in behaviors. My brother spends some of his free time playing basketball, swimming, or playing tennis. The behaviors are different, but I can see a common athletic element in the various behaviors; the activity is consistent and forms a kind of pattern.

We also look for some common theme in intentions. Of course, no such person exists, but suppose someone over a period of time said the following things: "Norma, you look terrible today—a complete mess!" "Why do you go around the office looking so sloppy, Tony?" To someone who had just been terminated: "You should have expected to be fired; you are incompetent." To a fellow-worker: "Cal, I thought I ought to tell you that nobody around here likes you." Do you detect a consistency in purpose? Do you think this person keeps trying to hurt other people's feelings?

If an acquaintance of yours ridiculed your scholastic ability in front of a group of your friends, suggested to one of your instructors that it might be wise to watch you on exams, and told your lover that you are unfaithful, would you find some consistency in intentions? What would you decide that person's consistent purpose was?

Although people's feelings vary from time to time and their moods may fluctuate greatly, we look for consistency here also. We try to find patterns of emotional states. I have learned not to ask one of my friends how he is or how things are going. Almost evey time I did, I got a response like: "Don't ask!" "Certainly could be better." "Oh, Lord, Bob, it's awful!" Or, at best, "Just fair. I'm barely surviving!" I detected a consistent pattern and quit enquiring.

We look for consistency in attitudes as well. We try to structure patterns that make sense out of the various attitudes that we infer a person has. Do you find a consistency (as far as attitudes are concerned) in the following statements uttered by a person over a period of time? "The laws in America are encrusted with Puritanism." "The Puritan influence on our laws is a noose around the neck of freedom." "The Roman Catholic Church should not interfere in the legislative process with lobbying." "The Baptists and bootleggers pushed Prohibition through and keep our county 'dry' still!" "Sunday blue laws are a result of churches literally minding everybody's business." The subjects discussed are perhaps different in each case, but you may be able to detect a consistency in attitude. Is it directed toward particular churches or toward organized religion in general?

Categorizing and Generalizing

If one finds consistency in another person's behaviors, intentions, emotional states, or attitudes, then the person is classified. One *generalizes* from the perceived consistency and *categorizes* the person. One labels the person—based on what one believes are consistent characteristics. Having "found" attributes that do not vary, one classifies the person.

I classify my brother as athletic; his behaviors provided me with that category. Would you categorize the person who keeps making "vicious" remarks as hostile or mean? Would you think the person who ridiculed you, poisoned your instructor's mind, and tried to break up your love relationship was your enemy? How would you classify the "oh, Lord, Bob" person? Unhappy, wretched, depressed, despairing, or just discontented? And what label would you attach to the person whose remarks on organized religion and the law were quoted earlier?

Our classifications are rather general and abstract, because they must cover a wide range of circumstances, behaviors, intentions, emotional states, and attitudes.

If a person throws a tantrum today at work, pouts over an imagined slight tomorrow, and refuses responsibility (making all sorts of excuses) for something he did yesterday, I may find some consistency in that group of behaviors and label the person "childish" or "immature." Both are very general or abstract terms, but they must be to cover the wide range of behaviors I am lumping together.

Think of the kinds of categories you put people into. The easiest way to do that is to think of the adjectives we use to describe (or differentiate among) people. An incredibly long list, isn't it? Probably runs into the thousands. Add in the nouns too. A staggering list of categories and labels.

We label people on the basis of their enduring characteristics, their permanent attributes, their personality traits, their dispositions. I think of this person as "intellectual" but that person as "slow." I label Jo-Ann "dynamic," but Ann "lethargic." I classify Gus as "ambitious," Valerie as "aggressive," Billy as "passive," Jerry as "domineering," Carmen as "pompous," and Steve as "obnoxious."

Today, I infer that Walter is sad, but then he is always "depressed." Yesterday Laurie was sad, but today she is elated; last week she wanted to quit, and this week she loves her job. What can one expect, since she is "unstable"? This week, Randy wrote an excellent article in the school paper; last week, he made the highest score on a chemistry exam; but, of course, Randy is a "capable" person. We classify and categorize other people.

If we ascribe consistency in behavior, we classify the person according to traits. If we "discover" consistent intentions, we label the person's character. If we "detect" consistent emotional states, we place the person's personality into a pigeonhole. If we believe a person's attitudes are consistent, we note the person's dispositions or predilections. Indeed, we may find consistency in the person's communication in general and classify the person's complete world view (beliefs, values, and attitudes together). I repeat: Each of us may do it a little differently, but we all classify and categorize other people.

Making Predictions

We use the categories we have formed in our own heads to predict the behavior and responses of the other person(s). We *make predictions* based on the other five things we have done in the people perception process. Having formed an impression (perception) of the other person, we use that impression to predict how the person will react to our efforts to communicate. It is at this step that we apply the perception we have developed of the other person.

All intentional human communication involves an effort to elicit a response from human beings. How can I send a message that will get the response I am aiming for unless I know (or think I know) what you will respond to and what bases you react on? I must be able to predict your response, so I use the image I have formed of you as the basis of my prediction. I speak to the picture I have of you in my head. In a very real sense, I do not talk to *you*—the real you, but to my image of you. Of course, you do not listen to *me* either—the real me—or even my image of myself; you listen to your image of me. That's who you get messages from.

As you can see, there are mammoth potential problems here. When you and I talk together, the I-I-think-I-am talks and listens to the you-I-think-you-are, and the you-you-think-you-are listens and talks to the me-you-think-I-am. The communication transaction, then, involves not two people but four!

The four people involved when two people communicate

In a very real sense, when I talk to you, I really am talking to myself. Since I am addressing my image of you (and that image exists in my own mind), I am talking to something that is very much a part of *me*. Do you see the sense in which I say I am talking to myself?

The listener also has perceptions of the other person—the talker. And the messages the listener gets come from the listener's *image* of the speaker. In that sense, the listener is listening to himself or herself—to a person who exists in the mind of the listener.

Confused? I hope not. Let us look at those four people I mentioned:

the I-I-think-I-am
the me-you-think-I-am
the you-I-think-you-are
the you-you-think-you-are

First, we have my self-image; next, we have your image of me; then we have my perception of you; and finally, we have your perception of you. It would be so much easier if you could communicate with my perception of me directly and I could communicate directly with your perception of you. Unfortunately, that is not possible. The reason that it would be much better, of course, is that we send, receive, and respond to messages in terms of our own self-perceptions. If the other person knew or shared those perceptions, the other person could understand and predict responses with much more accuracy.

We talk and listen to our images of other people. If our images of them are significantly different from the images they have of themselves, we are likely to have major communication problems. It is equally true, of course, that if their images of us are significantly different from our images of ourselves, we are also likely to have major communication problems.

Can I ever hope to understand your you, and can you ever hope to know my me? Probably not completely. But the more I am able to talk to your perception of you than to my perception of you, the more efficient and effective my communicative efforts are likely to be. The more I understand your perception of your self, the more accurate will be my predictions of your behavior and your responses. "How can this necessary mutual understanding be achieved?" I hear you saying. Through empathy, which we will discuss very soon. But first, we must acknowledge one other problem related to predictions.

One of the steps in forming a perception of the other person involves making judgments, you remember. That presents some difficulties we must face.

When we discussed self-perception, we noted that each person not only has an idea of what kind of person he or she is (the self-image); that person also has an idea of what kind of person he or she should be (the ego ideal). And each person judges his or her own self against the standards set by the ego ideal. How the person measures up results in a degree of self-esteem. The ego ideal is a very personal thing; the standards used in judging the self have been learned over the person's lifetime. They may or may not be shared by other people the person encounters and communicates with.

When we judge other people, we use the standards we have learned. We use *our* standards, our criteria, our rating system to evaluate the other person. And other people use their own standards when they rate us. Just as my image of you may be quite different from your image of you, so too my standards for judging you may be quite different from your standards for judging you. And your bases for evaluating me may be markedly divergent from the criteria I use in evaluating my self.

Think for a moment of the criteria you use in judging other people. What kinds of behavior do you approve of and what kinds do you disapprove of? What kinds of communication do you accept, and what kinds offend you? What kinds of physical appearance (or physical attributes) do you like, and what kinds do you dislike (or find unattractive)? What kinds of intentions or purposes do you think worthy and what kinds do you think unworthy (or wrong)? What kinds of emotional characteristics (personalities) do you admire, and what kinds do you look down on? What kinds of beliefs, values, and attitudes do you find acceptable, and what kinds do you find unacceptable?

Whatever answers you gave to those questions, rest assured there are many other people who would give quite different replies. And you will be communicating with those people from time to time. You are going to be judging them on the basis of your rating system, but they are going to be judging you on the basis of their own rating scales. Our perceptions of other people include both our ideas about what the other person is like (image) and our judgments, our evaluations, of what we think the other person is like. If our internal rating scales are significantly different from the rating scales of those with whom we are communicating, we may encounter major communication problems.

How can we possibly ever come to some mutual understandings? How can we commune? As I mentioned earlier, through the development of empathy. Empathy is the vicarious experiencing of the thoughts, feelings, and attitudes of another person. It is putting oneself into the place of the other; it is looking at the world from the other person's point of view.

Actually, it is not transplanting my self whole into the position of the other person. If I imagine myself in the spot someone else is in, it is *me* I see there, and it is my eyes I look out from. I would still see the situation from my own set of beliefs, values, and attitudes. That is not empathy at all. Empathy is trying to see the world through someone else's eyes—looking at the situation from the vantage point of the other person's set of beliefs, values, and attitudes. It is the attempt to put on some other person's filters.

The American Indian prayer, "Great Spirit, grant that I may not criticize my neighbor until I have walked a mile in his moccasins," is a prayer for the power of empathy.

empathy

Empathy is different from sympathy. Sympathy is based on two Greek words (σύν + πάϑοσ) that mean *feeling with*. If you have sympathy, you stand with the other person. You stand beside the other person. You indicate that you care when the other person is hungry or angry or hurt. You feel something for them; you care about their hunger or anger or pain. But it is still *their* hunger and anger and pain; it is not yours. You are compassionate; you care that they are feeling these things. But you are not feeling them.

Empathy goes deeper than sympathy (as admirable as sympathy may be). Empathy is based on two Greek words (ἐν + πάϑοσ) that mean *feeling in(side)*. If you have empathy, you do more than stand beside the other person; you try to get inside the other person. With empathy, you do not feel *for* their hunger, anger, or pain; you *feel* the hunger, the anger, the hurt the other person is feeling. With empathy, you not only try to understand what a person does, but why the other person does it. You try to see what the other person believes, what values the other person applies in making judgments, what attitudes and loyalties the other person has, what emotions

Sympathy

the other person is experiencing, and what reactions are characteristic of
the other person.

Syndicated columnist Sydney J. Harris, writing in his column "Strictly
Personal," which appeared in *The Courier-Journal and Times,* Louisville,
Ky., 26 December 1971, demonstrated an understanding of and presented
a plea for empathy:

> During the question period following my talk at a Midwest college
> recently, a woman in the audience stood up and asked: "Do you approve of
> the sexual permissiveness that young people are engaging in today?"
>
> What a quaint way to phrase the question: Do I approve? Who cares
> whether I approve or not? What young people are going to listen to my
> disapproval, if I disapprove? I might as well save my breath to cool my
> porridge.
>
> If we don't begin by asking the right questions, we can't end up with any
> satisfactory answers. If we begin with our own attitudes, we can't understand
> the attitudes of others. If we make judgments based solely on our own
> experiences and preconceptions, we will fail in even reaching a common
> meeting-ground with those whose experiences and conditioning are different.

Empathy

Whether I approve or not is of no consequence. What is important is why they are doing it, what it means to them. . . .

Sydney Harris is quite right: An empathic person asks the questions, "What does it mean to them?" rather than "What does it mean to me?" and "What do they (the other persons) think about it?" instead of "What do I think about it?" An empathic person focuses attention on how the other person feels about something rather than on how he or she feels about it. An empathic person tries to look at another human being's world through that other human being's eyes.

Empathy requires:

Involvement
Imagination
Insight
Identification
Interaction

If you are going to empathize, you must be willing to get involved with another human being. No withdrawal. No indifference. No escape. No isolation. No apathy. No callousness. No disdain. You obviously cannot cut yourself off from other people and have empathy with them. You must be willing to establish a relationship with them—to deal with them as human beings. Involvement implies your acceptance of the person-ness of the other person. You may not agree with that person or approve of everything that person does (or is), but you accept that person's right to be, and you are willing to deal with that person on a person-to-person basis.

Involvement

Each of us has a different background; each of us has a different set of experiences that have shaped our lives. I have not lived through your prior conditioning, and you have not lived through mine. I have not belonged to the identical set of reference groups you have, and you have not been *norm*alized in the same groups I have. We must, then, use imagination to get some approximation of how the world looks through someone else's filters.

Imagination

We must not only be able to imagine what kind of life the other person has lived, what kind of experiences he or she has had; we must also be able to gain some insight into that person's thought processes. We must be able to understand (without judging) what the other person believes and values and in what directions the other person leans (attitudes). We must be able to understand how the other person's mind works.

Insight

Insight has to do with clarity of understanding. Are the other person's beliefs clear to you? Could you explain them as the other person would? Could you report them without any trace of your own beliefs and values and attitudes showing through? Think of some friend you disagree with about some issue. Can you explain fully and fairly the other person's position? You might try it. See if your friend says, "That is exactly the way *I* would have explained what I believe!"

Do you understand the values the other person uses to evaluate everything? Do you understand the standards the other person utilizes in making judgments (or ratings)? Could you report what the person thinks is right or wrong, good or bad, noble or ignoble, admirable or despicable, moral or immoral, acceptable or unacceptable? More important, can you explain *why* the person gives the ratings he or she does? That is part of insight.

Do you understand the other person's attitudes? What does the person lean toward and what does the person lean away from? What is the person for or aganst? What loyalties or sentiments does the person have? Even if you do not share someone's attitudes, can you understand what they are

155

and why the person holds them? That too is part of insight, and it is a necessary ingredient of empathy.

Last year, at a small, church-related college in Texas, a widely respected professor of religion from Florida gave a lecture series. After the first lecture, the first question from a student during the question period was: "You are a Floridian and a professor of religion. What do you think of the views of Anita Bryant?" Ms. Bryant had become embroiled in a controversy over the issue of legal rights of sexual minorities in the United States. The professor answered, "I do not agree with Ms. Bryant's views. But I understand the assumptions on which her beliefs are based, I understand the values she cherishes, and I understand the attitudes that derive from those beliefs and values. Though I come out of the same background as Ms. Bryant, I do not share her underlying assumptions, which result in her beliefs and attitudes." That professor had insight into the mental processes of someone with whom he differed.

Identification

Each of us has his or her own behavior patterns, purposes, and feelings. If you identify with me, you accept my behaviors, purposes, and feelings as if they were your own. Indeed, you may imitate my behaviors and associate yourself with my purposes and feelings.

Have you ever been at a boxing match or wrestling match and watched the spectators? Did you see many so caught up in what they were seeing that they were physically exerting themselves? Were their muscles tensed and their fists clenched? Were they punching the air? They were identifying with the athlete they were watching; in their minds (and bodies), they associated themselves with the other person. That is what identification is about—associating oneself with the other person.

Of course, we not only can associate ourselves with another's physical activity (I come away from watching football games exhausted); we also can associate ourselves with another person's intentions and feelings. That too is identification, and it is an integral part of empathy.

Interaction

Empathy is impossible unless one opens oneself up to the other person enough to permit mutual exchange and mutual influence. Think about what it means to *inter*-act with other people and, indeed, with the rest of the world! There is a risk involved in attempting empathy. It opens us up to the possibility of change; it assumes that we are capable of growth and learning; it operates on the principle that we human beings can learn from each other. We must be willing to be influenced as well as to influence; we must be willing to learn as well as to teach; we must be willing to let live as well as to live.

Interaction requires us to recognize that we are all human beings. We are not devils or angels or gods. As human beings, we have a great deal in common; we all have hopes and fears and needs and desires. We are all capable of hurting others and equally capable of being hurt. We are less likely to hurt those we perceive to be similar to ourselves (so more empathy would make the world better for all of us!).

Through interaction, we experience each other; through interaction, we have the opportunity to learn about other people's perspectives. Through interaction, hopefully, we will become more conscious of other people's humanness—and our own as well. Through interaction, which is, after all, reciprocal stimulation and adaptation, we expose ourselves to the opportunity of knowing another and of being known.

If empathy is the goal of perceiving other people, there are some pitfalls and dangers we must recognize along the way. Few people seem to realize they are forming perceptions of other people all the time. Of those who do recognize they are forming such impressions, many people do not seem aware that their perceptions may be quite mistaken and are, at best, incomplete.

Some people are better people perceivers than others are. We vary in our relative abilities to form somewhat accurate impressions of others. And even the most perceptive of us are more successful at the person perception process sometimes than at others. How can we account for these differences?

factors that affect the person perception process

Remember that, in the person perception process, we were required to do six things: observe cues, make inferences, make judgments, look for consistency, generalize (into categories), and make predictions. The predictions are really the outcome of the process. How closely my perception of you resembles your perceptions about you will govern how well I can predict your behavior and responses. And how much my perception of you will resemble your perception of you depends on five things: (1) the adequacy (or clarity) of the cues, (2) the degree of commonality in our backgrounds, (3) how much experience I have had with you, (4) my intelligence, and (5) my mental health.

Adequacy (or Clarity) of Cues

Since I form my impressions out of the *cues* I get, the better the cues, the better chance I have of making accurate impressions. Sometimes, cues are ambiguous or downright misleading. To develop accurate perceptions about you, I need clear, consistent, adequate cues.

Degree of Commonality in Background

I have a better chance of forming an accurate impression of someone if that person's *background* is similar to my own. That makes sense, doesn't it? We can make guesses more easily about people who have lived through the same kinds of experiences we have. If we have been conditioned in much the same way, we will likely share the same language, the same general meanings, the same behaviors, the same norms, the same beliefs, the same attitudes. If not the same then similar! And that similarity makes inferring, judging, generalizing, and predicting easier.

Experiences with the Other Person

Of course, *experience* is a help in forming perceptions. If I have a history of contact with you, I have had the opportunity to check my perceptions over a period of time. I have many more cues to put together; I have had a better chance to look for consistency (or inconsistency) and to group your behaviors, intentions, and emotions into categories. Do you think your impression of the instructor in your human communication course is more accurate now than on the first day of the term? Is it appreciably different from that first impression? If it is different, is that difference the result of your experience during the term with that instructor?

Some people seem to be more perceptive than others; they have a better track record in perceiving other people. What capabilities are required for perceiving other people accurately? Two, primarily: intelligence and mental health (maturity).

Intelligence

One's skill in perceiving other people depends in part on one's *intelligence*. I cannot define intelligence satisfactorily, but I am sure there are three capacities related to intelligence that one needs in perceiving others: the ability to abstract qualities, the ability to form categories and principles, and the ability to draw inferences.

We must be able to abstract qualities. We observe people, but we must be able to consider their qualities apart from the people themselves. We must be able to separate out the idea of a quality from the thing the quality is found in. Abstraction involves isolating the properties of objects (including people); it involves noting the aspects or characteristics of things (including people).

If I see you push an old lady out of your way as you charge for the waiting bus, I may label that an unkind act. I have abstracted the quality, the aspect, the characteristic *unkind.* That unkindness now exists in my mind apart from you; I have pulled out the idea *unkind,* and I can think about it as separate from the observed act and the observed person.

In abstraction, I move beyond mere observation. I do not observe "unkindness." I observe acts. "Unkindness" is an abstract idea that I cannot observe directly with my senses. But it is a quality or characteristic of some acts that I am able to pull out and think about. The ability to abstract such qualities is related to intelligence and is needed in the process of people perception.

We not only need the ability to isolate specific characteristics of what we observe; we also need the ability to form general categories and principles. I must be able to recognize that these qualities, aspects, or characteristics may be ascribed to several different objects (or people). We move beyond recognizing characteristics to classifying things according to their characteristics. We form general categories or classes of things (and people) in our minds.

Do you believe there is such a category (in your mind at least) as "unkind people"? What characteristics do they have in common? Note how far we have moved from: (1) He is pushing that old lady out of the way. (2) That is an unkind act. (3) He is an unkind person! The ability to form general concepts is related to intelligence and is needed in the process of person perception.

A third capacity related to intelligence plays an important part in perceiving other people. That is the ability to make valid inferences. If one has learned to reason well—to draw sensible conclusions from what is observed—one will be better than average in person perception. Guessing right is crucial! Look back over the material on inferences in the people perception process (pp. 143–145). Also look ahead to the material on reasoning considered in Chapter 12. We can improve our reasoning power; it is a capacity that can be developed. Each of us should work to insure that, every time we make an inference about another person, that inference is grounded in sound principles of reasoning.

Mental Health (or Maturity)

The last of the five factors that affect the person perception process is the *mental health* or *maturity* of the perceiver. What I see is not necessarily what I get. Rather, what I see is greatly influenced by what I am! If I do not know myself, if I cannot face (and accept) myself, and if I do not like myself, I will have great difficulty dealing with other people's selves. How can I accept others if I have not faced and accepted my own nature? Won't my high or low self-esteem affect my reaction to (and impression of) other people? Of course.

A gay (homosexual) friend of mine recently said, "Beware the closet queen! What he dislikes in himself, he will hate in others; what scares him about his desires will terrify him when he sees it in other people. Folks like that who can't cope with their own true natures are dangerous!" An interesting comment. How does it relate to what we have said about the need for healthy self-acceptance as a basis for perceiving other people?

Nietzsche wrote that "we must fear him who hates himself because we shall be the victims of his revenge." Arthur Jersild often said that if one loves his or her own self, one is more likely than not to be able to love other selves and that if one hates his or her own self, one is more likely than not to hate other people. I learned a great deal from that wise psychologist at Columbia. Though I have conducted no scientific studies to test his thesis, I am convinced it is correct.

One reason that mature people are more adept at accurately perceiving other people, according to Dr. Jersild, is that mature people do not need human gods to worship or human devils to blame. Having faced their own humanity (with its attendant strength and weaknesses), they can face the humanity of other people. They are not unnerved to discover that "good people" have faults and that "bad people" have virtues. They do not classify people as either heroes—models of perfection—or scapegoats—paragons of evil. In the musical play *Lost in the Stars,* Stephen demonstrates this kind of maturity when he says, "All men do evil, I among them—and I wish all men to do better, I among *them.*" The old adage put it: "There is so much good in the worst of us and so much bad in the best of us it ill behooves any of us to speak ill of the rest of us!"

A mature person can deal with other persons as they really are (and as they think themselves to be), in part at least, because he or she has learned to deal with his or her own self on a realistic and accepting basis. Further, a mature person does not need to distort the impression of another person to protect his or her own fragile, easily upset self. If I know, accept, and like my self, it is unlikely that I am going to find you (whoever or whatever you may be) disgusting or dangerous (a psychological threat) to me. I will not need to protect my self from you by doctoring my image of you.

pitfalls and dangers in the person perception process

True as it is that some people are more skillful people perceivers than others, it is equally true that all of us face pitfalls and dangers in the person perception process. Let us look at some of those problems. You will note that several of them are related.

Stereotyping

The word *stereotype* was originally a printing term. A stereotype is a metal plate. The type is not movable, but everything is molded together into one plate. Once the plate is cast, it is difficult to change. And, unlike the old handwritten books (each one of which was different and slightly unique), the same image is printed every time. Every time that plate (the stereotype) comes down, it makes the same impression. Do you see why Walter Lippmann used the term to refer to a simplified classification system in perceiving people?

A stereotype is a ready-made compartment for classifying people. If you use stereotyping in your person perception process, you find a premolded category in which to place the person, and you assume that the person has all the characteristics associated with people in that category. In a sense, then, stereotyping is a kind of simple filing system. You locate the pigeonhole the person fits in, file the person in it, and you have a ready-made impression of the person.

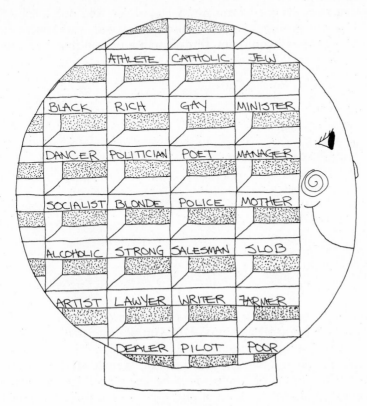

Stereotyping

The word stereotype is extremely fitting as a metaphor for this classifying system. Just as in the case of the printing stereotype (molded plate), once a personal stereotype is cast, it is very hard to modify, and when a stereotype comes down it makes the same impression! The impression may be dead wrong, you understand, but it comes out the same each time the stereotype is applied.

Stereotyping is quite convenient, of course. You don't have to bother to get to know a person; just find out what category he or she fits into and you "know" all you need to know about the person! No interaction necessary, no time wasted in communication, no real effort expended. You can form an impression (perception) of the other person so quickly and easily, and it requires almost no thinking at all.

Though we should resist the temptation to use this shortcut method of perceiving people, we all use it at times. Check to see if you are prone to rely on this simple, but fallible system of stereotyping. Do you ask people,

"What's your sign?" Do you think there are characteristics associated with people labeled Libras? What kind of people do you think Leos are? Those *are* stereotypes, aren't they? Convenient pigeonholes to classify people into. And popular too!

If you had not yet met someone but had been told one piece of information about the person (a label), would you have an impression about the person? Try it. What would you think about a person if a friend told you:

> He is an athlete.
> She is a devout Roman Catholic.
> He is Jewish.
> She is Black.
> He is homosexual.
> She is wealthy.
> He is a professional dancer.
> She is a minister.
> He is a politician.
> She is diabetic.
> He is a weight lifter.
> She is Hispanic.
> He is alcoholic.
> She is blonde.
> He is a policeman.
> She is a Socialist.

Did you form a complete impression of the person based on the category the person had been placed into? Did you assume that people in these categories are alike in essential ways?

What picture do you have in your head of "a male athlete"? Is he smart or dumb? What kinds of grades does he get in college? What kinds of courses does he take? What kind of physique does he have? Is he interested in art or music or politics? Is he well-informed on current events? Is he socially mature and poised? What kinds of speech patterns does he have? What kind of language does he use? Does he have a large, educated vocabulary? What kinds of clothes does he wear? What kind of manners does he display? Would you call him polished and urbane? What are his attitudes on sex? On love? On women? On life in general?

If you have such a picture—whatever the picture is—in your mind of "an athlete," then you have a stereotype, a ready-made impression, stored away, waiting to be applied to someone you meet "in that category."

Did you have a mental image to associate with each of the "categories"? You do not have to tell anyone what the impressions are, but beware. Stereotyping provides shortcuts that take a lot less effort than getting to know people one at a time, but those shortcuts can lead us to very mistaken perceptions.

For all its convenience, stereotyping has two great flaws: it assumes similarities and disregards mammoth differences and it imposes unnecessary limitations on the people thus categorized.

Stereotyping is based on one common aspect. You must select some basis for grouping the people together into the same category. "She is Black." Then you have a category "Black"; it is a general category for people who share "Blackness"—whatever that is in your mind. All the people in the same category will share at least one characteristic or feature (or label). But stereotyping does not stop there. It goes on to assume that all the people with that one characteristic in common will have a lot of other characteristics in common also. There is the fallacy! It is the "all" fallacy. Check yourself honestly. How would you complete the following statements:

All athletes are . . . .
All Roman Catholics are . . . .
All Jews are . . . .
All Blacks are . . . .
All homosexuals are . . . .
All rich people are . . . .
All professional dancers are . . . .
All clergy are . . . .
All politicians are . . . .
All diabetics are . . . .
All weight lifters are . . . .
All Hispanics are . . . .
All alcoholics are . . . .
All female blondes are . . . .
All police officers are . . . .
All Socialists are . . . .

The list is just to suggest to you whether you are tempted to fall into the "*all*" fallacy. If you do, you might want to consider the logical weakness of that fallacy.

Are all people of Irish extraction alike? Are all people who smoke marijuana alike? Are all people with the same skin color or eye color or hair color (I don't know what matters to you in these very important matters!) the same? *All* teachers, preachers, priests, psychologists, lawyers—pick your category because the principle will apply to any category you pick—are *not* alike in essential respects. The differences from person to person inside the group will be far greater than the similarities. That is the weakness of stereotyping. It leads us to ignore those differences and focus on the one common feature. It blurs individual distinctions; it sees all people with the same label as the same. It does not permit us to see individual persons; rather, we see a fixed impression of a group—a group we have created in our own minds.

The other great flaw of stereotyping is that it imposes unnecessary limitations on the persons thus categorized. If our perception of someone is based on a stereotype, we treat the person as if he or she had the characteristics we associate with the stereotypical category. The perception of the other person as a group member rather than an individual person affects the perceiver's communication with the other person.

Stereotypes are based on incomplete and often inaccurate information. But this incomplete and inaccurate "knowledge" will govern our communication with the other person when perceptions are shaped by stereotypes. If you believe that New Yorkers are cold, haughty, rude, pushy, and unfriendly, how will you treat me if you discover I am a New Yorker? You will treat me like you would treat any cold, haughty, rude, pushy, and unfriendly soul. Frankly, I might even respond to your treatment with unfriendliness and coolness at least. And you would say, "Aha! He's just like all the rest of them—cold, haughty . . . ."

When a person stereotypes another person, he or she puts the other into a category with a long list of presumed characteristics attached to it. Once the other person is placed in that category, then the person starts looking for the characteristics that are supposed to go with the classification. And it is easy to find something there if you are looking for it! Behavior that would be unnoticed in someone else gets noted if you are looking for it; behavior that would be explained away in someone else becomes very significant—if you are looking for it. An Anglo friend says "Dammit," and you say, "What's wrong?" But a Hispanic says "Dammit," and you say, "You see how emotional they are—just can't control their feelings." Your stereotype has imposed a limitation on the person you classified; that person's behavior is not being evaluated in the same way as everybody else's. Looking for corroborating evidence, you find it, and the stereotype is perpetuated.

One of my students, Barbara Johnson, has given permission for me to use her poem "The Dude Who Had No Sign." In this poem, she spoofs the stereotyping based on signs of the zodiac.

It was Gemini Jim and Scorpio Sal
  In a crib by the Golden Gate,
Freezing their nose and wearing strange clothes
  And dealing every way but straight.
They had a Leo dog and a Capricorn cat
  And things were going just fine
Till into their life on a pitch black night
  Came the dude who had no sign.
"Look out, Momma, he's heading this way"—
  One eye yellow, the other one gray,
Looking for a soul—"But he won't get mine!"
  He's the dude who has no sign.
Well, he walked right in and sat right down
  And rolled him a righteous smoke.
He hit his roach with a lightening bolt,
  And he took a drag and spoke.
He said he was born in astrological form
  When the moon refused to shine,
On the edge of nowhere and the cusp of so there—
  A dude who had no sign!
Then he told his tale of an endless trail
  To find his missing part.

And Sal, she grins and smiles at him
　　And tries to do his chart
Till Pisces Ben, who's Jim's best friend
　　Said, "Man, you must be blind,
Your woman's lost, 'cause her star is crossed
　　By the dude who has no sign."
Late that night six shots rang out
　　From Jim's old thirty-two.
He had caught his woman and that no-sign no man
　　Doing what they shouldn't do.
When folks got to the shed, there was Jim by the bed
　　Where Scorpio Sal was dyin',
But a blood red stain was all that remained
　　Of the dude who had no sign.
The arrest was made by Bobby Slade,
　　An Aquarius through and through.
The jailer was a Sagittarius,
　　So he beat Jim black and blue.
They snatched Jim up the courthouse steps,
　　And said, "Bud, what's your plea?"
He said, "Man, the moon's in Virgo,
　　So don't whip the blame on me!"
The jury was all Libras, so you know
　　They were more than fair.
But his lawyer was an Aries,
　　And Aries men don't care.
The judge—he was a Cancer,
　　And Cancers have no friends,
The hangman was a Taurus.
　　With him, the story ends.
So late at night, when the stars are right,
　　And the moon is gray and dim,
The shadows roll around the knoll
　　Where's the grave of Gemini Jim.
One is the ghost of Scorpio Sal,
　　As she cries and shrieks and grinds;
The other is the juice that keeps her loose
　　From the dude who had no sign!

　　　　THE DUDE WHO HAD NO SIGN
　　　　　　　—Barbara Johnson

Epithets

Stereotypes depend on labels—the names we have for the categories we classify people into. We have to have labels to put under the pigeonholes in our minds. We have to be able to file people according to the

He is a . . . .
   and
She is a . . . .
   formula.

The blanks are the labels we attach to the groups we have made in our heads. Some of the labels are rather neutral. The label "basketball star" does not carry a stigma in most circles, for example.

We do have a number of labels, however, that are clearly not neutral. They are, and indeed are meant to be, quite derogatory. We call those labels *epithets*. How many can you think of offhand? Are there categories' labels you can think of for national groups, religious groups, racial groups, professional groups? What others can you recall?

Epithets are labels with negative connotations (attitude and feeling) built in. These names are definitely not meant by the labeler to be complimentary.

Honky	Dixiecrat
Spic	Bleeding heart
Nigger	Do-gooder
Wop	Shrew
Kike	Yenta
Polack	Busybody
Terrorist	Goyem
Kraut	Radical
Jap	Reactionary
Chink	Cross-back
Mick	Piece (also: piece of ass)
Cracker	Gook
Red	Pig
Commie	Fag (variant of faggot)
Jig	WASP
Shyster	Junkie
Pinko	Wetback
Fanatic	Jock
Limey	Fascist
Quack	Whitey
Queer	Pusher
Dyke	Pimp
Canuck	Hooker
Damnyankee	Heathen (or pagan)
Hebe	Punk
Greaser	Pervert
Bohunk	Ex-con
The Man	Broad
Rebel	White trash

I am sorry to say you can probably add to this list many more such epithets. These negative labels contribute to the practice of stereotyping, because they give ready-made names to attach to the pigeonholes human

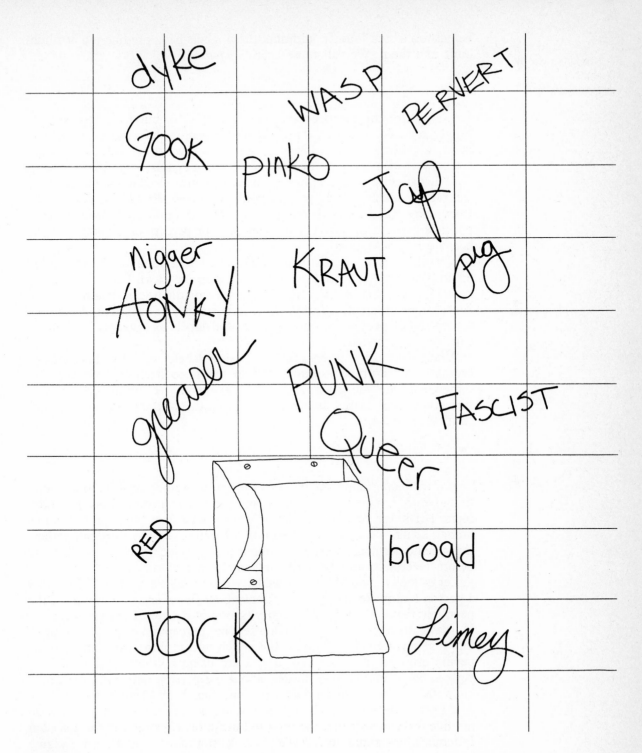

Epithets

beings are tossed into. In addition, these labels have predigested attitudes built into them. We call these attitudes *biases*.

Bias

We have already discussed bias (see pp. 77–79), but it is necessary to briefly review the concept in relation to people perception. Biases are inclinations or leanings. They are attitudes toward or away from some category or idea. Are you inclined to be for or against organized religion? Will that affect your perception of someone you are told is a member of the clergy? Obviously. What are your political biases? (*Bias* is not a bad word. Everybody has biases—leanings one way or another!) Whatever your political biases are, wouldn't they affect your perception of someone you heard called a Marxist?

Not all labels are negative, and we can be biased in favor of some group (or idea) as well as biased against that group (or idea). I have no way of knowing your biases on such subjects as medicine, or health care in America, or psychiatry. But those attitudes that you have will affect your perception of people who get such neutral labels as "doctor," "pharmacist," or "psychiatrist."

When you use epithets, you are using labels with the bias clearly revealed; the attitude is embedded in the term itself. If you react to someone before you get to know that person—based almost certainly on stereotypes and biases and possibly on epithets—then you are demonstrating *prejudice*.

Prejudice

The word *prejudice* means literally the act of prejudging—judging something before having enough information to use as a sound basis for judgment. If I judge you before I know who or what you are as an individual human being, if I decide what kind of attributes you have without gathering specific personal information about you, if I decide whether I like you before I get acquainted with your you, I am prejudiced.

Let us look at how the terms we have discussed are related. If I classify a person and make some assumptions about the characteristics of all the people in that classification category (group of people), I am stereotyping. If I have attitudes or leanings that affect my perception of people grouped into that category, I am biased. If I attach uncomplimentary labels to the people grouped into that category, I am using epithets. If I react to a person, based on my assumptions about the person, before I even get to know that person first-hand as a person, then I am prejudiced.

If I get to know you—understand you and accept your right to be, but do not like you (do not hold you in high esteem or feel affection for you), am I demonstrating prejudice? *No.* We do not have a word for judging someone *after* the information is in, but it is certainly not prejudice. I suppose a good word would be *post*judice! One is not obligated to like everybody, but it is irrational and self-defeating to decide your reaction to a person without knowing the person accurately.

Is prejudice always negative? Is the decision or reaction always one of dislike? Again the answer is *no*. What makes prejudice prejudice is not what the reaction is but when the reaction is made. To be prejudice, the decision must be made *before* personal information is gathered about the individual being "perceived." Even if you decide you *like* someone, if the decision is made before getting to know the person, you are demonstrating prejudice.

A friend of mine provided a good illustration of favorable prejudice a few years ago. Having arrived at LaGuardia Airport in New York City, he got into a cab for the ride to the center of the city. He knows the city well. It soon became apparent that the driver was taking him out of the way and running up the fare on the meter. He said nothing. Though he knew the way and knew what was happening, he did not complain. At the end of the trip, he made no comments about the extended ride and paid the fare without a murmur. Indeed, he admitted to me that he gave the crooked taxi driver a handsome tip besides. Incredible, you say! Well, my friend groups people by race: he is a Southern white, and he is strongly biased in favor of Black people. The cab driver was Black, and my friend decided he liked him even before the ride started. In spite of his experience with the driver, he did not change his reaction. Though it is prejudice in *favor* of the person, it is no less prejudice (and in this case, I think, racism) than negative reactions would be. My friend did not respond to the person as a person—on the basis of his experience with the person. Rather, his reaction was to a group member—a symbol—a thing. And that reaction was determined before personal information was gathered. That is prejudice!

If I decide that a person cannot be accepted as a person, I am demonstrating *intolerance*.

Intolerance

If I am intolerant, I do not accept your right to exist. I cannot abide you. I do not want you in my world. I deny your very being. I cannot tolerate you.

The person who says, "I don't want those people around me," or "I don't want them in my school," or "let them go to their own church," or "they have no right to move into our neighborhood because they have a neighborhood of their own" is demonstrating intolerance. He or she denies the humanity of the people perceived; they are viewed as so different that they are less than people.

Do you think the code of the U.S. Military Academy (West Point) teaches or promotes intolerance? Isn't their code: I will not lie, steal, or cheat, and I will not tolerate among us those who do? Does that code presume that one can be faultless (absolutely sinless—with emphasis on the word *absolute*) and that people who err are intolerable (should not be tolerated)?

To check out whether you are intolerant of some "kinds of people," you might try completing these sentences:

I do not want to live in the same house with . . . .
I do not want to go to the same school with . . . .
I refuse to be in same fraternity, sorority, or club with . . . .
I would not want to be on the same team with . . . .
I do not want to live in the same neighborhood with . . . .
I refuse to associate with . . . .
I do not want to be seen with . . . .
. . . should stay away from me.
I prefer not to work with . . . .
I want . . . to stay out of my sight and out of my life.

If one is intolerant of a group of people, he or she does not want those people around. It was best illustrated for me a few semesters ago. My class in small group communication had completed its meeting; the discussion had been animated, and I had closed with a plea for tolerance and an endorsement of free speech. A student came up to me and said, "Dr. King, that's the difference between me and my friends and you and your friends. You and your friends think there is room in the United States for me and my friends, but me and my friends do not think there is room in the United States for you and your friends!" That's intolerance!

If you go beyond not wanting a group of people around and actively seek to harm them, you are demonstrating *hostility*.

Hostility

Anger and hostility are not the same. If you do something to me that I do not like, I may get angry with you. I may indeed get furious with you or go into a rage. But the emotion has been triggered by something you did, or at least by something I thought you did, and that emotion is temporary. It is not a permanent state. Hostility, on the other hand, is more durable. It persists; it abides; it indwells the person. And it affects our perceptions.

If I am hostile to some group of people (some category that exists in my mind), I attach my grievances to everyone labeled as a member of that group. In a sense, I keep fighting old battles (real or imagined). I perceive someone I have just met or someone I am dealing with right now to be as guilty of having hurt me as someone who did hurt me in the past. I feel about the new people the same way I did about the past "enemies." I am attaching my old grievances to new persons and new situations.

This kind of irrational hostility may lead me to fight unnecessary battles and make unnecessary enemies. It may lead me to be combative or cruel to people who have done nothing to me and intend to do me no harm. This kind of misperception closes doors that could have been open and kills relationships that could have been beneficial to both people involved.

I am sure you can think of many examples of this abiding, irrational hostility, but I offer one story a friend recounted. He was riding a bus and began talking to the person sitting in the next seat. Eventually, the other person (a young man) said, "Are you Italian?" My friend said he was of Italian descent and quickly found himself facing a drawn knife. "What's this about?" he blurted out in shock and fear. "I met an Italian once," said the young fellow, "and he robbed me!" He was hostile to all "Italians." It took some fast talking to overcome that hostility and keep the peace.

Are there any groups that you bear a grudge against? Can you think of any group of people, a member of which, if you met, you would want to harm or get even with? If so, that's hostility, and you ought to examine it. Is every member of the group responsible for whatever grievance you have against some member of that group?

If you feel that some person endangers you in some way, you may demonstrate *defensiveness.*

Defensiveness

Believing that your self, your beliefs, your values, your attitudes, your memberships (loyalties), your behavior, your intentions, and your feelings are under attack (or are about to be attacked), you concentrate on protecting yourself. Your attention is directed toward alleviating your anxiety, and your energy is expended in defending yourself.

As Jack R. Gibb has noted, the more defensive a person is, the less able that person is to perceive the other person accurately. Gibb has analyzed tape recordings of group discussions, and his findings indicate that when defensiveness increases, efficiency in communication decreases. Other people's messages were received in quite distorted states by defensive listeners. Wouldn't you expect that? After all, the defensive person is preoccupied with himself or herself. If you are focusing your attention on how you are going to defend yourself, your behaviors, and your views, how can you give needed attention to others—their behaviors and their views? If you waste a lot of time and effort getting ready to strike back, there will be too little time and energy left to work at understanding the other person!

Defensiveness is more than just a waste of time and effort. It is a problem because it causes distorted perceptions of other people.

One illustration should suffice. The class was taking an exam. In the middle of the exam, I remembered that I had found a notebook belonging to one of the students after the preceding class. I simply announced from the desk, "Terry, would you see me after class, please?" His reply indicated his defensiveness. He said: "I'm not cheating; I'm just looking off into space!" Then we had to waste time clearing up the misunderstanding. He evidently had a perception of me as detective rather than professor. That perception of me certainly differs from my own perception of myself in the classroom.

There is one other pitfall or danger connected with perceiving other people that we should note briefly. It is *projection.*

Projection   If I assume that another person has beliefs, values, attitudes, interests, loyalties, intentions, and feelings exactly like my own, it is likely that I am projecting. The metaphor, of course, is that of a slide projector, which projects an image that is inside itself on a screen that is separate from itself. If I see my own image in you, I have probably projected it onto your screen/personality; I am looking at my own reflection!

The point is that we can misperceive other persons by attributing our own traits (as we see them, of course) to them. The danger lies in the fact that the perceiver does this attribution unwittingly, unknowingly.

I recently met someone who was suspicious of everyone; he thought everyone else in the world was dishonest. Frankly, I had doubts about that person's honesty, because I thought he was projecting on others what he saw in himself! Have you ever known someone who misperceived another person because he or she assumed the other was exactly like himself or herself? That person perception pitfall is projection.

Well, there it is. We have looked at five things we do in the process of perceiving others, at the goal of empathy and five aspects of empathizing, at five factors that affect one's capacity to form accurate impressions of others, and at eight pitfalls to guard against. I hope this study will help each of us improve our ability to see others as they see themselves.

SUGGESTIONS FOR FURTHER READING

BERSCHEID, ELLEN, and ELAINE HATFIELD WALSTER, *Interpersonal Attraction* (Reading, Mass.: Addison-Wesley, 1969).

CANTRIL, HADLEY, "Perception and Interpersonal Relations," *Readings in Interpersonal Communication*, Kim Giffin and Bobby R. Patton, eds. (New York: Harper & Row, 1971).

COOK, MARK, *Interpersonal Perception* (Baltimore: Penguin, 1971).

GIBB, JACK R., "Defensive Communication," *Basic Readings in Interpersonal Communication*, Kim Giffin and Bobby R. Patton, eds. (New York: Harper & Row, 1971).

HARRIS, THOMAS, *I'm O.K., You're O.K.* (New York: Avon, 1973).

HASTORF, ALBERT, DAVID SCHNEIDER, and JUDITH POLEFKA, *Person Perception* (Reading, Mass.: Addison-Wesley, 1970).

KELTNER, JOHN W. *Interpersonal Speech-Communication: Elements and Structures* (Belmont, Calif.: Wadsworth, 1970).

MILLER, GERALD R., and MARK STEINBERG, *Between People* (Palo Alto, Calif.: Science Research Associates, 1975).

SCHEIDEL, THOMAS M., *Speech Communication and Human Interaction*, 2nd ed. (Glenview, Ill.: Scott, Foresman, 1976).

STEINFATT, *Human Communication: An Interpersonal Introduction* (Indianapolis: Bobbs-Merrill, 1977).

SUDNOW, DAVID, *Studies in Social Interaction* (New York: The Free Press, 1972).

TAGIURI, RENATO, and LUIGI PETRULLO, eds., *Person Perception and Interpersonal Behavior* (Stanford, Calif.: Stanford Univ. Press, 1958).

WARR, P. B., and C. KNAPPER, *The Perception of People and Events* (New York: Wiley, 1968).

6
TRANSMISSION: SENDING ORAL MESSAGES

general goal:

To learn what is involved in transmitting oral messages and to examine and evaluate your own transmission skills.

specific objectives:

After completing this unit, you should:

Understand the four processes · by which speech is produced.

Understand the relation of mental activity to transmission.

Understand the four attributes of voice used in transmission.

Understand four basic principles of using your voice in transmission.

Understand three categories related to physical activity in transmission.

Understand four basic principles of physical activity in transmission.

Have examined and evaluated your own transmission skills and their effect on your ability to communicate efficiently and effectively.

IN THIS CHAPTER, we want to look at the skills needed by any human being to send messages—oral messages—efficiently. If you send a message, you certainly want it to "get through." You want it to be understood and accepted by the receiver.

In the very first chapter of this book, we defined *speech* as a series of bodily movements made visible and audible. To transmit messages by speech, we make our bodies *do* things to get the messages out; we turn our bodies into transmitters. We use parts of the body that have other basic functions; we have learned how to borrow those parts of the body and put them together into our human transmitter. Transmitting is a complex and difficult process, and it requires great skill. In fact, it requires many skills. That is what this chapter is all about.

Now, I know what you are probably thinking: "I have been talking since the age of one and a half. I certainly do not need any advice, assistance, or coaching on sending out spoken messages at this late date!" Or maybe you are thinking, "I do not need to waste my time reading a chapter about speech skills when I speak as well or better than the next person. I don't mumble, and my friends can understand every word I say!" Maybe, but this is not a long chapter, and it *might* have something in it that would be practical or helpful for you. Check it out.

the processes by which speech is produced

First, you really ought to know the processes by which speech is produced. Have you ever analyzed *how* you transmit messages—the processes involved? There are four processes that we utilize to speak: respiration, phonation, resonation, and articulation.

Respiration is the breathing process; we use it mainly to keep the body supplied with oxygen. We also use it, however, to provide the motor force behind our transmission. Lung power is essential for transmission, because we speak on the exhaled air stream.

Respiration

Phonation is the process of producing a buzzing noise at the vocal folds. These little membranes are at the top of the wind pipe and are used in swallowing and defecating; we borrow them and incorporate them into our transmitter. We can set them vibrating, and they produce the sound of our

Phonation

voices. These sounds are very weak and have to be amplified if our voices are to carry.

Resonation

The process of amplification is called *resonation.* We use the bony cavities of the head and chest to echo the basic tones and some of the overtones produced by the vocal folds; we human beings have our own amplifiers built in. Of course, we have to learn how to use these amplifiers, just as we have to learn how to make the most effective possible use of our lungs/ motor and our vocal folds/vibrator.

Articulation

The last of the four processes by which speech is produced is *articulation*—the chopping up of the outgoing air stream into specific sounds of the language. We stop or hinder the outgoing air stream to make such sounds as /b/ or /g/ or /v/; that process of interference is called articulation. Its name is based on a Latin word for *joint,* a place where two things come together. Since we bring two things together to stop or hinder the air stream (such as our two lips or our lips and teeth or our tongue and teeth), we "joint" or articulate the sounds. Each of us learns to articulate sounds. If you articulate your sounds clearly and precisely, you will have "good diction" or "clear enunciation." [1]

three kinds of activity involved in transmission

Some of you may have gotten impatient already with that extremely brief discussion of the four processes involved in speech production ("speech here does not mean "*a* speech" but "speaking—talking"), and you may be wanting a more practical approach to the business of message-producing, to the skills of speech transmission. This approach, then, may be better: There are three kinds of activity involved when we human beings send oral messages: mental activity (using your brain), vocal activity (using your voice), and physical activity (using your body). Hopefully, the first kind of activity will precede and accompany the other two! We will look at each of these kinds of activity briefly.

In the first chapter, you will remember, we discussed three elements of human speech communication—three components that make up speech.

---

[1] If you need to work to improve your own transmission skills of voice or articulation, you might consult *Articulation and Voice: A Communication Approach* by Robert G. King and Eleanor DiMichael (New York: Macmillan, 1978).

They were the verbal (symbolic) element, the vocal element, and the visible element. These three elements are the product of human speech transmission. We are now looking at the three kinds of activity that produce the three elements. Mental activity produces the verbal (word) element; vocal activity produces the vocal, paralinguistic element; and physical (bodily) activity produces the visible, kinesic element. Well, it is not *quite* that neat and simple, because we use the voice to produce the sounds of speech that make up our spoken words, so vocal activity is used to transmit both the verbal and the nonverbal, paralinguistic elements. But at least we can say truthfully that mental activity is directly related to the verbal element produced, that vocal activity is directly related to the paralanguage features produced, and that bodily activity is directly related to the visible, kinesic element produced.

When I have taught this course on human communication and come to this brief unit on transmission, I have always begun that class period by asking, "What activities are involved in talking? What do you use when you talk?" All my classes have mentioned that, as speakers transmitting messages to others, they use their voices. After a bit of thought, they also note that they use their entire bodies when speaking. But not all my classes have rememered that they use their brains. Until they are reminded with hints, at least!

Mental Activity

Mental activity is primary in transmission. It is the brain that controls the rest of the body; it is the brain that sends out the messages (intrapersonal communication) to the parts of the body involved in transmission and commands them to perform their functions in the act of transmission. It is the brain that registers the stimuli to which your outgoing message is a response; it is the brain that stored the code you will use and stored the words from which you will select. It is the brain with which you select your purpose and analyze your listener(s). And you use your brain in deciding how to put your message together. Mental activity is not only essential to the act of transmission; it is central to it.

Can the listener judge whether you are using your brain or *how* you are using your brain when you speak to him or her? Of course. We cannot see the chemical and electrical changes in your brain, but we can judge your mental activity from its results! We can tell whether your purpose was clearly defined; we can tell whether you chose appropriate words to convey the message; we can tell whether you have an adequate store of words from which to choose; we can tell whether you organized the message (remember, we are not talking about a speech, but about a message—any message—a spontaneous, brief, perhaps only one-sentence message) clearly and logically.

Here, then, are a few helpful hints on mental activity in transmitting messages. They are not rules, but they are basic principles. The first, of course, is: Think before you speak! The next is: Decide on the purpose you want to accomplish with your message. What is your specific goal? What do you want your message to do? What response do you want from your listener(s)? Next: Decide what strategies will best accomplish those goals or that clearly defined purpose—with *this* listener or with *these* listeners. What kind of message will work in this situation? Then: Decide how you will organize that message. Remember that a clearly structured message is both more efficient and more effective. Organize the message so your receiver(s) can grasp and hold on to it easily. And, finally, decide how you will word the message (or symbolize it). Of course, you must pick the wording of the message with your receivers in mind; what would be appropriate words for one listener might be totally *in*appropriate for another listener. We will take a closer look at word-picking in Chapter 8.

Vocal Activity

The second kind of activity used in transmitting oral messages is *vocal activity,* using one's voice. We have already looked at the four processes involved in speech production. We expel air from the lungs, we set our vocal folds into vibration, we amplify the sound in the throat, mouth, and nose, and we impede the outgoing air stream to articulate speech sounds.

FOUR ATTRIBUTES OF VOCAL ACTIVITY

"What control do we have over our voices?" You may be asking. Or, what can be varied or changed in our voices to give them vitality, variety, and meaning? There are four attributes of voice that can be manipulated: pitch, volume, rate, and quality. Let us look at each of these elements.

Pitch.   *Pitch* can be varied from low to high. If you have a musical instrument, you can play two different notes and compare them. One will be higher up the scale than the other one. We do not need to go into any discussion about frequencies and cycles per second here. It is enough for you to know that we can hear pitch differences and recognize when a tone is higher or lower than another tone. Pitch changes are essential to melodies in music, of course, but they are also essential to speech comunication in English. We use pitch changes to convey meaning and to denote emphasis. Certain kinds of sentences have certain kinds of pitch patterns (melodies or intonations). If you are going to communicate effectively, you must know and use the conventional melodies (pitch patterns).

The pitch patterns are based on relationships between pitches rather than on absolute pitch values. A man with a bass voice will not use the same pitches as a woman with a soprano voice, but the two will use the same pitch *relationships* when they each say the sentence, "Will you go?" The first two words will be about the same in pitch and the third will begin at a higher pitch and rise even higher. The *key* in which each speaks will be different, but the *pattern* of the pitches will be the same.

Some people speak in too high a key all the time, and other people speak in too low a key all the time. I would advise against your doing anything about changing your key of speaking unless you are working with an excellent, well-trained voice therapist/speech pathologist.

On the other hand, some people tend to speak within too narrow a range of pitches. Lay persons talk about such people speaking in a monotone; of course, they do not really speak on one pitch (mono-tone), but they lack enough variety in pitch to be interesting to listen to. If your instructor tells you that you have this problem, the instructor may help you to improve your transmission with more vocal variety in pitch. You should be warned, however, that you can overdo a good thing. In fact, there are some people who use too wide a range of pitches. They vary the pitch range so much that the result may be ludicrous. I recently heard a member of the New York City Council who has this problem, and her listeners laughed at her excessive pitch shifts. Her transmission sounds greatly exaggerated because her pitch jumps exceed conventional expectations. You want variety in pitch, but you do not want to sound as if you are telling a hyped-up version of some wild story to a little child!

Volume.   *Volume* can be varied from loud to soft. You probably know someone who speaks as if all the world is deaf, and you also probably know someone whose transmission is so weak and muted that others have difficulty hearing all he or she says. We use increased loudness for emphasis, although we can also indicate the importance or solemnity of a message by lowering the volume when we say it.

If you have a problem with the general level of volume in your transmitting, others will have to tell you so, and you will have to rely on that feedback to correct this transmission defect; it is likely that you are unaware of it and the message sounds loud enough or not too loud to you. Don't try to fool yourself by assuming that "this is the way I am; I was born this way; and this is the way I speak." And don't tell yourself that "this is my personality; I am a quiet (or a loud) person!" You have learned to use your loudness level, and you can learn another level if you need to. Since you send messages to affect your listeners, you must adjust the loudness to their needs. If your listeners say, "I can't hear you," or "I can barely hear you," or "I can hear you but I have to strain to do it and it is uncomfortable to have to listen to you very long," or "you talk so loud I want to back off and get at a more comfortable distance," then you need to work on the loudness of your voice.

Rate. *Rate* can be varied from fast to slow. You should vary the rate of your messages to reflect the ideas and the feelings expressed in those messages. We use variations in rate, including pauses, to highlight and emphasize important words or concepts, to indicate different parts of the message, and to color in words with emotions. The speaker, the message-producer, should transmit in such a way as to make the listener's task as easy as possible. If the transmitter varies the rate (and the other attributes of voice) meaningfully, the listener is given the needed assistance; if not, the listener's job is made unnecessarily difficult.

Occasionally, a person will consistently use a rate that is too slow for easy listening. Speakers who drag everything out to tedium and exasperation for listeners are rare, however. It is far more common to find people whose transmission is too fast for listeners' comfort. Although there is no absolute rule on rate (words per minute), most speakers who speak clearly and interestingly speak at about 150 to 200 words per minute. You might time your own rate by reading a passage of 200 words and timing yourself to see how long it takes you. More helpful would be the honest feedback of those to whom you talk—especially teachers and new acquaintances, since family and friends are probably used to the rate you already use. If you *do* speak too fast, chopping the words apart with pauses will not be an improvement. You may need to work on the duration of the sounds in the words, holding on to such sounds as /m/, /n/, *ng,* /l/, and /z/ (especially at the ends of syllables) and to the long vowels and diphthongs such as ē, ī, ō, ā, and o͞o. You may need some attention also to getting all the sounds in (if you have a tendency to leave out sounds, especially at the ends of words). Your instructor can assist you if you have this problem with rate.

Quality. The *quality* of your voice is the character of the sound of your voice, its timbre. Your voice can vary a great deal in quality—from mellow to harsh, from throaty to whispery, from nasal to denasal (a cold-in-the-head quality). We deliberately change the resonance of our voices to reflect the meaning and mood of our messages. Resonance largely determines the quality produced. It may be, however, that you *consistently* have a voice quality that irritates or distracts your listener(s). If you have that problem, you may need to get help from a good voice therapist/speech pathologist.

FOUR BASIC PRINCIPLES OF VOCAL ACTIVITY

Fearing that you are beginning to get a bit restless and are eager to get to the helpful hints for vocal activity, I will give them immediately. There are at least four basic principles for vocal activity in transmission. They center on: *audibility, intelligibility, unobtrusiveness,* and *appropriateness.* Let's look at each of them briefly.

Audibility. If something is audible, of course, it is capable of being heard. The basic principle here is that your voice ought to be able to be heard. Now that may seem a little obvious to you, but the obvious often is taken for granted and thereby ignored. No communication will take place if your intended listener cannot hear you. Your transmission must be loud enough to be heard! So use your voice in such a way that the sounds will reach that intended receiver.

Intelligibility. Here the question is not whether your voice can be heard, but whether your spoken message can be understood. If your oral message is intelligible, it was spoken clearly enough for the listener to understand it. Try to avoid speaking in what John Davenport cleverly dubbed "Slurvian."[2] That is what he called the sloppy, careless, slovenly enunciation of the lip-and-tongue-lazy among us who say such things as "prayed" for *parade,* "sport" for *support,* "nitly" for *in Italy,* and "beans" for *beings.* We listeners may be able to decipher Slurvian if you speak it to us, but we will have to work hard at it, and there is just the chance we will not be able to understand it at all. Work for clear, correct (conventional), precise articulation; that is the key to intelligibility.

Unobtrusiveness. This may not be an everyday word for you. If something obtrudes or protrudes, you know, of course, that it sticks out. If something is *un*obtrusive, then it *does not* stick out. And anything in your use of voice (pitch, volume, rate, quality—anything, even such meaningless verbal crutches as "yuh know," "you see," "like I mean," and "like man") that sticks out is a distraction. The question you should ask yourself is this: Is my way of speaking calling attention to itself and away from the message I am trying to convey to my listener? The way you use your voice in transmitting your message should *not* call attention to itself; it should not stand out; it should be unobtrusive.

When we were discussing the principle of intelligibility, we noted the danger of sloppy, careless speech habits. We should note, however, that exaggerated precision, perniciously precise articulation, calls as much attention to itself as slack articulation does. *Anything* in your use of voice that distracts the listener's attention from the message is a hindrance and should be avoided!

Appropriateness. This principle, like the others, is just common sense: Your use of voice should be suited to the message and to your purpose. The variations in pitch, volume, rate, and quality should all be appropriate for the meaning and mood of your message; they should reflect and underline the intellectual and emotional content of your message.

If you are using your voice appropriately, your voice will sound considerably different when you are uttering professions of undying love to your beloved and when you are in one of those infrequent arguments with him or her.

Physical Activity

The third kind of activity used in transmitting oral messages is *physical activity,* using one's body. When we defined speech, we noted that something was produced that was heard and seen. The use of the entire body is an integral part of speaking; it is not overlaid or added on to speech, but is a vital part of speech transmission.

The old adage says, "Actions speak louder than words," but what does

[2] John Davenport, "Slurvian Self-taught," *The New Yorker,* June 8, 1949, p. 26.

bodily activity say and how does it say it? We are indebted to Ray Bird-whistell for beginning the systematic and scientific study of bodily move-ment as communication.[3] He called this area of study *kinesics* and at-tempted to construct a consistent theoretical structure for its study. One need not agree with Birdwhistell's theoretical system (based on an analogy with language structure) to recognize the importance of what has come to be known popularly as "body language."

THREE CATEGORIES OF PHYSICAL ACTIVITY

We use the entire body to communicate, and we never speak without sending out bodily signs. Receivers react to these bodily signs and attach meaning to them—or at least to some of them. Doubtless, receivers react to a total impression rather than to isolated component parts (that is especially true, I think, of the sender's physical behaviors), but for the sake of convenience let us divide the sender's physical activity into three categor-ies: appearance and stance, body movement, and facial expression.

Appearance and Stance. You may think that a sender's (speaker's) physical appearance should not be listed under the category of physical activity. But we are concerned with what the message-receiver *sees* and attaches meaning to. How you look when you speak is, for better or worse—mostly worse—perceived as part of your speaking; it transmits messages; listeners infer meanings from that appearance. If this were indeed the "best of all possible worlds," then people would not attach meanings to a person's physical features. But they—that is, *we*—do! However illogical or misguided this tendency may be, it exists and we must face it.

In his excellent book *Nonverbal Communication in Human Interaction,* Mark L. Knapp devotes a chapter to "The Effects of Physical Appearance and Dress on Human Communication."[4] He presents evidence that phys-ical appearance significantly influences interpersonal responses and that meanings attached to physical features significantly affect our perception of the other's intelligence, personality, credibility, and ability.

Some of the body features that affect receivers' responses are character-istics over which we human beings have little or no control—the shape (body type), skin color, and amount of body hair. But many of us recognize that these and other body features are important in interpersonal relations because we do all we can to alter them and make ourselves "more attrac-tive." Witness the amount of time, effort, and money we Americans spend each year on health spas, weight-loss programs, cosmetics, lotions, deo-dorants, colognes and perfumes, facelifts and hair transplants!

[3] R. L. Birdwhistell, *Introduction to Kinesics* (Louisville: University of Louisville Press, 1952). R. L. Birdwhistell, *Kinesics and Contexts* (Philadelphia: University of Pennsylvania Press, 1970).

[4] Mark L. Knapp, *Nonverbal Communication in Human Interaction* (New York: Holt, 1972).

Not only is a listener influenced by a speaker's general appearance; the listener is also affected by the speaker's stance. By stance I mean the position of the body—one's posture. Is the body rigid or relaxed? Is the body erect or slouched/slumped? Is the body standing, supine, prone, or kneeling? Rightly or wrongly, we make inferences from the posture of the sender; we attach such meanings as alert, withdrawn, aggressive, defensive, indifferent, hostile, receptive, seductive, resistant, arrogant, repentant, and subservient.

Of course, these meanings may be unintended by and totally unknown to the speaker/sender, but meaning—like beauty—is in the eye of the beholder! G. W. Hewes says that human beings have over 1000 different steady postures available to them, but he points out that the postures we choose are determined primarily by cultural influences.[5] Like all other forms of communication, posture is culturally determined and culturally interpreted. A posture that is acceptable for a male in the United States, for example, might be offensive somewhere else in the world. And the "wrong ("unmasculine") way" for a male to cross his legs in the United States is perfectly acceptable and considered quite masculine in Great Britain. Body language is learned behavior; it varies from one culture to the next.

Body Movement. I deliberately called this category "body movement" rather than "gestures," because to most people the word "gestures" conveys only the idea of hand and arm movements. And we use the whole body! We move the whole head, our shoulders, arms, hands, fingers, legs, feet, torso, and pelvis. We can also move the entire body. We can shift from one stance or posture to another. We can take a step forward or a step backward; we can shift the body from one side to another or rock back and forth. The possibilities are seemingly endless.

We use body movement as part of speech to underline and reinforce the verbal message as well as to convey feelings and attitudes. Some gestures are social conventions and are therefore signals. That is, they have a meaning recognized within the culture, and the response of the receiver is usually clear-cut and immediate. Because of the one-to-one relationship between the sign and the meaning, the significance of the gesture (movement) is not ambiguous—in that particular culture. A few years ago, then Vice President Nelson Rockefeller was speaking at a public gathering and was insistently heckled by a young person in the audience. Giving vent to his irritation and frustration, Mr. Rockefeller leaned forward over the podium and raised his middle finger in the direction of the heckler. Although they had not heard the speech, the heckling, and the verbal exchange, few American newspaper readers who saw the picture of Mr. Rockefeller's gesture failed to understand his meaning.

Contrary to what "common sense" might lead you to believe, gestures

[5] G. W. Hewes, "The Anthropology of Posture," *Scientific American,* **196** (1957), pp. 123–132.

are culture-bound. Within a culture, a gesture may become such a social convention as to become a signal, but such signals do not have universal meaning; they are not recognized and interpreted the same all over the world. I often begin this section of the course with a question to my students. I am sure they would agree that words are not universal (world-wide) in use or meaning, but I ask them if they believe gestures would be interpreted the same all over the world. Sometimes I pose the question as a problem: You have crashed in a plane in a country whose language and customs you do not know. Would you try to communicate with the natives through sign language? Would you assume that sign language would be perfectly clear and unambiguous? Would you assume that your gestures would mean exactly the same things to the natives as those gestures meant to you? Many students answer yes to all the questions.

What about you? Do you believe that a nod of the head would mean "yes" all over the world? Do you believe that a forward overhand motion of the arm, with the forearm and hand swinging forward from the elbow, would mean "Come on, friends," all over the world? Do you believe that an open hand raised, the fingers extended and the palm toward the message-receiver, is a sign of greeting or friendship all over the world? If you have answered yes to any or all of these questions, we need to discuss body movement and gestures a little bit more!

Because gestures do not mean the same thing all over the world, one must be very careful in the use of gestures when moving into another culture. The chance of unintentional offense is great! A nod does not mean "yes" in Greece, but the opposite; I have visited that country many times, but the raising and lowering of the head to mean "no" (a definite nod) still seems a little strange to me. But I try to remember not to nod when I say "yes" in Greece; I certainly do not want to confuse my listeners with *modality splitting* (conveying one message in one mode and a contrary or contradictory message in another mode).

One of my students who had served in Vietnam and Laos told me that he had an interesting and potentially dangerous experience in cross-cultural problems with gestures. He was leading a small group of Montagnard tribesmen down a jungle path. He did not speak their language and had to communicate with them verbally through an interpreter. Since the path was through enemy territory, he did not want to speak directions or instructions anyway. He relied on hand signals. To speed the men up a bit, he motioned, using the overhand gesture we Americans use for "come on." It is a rather large gesture, using the entire arm with extra movement of the forearm and hand in an arc downward. When he turned around to see if the men were indeed speeding up, he found them so angry they were ready to shoot him. He did not understand what the trouble was. The interpreter had to explain to him that the gesture he had used was used in Southeast Asia only for animals, never for human beings. One might signal to a dumb water buffalo to come on in that fashion, but one did not use such gross overhand gestures at a human being. The meaning the men got was that he considered them animals, and they were ready to turn on him. He quickly got instructions in the "proper" way to signal for human beings (in that culture) to "come on, friends!" Last year I read that some of the teachers in Louisville, Kentucky, were having some difficulty understanding the behavior of the new Vietnamese children who were in their classrooms. According to a report in the newspaper, the children would sometimes burst into tears for "no apparent reason." You guessed it! The teachers had been using conventional American gestures (including gross, large overhand gestures asking the students to come forward to the desk or to the front of the room) as they spoke to the Vietnamese students. The children were deeply hurt and humiliated and often cried when "spoken to in that way" (with the to-them gross gesture). The school system held special workshops for teachers who had the new children in their classes in order to alert them to the communication problems they were facing.

If you saw the poster advertising the movie *Pumping Iron,* you saw a large picture of Arnold Schwarzenegger waving both hands over his head, the palms toward the viewer and the fingers extended. Those of you who still remember Richard Nixon may recall that he often used that gesture when campaigning—stretching both arms high overhead and waving both hands, palms forward. What does that gesture mean? Well, it depends on where you are! A few years ago, I saw some young American exchange students on a beach in Greece running around giving the "peace sign" to everyone. I suggested to one young lady that it might be best not to do that. She was dubious and a little resentful of the interference of a stranger in her effort to establish friendly contact with the local Greeks. I told her the gesture did not mean exactly the same thing on that beach in Greece it did back home. She remained skeptical, but asked, "What does it mean here?" while she continued to raise the two fingers aloft, the palm toward her intended receivers. I said, "Do you know what one finger means?" She lowered the hand and said she did. "Here," I said, "the two fingers raised would just mean: 'double!'" Putting the palm toward someone in Greece is extremely rude; it is even vulgar. I went on to explain that if you wanted to insult your adversary even more than double you could open the hand and extend all five fingers. Probably the worst you could do to him would be to raise both hands, palm forward, and extend all five fingers of each hand. Indeed, one of my Greek friends was given a ticket a few years ago in Athens (he paid the fine without a contest) for "public obscenity." He was driving in downtown Athens when another driver cut in front of him in his lane. He said nothing, but he stuck his hand out the window—palm forward and all five fingers extended. It was not interpreted by the policeman on the corner as a friendly, or even a polite, gesture. He gave my friend the citation for a gesture that would have meant either "stop" or "hello" in the United States! Gestures are culture-bound; one must be cautious in their use when moving from culture to culture.

Facial Expression.   It is no accident that we talk about "face-to-face" communication; we use the face more than any other part of the body when we speak. For one thing, whenever possible, we "face" each other when conversing. The face is one part of the body that we do not usually cover up with clothing; its interesting, expressive changes are open and exposed. Cosmetics provide no adequate mask for one's facial expressions!

Think of the different parts of the human face. True, we get a general impression of your overall expression, but the various parts of the face can be used separately to vary that impression. Your forehead can be smoothed out, wrinkled, furrowed or wiggled. Your eyebrows can be raised, lowered, arched, cocked, or wiggled. Your ears may be somewhat movable, but mine are pretty immobile; they can blush, however. Your mouth can be tensed, relaxed, pursed, puckered, lifted into a smile, or dropped down into a pout. Your nose can be pinched in, flared out, or pulled up. Your cheeks can blush, and you can jut out your chin or tuck it in. And your eyes are so important and interesting that we will deal with them at more length.

Where do we get facial expressions? Are they natural—innate, inborn, instinctual? Some people still believe that some expressions are natural reactions to stimuli, but most researchers believe that we *learn* to express our emotions with our faces. Birdwhistell has studied many cultures, and he has concluded that there are no universal facial behaviors that mean the same thing in all cultures. Nature (genetics) may give us our bodies, but in a very real sense we learn our looks! Of course, the features we have affect those looks, but the manipulation and display of those features we learn from those around us. We pick up the facial expressions of the culture in which we are reared and of the family and friends with whom we associate. At least to some extent, we learn to control our facial expressions, and even the expressions we do not consciously control were conditioned by previous experience. Just as we have learned how to manipulate our faces to convey emotions, we have also learned how to manage our faces in an effort to mask our feelings. To what extent we are successful in that masking effort varies greatly!

But let us turn our attention back to the eyes. The eyes have been called the most expressive part of the human face, "the window of the soul." St. Jerome wrote, "The face is the mirror of the mind, and eyes without speaking confess the secrets of the heart." There has not been enough research on eye behavior in human communication, but research and observation make possible some generalizations.

First, expansion and contraction of the pupils of the eyes (one of the autonomic processes over which we have no conscious control) is affected by our emotional states. Our pupils expand in low light so more light can come into the eyes; our pupils also dilate when we look at something that interests us, appeals to us, or is pleasant to us. Pupil dilation is probably a reliable indicator of how well we like what we are viewing. I do not know anyone who can monitor pupil sizes during conversation and thus detect true attitudes; that is probably fortunate for all of us.

Eye behavior, like all communication activity, is culturally conditioned. We must, therefore, identify the culture when making generalizations about the use of the eyes in communicating. In North American society in general, there are certain norms that regulate eye behavior in communication. Let us look at some of them; I am sure you can think of examples of each of these behavior patterns from your own experience.

We use eye contact to register recognition, to invite interpersonal contact, and to encourage involvement. Don't you look into the eyes of someone you know more than into the eyes of a stranger when you encounter that person on the street? Unless, of course, you would *like* to know that stranger. Then you may be apt to look into the eyes as a kind of invitation to acquaintance.

On the other hand, we use the lack of eye contact to register disaffiliation and withdrawal. We curtail eye contact in an effort to curtail social contact.

We use eye behavior to regulate who speaks and who listens; through the use of our eyes, we indicate the opening and the closing of channels of communication. The listener is expected to look at the speaker to indicate attention and interest, but the speaker is not expected to look at the listener all the time. Indeed, the speaker will look at the listener at the end of the transmission to give the cue that the transmission is over. Looking at the other person gives the cue that it is now that person's turn to talk. If you stop talking and do not look at the other person, that person will probably think you are just pausing for a moment. It is the look that says, "Transmission ended; channel open!"

This use of the eyes to control who talks and for how long has been called the regulatory function of eye behavior. The fact that the speaker does not maintain eye contact while the listener is expected to look at the speaker may explain some rather surprising research recently done in England. That research indicates that, when two people meet, the one who first averts his or her eyes is the more aggressive of the two! The more dominant person looks away first. Maybe further research will clarify these findings.

We use eye behavior to express emotions such as anger, embarrassment, dislike, or tension. We usually look away if we are angry or embarrassed or if we are irritated or tense. On the other hand, an interested listener is expected to look at the speaker almost constantly; we express our interest with our eyes. In our culture, we are taught very early that the listener should look at the speaker. Did your mother or father ever say, "You look at me when I am speaking to you!"?

We look into other people's eyes for other reasons, too. We establish eye contact when we are seeking feedback—when we are trying to find out others' reactions to something we have said or done. Our eyes send out the message, "What do you think?" And we may use eye contact as a kind of visual aggression. Staring at another person can produce anxiety. Our relatives, the great apes, also use stares to express hostility and aggressiveness, according to Desmond Morris.[6]

Finally, we use eye contact to compensate for spatial distance variations. If there is a greater distance between us while we are speaking, we will probably increase the amount of eye contact; on the other hand, when we are very close to one another, we will probably reduce the amount of eye contact. We use space distance and eye contact, then, in inverse ratios to maintain some sense of psychological distance between us when we communicate.

The generalizations we have been discussing apply to North Americans, but they may not apply at all to other cultures. To assume that these norms are universal is to invite communication breakdowns. One illustration might illuminate the point.

A Puerto Rican young man in New York was brought before a judge and accused of a theft. "Just tell me what happened," said the judge. The young man hung his head and looked at the floor as he began to speak. The judge did not believe the young man's version of the events. "I could tell just by looking at him he was guilty," he said later. "He couldn't look me in the eye!" The young man's averted gaze meant sneakiness, dishonesty, and a sense of guilt—to the non-Hispanic judge. But to the Puerto Rican young man, the averted gaze, the downcast eyes, showed his respect for one in authority. His lowered eyes—to him—meant courtesy and humility.

There is probably much greater danger of cross-cultural misunderstanding based on physical activity (the visible component of speech) than from either the vocal or verbal speech components.

"Well," I can hear you saying, "as long as you are talking about facial expressions, I know one that is universal: the human smile—the worldwide sign of friendship and affection!" But no. Even the smile offers the chance to issue the warning again: Not only is there a real danger of offending people from other cultures, unintentionally and unknowingly, with physical activity appropriate in our culture but not in theirs; there is also the danger of misinterpreting the physical activity people from other cultures use.

I remember reading a few years ago about some missionaries who went to the upper reaches of the Amazon River to convert the natives to Christianity. They went, of course, in peace and were filled with good will. Unfortunately, when they saw their first tribesmen, they smiled to indicate their warm friendship. They were immediately killed for demonstrating their "hostility"! It seems that among some of the tribes of the Amazon region a smile is a sign of hostility and imminent attack. Baring the teeth there is not a friendly gesture. The missionaries incorrectly assumed that the facial expressions that meant openness and friendship to them would

---

[6] Desmond Morris, *The Naked Ape* (New York: McGraw-Hill, 1967), pp. 33–34.

also mean openness and friendliness to the tribesmen steeped in another culture. Even a smile is *not* a universal sign of friendship!

When we human beings transmit messages, we send out many cues—verbal, vocal, and visible. The receiver must look at all these cues in context—holistically, rather than isolating one cue and fixing on that alone as the basis for interpreting the message. The public has become very interested in body language in recent years, but some writers have presented a vastly oversimplified approach to this complex subject. People have been led to believe that there is a signal relationship in body language—a one-to-one relationship of *this means that.* Although it is true that body activity conveys meaning, it is not true that each separate movement has one meaning and one meaning only. Reading body language is just not that easy! The words we use (the verbal component of speech communication) do not have one meaning and one meaning only; neither do our stances, our body movements, or our facial expressions. We must learn to interpret physical activity *cautiously.*

But what about *using* physical activity in transmitting messages? Are there helpful hints or guidelines about its use? Briefly, here are four principles. The visible component of speech communication should be: appropriate, well-timed, unobtrusive, and natural.

FOUR BASIC PRINCIPLES OF PHYSICAL ACTIVITY

Appropriateness.   The purpose of the physical activity is to underscore and reinforce the ideas and mood of the verbal message. It is important, then, that you not send out contrary or contradictory cues with your body. Surely you would not propose marriage or cohabitation with your fist clenched and your face twisted into a grimace, but sometimes our bodies do send out incongruous messages.

Timing.   Body movements must be timed to accompany the idea words and not precede or follow them. A comic effect can be achieved by the right gestures made at the wrong time.

Unobtrusiveness.   Your stance, body movements, and facial expressions should support your ideas—not compete with them. Your physical activity should not *stand out,* but *fit in.* If you have physical mannerisms that detract from what you are saying and distract the listener's attention, they should be toned down or eliminated.

Naturalness.   Your physical activity should not appear artificial, planned, phony. Rather, it should appear natural, spontaneous, and sincere—unstudied and unaffected. The best way to achieve this is to let the physical activity come naturally and concentrate on what you have to say and on your listener-receiver.

ANDERSON, VIRGIL A., *Training the Speaking Voice,* rev. ed. (New York: Oxford, 1961).

BIRDWHISTELL, R. L., "Some Body Motion Elements Accompanying Spoken American English," *Communication: Concepts and Perspectives,* Lee Thayer, ed. (Washington, D.C.: Spartan Books, 1967).

BRODNITZ, F. S., *Keep Your Voice Healthy* (New York: Harper, 1953).

BRONSTEIN, ARTHUR, and BEATRICE JACOBY, *Your Speech and Voice* (New York: Random House, 1967).

FISHER, HILDA B., *Improving Voice and Articulation,* 2nd ed. (Boston: Houghton Mifflin, 1975).

KING, ROBERT G., and ELEANOR M. DIMICHAEL, *Articulation and Voice: Improving Oral Communication* (New York: Macmillan, 1978).

LESSAC, ARTHUR, *The Use and Training of the Human Voice* (New York: DBS Publications, 1968).

MOSES, PAUL, *The Voice of Neurosis* (New York: Grune & Stratton, 1954).

OLIVER, ROBERT T., *Making Your Meaning Effective* (Boston: Holbrook Press, 1971).

RIZZO, RAYMOND, *The Voice as an Instrument* (New York: Odyssey, 1969).

SHAPIRO, J. G., "Responsivity to Facial and Linguistic Cues," *Journal of Communication,* **18** (1968), pp. 11–17.

7
LANGUAGES AND HOW THEY WORK

general goal:

To learn some basic linguistic principles and the part language plays in human communication.

specific objectives:

After completing this unit, you should understand:
What language is.
What languages are.
What the basic elements of any language are.
What social and regional dialects are and their role in American English.
What "standard" American English is and what "nonstandard" dialects are.
What idiolects are and something about your own idiolect.
What functional varieties of language are and how they operate.

Πῶς εἶσθε; Καλά; Πολύ καλά;
Comment allez-vous? Bien? Très bien?
¿Cómo está usted? ¿Bien? ¿Muy bien?

I HAVE JUST sent you a message. I used written symbols to represent spoken words because I cannot talk to you directly. The message I tried to send you is a simple one. I hope you understood it. In fact, I sent the same message several times. In each of the lines above, the message is the same. Each time, however, I used a different code to send the message. We call those codes languages. If you don't know a language, then it is a *secret* code, isn't it? How many of these codes were unfamiliar to you? If they all looked like secret codes, here is the message for you: "How are you? Well? Very well?" Simple, right? Well, it is simple *if* you know the code—the language.

You learned your first language so long ago you have probably forgotten how you did it. And you probably take it for granted. It is true, as many have said, that human beings are tool-making animals. But it is equally true, I think, that language is the most sophisticated tool we have made!

Think about how we use language. To represent what we think, we talk. We can represent what we say by writing. And we can talk about what we write. It (the use of language) is a complicated business! The spoken word is the symbol for an idea; the written word is a symbol for the spoken word; and the spoken word can be used to discuss (symbolize) the written word.

If I want to represent (symbolize) or remind you of a particular class of objects, I can use the name for that class of things, the word (verbal symbol) for that category (concept). I can say the word for it. Of course, the word I pick will depend on what code (language) I am using to transmit my message to you. Hopefully, we will share the same code. If I want to remind you of a piece of furniture consisting of a smooth, flat slab on legs, I would say the word *mesa, tish, τραπέζι,* or *table,* depending on what code I chose. In order to preserve what was said, I could write the words down. Then we could look at the written sentence and talk about it. You could say, "You have misspelled the word *table* in that sentence," or "The *t* at the beginning of the word *table* looks like an *f.*" Look at what has happened in the use of symbols. We started with oral symbols for ideas. Then we used written symbols for the oral ones. Then we used oral symbols for the written ones. I told you language manipulation is a complicated business!

defining "language"

The word *language* is a general term; we use it to refer to the use of verbal symbols (words) to stand for ideas. When we talk about the verbal symbols of the human race collectively, we use the word *language*. Not *languages,* but *language.* The idea of language involves using words, no matter which of the world's languages the words are in. Like the words *law, medicine,* and *painting, language* symbolizes a concept—a generalized category. Law refers to an area of study related to the governing of human conduct; medicine refers to an area of knowledge related to the preserving or restoring of health; painting refers to the practice of those who make visual representations (paintings). The general term *language* refers to the use of words to represent things, actions, relationships, feelings, and ideas.

Language in the collective sense is one thing. Specific *languages* are something else. Just as there are laws, medicines, and paintings, so there are specific languages. Laws are specific regulations; medicines are specific remedies; paintings are specific products of a painter's skill and imagination. *A language* is a specific verbal code—a code made out of words.

Any code is a system of signs (things that stand for other things). There are many different kinds of codes. American Indians used smoke signals to send coded messages; in Africa, drumbeats were used to code messages; navies used to use lights and flags for the signs in their codes. Hoboes invented a code that they used during the Depression in the United States; it was a system of line drawings. Prisoners have devised wall-tapping systems to use for coded transmissions. I am sure you can think of many other examples of codes.

The word *code,* of course, is a more general term than *languages;* languages are just one kind of code. All codes have two things in common: they are systematic (there is some kind of pattern involved), and they utilize signs (some things that stand for other things).

"Enough," I hear you saying! "I know that a language is a kind of code. But give a straightforward definition of a language. What is it?" All right. A *language* is a *conventionalized system of arbitrary vocal signs.* Although the definition seems a little complicated, every word in the definition is essential. There are five key words in that definition; each of them reminds us of some important aspect we need to understand about languages.

System

First of all, a language is a *system.* Like any code, it has a pattern. No language is a random collection of words. It is organized. It has structure. There is order to any language, which means that a language can be analyzed. It also means that a language, once you have figured out the patterns, is predictable. Each language has a system. To learn a language, you must find out what the system is.

If you do not know the system, a language is a secret code. Perhaps you, like I, know how frustrating it is to be in a country where everyone around you is sending, receiving, and apparently understanding spoken coded messages and you haven't the vaguest idea what is being said. To those other people, the code is not secret or mysterious at all; they have broken the code—figured out the patterns and how they work. But there you stand, hearing everything, seeing everything, and understanding nothing! You've got to learn the system. There is regularity there—if you can just discover it.

Signs

A language is a system made out of *signs*. Signs, as we have noted earlier, stand for something else. They represent meanings—ideas. Languages are codes made out of verbal symbols: words. Each language has its own set of words. If you grow up in a language community, you learn the words, and you learn what meanings to attach to those words. Words (no matter what the language) do not carry meaning; rather, they stir up (stimulate) meanings (in the minds of the listeners/receivers) and represent or stand for meanings (in the minds of the speakers and listeners). It is important to remember that meanings do not inhere in the words themselves, but exist locked up in the minds of the people who use the words. If the meanings were part of the words and were transmitted in, through, with, or by the spoken words as they are uttered, each of us would be able to understand all the languages of the world. There would be no secret codes, so far as languages are concerned. The spoken word, no matter what language it was in, would bring the meaning to us—*if* the meaning were *in* the word. But words are *signs:* they stand for meanings; they are the representatives of our ideas. They are not the ideas themselves or even the embodiment of our ideas.

The word *signs* in our definition of a language reminds us that each language system is constructed of verbal symbols (words) that stand for ideas in the minds of senders and receivers.

All right. A language is a system made out of signs. So is any other code. What makes the signs in a language distinctive? Note that there are two words in the definition used to limit (describe) the word *signs: vocal* and *arbitrary.* Now we are getting somewhere! All codes do not use vocal signs; all languages do.

Vocal

By vocal signs, I mean spoken symbols. So all languages are systems made out of *spoken* (oral) symbols. But, says a cynic, that does not include the written language. And what we *write* is the language, isn't it? No, no, ten thousand times no. We *speak* a language, and a language does not need a written form to be complete. In fact, many of the world's languages have no written form. The written form is not the language; the written form is an attempt to represent the language. It is a symbol system representing a symbol system! The language itself is made up of words spoken and heard. A language (any language, all languages) is made up of vocal signs—oral (spoken) symbols.

Arbitrary

Our definition describes those vocal signs (that languages are made out of) as *arbitrary*. That concept is important. The word *arbitrary* means "random and unpredictable," "not logically supported," "not based on reason," and "capricious." In what way are the words of a language (any language) *arbitrary?* Well, a tangential illustration might help. One of my students came in to class one day and said, "Why are we going to have an exam today?" And I replied, "Because we are." She persisted: "But *why?*" "Because that's the way it is," I said. Undeterred, she asked, "Why is that the way it is?" And I, playing the autocrat, came back with: "Because I said so." To which she responded: "Why do you say so?" My enlightening answer was: "Because we are." Her comment broke the pattern as she exclaimed, "You're being *arbitrary!*" "Exactly!" I said.

If something (or someone) is arbitrary, you can give no other reason for it except "that's the way it is." It is not that way because of some logical planning or cosmic purpose. It's that way because of whimsy or accident.

Am I saying that the words in each language are arbitrary symbols? Exactly. There is no logical connection between the word (the sign/symbol) and whatever that sign represents (the meaning/idea). The names of things are arbitrary names, chosen at random for no apparent reason. One name for a thing makes just as much sense as another. Oh, we can trace the history of a word in a language, giving its "roots." But when we finish tracing the word's ancestry, we arrive at the same place: there is no logical reason for the word(s) from which this word descended.

Let's go back to that piece of furniture consisting of a smooth, flat slab on legs. What is the logical name for that object? Is there any sensible reason to call it a "table"? (And did you pronounce that word in English or French? That spelling represents two different words in two different languages.) Isn't it just as logical to call it something else—such as *mesa* or *tish* or *mother,* for that matter. (If the customary name for that object were *mother* in English, I would put food on my mother and no one would think it strange.) Is the Spanish name (*mesa*) or the German word (*tish*) any more logical (or less logical) than the English word? No. Is any one language's word for that object any more accurate or appropriate or sensible than any other language's word? No, again. What is the *right* name for the thing? A foolish question, because the spoken symbols (words) of a language are *arbitrary.*

Conventionalized

There is one other word in our definition of a language that we have not discussed. We have noted that a language is a *system* (code) made of *arbitrary vocal signs.* But there is one other factor we must take into account. That system is a *conventionalized* system.

If you say to someone that his or her behavior is not conventional, what do you mean? If a person does not observe the conventions, what has that person disregarded? That's right: Something that is conventional is customary. If someone breaks out of conventional behavior, that person has done something that is not customary in that group of people.

A system that is *conventionalized* is one that is based on the customary usage of some group of people. It developed, as did other kinds of customs, within a group of people. After all, each group develops its own set of customs—including its customary language patterns. Those patterns are neither right nor wrong, good nor bad; linguistic patterns are just conventionalized—customary.

There is our definition of a language: A language is a conventionalized system of arbitrary vocal signs. And here is how we have translated that definition: A language is a structured code, based on the customs of some group of people, made up of spoken symbols chosen at random.

The scientific study of language (in general) is called *linguistics.* Related to the study of language are several disciplines. Some scholars have studied the sounds of speech; that area of study is called *phonetics.* One may study the sound system of a particular language; one would then study the *phonemics* or *phonology* of a specific language. *Grammar* is the study (description—not prescription) of the patterns used in forming words and sentences. Grammar, therefore, has two subdivisions: *morphology,* the study of word-formation, and *syntax,* the study of sentence formation. A maker of dictionaries is called a *lexicographer,* and the field of study—the study of words as expressions of ideas—is called *lexicology.* There are two subdivisions in the discipline of lexicology: *etymology,* the study of the derivation (history) of words, and *semantics,* the study of the meaning of words.

Don't be alarmed by all those terms. You need not memorize them, but you should at least have been introduced to them. As you can see, there are many aspects to the study of language and languages.

the three components of any language

So far, we have talked about what a language *is.* Now we should examine what all languages *have* or consist of. All languages—no matter how complicated (such as Navajo) or how simple (such as English)—have three basic elements:

1. A set of significant sounds, called phonemes.
2. Regular patterns, called grammar.
3. A collection of words, called vocabulary.

If we are to understand the nature of any language (including our own), we must look at each of these three elements in more detail. "Must we?" I hear some reluctant scholar saying. "I already speak a language. Why must I analyze it in this way?" The answer is that you cannot possibly understand the way human communication works if you do not know some basic bits of information about language.

We can stir up feelings in other people without words (nonverbal communication). We can express our own feelings without words. But when it comes to representing intellectual (conceptual) meanings, we must turn to words. Language plays a crucial part in human communication, and we need to know how it functions.

If you doubt the importance of language in human communication, try to explain without words (nonverbally) your concept of *democracy* to a friend. Or, for that matter, try to explain your understanding of the meaning of *love* without words. We rely on language when we try to communicate about the complicated things in our heads. Let us look, then, at the three elements found in any langauge.

Phonemes

Remember that when we talk about language we are talking about the spoken language. Every language uses a set of significant sounds, out of which words are made in that language. Different languages use different sounds. American English has about 42 sounds (phonemes), and Spanish uses approximately 32 sounds (phonemes). We have some sounds in English that do not occur in Spanish—the vowel sounds in the words *shut* and *book*, for example. And Spanish has some sounds we do not have in English—the great trilled sound of *rr* in such words as *perro*, for instance. In my unsuccessful attempt to learn modern Greek, I had great difficulty with two phonemes, because the two sounds (for χ and γ) are different from any we have in English. And I was determined not to substitute the English sounds of /h/ and /g/! I wanted to use the Greek sounds.

Phonemes are not just sounds; they are speech sounds that are significant—sounds that make a difference, sounds that matter. A *phone* is a sound—any speech sound; that is why the study of speech sounds is called phonetics. A phoneme, however, is a sound that can change the meaning of a word. To be significant, a phoneme must be able to make the difference between one word and another.

Phonemes: Significant speech sounds

Let's suppose that you did not know English, but were trying to figure out the phonemic system in that language. You would listen as people said words (just as you did when a baby), and you would hear the sounds in the words. Eventually, you would be able to tell that the difference between the words *mate* and *meat* has to do with the sound in the middle. Are they the same sounds or not? No, you decide. You can *hear* a difference between the two sounds. So they are different *phones*. But you would have to discover whether that difference was significant—whether it changed the meaning or not. You would check to see if a lady saying the word *mate* pointed to the same thing as when she used the word *meat*. And you would discover that the referents are different. So they are different words. And that means the *ā* and *ē* sounds are separate phonemes in English; they are not interchangeable. If you substitute one for another, you have changed the word.

Phonemes are speech sounds that distinguish one word from another word. In my city, there is a section named Forest Hills. I have heard some people call it *Far*est Hills, and I have heard others call it *Fawr*est Hills. I could hear the difference in the sounds. Try those pronunciations out loud. Does the change make a difference in the meaning of the words? Is the referent the same? If you directed someone to the place, would he or she go to the right place—no matter which pronunciation you used? Yes. The difference in sound makes no difference in meaning. So the variation is not phonemic; the two *phones* are not different *phonemes*.

In order to master any language, you must learn the phonemes of that language and learn to produce them in the conventional ways. As you have already guessed, however, many phonemes have several different variations. These variations are called *allophones*, a word based on the Greek words for *other* and *sounds*. If you are going to learn a language, then, you must not only learn the basic phonemes, but you must also learn all the variations of each phoneme and when to use which variety.

If you speak American English, you will have five different varieties of the /t/ phoneme, and you will use each of these allophones in a different sound context. Let me prove it to you. Pronounce the words *top, stop, pot, city,* and "*fight* the good fight" aloud. Check to see if the *t* sound in each of these words is exactly the same. The *t* is a stop-plosive speech sound; the air is stopped completely and then exploded in a little puff. But, on the first three words, does the *t* have the same amount of explosion when you pronounce the words? Check it out again. If necessary, put a lit candle about four inches in front of your mouth. The more explosion (the bigger the puff of air on the *t*), the more the candle flame will flicker. Which of the *t*'s had the largest burst of air? That's right. The first one. It should also have been the same if you had said the word *atop*. In both instances, the *t* started a stressed syllable. After an *s*, the *t* has less plosiveness, and at the ends of words and phrases in American English, we often have no explosion at all on plosive sounds such as *t*. There are three different allophones of the *t* already. The fourth allophone of this sound resembles a *d*. It is not a *d*. We can tell the difference between the words *matter* and *madder*, even though the *t* in the middle of *matter* will be a little *d*-ish because, between vowels at the beginning of an unstressed syllable, the vocal folds vibrate somewhat. If that explanation just confused you, ignore it. It is enough for you to know that the *t* in such words as *city, pretty, butter,* and *betting* is a different allophone from the first three we noted. As for the fifth allophone, it occurs before either of the two *th* sounds in English. Usually (on the other four allophones), the *t* phoneme is made with the tongue-tip touching the gum ridge behind the upper teeth. Before either of the *th* sounds, however, the *t* is made with the tongue at the bottom of the upper teeth. Check to see where your tongue goes when you make the *t* in the phrases "no*t* thin" and "righ*t* there." Isn't it on the teeth? That's a fifth variation of the *t* phoneme in American English.

We are not going to analyze all the 42 phonemes of our language to establish that there are such things as allophones. Just examining the one sound *t* should have clarified the allophone concept.

Grammar

Grammar is not the "thou shalt's" and "thou shalt not's" some antediluvian teacher prescribed in elementary school. Such teachers got confused; they were preoccupied with prescribing rules of "what should be" instead of analyzing "what is." To make matters worse, many of the "rules" had no foundation in the actual structure of our language at all.

I was taught that one must not "split an infinitive" or "end a sentence with a preposition." Why not? Because it was a "rule of grammar." My teachers found it difficult *to completely convince* me that a preposition was not a word which I could end a sentence *with.* I obeyed, for fear of failing English, but those "rules" never did make sense to me. Small wonder! They were not derived from the way the English language actually works. They resulted from the attempt to impose the grammar (structure) of other, classical languages (Greek and Latin) onto the presumably inferior English language!

So far I have concentrated on what grammar is not. What, you are asking, *is* it? All languages have regular patterns; those patterns in a language are called its *grammar.* Grammar, then, is a *description* of the structure of a language. It is not a prescription of what the patterns ought to be; it is a description of what the patterns are. Every language has its own patterns. If you want to call those patterns "rules," fine—provided you understand that the "rules" are presently accepted customs and may be changed. They are certainly not like the laws of the Medes and Persians, which, you remember, could never be changed.

My friend, Dr. Dimitri Manouskos, who learned four other languages before learning English, recently said to me, "English is so simple; it has no grammar at all!" Of course, that was a joke. All languages, including English, have grammar; they have regular, predictable patterns. He simply meant that English grammar is much simpler than the grammar of the other languages he knows. The simplicity of our grammar, in my judgment, has helped make English the world language it is today. I have been at many parties with people from many different countries where English was the one language common to all the people present.

In any class in which I refer to English as an easy language, I face students' objections. Remember, however, that I am talking about the language—the *spoken* language. The attempt to represent the language in writing *is* a mess, I agree; our spelling is not phonetic and is very difficult to learn. But the grammar of English is relatively easy. There are far fewer patterns to learn than in most other languages.

Grammar is the study of the patterns used in forming words and sentences in a language. As I noted earlier in this chapter, there are two subdivisions of grammar: the study of patterns for making words, called *morphology,* and the study of patterns for making sentences, called *syntax.*

The reason the study of word formation is called *morphology* is that words are constructed of meaning units called *morphemes.* Individual sounds (phonemes) do not mean anything. When I am teaching phonetics and produce a lone sound for the class, the class often laughs. The sounds by themselves sound funny. They don't mean anything in isolation. They *change* meaning, but they do not *have* meaning. Morphemes, on the other hand, are units that do have meaning.

Morphemes are the building blocks that we put together to form words. You may think of them as roots, prefixes, and suffixes. The word *unthinkable* is made up of three meaning units or building blocks: *un* (which means "not"); *think* (which means "to consider"); and *able* (which means "capable" or "having the capacity"). If something is unthinkable, then, it is "not capable of being considered" or "not able to be considered." There was a root (*think*), a prefix (*un*), and a suffix (*able*). The root is the core of the word; a prefix is put in front of a root; and a suffix is attached after a root.

Morphemes

What is the pattern that the word *unthinkable* is made by? If someone knows that pattern, could they make other words they have never heard?

Indeed they could. All you would need is a verb and the pattern. If you know that *know* is a verb (something that gets done), couldn't you construct the word *unknowable* from this word pattern? Yes, and *unspeakable* too. If I give you any more examples, you may think it *unpardonable!*

A word need not have all three kinds of morphemes. How many morphemes are there in the word *announce?* Yes, there are two syllables (pulses), but you are correct: only one morpheme. What about the word *announcement?* Right. Two: *announce + ment*. A root and a suffix. Or how about *unwed?* Right again. Two: *un + wed*. This time it is a root preceded by a prefix.

A word may have more than one prefix or suffix. I know you are getting tired of this, but let me give you just one example. What is the morphemic pattern of the word *incurably?* How many morphemes are there, and what are they? Be careful. Our spelling may confuse you. Remember that morphemes are spoken units, and our writing system may mislead you. Pronounce the word *incurably*. Now analyze what was put together to make that word: *in* (meaning "not") + *cure* (meaning "to make well") + *able* (meaning "capable") + *ly* (meaning "the way" or "manner"). If one is incurably ill, then, one is sick "in a *way* that is *not capable* of being *made well*." Four morphemes. But there are only three kinds of morphemes. True, but in this word there are two suffixes: *able* and *ly*.

You have to know morphemes (the units themselves) and patterns to be able to construct words. What does the suffix *-er* mean, for example? Well, in the word *teacher*—made out of *teach + er*—what is the meaning of *-er?* Of course, it is one who does something. If you know that morpheme *-er* and the pattern *verb + er*, you can make up words you have never heard of. You could build the words *worker, farmer, consumer, singer, educator, actor,* or *invader*—whether you had ever been taught those specific words or not.

Someone is sure to wonder about *actor* and *educator*. Yes, those words contain the same *-er* as the rest. Morphemes have to do with meaning—not with spelling. An *actor* is one who acts and an *educator* is one who educates. The fact that we spell the words with an *o* instead of an *e* is irrelevant.

How many syllables a word has or how the word is spelled is no guide to its morphemic construction. Compare the words *singer* and *finger,* for example. They look a great deal alike and sound a great deal alike. Both words have two syllables, but the *-er* of *finger* is different from the *-er* of *singer*. *Singer* is made up of two morphemes: *sing + -er,* but the word *finger* is indivisible; *finger* is one morpheme. A singer is one who sings, but a finger is not one who fings!

A morpheme is the smallest language unit that has meaning. But, just as phonemes could have variations called allophones, so morphemes can have variations. Those variations are called *allomorphs*.

To illustrate the concept of allomorphs, let us go back to the pattern: NOT prefix + VERB root + ABLE suffix. If the verb is *bear,* what word will result from that pattern? *Unbearable,* right? But think of what word you will form if the verb is *cure. UNcurable?* No, *INcurable*. What if the verb is *reverse? UNreversible* or *INreversible?* Neither. *IRreversible!* Finally,

Allomorphs

what if the verb is *limit?* Right: *ILlimitable.* All of those prefixes mean "not"; *un-*, *in-*, *ir-*, and *il-* are all variations of the same negative prefix morpheme. They are allomorphs of that one morpheme.

Can you figure out how many allomorphs there are of the plural morpheme in English? What about the past tense morpheme for verbs in English? The answer to both questions is the same. There are three allomorphs of each of those morphemes. Can you figure out what the allomorphs are? You use them all the time without thinking about them, so you had to learn them at one time. Now you are so familiar with them, you take them for granted and pay no attention when you use them.

To construct words, you must know patterns, morphemes, and the allomorphs of those morphemes.

The second subdivision of grammar is *syntax,* the study of sentence formation. The word *syntax* comes from a Greek word that means "to put together in order" or "to draw [soldiers] up in line in battle order." Just as there are patterns for making words out of morphemes, so there are patterns for making sentences out of words. Syntax analyzes those patterns for making sentences in a particular language.

English has specific patterns for sentences. Other languages may have completely different patterns. One sentence pattern in English, for example, is "I like you." In Spanish, however, if you followed the pattern customary in that language, you would say *"Yo te quiero."* (I you like.) Neither pattern is right or wrong; each pattern is customary in that particular language. Obviously, you cannot automatically transfer a pattern from one language to another.

In Spanish, it is customary (it is the accepted pattern) to pile up negative words to make the declaration more intense and strong. One could say, "I don't never say nothing to nobody." In English, on the other hand, such a sentence does not follow the customary (standard, accepted) pattern. We say, "I don't ever say anything to anybody." The idea is the same, but the pattern for putting the words together into a sentence—the syntax—is different.

To construct sentences, you must know syntax—the patterns for making sentences in that language.

Vocabulary

Words are spoken symbols. They stand for ideas. Every language has a collection of words; the total stock of words in a language is its *lexicon*. That name comes from a Greek word for "word."

Each person has a collection of words that he or she knows. That is our vocabulary. I doubtless know more words in my "reading vocabulary" (the words I recognize on paper and can attach meaning to) than I do in my "speaking vocabulary" (the words I use when I transmit messages out loud).

To send and receive messages in a language, you must know the words for things in that language. You must master a basic vocabulary.

So far, we have defined language and languages, and we have looked at the three basic elements of which all languages are composed. We now turn to three other important concepts related to language: dialect, idiolect, and functional varieties.

dialect: variations of a language

Languages, like people, are born, live, change, grow, and sometimes they die. In the fifteen-hundred-year history of English, it has changed radically. It began with the Germanic tribes (Angles, Saxons, and Jutes) who invaded and took control of the British Isles in the fifth century A.D. They brought their forms (dialects) of German with them. In the sixth century, Christian missionaries from Rome arrived. They set up both churches and schools, and they imported the Latin language and its alphabet. The reliance of the Roman Catholic Church on Latin exerted a strong influence on the Old English language. As long as a language is alive and in use, it is dynamic—continuously changing and evolving. By the time William the Conqueror, Duke of Normandy, invaded and conquered the British Isles in 1066, the language had already become quite different from the Germanic dialects of its origin some six hundred years before. William's conquest brought even greater changes to the language. He brought Normans from the continent to settle in Britain. While Latin remained the language of the Roman Catholic Church and its schools, French became the language of the royal court, the court system, and the aristocracy. Under Norman rule, which lasted over two hundred years, French was the language of the upper class—the nobility and businessmen. The masses continued to speak English (we are now in the Middle English period of the language's life), but many French words were incorporated into the English language. When Norman rule ended, the use of French declined, but French had made an indelible mark on the English language.

By about 1500, there had occurred a rather drastic change in the pronunciation of words in English, mostly involving the vowel sounds in the words. The words sounded much more like the way we pronounce them today than they had in the previous period. The Modern English period had begun.

Throughout the history of our language, there have been variations of the current language spoken by various groups. No matter what period of time one examines, not all speakers of a language will talk alike. There will be variations of the language spoken by groups of people who associate together. Often these groups associate because they live in the same region of the country. In the Middle English period, for example, there were four principal regional varieties of the language in the British Isles.

A variation of a language spoken by some group of people is called a *dialect.* The group may be regional or social, but for some reason the group members interact and tend to speak the language in the same way. Dialects differ enough from each other to be noticeable; the differences are not great enough to call them different languages.

The distinction between a different dialect and a different language is not absolute; indeed, it is not always even clear. Sometimes the distinction is based as much on political and national considerations as on more linguistic and scientific ones.

I have often been told that the difference between a different language and a different dialect has to do with understanding. If a receiver notices the linguistic differences but still understands the speaker, the difference is one of dialect; if, on the other hand, the linguistic differences are so great that they prevent the receiver from understanding the speaker, they are speaking different languages. This distinction has some shortcomings. If a Dane who speaks only Danish talks to a Swede who speaks only Swedish, will the Swedish person understand what is said? Probably. And the Swede could reply in Swedish, which the Dane would probably understand. But, with much passion and pride, both would insist they were speaking separate and distinct languages. After all, they would tell you, citizens of Denmark speak Danish, and citizens of Sweden speak Swedish! Of course! But the "languages" of Danish and Swedish may be separated less by sounds, grammar, and vocabulary than by national boundaries.

In spite of such problems of definition, we do know what dialects are. They are variations of a language—whatever the language is.

Dialects vary in the same three ways that languages vary: (1) in sounds, (2) in grammar, and (3) in vocabulary. That is, if you speak a different dialect of American English from the one I speak, you may (1) use different sounds in words from the ones I use, (2) use different grammatical patterns from the ones I use, and (3) use different words for the same things.

Read the following word pairs, and listen to see how you pronounce the words:

oar	or
hoarse	horse
four	for
wore	war

Did the word in the right-hand column sound different from the one in the left-hand column, or did you pronounce them alike? If you are from the South, you probably make a distinction between the two words in each pair. The words in the left-hand column would be pronounced with ō, while the words on the right would be pronounced with ô. If you are from the North, however, you probably pronounce both words with the ô vowel. That dialectal difference, of course, is a *sound* difference.

If, in the same classroom, a teacher turns to one student and snaps, "What did you say?" eliciting the response from a student, "I didn't say nothing," and then the teacher turns to another student and demands, "What did you say?" to which the student replies, "I didn't say anything" or "I said absolutely nothing," what dialectal difference did you note? And the difference *is* dialectal! The dialect group is socioeconomic this time instead of a reginal group, but the differences are between groups of speakers of the language. The dialectal difference between "I didn't say nothing" and "I didn't say anything" (or "I said absolutely nothing") is a *grammatical* difference.

Recently a friend of mine called and said he wanted to borrow something to cook in. He said, "I think you Southerners call it a 'skillet.'" Before I told him he could borrow the object, I asked what he would call the same thing. "It's a frying pan," he said. Well, I call it that *too*, but I think *skillet* is a perfectly clear word. At least it is clear to me!

Some students of mine recently were discussing the strange names other people in various parts of the country call things. "At a ball game down South," one student related, "I asked at the concession stand for a 'frank.' The lady seemed confused, so I pointed. And she said, 'Oh, you want a *hot dog!*'"

What do you call drinks like Pepsi, Coke, Seven-Up, and Dr. Pepper? It probably depends on what dialect of American English you speak. If you are a New Yorker, you call them *sodas*. If you are a Southerner, you call them *soft drinks* (in contrast with hard liquor, I suppose). You may call them *tonic* or *pop*. These dialectal differences are *vocabulary* differences.

People who live, work, and socialize together develop common customs, including language customs. These customs, peculiar to the group, are the basis of a language's dialects. Differences in dialect may cause problems, but since the communicators speak the same language, they should be able to work those problems out.

There is one problem related to dialectal differences that we must face. Not all dialects of a language have the same status or prestige. Yes, one dialect is just as good as another, if it works to accomplish the purposes of the speaker and listener. But if your listener has a negative (or condescending) attitude toward the dialect you speak, you may have difficulty accomplishing your purpose. The dialectal difference may affect that listener's response to the messages you attempt to send.

There is a dialect of American English that is accorded more status or prestige than the other dialects. This dialect gets more respect than other dialects, not because it is linguistically superior in any way, but because it is spoken by the people with the greatest status and prestige in American society. This dialect is spoken by the upper-middle and upper classes—the people in power. For that reason, it has been called the *business and professional dialect.* More recently, it has been called the *career dialect* or *career speech.* Its most common name is the *standard* or *status dialect.*

Having a prestige dialect is not unique to American English, of course. In almost every country I have visited, native speakers of a language have distinguished between a respected variety (dialect) of their language and other, less respected (and often ridiculed) dialects of that same language.

In American English, "standard" speech patterns, like good manners in general, are not prescribed by law or decreed by any official authority. Rather, they consist of socially accepted (and respected) customs, established by the social leaders of our communities. These social leaders set the styles and fashions for most of our practices; what they do sets up the criteria for what is in "good taste."

As I said earlier, there is nothing in the status dialect itself—the sounds, grammatical patterns, or words used in it—that makes it better than any other dialect of American English. If the people in power spoke a different way, that way would be "standard."

Whether the status dialect is *better* than other dialects is really beside the point. This is the dialect spoken by those in status positions, and this is the dialect that is accorded the most respect. Too, those people who can speak the status dialect are given more respect than those who cannot. I grant that, in an ideal world, that might not be true. But this is *not* an ideal world, and it *is* true. We must deal with reality. And anyone who attempts to communicate in American English must face that reality because it may affect the outcome of communication transactions.

The status dialect (or standard dialect, if you prefer) is the dialect used—and expected—in education, business, and the professions. Although there are some regional modifications of that dialect (indeed, some writers believe we have standard dialects rather than a standard dialect), those regional variations are quite minor. And, thanks to the mass media of communication in this country, those minor differences are diminishing. If one speaks the status dialect, one can move anywhere in the country and be recognized as a speaker of standard American English.

We will not dwell on the subject, but nonstandard dialects are those that differ noticeably from the standard dialect. But who would notice? Speakers of the standard dialect—and some speakers of nonstandard dialects as well! What would they pay attention to? Major differences in the three elements of a language: sounds, grammar, and vocabulary.

Speakers of standard American English would notice if someone complained "Dis charge is unfair" for "This charge is unfair." They certainly would note the differences if someone said "oaf" for "oath," "deaf" for "death," "clove" for "clothe," "axed" for "asked," "oncet" for "once," "git" for "get," "purty" for "pretty," "once" for "ones," "loss" for "laws," "Ben" for "bend," or "athalete" for "athlete." These *sound* differences would be recognized anywhere in the United States as nonstandard.

We have already noted differences between the standard dialect and nonstandard dialects in terms of grammar. "I ain't got none" would not be viewed as customary in the status dialect anywhere in the United States; it is a *grammatical* difference that is nonstandard.

There are vocabulary differences, too, between the status dialect and nonstandard dialects of our language. The status dialect has held firm on some word taboos that are ignored in some nonstandard dialects of American English. Many of the taboo words are very old, and everybody knows them. But they are simply not uttered by "cultivated, educated speakers"—at least in polite society! (See pp. 225–226.) Any speaker of the standard dialect will notice if someone violates these word, or *vocabulary,* taboos.

As I said earlier, every language that is still in use is constantly changing. Like all social customs, languages change over a period of time. I can tell you what is "standard" today, but I cannot tell you with certainty what will be standard or nonstandard fifty or one hundred years from now. You and I will just have to wait and see!

idiolects: individual variations

Everyone who speaks a language speaks a dialect (regional or social variety) of that language. But each person also has distinctive speech patterns all his or her own. Those individual varieties are called *idiolects.* Although this word may seem new to you, you have doubtless seen *idio-* before. Think of the word *idio*syncrasies. Idiosyncrasies are traits, habits, mannerisms, or foibles characteristic of one person. This *idio-* comes from a Greek word meaning "one's own" or "one's self." An *idiolect,* then, is one person's own individual variety of a language.

Each of us speaks the way we do because of the many different influences that have been exerted upon us. Each of us puts together those elements of language in a unique and personal way. In some ways, each of us speaks a distinctive version of the language: his or her idiolect.

functional varieties

We speak in many different kinds of situations, and we adapt our speaking styles to the social situation we are in. Even a person who always speaks in the standard dialect of the language will not always speak in exactly the same way. The speech style will be adjusted to fit the formality or informality of the situation and to fit his or her relationship to the other communicators.

One does not speak the same way in the classroom as he or she does with close friends at a party. If you are giving a public speech at a formal occasion, you will use a different style from the one you use with your family around the dinner table. And the speaking style you use in a job interview will probably differ from both the public-speaking variety and the dinner-at-home variety.

These variations in degree of formality are called *functional varieties.* One varies his or her speech with the function to be served or the situation encountered. These varieties exist *within* a dialect.

Please keep in mind that *formal* is not a synonym for *standard* and *informal* is not just another word for *nonstandard.* A person who always speaks in the standard or status dialect of American English will use various degrees of formality within that dialect, depending on the situation.

"Cultivated, educated speakers" vary their speaking styles between two extremes: careful, precise, formal forms and casual, simple, informal forms. The speaker adapts to the situation: public, formal, and impersonal at one extreme and private, informal, and intimate at the other. A specific situation may fall somewhere in between the two extremes; in that case, one chooses a functional variety that falls in between the two extremes as well.

Some writers follow Martin Joos's classification system for these functional varieties. In his book *The Five Clocks,* Joos lists five "styles of communicating": frozen, formal, consultative, casual, and intimate. I am not certain the categories are that discreet or clear-cut. Rather, I think it better to picture a very flexible continuum stretched between two extremes. The general contrast between the most formal variety and the least formal variety is stated by King and DiMichael:

> The most formal variety (within the Standard Dialect) is marked by careful control: precision in the production of sounds, care in the construction of sentences (few, if any contractions such as I'll or can't, for example), and caution in the choice of words (avoiding slang and colloquial expressions). When using this variety, a speaker also demonstrates greater control of his or her voice—avoiding extremes of pitch, loudness, rate, and quality.
>
> The most informal variety (within the Standard Dialect) is casual and relaxed. Although articulation of the sounds is clear, it is less perniciously precise than in the most formal variety; sentence structure includes contractions and more informal, popular constructions (even Winston Churchill said, "It's me," on informal occasions); and, although outright taboo words are still avoided, slang and colloquial expressions are included. (In the formal variety, you would call him your "fiancé," but in the informal variety, you might refer to him as "the guy I'm going with"). When using this informal variety, a speaker will be more relaxed and "natural" in the use of his or her voice— letting the variations in pitch, volume, rate, and quality express attitudes and emotions more openly.[1]

One learns not only a particular dialect of a language; one also learns several varieties of that dialect—varieties based on the degree of formality or informality. If one wishes to speak the status dialect of American English all the time, for example, one must learn which informal varieties

[1] Robert G. King and Eleanor M. DiMichael, *Articulation and Voice: Improving Oral Communication* (New York: Macmillan, 1978), pp. 33–34.

210

FUNDAMENTALS OF
HUMAN
COMMUNICATION

lie within that dialect and which ones *are* nonstandard. And if one wishes to adapt to his or her environment sensibly and use communication appropriate for that environment, one must be able to select the functional variety that fits that situation.

I have attempted, in this chapter, to give you some inkling of what languages are and how they work. I provided a definition of a language and explained its terms; examined the three basic elements of which all languages are composed; and discussed three kinds of variations related to language: dialect, idiolect, and functional varieties. For the most part, I have used examples and illustrations from American English to help clarify the concepts. I hope I have been able to help you understand better the most sophisticated tool we human beings have made: language!

SUGGESTIONS FOR FURTHER READING

BARATZ, JOAN C., "Language in the Economically Disadvantaged Child," *ASHA*, **10** (1968), pp. 143–145.

BARBER, CHARLES L., *The Story of Speech and Language* (New York: Crowell, 1964).

BENTLEY, R. H., and S. D. CRAWFORD, *Black Language Reader* (Glenview, Ill.: Scott, Foresman, 1973).

CLARK, VIRGINIA P., PAUL A. ESCHOLZ, and ALFRED F. ROSA, eds., *Language: Introductory Readings* (New York: St. Martin's, 1972).

FROMKIN, V., and R. RODMAN, *An Introduction to Language* (New York: Holt, 1974).

GLEASON, H. A., *An Introduction to Descriptive Linguistics*, rev. ed. (New York: Holt, 1961).

HALL, ROBERT A., JR., *Linguistics and Your Language*, 2nd ed. (Garden City, N.Y.: Anchor Books, Doubleday, 1960).

HILL, A. A., *Introduction to Linguistic Structures: From Sound to Sentence in English* (New York: Harcourt Brace, 1958).

KENYON, JOHN S., "Cultural Levels and Functional Varieties of English," *Classics in Semantics*, Donald E. Hayden and E. P. Alworth, eds. (New York: Philosophical Library, 1965).

LABOV, WILLIAM, "The Logic of Nonstandard English," *Language and Poverty*, Frederick Williams, ed. (Chicago: Markham, 1970).

LABOV, WILLIAM, "The Study of Nonstandard English," *Language: Introductory Readings*, Virginia P. Clark, Paul A. Escholz, and Alfred F. Rosa, eds. (New York: St. Martin's, 1972).

LABOV, WILLIAM, "Academic Ignorance and Black Intelligence," *Atlantic Magazine*, June 1972, pp. 59–67.

LABOV, WILLIAM, *Sociolinguistic Patterns* (Philadelphia: University of Pennsylvania Press, 1972).

LAIRD, CHARLTON, and ROBERT M. GORRELL, *English as Language: Backgrounds, Development, Usage* (New York: Harcourt Brace, 1961).

PEI, MARIO, *The Story of Language*, rev. ed. (Philadelphia: Lippincott, 1965).

SALUS, PETER H., *Linguistics* (Indianapolis: Bobbs-Merrill, 1969).

SAPIR, EDWARD, *Language: An Introduction to the Study of Speech* (New York: Harvest Books, Harcourt Brace, 1949).

WILLIAMS, FREDERICK, *Language and Speech* (Englewood Cliffs, N.J.: Prentice-Hall, 1972).

WISE, CLAUDE M., *Applied Phonetics* (Englewood Cliffs, N.J.: Prentice-Hall, 1957).

WISE, CLAUDE M., *Introduction to Phonetics* (Englewood Cliffs, N.J.: Prentice-Hall, 1958).

WOLFRAM, WALT, and RALPH FASOLD, *The Study of Social Dialects in American English* (Englewood Cliffs, N.J.: Prentice-Hall, 1974).

8
STYLE IN LANGUAGE: CHOOSING WORDS

general goal:

To learn how a speaker's language choices may affect communication.

specific objectives:

After completing this unit, you should understand:
What style in language is.
The basic principles of effective style.
The most common problems related to word choice.

WHEN SOMEBODY SAYS to you, "Baby, I like your style!" they're saying they like the way you do something—the way you dress, the way you carry yourself, the way you perform, the way you talk. That's what style is—the way of doing something that is especially a person's own. We've all got style. And each of us has his or her own style. If that person is talking about your style in clothes, the person likes the items of clothing you pick out to wear and the way you combine the various items of clothing into an outfit. If the person is talking about your style of speech, he or she probably means the words you pick out to express yourself and the way you put those words together into sentences. At least that is what *I* am talking about in this chapter on style in language.

Any style depends on choices. There are lots of kinds of clothes to choose from when you put together a wardrobe. There are certainly lots of words in the English language to choose from when you want to express an idea. The words you pick out, from all the options open to you, to say what you want to say is your style.

some basic principles for picking words

Choosing words, like choosing clothes or choosing houses or choosing cars, is a very personal thing. Your choice of words will probably be based on how you feel, your image of yourself, the idea you want to express, and what you think is appropriate for the intended receiver and the situation. Nobody can tell you what the "right" choices are. I am certainly not going to try! But each time you try to symbolize an idea with words, you will try to find a style that suits the message and the situation. You will probably have more than one style, because the style must be tailored (like clothing again) to the occasion. Although I cannot give you absolute rules for picking words, I can give a few general principles to consider when choosing words. In general, it is better to pick words that are

CLEAR

CONCRETE

CURRENT

CONCISE

COLORFUL

CAUTIOUS

215

Clear

Common sense tells you to pick words that the person on the receiving end of your message can understand. Of course, you have to know something about that person or those people and have an idea of the range of their vocabulary if you are going to pick words that will be clear to them. If I were going to discuss speech therapy techniques for laryngetomized patients with a group of physicians, I would doubtless use different words than I would use with a group of lay relatives of the patients. The content, or information, might well be exactly the same, but the words—the style—would be different. The technical vocabulary, quite familiar to the physicians, would not be clear to the patients' families. Remember that something is clear if it is known. And also remember that just because a term is clear to the message-producer does not necessarily mean it is clear to the message-receiver! Pick words that are clear—familiar and understandable—to your receiver(s).

Concrete

If at all possible, pick words that are exact, specific, precise. Words stake out boundaries, so pick words that are limited to exactly what you mean. Don't pick a broad word if you can find a narrower one. Why say "some guy" when you can name "Seymour Kleerly"? Why say "gun" when "pistol" is more accurate? Why say "pistol" when "44-caliber revolver" is more specific? Why say "not too much longer" if "ten minutes longer" more specifically identifies what you are talking about? Nail down what, where, when, why, who, how much; in fact, pin down every idea you can with a specific, exact word. Concrete is solid, something you can get hold of—the kind of words to choose whenever possible.

Concise

Be economical with your words. Say what you mean in as few words as possible. "Brevity is the soul of wit"—and the heart of good style. Make your point; don't hide it under a mountain of words. Make your style muscular; chop out the fat.

The touchstone of elegant style is not found by piling polysyllabic words atop each other in superfluously padded sentences! In brief, do not try to mimic the style of Howard Cosell—who never clarifies, if he can elucidate; who never predicts if he can offer a modest prognostication; and who never evades or lies, though he may present an exercise in circumlocution and prevarication. Enough? The point is: Get to the point. Quickly. Simply. That's being concise.

Colorful

Pick words that are interesting, lively, fresh, stimulating. Choose words that grab the receiver's attention and rivet that attention on your idea. Colorful words stir the receiver's imagination, reminding him or her of how something looks, sounds, feels, tastes, or smells. "He staggered into the room," or "he shuffled," or "he stumbled," or "he strode," or "he swaggered" paints a more striking picture for the listener than "He came into the room." General Douglas MacArthur certainly had a colorful style. When he was about to disembark and wade ashore, he did not say, "My men think I am infallible, but I am not." Instead, he commented, "My men are about to discover I cannot walk on water."

Don't rely on the old tried and true, trite phrases that each and every one of the other people in this old world uses day in and day out, time and time again, and has used from time immemorial! Instead, look for the striking words that have not been rubbed smooth from overwork.

Current

Language is constantly changing because life is constantly changing. Words drop out of usage as other words come into use. When picking out words, be sure you are up to date. If thou dost discern my meaning.

Cautious

We choose words with our receivers in mind. Remember that some receivers have strong feelings about certain words. They just don't want to hear words they consider "profane," "obscene," "vulgar," "taboo," "dirty." Whether we agree with those designations or not, we should be cautious about using such words—not only in consideration of the feelings and attitudes of our listeners, but also because their reactions to the words may short-circuit their responses to our message. When we send any message, we are trying to get a particular response. If expressing my idea in particular words will sidetrack the listener from the idea and get a reaction (to the words) that I do not want, why use those words?

Back in the sixties (it seems so long ago now), I was participating in a march down Broadway in New York City. Our message was: *End this illegal and immoral war!* At the time, that message was not very popular, and we were seeking to enlist more support for our position. It was lunch hour, and the sidewalks were filled with onlookers, mostly middle-class workers from the stores and offices along our route of march. Behind me, a group of students began to chant, "One, two, three, four; we don't want your f—ing war" over and over again.[1] I looked out at the faces of those solid, middle-class citizens as we walked past. If I read their reactions correctly, they heard little or nothing about the war. What they heard was one taboo word, and that turned them off. The use of that word confirmed what they had thought about those antiwar hippies—foul-mouthed, foul-minded, low-valued, and *wrong!* Maybe, just *maybe*, if the students had

---

[1] In an effort to avoid offending people and to be consistent with the principle being discussed here, we are not printing the full taboo word.

been more cautious in their choice of language, we would have had a better chance of getting our message heard and considered. And after all, that was our real purpose, wasn't it?

some warnings on picking words

Nobody can tell you exactly the right word to choose, and nobody can tell you exactly what words *not* to choose. But there are some kinds of words you should be careful about. Perhaps you will want to use some of these kinds of words for effect or because they suit your particular purpose or receiver(s), but generally you should be wary of using them:

SLANG

JARGON

CLICHÉS

OUT-OF-DATE WORDS

GOBBLEDYGOOK   **(VERBOSITY)**

TABOO WORDS

AMBIGUITIES

VAGUE GENERALITIES

Slang

Slang is informal, in-group language. It is designed to be fully understood only by the "initiated." It separates "us" from "them." Slang words are usually short, forceful, lively, vivid, and maybe even brash. Although some slang words stay in fashion for a long time and some actually become standard usage, most slang words are fads—very popular in the group for a while and then discarded in favor of other words. They get discarded when they can no longer serve their function as in-group language. Once a group hears its special, lively style used by just anybody—by outsiders—then the group doesn't want it anymore. Remember when it was "cool" to be "hep"? Probably not. That was before your time! Now it is "cool" to be "hip." Who knows how long it will be good to be "bad"? A generation ago, you would have worked for "dough"; now you work for "bread"; and your children will probably have a different slang term for it (maybe "crumbs") when they come along.

Notice that slang usually uses ordinary words in an un-ordinary way. Think of some of the common slang terms used today. "Hip" has nothing to do with a part of the body; "short" has nothing to do with height; "grass" doesn't need cutting; "hogs" are found on streets instead of farms; and one can "dig it" without a shovel or a hoe.

One danger with using slang is that your listener may not be among the initiated; he or she may not be "with it." If you ask your father to help you fix your "short," you may get confused looks and no help. If you really want him to help, you'd better ask for help on the car—a once-slang word he is sure to know.

Another danger is that slang words are often overused while they are in fashion. "Hey, man, what's happening?" is not the most original way to say hello nowadays. And some people describe everything and everybody as "beautiful." Slang words may add life and forcefulness to your speech, but "they can also be a drag, man!"

In the anonymous poem, "A Verse for Those Over Thirty," the author commented (as an outsider) on the slang of contemporary young people. Here's the not-to-be-taken-seriously lament:

> *Remember when hippie meant big in the hips*
> *And a trip involved travel in cars, planes or ships?*
> *When pot was a vessel for cooking things in*
> *And hooked is what grandmother's rugs might have been?*
>
> *When fix was a verb meaning mend or repair*
> *And be-in meant simply existing somewhere?*
> *When neat meant well-organized, tidy and clean*
> *And grass was a ground cover, usually green?*
>
> *When lights and not people were turned on and off*
> *And the pill was intended to help cure a cough?*
> *When groovy meant furrowed, with channels and hollows,*
> *And birds were winged creatures like robins and swallows?*
>
> *When fuzz was a substance, all fluffy like lint*
> *And bread came from bakeries, not from the Mint?*
> *When a roll was a bun and a rock was a stone*
> *And hung-up was something you did to the phone?*
>
> *When chicken meant poultry and bag was a sack*
> *And junk was just cast-offs and old bric-a-brac?*
> *When cat was a feline, a kitten grown up,*
> *And tea was a liquid you drank from a cup?*
>
> *When swinger was someone who swung in a swing*
> *And pad was a sort of a cushiony thing?*
> *When way-out meant distant and far, far away,*
> *And a man couldn't sue you for calling him "gay"?*
>
> *Words once so sensible, sober and serious*
> *Are making the scene, man, like psycho-delirious.*
> *It's groovy, dad, groovy—but English it's not.*
> *Methinks that the language is going to pot!*
>
> —Anonymous

I first saw a copy of this poem in the *International Herald Tribune* of August 21-22, 1971. How many of the slang words used in this poem are no longer still in general use? Well, I told you slang words were discarded quickly!

Jargon

Slang is social in-group language; jargon is professional in-group language. Every kind of job or profession has its own "shop talk." That technical vocabulary is called *jargon*. Unlike slang, which is usually short-lived, jargon is more stable and enduring, because it serves a useful, but not exclusionary purpose. People in particular occupations develop their own spoken shorthand, using shortened words or abbreviations in place of complicated, complete words or phrases. Your teacher in this class may ask a technician to record you on a VTR; the waitress may order a BLT for you at lunch; and if you become ill, you may be taken from the hospital ER to the OR and given an IV!!

Jargon is useful, of course, for people inside the same trade or profession. But we run into problems when we use it (usually without thinking about it) with people who are not from our profession. Shop talk should be reserved for shop people; everybody else will probably need a complete translation—not just the shorthand.

Judge Justin C. Ravitz of the Detroit Recorder's Court refuses to speak in Legalese—the "silly jargon" of lawyers and judges—in his courtroom when he is talking to lay persons. When he explains to a defendant his or her rights, the young judge uses everyday, conversational American English. "Do you think if you went to trial you'd have to testify?" he will ask a defendant. Often the defendant says he or she doesn't know, and the judge will say, "Well, I'm telling you you don't." He will then explain: "You are presumed to be innocent, and you could look over at the prosecutor and say, 'You brought me in here, and you have to prove me guilty. I don't have to do a thing.' And if you didn't testify, it couldn't be held against you. But you can testify if you want to. Do you understand that?" Judge Ravitz knows the legal jargon, but he uses it only when talking to fellow members of the legal profession. A judicious decision!

Clichés

Clichés, as you know, are old, worn-out words and phrases that have lost their punch from overuse. Unlike slang words, which seem to flourish briefly and then disappear, clichés have the unwelcome ability to endure. Though overworked, they refuse to die. The word *nice* stubbornly refuses to give up its place in the language, though *each and every time* I hear it, I urge the speaker to *avoid it like the plague—to no avail, sad to say.*

When we speak (and when we write), we want to get beyond clichés. It is not easy. *In the first place,* I learned *early on* that we human beings are likely to be lazy *from time to time,* and clichés are an easy substitute for original thought. If you are tempted to use clichés, you should *buckle down and work harder.* (I know you would not want me to *pull my punches* with you!) And though you may not be able to escape clichés completely, *there's no harm in trying* and remember, *nothing ventured, nothing gained.*

Commencement speakers, in overwhelming numbers, seem to be addicted to the cliché. Here is an example of such an address, attributed to Dr. U. R. Gross:

> My fellow graduates of this glorious old school and fellow-travelers on the road of life, it is indeed a great pleasure and privilege for me to be here today to address you on this auspicious occasion. As I look down into your happy and smiling young faces, I feel confidence in the future of this great land of ours. In the world of today, there are problems all over this old world, but in my heart I know that you—the citizens of tomorrow, the youth of today—will face those problems and will move onward and upward in mankind's struggle to make this a better place in which to live.
>
> We of the older generation have faced these problems too. We have tried to lay a foundation, so you young people could build on it. We have tried to put into your hands the tools with which to build. And the greatest tool is education. We have been involved in the great struggle against the problems of poverty, and war, and pollution. But soon we must turn the battle over to you. We have only started to fight. You must take up the weapons we have left on the battlefield and fight valiantly on. We have taken the first steps in the march toward victory over these obstacles; you—tomorrow's leaders—must continue the advance.
>
> Each and every one of you must decide what path he or she will take. Life is no bed of roses. Nor is it a bowl of cherries! It is a game to be played—and played to win! We pass the ball to you, and you will be judged on how you catch and run with it. Remember, you can't expect George to do it. You have to carry the ball yourself. And as you play the game of life, stick to the rules of the game. Play fair. Play square. But play hard!
>
> Today is not the end of your education. It is, as the program so aptly says, a commencement. Today you commence your adult responsibilities. And I just want to leave you with this final inspiring word: You can't be a spectator in the great game of life. You've got to get down there on the field and fight for what's right and decent and good. As the old song says, "It's a Long Way to Tipperary!"

Out-of-Date Words

Words come and go in the language. If you went around talking as people did in Shakespeare's time, you would certainly be noticed and you might or might not be understood. In his day, *prevent* didn't mean "stop"; it meant "to go before, to precede." And imagine saying, "Dost thou know me?" to someone you haven't seen for a long time. Things have changed in the last four hundred years, the language along with everything else.

A language is constantly changing. Some words that were commonly used fifty or even twenty years ago would seem strange to our ears now. People today don't *fetch* anything very often, they don't sit in the *parlor*, and though they still worry a lot, they don't *fret* much. Would any of your friends understand you if you used the word *doughboy* to mean "soldier?"

Gobbledygook

Did you ever notice anyone laying down a smokescreen of words? Words can be used to impress, confuse, and bewilder; they can hide ideas as well as reveal them. Gobbledygook (piling up words on top of words for their own sake—mere verbosity) *seems* to say something, but when you blow the fog away to find the meaning, there is little or nothing left. Gobbledygook is a thick, confusing, billowing cloud of words—"full of sound and fury, signifying nothing!"

It is not really as difficult as it seems to speak good gobbledygook. Just follow these four simple rules:

1. Pick out the biggest words you can find—the more syllables the better.
2. Pick out the most abstract words you can find—the more obscure and esoteric the better.
3. Use as many words as possible to express an idea—even if only one word would be enough.
4. Put all these words together in long, complicated sentences.

The word *gobbledygook* itself was coined by Congressman Maury Maverick of Texas to refer to the extra verbiage used by government bureaucrats in their reports and correspondence. The word is now used to refer to long-winded and pretentious style in general.

Many people who speak gobbledygook are laboring under the delusion that bigger words carry heavier meanings and longer, more involved sentences are bound to be more profound. Some speak gobbledygook, of course, without such delusions; sometimes one must say something even when he or she doesn't want to communicate anything. In such instances, a clever person may resort to gobbledygook. (I am not mentioning this fact so you will use this device, but so you will be aware of it! You *know* I would never advise you to use speech communication to confuse your listener(s) or to evade difficult questions or to avoid taking stands. But you certainly should be aware that some people *do* use gobbledygook for those very purposes.)

At a press briefing on March 24, 1973, a reporter asked Ronald Ziegler, the President's press secretary, whether John W. Dean, the President's personal counsel, had called L. Patrick Gray, nominee to be head of the FBI, to ask him to change his testimony offered to a Senate committee. Mr. Ziegler "replied":

> The statement that Mr. Dean called Mr. Gray is absolutely correct. And I suppose I would do the same thing if it was suggested—that—well, I suppose any individual would make a phone call such as that if it had been indicated that the individual, as the exchange stated, probably lied for the purpose of making sure that those who were involved in that discussion, as discussion which resulted, of course, in extensive reports of that—and I am not being critical of that—said that Mr. Dean probably lied.

Now, did Mr. Ziegler say that Mr. Dean did or did not call Mr. Gray and ask him to change his testimony? Gobbledygook. In fact, the Committee on Public Doublespeak of the National Council of the Teachers of English gave its first annual Doublespeak Award to Mr. Ziegler in November 1974 for this "statement" about the safeguarding of the Watergate tapes:

I would feel that most of the conversations that took place in those areas of the White House that did have the recording system would, in almost their entirety, be in existence, but the special prosecutor, the court, and, I think, the American people are sufficiently familiar with the recording system to know where the recording devices existed and to know the situation in terms of the recording process, but I feel, although the process has not been undertaken yet in preparation of the material to abide by the court decision, really, what the answer to that question is.

Gobbledygook is certainly not limited to politicians or their spokespersons. Thomas H. Middleton reported in the *Saturday Review* of April 19, 1975, that Dr. Lois DeBakey, professor of scientific communications at Baylor College of Medicine, is attempting to immunize future physicians against gobbledygook. But, she confesses, "Physicians . . . usually favor *cholelithiasis* over *gallstones, pyrexia* over *fever, deglutition* over *swallowing.* . . . A patient will probably react differently if told he must be treated for *cephalalgia* than if informed that he will be given something to relieve his *headache.* (He may, however, be unwilling to pay a large fee for medication for the simple headache.)" The clear implication is that services cloaked in big words are worth more than the same services wrapped in everyday words. Dr. DeBakey will have a difficult time forcing physicians to give up gobbledygook if it really impresses their patients and fattens their purses and wallets.

Lawyers, banks, and insurance companies have used gobbledygook successfully for years. Only recently has there been a real trend away from the gibberish. In fact, New York State has passed a law requiring that many legal documents (such as loan forms) be written in clear, direct, everyday American English.

I am sorry to have to admit that professors are often also guilty of using gobbledygook. The folks back in my home state know that muddy water is not always deep, but some professors seem to have confused muddiness with depth anyway. One of the Doublespeak Award recipients in 1974 was Professor Donald Jay Willower, professor of education at Pennsylvania State University. He won for the following "analysis":

> Yet, the most basic problems that arise in connection with knowledge utilization may be those that stem from the social and organizational character of educational institutions. A few university adaptations already have been highlighted. Public schools display a myriad of normative and other regulatory structures that promote predictability, as well as a host of adaptive mechanisms that reduce external uncertainties.

Thomas H. Middleton, in the *Saturday Review* of May 3, 1975, passed along this masterpiece by an anonymous instructor of sociology at UCLA. He was never able to make sense of it. Can you?

> In doing sociology, lay and professional, every reference to the "real world," even where the reference is to physical or biological events, is a reference to the organized activities of everyday life. Thereby, in contrast versions of Durkheim that teach that the objective reality of social facts is sociology's

fundamental principle, the lesson is taken instead, and used as a study policy, that the objective reality of social facts *as* an ongoing accomplishment of the concerted activities of daily life, with the ordinary, artful ways of that accomplishment being by members known, used, and taken for granted, is, for members doing sociology, a fundamental phenomenon. Because, and in the ways it is practical sociology's fundamental phenomenon, it is the prevailing topic for ethnomethodological study.

I hope you agreed with Middleton. Recent research indicates that many "educated" people cannot see through gobbledygook and are taken in by it. Psychologist Phil Reidda reported his discouraging findings in *Human Behavior*. In a group of graduate courses in psychology, students were given a 350-word paper written in pseudopsychological style, but really meaningless. The students were asked to read the paper and write a critique either defending or attacking the incomprehensible paper. Of the 29 students given the assignment, only six admitted they could make no sense of the nonsense. The other 23 wrote the assigned papers and commented at length on the paper's "major points." They were unable to admit that they could not understand gobbledygook if a professor gave it to them and seemed to expect them to understand it! But, as St. Paul once said, "I believe better things of you!"

Actually, since anyone can develop the periphrastic arts (if properly instructed in the circumlocution formulation process, of course), anyone ought to be able to see through it. To discover how easy it is to generate absolutely first-class gobbledygook, you could use the following Gobbledygook Generator:

instant gobbledygook generator

Select one term each from Columns A, B, and C. You may combine these terms by selecting a numbered term from each column. For example, the sequence 10-4-7 gives "Programmed Implementation Module." All the possible combinations make about the same amount of sense.

	A	B	C
1	Subliminal	Communication	Subsystems
2	Behavioral	Interorganization	Proclivities
3	Cognitive	Curricular	Assessment
4	Affective	Implementation	Evaluation
5	Intrapersonal	Participation	Considerations
6	Hyperactive	Examination	Resources
7	Interdisciplinary	Simulation	Module
8	Interstellar	Stimulation	Validation
9	Multidimensional	Innovation	Infrastructure
10	Programmed	Research	Objectives

Every group has its own standards; every group has its own set of taboos. Taboos are forbidden behaviors. Just as there are acts that are no-nos, so there are words that are no-nos also. Like all norms, taboos are relative (hold true) to the cultural group, and they vary from group to group.

The middle class in the United States sets the prevailing fashions (styles), and it is their taboos that are of most interest and importance to us. The middle-class usage makes a dialect "standard." The words that are taboo in "standard" American English are often divided into profane words and obscene words. Profane words are those that treat "holy" or "sacred" things irreverently. To invoke the name of God in a curse is an example. Obscene words are those, according to the *Random House Dictionary,* that are "offensive to modesty and decency." A rather vague standard, as the courts have learned. Generally, the "obscene" words are Anglo-Saxon words dealing with the sexual act or bodily parts or functions. Latin-root words for the same acts, parts, or functions are not taboo. In "polite society," you can say *intercourse* or *fornicate, defecate, anus,* or *urinate* without violating the verbal taboos, but their simpler Anglo-Saxon synonyms are "offensive to modesty and decency!"

Lenny Bruce, a social critic who performed as a night-club comic in the 1950s and 1960s, talked about taboos in American English, ridiculed them, and violated them. He was harrassed, arrested, and prosecuted for "obscenity." Although he was never ultimately convicted, his ordeals bankrupted and destroyed him. More recently, comedian George Carlin was arrested for saying "dirty words" in a public monologue. Ironically, Carlin's monologue is a brief lecture on taboo words (I play the recording for my classes) called "Seven Words You Can Never Say on Television."[2]

In a sense, taboo words may be thought of as *magic* words. They are residues of belief in witchcraft, when words were thought to have power to curse and bless, to conjure up spirits and dare the gods. We still use the taboo words that way. When fate has been unkind to us, when something has gone wrong, we may be tempted to utter a taboo word. If the gods are going to be cruel, then we will get even by violating their old word taboos. And so we let off steam! If I strike my finger with the hammer, instead of striking the nail, I might emit the taboo word "damn!" The greater the hurt (unkind fate has dealt me), the greater is likely to be the taboo I violate. If I have really smashed the finger, I may embellish the "damn" with other taboo words—the greater the pain, the more daring the embellishments.

In another sense, too, taboo words are magic words. They may not have the power to conjure up evil spirits or apply devastating effects with a curse, but they still do have the power to stir up some folks emotionally! (Were not many people in the United States more disturbed by what the

[2] George Carlin, "Seven Words You Can Never Say on Television," Little David Records #LD 1004, Atlantic Recording Corporation (1841 Broadway, New York, New York 10023), © 1972.

White House tapes revealed about President Nixon's language than what they revealed about his legal lapses?) A word with the power to shake people up so much is a *magic* word! No magician's "abracadabra" has that kind of power!

Ambiguities

Ambiguities are words or sentences with at least two possible meanings. Although the context will usually tell your listener what you mean, an ambiguous word or sentence can cause confusion. Be wary of words or sentences that can be interpreted in more than one way.

When Bea Schure tells you, "I saw the man with the binoculars," can you be certain whether Bea or the man had the binoculars? Did she use the binoculars to see the man, or did she see the man who had the binoculars? The sentence is ambiguous. In fact, almost all sentences in English constructed in the same way (noun-verb-noun-preposition-noun) are ambiguous. Look at these examples, all constructed from the same pattern:

> I saw the girl in the bar.
> Jack hit the child on the bike.
> Joan hit her husband with a case.
> Her husband caught Joan with a trick.

Can you see *at least* two meanings possible in each of those sentences? They are all ambiguous.

Words themselves can have two meanings. When Dr. Ed Hugh Kated comments, "The students are revolting!" the ambiguity lies in the word *revolting*. That word, of course, can mean either "engaged in a revolution" or "disgusting" and "stomach-turning." Which meaning Dr. Kated intends to convey will have to be conveyed vocally (with paralanguage) or kinetically (with body language) or (better yet) both.

If a word has two meanings and one of the meanings is risqué (considered vulgar or "obscene"), the word or phrase is a *double entendre*. I considered giving you some examples, but I have thought better of it. I am sure you can think up your own examples to illustrate the point.

Vague Generalities

Sometimes, or at least every once in a while, somebody says something more or less vague and general about some topic or other and somehow almost never seems to get down to specifics. The sentence you have just read is an example of vague generalities. It's exaggerated, of course, but it serves to remind us of the problems that vague generalities give us in communicating with each other.

Some people may use vague generalities without being aware of doing so. The message seems clear to *them! They* know what they mean! Listeners, however, need concrete language—specific details—rather than general or abstract language. There are times, perhaps, when one uses vague generalities deliberately, as a means of evasion. If your mother asks,

"Where are you going?" and you say, "Out," and she adds, "Where will you be?" and you reply, "Around," and she persists, "Who will you be with?" and you answer, "Some of the gang," and she asks, "How long will you be gone?" and you tell her, "Not too long," you are talking in vague generalities. Too bad for your mother; she never got the information she so diligently sought. Consider this, however: If you come home and your brother Elmer informs you, "Somebody called a while ago and said to tell you something," but gives no more information, your own kind of vague generalities are coming back to you. You want specific, exact, accurate reporting—not vague generalities; you *need* specific, exact, accurate reporting. So does everybody else. Remember Elmer, and beware of vague generalities.

So far, we have looked at what style in language is, at a few guidelines for effective style, and at some common dangers in word choice. As a brief review, fill out these exercises:

In the blank, write whether the sentence contains slang, jargon, clichés, vague generalities, ambiguities, taboo words, out-of-date language, or gobbledygook:

_____ 1. "I plight thee my troth." —I. U. Wedd
_____ 2. The pressure increased from 10 p.s.i. to 25 p.s.i.
_____ 3. "Some time back, some of them said something to that effect." —I. D. Claire
_____ 4. "Speaking clearly and candidly with reference to the issue that divides us, I want to say that I am very supportive of any of those measures that will reduce the controversy and minimize the hostilities, although I will *never* retreat from my principles nor forsake my positions or my promises." —Hugh Briss
_____ 5. Jerry may have been down on his luck lately, but he's going to be fit as a fiddle soon.
_____ 6. Let us join hands together and face the challenges of tomorrow's world united in faith in the basic goodness of our fellow man.
_____ 7. "This joint is real bad. Can you dig it?" —U. B. Goode
_____ 8. "I shot the man with the gun." —Harry Tales
_____ 9. "Some people seem to believe that masochism and morbid sadness are the essence of Christianity. Bullshit!" —Rev. Al Carmines
_____ 10. Our company has adopted MBO.

Each of the following examples violates one of the guidelines for effective style. In the blank, write whether the example is not *clear,* not *concrete,* not *concise,* not *colorful,* not *current,* or *not* cautious:

_____ 1. Somebody ought to do something about it sometime.
_____ 2. "If you have that disease, it burns when you piss." —High school student being interviewed on TV documentary about sex education

—————————— 3. Forsooth, knave, get thee hence!

—————————— 4. Mrs. Roosevelt made this old world a better place in which to live.

—————————— 5. "Any variation or novelty, whether in the parameters of the same modality that originally caused it or not, will revive the orienting reflex." —R. U. Schure

—————————— 6. "I have been asked to state my position on the controversial subject of whiskey and other alcoholic beverages. There are different ways of looking at this subject. One may think of whiskey as a poisonous scourge that defiles innocence, dethrones reason, promotes debauchery, and causes poverty. On the other hand, one may think of whiskey as a soothing balm to jangled nerves, a pleasant assistant to social intercourse, a token of friendship and good cheer. This is my position, and I do not hesitate to state it publicly." —Gerry Mander

SUGGESTIONS FOR FURTHER READING

BLANKENSHIP, JANE, *A Sense of Style* (Belmont, Calif.: Dickerson, 1968).

BLOOMFIELD, LEONARD, "Literate and Illiterate Speech," *American Speech,* **II** (1927), pp. 432–439.

BORCHERS, GLADYS, "An Approach to the Problem of Oral Style," *Quarterly Journal of Speech,* **27** (1936), pp. 114–117.

CHASE, STUART, *The Power of Words* (New York: Harcourt Brace, 1954).

FERNALD, JAMES C., *Standard Handbook of Synonyms, Antonyms, and Prepositions,* rev. ed. (New York: Funk & Wagnalls, 1947).

GLEASON, HENRY, *Linguistics and English Grammar* (New York: Holt, 1965).

JOOS, MARTIN, *The Five Clocks* (New York: Harcourt Brace, 1967).

KENYON, JOHN S., "Levels of Speech and Colloquial English," *English Journal,* **XXXVII** (1948), pp. 25–31.

STRUNK, WILLIAM, JR., and E. B. WHITE, *The Elements of Style,* 3rd ed. (New York: Macmillan, 1979).

9
SEMANTICS: MEANING IN LANGUAGE

general goal:

To learn to identify and overcome problems in communication related to meaning (semantics).

specific objectives:

After completing this unit, you should understand:
- What meaning is.
- How meanings may change over a period of time.
- Three kinds of meanings.
- Some basic principles of semantics.
- What dictionaries are—and are not.
- The conceptualizing process and the problems related to it.
- Variations in degree of abstraction.
- The relation between language and thought and culture.
- Problems in communication that can result from the process of attaching meaning to words.

HAVE YOU EVER BEEN LISTENING to a lecture by one of your favorite professors and felt like interrupting with, "What does that indecipherable word mean?" Or, if you have had courage enough to ask some professor the meaning of a word, has that erudite soul instructed you to "look up the meaning in your Funk and Wagnall's" (or Webster's, as the case may be)? We often talk and wonder about "what words mean." This chapter deals with problems related to meaning in language.

five myths about meaning

We will look at two sides of the same problems. First, we will face some mistaken, but widespread, myths about meaning. And then we will look at some basic, simple, but important principles of meaning in language.

MYTH 1: Every word has a meaning.

The question, "What does that word mean?" includes a built-in assumption: that words mean. Or, put a different way, that words have meaning. The only thing wrong with this question is that the assumption is false. Words do not have meanings; they do not possess meanings; they do not contain or include meanings. Meaning exists, but it is not in, with, by, or on the words.

The mistaken idea that words contain meanings leads to the equally mistaken notion that meanings are transmitted or meanings are transferred. We have discussed that misunderstanding before. (See pp. 9, 48–49.) We transmit messages. When we speak, we transmit audible and visible behavior (sounds and bodily activity). Our behavior stands for meaning; it represents meaning; it is an attempt to stir up meaning; but it is *not* meaning. Meaning does not go through the air from person to person. We say words—successions of noises—but those words do not *have* meaning of themselves.

MYTH 2: Every word has A meaning.

This belief is built on the first myth. But it goes beyond that first myth. Not only does it assume that words contain meaning; it asserts that each word has only *one* meaning. Haven't you heard someone say, "What is the meaning of . . . ?" Note: "*the* meaning"! There is only one, isn't there? Well, not really. How many different meanings can you think of for the word *pot,* for example? (I will not ask which meaning you thought of first!) Even if words *did* possess meanings (and they do not), each word is not limited to one meaning. When it comes to meanings, it is definitely not "one per customer."

MYTH 3: Every word has a right meaning.

This myth is based on the mistaken assumption that there is a logical connection between the thing a word stands for and the word itself. When one uses a word, according to this myth, it must refer to the thing—the one thing—it is logically connected with.

I recently saw a television program on which a group of people lamented the dreadful state of present-day language usage. People are using words in a different way today, they bemoaned. (There was no linguistics or semantics scholar among the group, of course.) All the members of this panel agreed that words were in a very bad way—in the hands of such Philistines as we. We are using *like* where we should (according to these self-appointed "experts") be using *as;* to my chagrin, I discovered from them that we are using *hopefully* to mean what it does not mean at all! The fact that everyone today is employing the word to mean this "wrong" meaning was irrelevant to them. And, they said, people are committing the unpardonable sin of using nouns as verbs and adjectives! We are talking about trying to *contact* someone, to *book* a play, to *host* a show—all of which they considered gross misuse of the words. As for using nouns as adjectives, we might call someone or something "a *contact* high" (a compound sin with a noun for an adjective and an adjective for a noun!), "a *book* salesperson," or a "*host* country." Words, they assumed, should be confined to the labels and functions assigned them by the English teachers who taught them in elementary school. After all, (myth 3) "every word has a right meaning," and usage should conform to that correct meaning!

This myth is not based on sound semantic principles, as we shall soon see.

MYTH 4: To find the correct (right) meaning of a word, look it up in a dictionary.

This myth is based on the assumption that dictionaries are arbiters of meaning. "But," I can hear some shaken soul muttering, "dictionaries *are* the authorities on meaning, aren't they? Don't the dictionaries tell us the *real* meanings of words?" Sorry, no. There isn't *one* right meaning for a word; there isn't even a group of right meanings for a word. And, whatever dictionaries do, they do not set up authoritative statements about what words mean and how we should use words.

MYTH 5: The right meaning of a word is fixed—permanent.

This myth leads us to believe that, once we find the right meaning for a word, we *know* it. We've got it, because it (the meaning) is an unchanging and unchangeable entity to be acquired. Once we acquire it, of course, we have it for all time! The only problem with this myth is that it fails to understand the dynamic nature of language. A language is a living thing; it keeps growing and changing. Words do not stay forever the same, as if they were frozen or petrified.

All right, you say, there are the myths. But accentuate the positive. What are the principles we need to know about semantics? And don't just give us the old platitudes of know what you mean, say what you mean, and mean what you say. We've heard all that before!

All right. The study of meaning is called *semantics*. Just as linguistics, the study of language, can study language development over a period of time (*diachronic* linguistics) or the nature of a language at a given point in time (*synchronic* linguistics), so also semantics can study the changes in meaning of words over a period of time (diachronic semantics) or the nature of meaning at a specific time (synchronic semantics).

four kinds of meaning change over a period of time

A semanticist is concerned with changes in meaning over a period of time. Such changes have been classified into four types: (1) widening, (2) narrowing, (3) raising, and (4) lowering. If the number of meanings is expanded to include more possible applications, then meaning has been *widened*. If the possible meanings are reduced in number or scope, then meaning has been *narrowed*. If meanings change to become more positive, then meaning has been *raised*. And if meanings change to become more negative, then meaning has been *lowered*.

Widening

Professor William Walter Duncan offers this example of widening: "The word *frock* was for centuries applied to a loose outer garment worn by men. Priests, for example, wore frocks, and of course we still speak of clergymen being unfrocked. Today, however, the word can apply to women's clothes, children's attire, the uniforms of various professional groups such as nurses, and the like." You can see that the term *frock* is now applied to a wider variety of items than previously; possible meanings have been expanded and extended.

Narrowing

What do you think of when I use the word *doctor*? At least, what is the first meaning that comes into your mind? You probably think of a physician, someone with an M.D. degree. That is certainly the most common use of the word today. Originally, however, the word was used to include anyone with a doctorate from a university—Ph.D., LL.D., Th.D., or some other such degree. Although the word *doctor* is used in its broad sense inside universities, the more restricted meaning is more prevalent generally. (I remember a lady in Queens, New York, who desperately wanted her daughter to marry a "doctor." She wanted, she said, a "real doctor"—an M.D.—"not an almost doctor"—a D.D.S.—"or a phony doctor"—a Ph.D.!) The word *doctor* offers a good example of narrowing.

Raising

The word *nice* has been elevated from the lowly state in which it began; it offers a good example of raising. *Nice* comes from a Latin word meaning "ignorant." In Middle English, it had come to mean "foolish"; by the time of Izaak Walton (the seventeenth century), it meant "finicky." And today it is admirable to be *nice*! Another good example of raising is to be found in the history of the word *pretty*. The Old English word *praetig* was the word for "deceitful" or "sly." The word had changed into *prati* by Middle English and the meaning had changed to "cunning" or "clever." That meaning evolved into "ingenious," and today someone pretty is quite attractive.

Lowering

The word *fool* provides a clear example of lowering. The word once referred to the court jester, who was a performer and entertainer. Today, if you call someone a *fool*, that person will not think you are calling him or her a comedian, but a person lacking good sense. The term has become more negative in its meanings.

three kinds of meanings

A semanticist is not just concerned with historical changes in meanings of words, but with contemporary meanings as well. The study of semantics recognizes at least three kinds of meanings: (1) denotative meanings, (2) connotative meanings, and (3) structural meanings.

Denotative Meanings

All meanings are associations made in the mind of a human being. We make (or construct or see) connections between things. We attach significance to something (no matter what the "thing" is), and that something takes on meaning for us. The different kinds of meaning differ in terms of the relationships of the associations in our minds. Or, put another way, the different kinds of meanings depend on what we connect with what in our minds.

Denotative meaning depends upon a person seeing a relationship (an association) between a symbol and a referent. A symbol is something that stands for something else, and a referent is the thing to which the symbol points or refers. Although this meaning is inside the person making the association, the person is not very emotionally involved. These associations are often called objective rather than subjective meanings; they focus on the symbol and the *object* symbolized rather than on the person (the *subject*, the *I*) himself or herself.

When we attach denotations to a symbol in our minds, we are reminded of some object, condition, process, or event. And we keep our attention on the object, condition, process, or event rather than on our feelings about the referent. Denotation centers on external reality; that reality may be

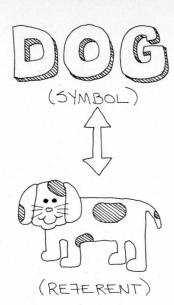
(SYMBOL)

(REFERENT)

Denotation

physical or social, but it is largely objective. Denotative meanings acknowledge something's existence; they do not evaluate it or assume an attitude toward it.

If you were asked to give an unemotional, uninvolved (objective) definition of the word *mother*, what would you say that word means to you? Try it, and then check your meaning for emotional overtones. Did you keep yourself out of the meaning? Did you confine your meaning to an association only between the symbol (the word *mother*) and the concept it represents? If so, your definition is probably something like this one: "female parent." That is denotative meaning. It is as objective as we can get—and still use words.

To get more "objective" than that, we would have to resort to pointing to physical objects in sight. "That is a *ball*. That is a *chair*. That is a *foot*." We could make the association between the name (the symbol) and the referent (the visible object) without the use of other words (for definitions). If we have enough experiences of that sort with the same specific object, we can use the symbol to remind us of the object, even if it is not physically present. Carol asks little Jenny, "Where is Uncle Bob?" and then informs her that I am away in New York. Little Jenny can picture me, even though I am not in sight at the time. That too is very objective denotation. But even that is not totally objective. Remember what we have said about the perception process. We do not associate the object itself with the symbol in our minds. Rather, we associate our own perceptions of the object with the symbol. As we have noted, those perceptions are very selective and highly personal. So "objectivity" is a relative term—and it is never absolute!

Connotative Meanings

Connotative meaning depends upon a person feeling a relationship among a symbol, a referent, and the person himself or herself. In this case, the person is very emotionally involved. Indeed, these meanings are highly personal; they are subjective instead of objective (self-oriented rather than object-oriented).

Connotation

When we attach connotations to a symbol in our minds, we are reminded of some object, condition, process, or event. But there is an added ingredient! We also include our feelings about that referent. Denotation, you remember, centered on external reality (so far as that is possible), but connotation centers on internal reality. Connotations go far beyond acknowledging something's existence; they include an evaluation, a judgment, an attitude, some emotional overtones toward that thing.

All meanings are learned, but, of the three kinds of meanings, connotations are the most closely linked to an individual's personal experience. No two people have exactly the same set of experiences, and those differences come to the fore in connotative meanings.

Recently, I asked some students to write down what the word *mother* meant. I got an interesting variety of answers. Of course, we did not compare notes; each person wrote down his or her own individual meanings for the same word. Here are some of those meanings:

> the one who is always there
> the one who makes a house a home
> the one who nags incessantly
> the woman who smothers you with love
> a woman with apron strings of rope (or chain)
> someone who loves you no matter what
> a boss, a bully, a nag, a drag, a cook, a look, a crab
> the one who gives you life, love, and understanding

Had you been in my class, what meanings would you have listed? All these meanings, of course, are extremely personal. They reveal as much (or more) about the person's self as they do about the object being "defined." Each person's meaning was shaped by that individual's own experiences with some person (or people) called "mother." The meaning describes one's feelings about the object, condition, process, or event. That is connotative meaning.

Connotations have emotional overtones, and those overtones will be either positive or negative. Whether a word will be positively or negatively charged for you I cannot know unless you tell me. And you cannot know my private meanings for words either—unless we discuss them. These personal meanings pose problems in communication, as you can see. If I use a word and attribute to it some positive connotative meanings and you hear the word but attribute to it negative connotative meanings, our communication will be inefficient.

If I say that some person you do not know is a pious person, how will you picture the person? What meaning(s) do you have for the word *pious*? I have tried this experiment in class also. I have had students write their impression of the person I have so described. The answers have been quite different. Indeed, some have been directly contradictory! The reason for the opposite views of the pious person is that each person had a different set of connotations for the word *pious*. Without reading ahead, why don't you write your own description of that person. Then you can compare it with what my students have said:

> She is very religious, very devout. She goes to church every Sunday and takes an active part in the congregation's life. Religion is very important to her, and she talks about it and prays a lot.
>
> She is religious—and sincerely so. She practices her religion every day, every hour. She is good, kind, warm, loving. I would say she is a righteous person—living a good, clean, wholesome life—and practicing what the church preaches: love your neighbor as yourself.
>
> She is pseudo-religious; she is a hypocrit. Self-righteous and overbearing, she puts on a good show of religion. She thinks she is better than anybody else, and she thanks God she is not like the scummy sinners around her. She treats others with a kind of pity and contempt; she gossips constantly and is intolerant of others' faults. Of course, she thinks she has none of her own—being perfect and "pious."

These three descriptions really give each person's connotations for the adjective *pious*. Each has evidently known someone labeled with that adjective and conceives of piety in a different way. The second and third conceptions seem almost diametrically opposite to me; they are almost reverse images. How did the three compare with your own connotations?

Structural Meanings

As we noted earlier, all meanings are associations made in the mind of a human being. Denotation involves associations between a symbol and a referent; connotation involves associations among a symbol, a referent, and the self. Structural meanings are based on a person's seeing a relationship (an association) between or among symbols. In this case, meaning is derived from noting how the symbols are related to each other, or, put another way, how the symbols are put together into a structure. The form (or patterns) in which symbols are related gives us clues to meaning.

If one symbol (or word) helps me figure out the meaning of another word (or symbol), we have an instance of structural meaning. The meaning did not come from seeing how a symbol is related to some thing (as in denotation); rather, it came from seeing the relationship between two symbols. Look at these sentences:

What a grunchy picture!
Janet is really grunchy.
I wouldn't drive such a grunchy car.

I assume you have never heard the word *grunchy* before; neither have I. But can you figure out what it might mean? How did you get this meaning—with no prior experience with the word? Well, it must be a describing word (an adjective) because it is used to describe nouns—names for things. Do you think it carries good or bad (positive or negative) connotations for the people who have used it in these sentences? Negative, right? Sounds to me as if it is a synonym for *ugly*. I didn't get that meaning from a referent, and I didn't get it from my conditioning, having never encountered the word before. I got that meaning from the structure of the sentences in which it occurred.

If the sequence of the symbols helps me figure out the meaning, then we also have an instance of structural meaning. The meaning in this case does not come from the individual words (the symbols), but from the grammatical structure of the sentence in which those symbols occur. Look at these two sentences:

Mikie hit Matt.
Matt hit Mikie.

Are the symbols employed in the two sentences the same? Identically the same? Yes. Don't both sentences contain exactly the same words? Indeed they do. Now is the meaning of the two sentences the same? No, we agree. The two sentences do not mean the same thing to me. Well, if the words are exactly the same in both sentences, and the two sentences are not the same in the meaning attached to them, what accounts for that difference? Is it the referents—the things the symbols refer to (denote)? No, those are the same also. The difference lies in the word order. The words are not arranged in the same way in the two sentences, and that difference in structure is the crucial difference! If we have learned English syntax, we know that there is a formula for sentences:

SUBJECT — VERB — OBJECT

The first naming word is the doer; the action word is what gets done; and the second naming word is the doee—the one that gets done to. Switching the two names from one position in the sentence to the other (from subject to object) changes the meaning in English. That meaning is a kind of structural meaning.

To analyze structural meaning, we do not go to the external world to find the objects referred to. Nor do we go to our internal states to find the attitudes and feelings attached to the symbols. We analyze the form of our sentences—the relationships among the symbols themselves. Structural meaning, then, centers on formal or structural or symbolic reality.

Some writers speak of contextual meaning. Is that another word for structural meaning? Yes, because you are using surrounding words to guess the meaning of some unknown or ambiguous word. Look at these examples:

> She hit her husband with a case, and it came open, scattering papers everywhere.
> She hit her husband with a case, and it comes up in the next term of court.
> She hit her husband with a case, but the doctor cleared it up in no time!

So you have a different meaning for the word *case* in each of these instances? If so, where did you get that meaning? How did you figure it out? From the other words in each of the sentences. One (or more) symbol(s) gave you the clues to the meaning you needed for the word *case*. And for the word *hit* too, for that matter. If the meaning comes from seeing a relationship between symbols, then the meaning is structural.

We have examined very briefly some of the principles of the study of semantics. In this century, another, but related, discipline has developed. Scholars became interested in the ways semantics affects human behavior. This discipline, which grew out of the work of Alfred Korzybski and his students, Irving J. Lee, Wendell Johnson, Anatol Rapoport, and S. I. Hayakawa, is called *general semantics*.

seven important reminders about semantic problems

The field of general semantics has provided us with a number of important reminders about semantic problems in human communication. We will examine some of those principles. Note that many of them are related to the myths with which we began this chapter.

People, Not Words, Have Meanings

Instead of asking your professor, "What does that word mean?" it would be more accurate to ask, "What do *you* mean by that word?" For meanings are not in the words, but in the people who use the words. Meanings, after all, are ideas—thoughts. And thoughts are electrical impulses and chemical reactions in our brains. Those electrical impulses and chemical reactions stay in our brains; those ideas, those meanings, are ours; they are literally a part of us! Words represent meaning, but they do not *have* meaning. We have meanings. The speaker selects a word to stand for some intended meaning, and the listener selects a meaning to attach to the word. But each person has his or her own store of meanings to use in this communication process. So the meaning a speaker attaches to a word and the meaning a listener attaches to the same word may be quite different.

I am sure someone is saying, "The connotations may be different, but surely the denotations will be the same for both people in an interpersonal communication situation." Consider this instance: On a recent visit, my brother said to me, "I like fish." I replied, "So do I." It sounds as if we were in agreement. Unfortunately, we were not, as we later discovered. When I said, "So do I," I meant that I like fish to eat; I like them well prepared and on a platter. That was not what my brother had in mind at all. He meant he liked to raise fish—tropical fish—the tank, the bubbles, and dipping out the dead ones in the morning. As you may be able to detect, I would hate raising tropical fish; it is too much trouble. We were not in agreement at all! We were attaching quite different denotations (as well as connotations) to the word *fish,* and the structure did not help in clearing up the ambiguity.

People Attach Many Meanings to the Same Word (Symbol)

We human beings have an infinite number of things to think and talk about, but we have a finite number of symbols (words) to represent our thoughts. Having far more meanings than words, we solve the problem by using one word to represent many different meanings.

Although there may be as many as 600,000 words in the English language today, most adult speakers use only two or three thousand words in daily conversation. I am told that the five hundred words we use most frequently have a total of 14,000 definitions listed in a dictionary. Isn't that an average of 28 meanings per word? And we are talking now about denotative meanings. Connotative meanings aren't even counted in that number!

Various meanings for a single word

We have already discussed the idea that words are arbitrary symbols. (See pp. 193, 196.) There is no necessary relation between a thing and the word we use to represent that thing. Some general semanticists think it important to remind people that the word is not the thing itself, because some people tend to react to words (the symbols) as if they were the things (the object, process, event, and so on). There are certainly many people who believe (or act as if they believe) that there is a logical and necessary connection between the symbol and its referent. Such a misunderstanding leads to many problems in interpersonal communication.

When I say that meanings are arbitrary, I mean that one word (symbol) would work as well as any other to represent a particular concept. One word is not the right word or the "natural" name for something. But, true as that principle is, we cannot call things by any name we choose and expect to be able to communicate efficiently and effectively with others. We cannot, like Lewis Carroll's Humpty Dumpty, misapply this principle and disregard customary word usage. Humpty Dumpty's philosophy of semantics, revealed in a conversation with Alice, concentrated solely on the arbitrary nature of symbols:

> "I don't know what you mean by 'glory,'" Alice said.
>
> Humpty Dumpty smiled contemptuously. "Of course you don't—till I tell you. I meant 'there's a nice knockdown argument for you!'"
>
> "But 'glory' doesn't mean 'a nice knockdown argument,'" Alice objected.
>
> "When I use a word," Humpty Dumpty said, in rather a scornful tone, "it means just what I choose it to mean—neither more nor less."
>
> "The question is," said Alice, "whether you *can* make words mean so many different things."
>
> "The question is," said Humpty Dumpty, "which is to be master—that's all."[1]

Meanings Are Arbitrary in Origin, but Customary in Usage

[1] Lewis Carroll, *Through the Looking Glass, The Annotated Alice,* with an Introduction and Notes by Martin Gardner (New York: Clarkson N. Potter, 1960), pp. 268-269.

It is true that there is no necessary connection between a symbol and what that symbol represents. But it is equally true that we grow up in a language community which has developed shared, customary meanings for words. If we are to communicate in that language within that community, we must use the words in the customary ways.

Yes, words do mean different things to different people. And yes, we do use one word to mean more than one thing. But within the language community, there are shared words and generally shared meanings as well. Otherwise, we could not communicate in language!

We learn meanings. And we learn those meanings within the language community. The meanings that we have for words grew out of the experiences we have had with the people around us, the words they use, and whatever the words have been used to represent. We learn to associate meanings with symbols. Since I grew up at Fort Knox, Kentucky, USA, rather than near Fortalesa, in Puerto Rico, USA, I learned to associate a particular metallic element with the word *gold* rather than with the word *oro*. The word *gold* is not the "right" word or the "correct" word, but it is the *customary* word among speakers of the English language. However arbitrary that word may be, so far as logic is concerned, it is now the one in common use in English. If I want to communicate with other speakers of English (and there are over three hundred million native speakers of English), I must follow the customs and use the customary symbols (words).

Dictionaries Record Usage— Prior Shared Meanings

I know some people who seem to regard dictionaries as a kind of Supreme Court of word meanings—the final authority one appeals to on questions of meaning. That is not what dictionaries are, and it is not what they claim to be. Dictionaries do not establish the "correct" or "true" meanings of words. They are not prescriptive, but descriptive.

Writers of dictionaries *record* what people say and write. They note what words people use and how they use them. They note the contexts in which words are found. And they note changes in word usage over a period of time. Writers of dictionaries *report* what they have found out about the usage of a word in the past. They also report on the common spellings that have appeared in print and on the common pronunciations of the word. Observing what people seem to mean when they use a word, editors of dictionaries collect words that people use to substitute for the word and they report those synonyms and word phrases.

A dictionary is a very useful reference book, but it is not a sacred book or a book of laws. It takes a great deal of time to collect all the needed information and publish it—so much time that a dictionary is somewhat out of date by the time it is printed! Besides, it cannot give current information. Its approach must be historical. Since language is changing all the time, a dictionary cannot keep pace. It certainly cannot predict how people will use a word in a message to you tomorrow—or today.

Your best source of information about the meanings of words is the same source the dictionaries use—people. If you want to know how people in your language community are using a word, listen and learn—pronunciations, contexts, meanings.

Meanings Change over Time

I have already referred to the fact that a language is a living thing and, like any living thing, continues to grow, develop, change. We have already noted four ways in which meanings can change. (See pp. 233–234.) Both shared meanings (public or customary meanings, if you prefer) and personal meanings change over a period of time.

Indeed, personal meanings change more rapidly than do commonly shared meanings. Since we learn meanings from experiences, and we are constantly adding to our store of experiences, our personal meanings (connotative meanings) will be changing too. Meanings, after all, are associations in our minds, and we may make new or different associations when we have new experiences.

The Conceptualizing (Abstracting + Generalizing) Process Oversimplifies by Disregarding Differences

As we discussed earlier (pp. 95–97, 148–149), we form categories in our minds by pulling out specific characteristics to notice (abstracting) and then forming a group with those characteristics (generalizing). In this way, we are able to classify the many things we encounter into manageable groups of things. And we apply a label to the category or class of things. We now have a concept (the category) and a word to call it.

When we abstract, we focus on certain characteristics. But in that process, we ignore many other characteristics. It is a selection process, and while many characteristics may be present, few are noted. It is inevitable, then, that in the general class of objects we have classified together (on the basis of these selected characteristics), not all will be alike is every regard. Indeed, the individual objects in the general class will differ in many regards!

I assume you have a concept of *nation* and you call the concept by that name. All nations do have certain things in common. It is on the basis of their commonalities that we form that class of things. But I need not remind you of the great differences among the nations of the world to illustrate the point being made here.

Here is a short list of words. All represent categories we have formed in our minds. As useful as these words are and as valid as the classifications may be, we must not forget that the individuals that make up the class of objects are not all alike. If we fall into that trap, we are stereotyping.

teenagers
contraceptives
friends
books
love
men
injustice
students
beautiful
sweet
attack (verb)
reward (verb)
undo
fly (verb)
skip (verb)

Concepts and Words Vary in Their Degree of Abstraction

When I conceptualize, I think of a category—a class of things—with common characteristics. I have pulled out those relevant characteristics (abstracting), and I have noted that they are applicable to a group of things (generalizing). But some classifications or categories include more concrete, empirical data (more specific characteristics) than other categories do.

The more specific characteristics are included, the less abstract (think of it as subtracting if you like) is the concept and the word for that concept. The more concrete details are omitted, the more abstract and general will be the concept and the word.

This idea is probably easier to illustrate than to explain. I see an object. Actually, I see light reflected from the surface of the object, and I perceive the object. That object exists in a much more complex state than I am able to experience. I do not see it as a dynamic process of atoms and subatomic particles—though in reality, I am told, the object does exist at that process level. My own experience begins with my perception, and the perception process, you remember, is selective. I pick out some characteristics to notice and pay no attention to may others. But I do get an impression of that object. And I am able to attach a label to that object; I am able to find a name that stands for that object in my mind. The name is not the object; it is a reminder of my impression of that object. It has fewer details than the impression, which had fewer details than the object itself. I have been abstracting—selecting some details and omitting others. I need not stop, however, with naming the object; I can name the class of objects that the specific object fits into. And that class of objects will fit into a general category—broader, more inclusive, with more details omitted. If you leave out more details and thus make a more widely applicable category, you make a more general category. And so on and on.

Don't despair. Here comes the illustration:

MOST GENERAL CATEGORY:	wealth
EVEN MORE GENERAL CATEGORY:	asset
MORE GENERAL CATEGORY:	money
GENERAL CATEGORY:	coin
CATEGORY:	dime
LABEL FOR OBJECT:	a 1970 FDR dime
PERCEIVED OBJECT:	
PROCESS LEVEL:	dynamic process of atoms

General semanticists have called this kind of increasing abstraction and generalization *the abstraction ladder.* They see each level as higher than the one before (you must read the levels from the bottom up), with each level leading you further from the world of material reality. The higher on the abstraction ladder a word (or concept) is, the more vague and easily misunderstood the word is.

It has always been easier for me to picture the relative levels of abstraction and generalization in terms of increasingly large umbrellas than in terms of a ladder metaphor. You see, the broader category covers the next smaller category and more besides.

Here are four lists of words. I think I have arranged them in the order of their levels of abstraction and generalization. See if you agree. Again, read the list from the bottom up; each successive word should be broader and more general than the word below it in the list.

8.	living thing	living thing	living thing	justice
7.	animal	animal	animal	legal system
6.	farm animal	human being	human being	laws
5.	livestock (cattle)	foreigner	child	statutes
4.	cow	Englishman	female	federal statute
3.	"Bossie"	O. U. Kidd	Sandy Schore	H.B. 1046
2.	the object I "see"			
1.	The thing "as it is": a mass of atoms in motion			

Do not get the idea that words that are more abstract and general are better or worse than other words. We must keep in mind, however, that the higher a word is on the abstraction ladder or the broader its generalization umbrella is, the more possibilities are open for others to attach meanings

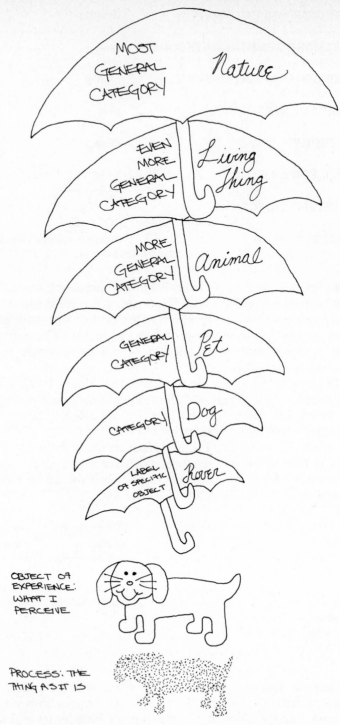

MOST GENERAL CATEGORY — *Nature*

EVEN MORE GENERAL CATEGORY — *Living Thing*

MORE GENERAL CATEGORY — *Animal*

GENERAL CATEGORY — *Pet*

CATEGORY — *Dog*

LABEL OF SPECIFIC OBJECT — *Rover*

OBJECT OF EXPERIENCE: WHAT I PERCEIVE

PROCESS: THE THING AS IT IS

Levels of abstraction and generalization

quite different from our own. When we are communicating, we must check to be sure we have similar meanings for our abstract and general words.

There are two other principles related to meaning in language that we should examine. These principles are two aspects of the same relationship, and we must look at them both: *Just as thought and culture influence language, so also language influences thought and culture.*

two principles on the relationship between thought and culture and language

Thought and Culture Influence Language

Language is a reflection of one's thoughts. The messages I send in words will not only represent my thoughts; they will be an indication of how I think. I choose words from the many options open to me. My word choice will give clues as to how my mind works. I must construct my messages using a wide variety of grammatical patterns and using some form (or structure) for the message as a whole. The syntax and message structures I choose will also give indications about how my mind works. Don't you get impressions about someone's personality from that person's use of language? I think we all do. A person's thoughts and feelings influence the language used by that person.

Language, like other aspects of human behavior, is culturally conditioned. It is learned in and from the groups one is a member of, and it will reflect the customs, priorities, and norms of those groups. The point is that language will not only reflect individual differences; it will reflect cultural differences as well.

I recently attended a state high school basketball tournament, where I sat among a group of strangers. A hawker came through selling programs. A young man about fourteen asked the price of the programs and was told they were a dollar. When asked if he wanted one, he shook his head and said, "Bullshit!" Do you think I made some inferences about the socioeconomic class from which that young man came? What inferences would you have made about his cultural background from his use of language? (Remember, *culture* simply refers to the customs of the groups that have influenced a person.)

A great deal, including several books, has been written in the last decade about one particular nonstandard dialect of American English: the Black Vernacular (folk dialect). Although this dialect is sometimes called "Black English," it is not spoken by all or even most Black speakers of the English language. It is the dialect of the economically disadvantaged Black people in the United States and has a great deal in common with the nonstandard dialects of other economically disadvantaged people in the South.

This dialect is consistent with itself, but has interesting and significant differences from the standard or status dialect. It differs in all three aspects of language: sounds, grammar, and vocabulary. It is one thing to recognize that language differences reflect differences in group memberships and quite another to judge those language differences (and group memberships) as inferior! Different is not degenerate, is it? And surely you don't think different is disgusting—or dangerous!

How do you react to reflections of cultural differences in language? Let's check. Suppose you are a high school English teacher. You have asked your class to read a short story, and you are going to discuss it with the class today. Your first question is: "What did you think of the character of George in the story?" A Black student raises his hand and answers, "Dat muvverfucker ain't worf shit!" What would you say? What would you feel? How would you react? Now, think about it for a minute. You asked a direct question. Did the student answer it? Did he answer it honestly, clearly, directly? Did he answer the question sensibly? I think he did. But he answered using the dialect of low-income Black people. He used the sounds of that dialect, the grammar of that dialect, and the vocabulary acceptable in that dialect. Can you pick out the differences in each of these respects from standard American English? More to the point, however, is this question: How would you react to this young man's message? Would you judge him and his message? How?

Unfortunately, many people (including some "professionals" such as educators and psychologists) seem to take these dialectal differences (culturally induced language differences) as manifestations of inferior cognitive ability (thinking) and linguistic deprivation (ignorance about language). They are nothing of the kind. But it may be easier to teach an extra dialect to the speakers of the Black Vernacular and other nonstandard dialects than to change the attitudes on language of those with such prejudices.

We have already discussed some problems in cross-cultural communication. It is obvious that semantic problems increase across cultural lines. Words do not mean exactly the same things to people in the same reference groups, but there are some important similarities in meaning shared by members of the same groups. When we cross those lines and communicate with someone from a different relevant reference group (see pp. 42–44), we may encounter differences in meaning that make efficient and effective communication much more difficult.

Language Influences Thought and Culture

It is true that how I think (and what groups have conditioned me) affects the language I use. It is also true that the language I know and use affects how I think. The language, by providing us with preset categories and labels for those categories, certainly influences the way we see the world.

If the society is sexist, will its language reflect its sexist beliefs, values, and attitudes? Well, think about it for a moment. Does your city or town have fire*men*, police*men*, and repair*men*? Does your favorite airline still have steward*esses*? Does your best restaurant employ bus*boys*, and does your baseball team have bat*boys*? Even though there are women in military service, my hometown newspaper still runs a column entitled "With Our Service*men*." The sexism of the language may well be a result of the sexism in the society, but it also helps create and perpetuate sexism, because it provides the linguistic framework for those biased views. Jean Faust has made the point well:

> All the titles, all the professions, all the occupations are masculine. They are weakened when they are made feminine by the addition of ess, ette. And man insists that these suffixes be used; he knows the power of language. He knows that language can control not only behavior, but thought itself.[2]

For that reason, there have been attempts recently to correct this sexist bias in American English, at least in official government publications. In the fourth edition of the Labor Department's *Dictionary of Occupational Titles,* the government's compilation of job classifications or categories, the job titles do not reflect sex or age. "Batboys" are now "bat handlers," and "repairmen" are now "repairers." The presumption of males filling those roles, built into the prior labels, is now gone. Will that affect the way Americans think if the words become generally used?

An interesting bit of evidence on the influence of language on thought patterns has been provided by Yu-Kuang Chu, Chairman of the Program of Asian Studies at Skidmore College. He has said that when he presided over academic meetings at a Chinese university with a bilingual international faculty, he used the Chinese and English languages for different purposes. If he wished to encourage the professors to deal with a problem directly, forthrightly, and objectively, following the regulations and applying rigid logic, he would use English. If, on the other hand, he wanted to encourage the professors to deal with the problem with an indirect approach and an emphasis on sentiment or feeling, he would conduct the discussion in Chinese. It was his observation that, as the faculty members spoke in one language or the other, they utilized two somewhat different sets of cognitive processes and conceptual habits. He also noted that this shift of approaches was true of both the Chinese and Western members of the faculty.[3]

Although one may not conclude that thought and culture are totally determined by the structure of a given language, surely one must concede that an individual's thought processes and the views and customs of the general culture are affected by the structure of the language spoken by that person and that society. Language helps shape our views of "reality."

We are indebted to Benjamin Lee Whorf for developing and illustrating this view of the relationship between language and culture. Although his

---

[2] Jean Faust, "Words That Oppress," *Women Speaking,* April 1970, pp. 4–5.
[3] Yu-Kuang Chu, "Interplay Between Language and Thought in Chinese," *ETC.,* September 1965, pp. 307–329.

theories have been widely disputed, and his theory may have been over-stated, the implications are important for human communication. Too often, we take our logic for granted and do not realize how deeply rooted it is in our language.

Let us try one last experiment to see how aware you are of the influence of language on your thought processes and on the views you share with others in your group(s). Do you find the following prayer unsettling? If you do, why?

> Our Mother who art in heaven,
> Hallowed be thy name.
> Thy Queendom come,
> Thy will be done . . .

Could you recite the Twenty-third Psalm this way without feeling un-comfortable:

> The Lord is my shepherdess;
> I shall not want.
> She maketh me to lie down in green pastures;
> She leadeth me beside the still waters.
> She restoreth my soul;
> She leadeth me in the paths of righteousness for her name's sake. . . .

Has the fact that only male pronouns have been used for God affected your thinking? How do you think it has affected this "Christian" nation—or Western culture generally? What influence, if any, has it had on the place of women in our society?

Just how sensitive are you to the predispositions language imposes on thought and culture? Will you be more on the lookout for this influence in the future? It is not that a person *cannot* think thoughts outside the limitations imposed by his or her own language system. The problem is that it is extremely difficult to do so—and oh, so much easier to use the ready-made categories and structures provided by our language!

SUGGESTIONS FOR FURTHER READING

ALEXANDER, HUBERT G., *Meaning in Language* (Glenview, Ill.: Scott, Foresman, 1969).

BENJAMIN, ROBERT L., *Semantics and Language Analysis* (Indianapolis: Bobbs-Merrill, 1969).

BUDD, RICHARD, "General Semantics," *Approaches to Human Communication,* Richard Budd and Brent Ruben, eds. (New York: Spartan Books, 1972).

CHASE, STUART, *The Power of Words* (New York: Harcourt Brace, 1954).

CONDON, JOHN C., *Semantics and Communication*, 2nd ed. (New York: Macmillan, 1974).

DUNCAN, WILLIAM WALTER, "How White Is Your Dictionary?" *Language: Introductory Readings*, Virginia P. Clark, Paul A. Escholz, and Alfred F. Rosa, eds. (New York: St. Martin's Press, 1972).

FABUN, DON, *Communications: The Transfer of Meaning* (Belmont, Calif.: Glencoe Press, 1968).

HANEY, WILLIAM V., *Communication and Organizational Behavior: Texts and Cases,* 3rd ed. (Homewood, Ill.: Irwin, 1973).

HAYAKAWA, S. I., *Language in Thought and Action,* 3rd ed. (New York: Harcourt Brace, 1972).

JOHNSON, WENDELL, *People in Quandaries* (New York: Harper & Row, 1946).

JOHNSON, WENDELL, *Living with Change,* edited by Dorothy Moeller (New York: Harper & Row, 1972).

LAFFEY, J. L., and R. SHUY, *Language Differences: Do They Interfere?* (Newark, Del.: International Reading Association, 1973).

LEE, IRVING, *Language Habits in Human Affairs,* rev. ed. (New York: Harper & Row, 1958).

OGDEN, C. K., and I. A. RICHARDS, *The Meaning of Meaning,* 8th ed. (New York: Harcourt Brace, 1946).

SHUY, R. W., and R. W. FASOLD, *Language Attitudes: Current Trends and Prospects* (Washington, D.C.: Georgetown University Press, 1973).

WHORF, BENJAMIN LEE, *Language, Thought and Reality,* John B. Carroll, ed. (Cambridge, Mass.: The Technology Press of M.I.T., 1956).

10 NONSPEECH COMMUNICATION

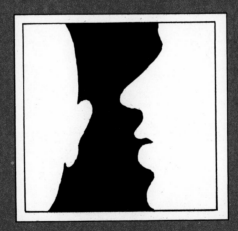

general goal:

To learn the nature, function, and importance of nonspeech communication.

specific objectives:

After completing this unit, you should understand:

What nonspeech communication is.

The various types of nonspeech communication.

Dangers (or problems) in interpreting nonspeech communication.

WHEN SOMEONE SPEAKS TO ME, I receive a three-fold message. Speech communication, as we noted in Chapter 1, contains three components: a verbal element, the words; a vocal element, the variations in the use of the sender's voice; and a visual element, the physical activity of the sender's body that is seen and noted by the receiver. Many books on human communication distinguish between verbal and nonverbal communication—that is, communication that uses words (verbal) and communication that does not use words (nonverbal). This distinction, though useful in some regards, has serious drawbacks as well.

Think about human speech communication for a moment. Does speech communication involve verbal or nonverbal communication? Right you are! It involves both. At the same time. And they are inextricably bound up together; they cannot be separated. How can you utter words (spoken sounds strung together) without using your voice? You can't. And how can you use your voice without varying your pitch, rate, volume, and quality? Right again. You can't. And those vocal characteristics are nonverbal! In a face-to-face situation with a sighted person, can you transmit spoken messages without giving off cues with your body (your physical activity)? No, even if you speak "deadpan," that will make some impression on the receiver and constitute part of the message received. You cannot separate the verbal from the nonverbal elements (except for the purpose of analysis) in speech communication.

defining nonspeech communication

We have already talked about the two nonverbal elements of speech communication in our chapter on transmission. We had to. You cannot analyze speech transmission without examining the vocal element (sometimes called *paralanguage*) and the visual or physical element (sometimes called *kinesics*).

Not all the messages we human beings receive are speech communication messages. We attach significance to other information gathered by our senses; we interpret other things than just speech as having meaning. It is those nonspeech messages that this chapter is about. All of these received messages will be nonverbal, but more important, I think, is the fact that all these meanings were stimulated without speech.

types of nonspeech communication

Those who have written about nonverbal communication are not in agreement on the categories we should use for analysis. I think the easiest way to classify nonspeech communication is on the basis of the channels used to pick up the "messages." The five senses, then, would give the categories for analysis. The only problem with this system, however, is that one important kind of nonspeech communication does not fall neatly into one of the five categories. We shall have to deal with it separately. In spite of this flaw in the system, let us look at five types of nonspeech communication: (1) touching, (2) tasting, (3) smelling, (4) hearing, and (5) seeing, and then note one multichannel type.

Touching

The first messages we human beings get are touch messages. The doctor spanks us, or, if a follower of Dr. Ferdinand Leboyer, rubs us, strokes us, and massages us. Our parents kiss, nuzzle, caress, embrace, cuddle, pat, and hug us. I'm told that these early tactile experiences are important in our later development as persons.

Touching

Communication through touch is not limited to infants or little children, of course. Linus may have grown attached to the feel of his security blanket, but I confess I have some things that give me messages of comfort and reassurance through touch also. And I get messages from touching people as well as things!

Think of the touching behaviors we use for communication. We shake hands in greeting; some folks seem to use kissing for greetings rather indiscriminately, while others are very parsimonious with their kisses. We hug—sometimes, some people, under some circumstances. We pat each other on the back, and sometimes we pat another person's behind. Again, it depends on the circumstances, doesn't it? With some people we hold hands. With others, we grasp hands rather than shake them. When we embrace, we may cling to each other. Occasionally, we get slapped—or slugged.

We learn to attach meanings to tactile behavior, and we learn the norms of our culture that govern touching other human beings. I remember how vividly the cultural differences were brought home to me by observing differences in tactile behavior norms. I was in Greece the first time, walking in front of the national Parliament building near the tomb of the Unknown Soldier. There were two of the royal guards (*evzones*)—the elite of the military units of Greece—walking in front of me. They were in uniform. They were walking up the street holding hands. I don't mean shaking hands. I mean *holding* hands! Of course, I see that same behavior fairly often now (almost twenty years later) in New York City, but it meant something different in Greece from what it might mean here. There were no sexual overtones to the touching in Greece between two men. Although it is a sign of friendship, it is not considered intimate behavior. When I visited Italy for the first time, I was also struck by the unaffected, unself-conscious touching between men. Men walked down the street with their arms around each other or with their arms on each other's shoulders. A strange sight in 1960 to one who had grown up in the United States.

In our (American) culture, touching is usually reserved for intimate personal situations and relationships. We are quite careful about touching each other. We have been conditioned, we have been taught, whom we can touch—and when and where. (The ambiguity is intended.) There have been hidden cameras set up to record movement patterns at busy cross-walks, and these studies show that we Americans maneuver quite a bit to avoid touching other people—even in these crowded circumstances! We have internalized the norms that prohibit touching (if it can be avoided) those with whom we are not on an intimate basis. And even with those folks, we are expected to limit our touching when we are in public.

Some demonstrations of elation and affection are spontaneous, and the norms are overcome. But the norms are still there. (I think they may be changing somewhat, but the changes are small and slow.) I am always interested in seeing the behavior of the other team members in football and hockey when a goal is scored. Often, team members exuberantly embrace and pat each other. If I am watching the game on TV, I know I will not be allowed to watch that behavior very long—if at all. The director will switch quickly to a view of the fans or the scoreboard. God forbid we should show the watching millions our masculine idols hugging each other and breaking the rules of touch in our society!

One of the instructors in our department has an interesting exercise. He gives each student a copy of a diagram of an outline of a human body. Various parts of the body are numbered. He then asks the students to keep a log for one day of who touches them—and where (using the parts-numbering system of the diagram). Although I have told that instructor I would refuse to turn in such an assignment if I were a student in his class, I think it is an interesting project. You might want to do it—and keep the resulting information to yourself.

Tasting

What messages do you get from taste? Can you get messages such as "I am concerned about you," or "I love you" from taste? When a child tastes a hearty meal prepared by the mother or father, does that child get such a message? What about a husband or wife? Isn't that what the old adage "The way to a man's heart is through his stomach" is all about? One can send a message of love through a tasty dish. At least you can send *me* a message of love through a savory gustatory delight!

Tasting

One may get messages of warning through taste as well. Don't you get the message "The milk (or meat) is spoiled" through taste? And in one episode of the excellent television series *I Claudius,* a woman looked up from her meal with a strange look on her face. The look in the eyes was one of terror. She had just received a message through her taste buds that she had been poisoned!

Smelling

We get interesting messages through smell. I walk into an elevator and get the message, "Jo-Ann has been here." The faint aroma of her delicious perfume has lingered behind. I got off the elevator in my apartment house recently and got a message about what we were having for dinner. Talk about delicious smells!

Smelling

I do not know whether you consider the sweet smell of marijuana delicious or not, but I did get a message about my neighbors recently when I stepped out into the hall near their doorway. As for warnings, you may not need to taste some food to get a message that it is spoiled; smelling the stuff may be enough for you. Can you think of other examples (and probably better ones) that illustrate messages received through the sense of smell?

Hearing

We get two kinds of messages through hearing: sounds and silence.

SOUNDS

We have already discussed paralanguage—the vocal characteristics that are part of speech communication. We are not talking here about the sound of the human voice; we are talking about the other, nonspeech messages we get from sound.

Hearing

Many sounds, of course, are used for signals. In our schools, bells signal the beginning and end of class periods. Bells may also indicate the need to vacate a building for a fire or some other emergency. Back in the late sixties at a college I have heard of, there was a certain number of rings for a fire and another number to alert people to a bomb threat. We can use buzzers for signals too. I summon my secretary with a buzzer. The message she gets from that sound is simple—"Help!" Do you have a smoke detector in your home? If so, can't you get a message from that buzzer, if it should go off? And do you have a Smokey detector in your car—a device that picks up radar emissions? What message do you get when that buzzer sound begins?

What other kinds of sounds can you think of that you get messages from?

Just as the presence of sound communicates information to us, so also the absence of sound (silence) communicates information to us. Or at least, it *can* communicate to us. The message we get may be a mistaken message; our received messages are inferences (guesses), after all, and we may guess wrong. But we do attach meaning to silences, don't we?

If I am a parent and my eight-year-old son is in the next room playing with a drum—banging away, and the banging stops and suddenly there is total silence, total silence for what seems like eternity, though it is only two or three minutes, do you think I will get a message from that absence of sound? What message might I get?

My mother came to live with me for a time. When she was not well, I was very concerned for her. She slept in the next bedroom, and I could hear her breathing (I hesitate to call it snoring) at night. During many nights I would wake up and listen for that sound. Once I heard it, I would go back to sleep, relieved and comforted. I feared listening and hearing a silence.

We often interpret silence from other people to mean withdrawal or coldness or hostility. Sometimes we use silence intentionally to convey exactly that impression. But silence is not always a reflection of anger or indifference. One day, lost in thought, I wandered up Fordham Road toward the IND subway. I saw no one I knew on the way to the train and spoke to no one. The next day before class, one of my students said, "So you are too stuck up to speak to your students out of class, eh?" I was dumbfounded. She said I had refused to speak to her when I passed her on the street. "You looked right at me," she said accusingly, "and you didn't speak!" She interpreted my silence as a deliberate slight.

One of my students told me this story. I am sure it is not uncommon. You may know of a similar experience. Her younger sister, a high school sophomore, wanted to go out to a movie during the week with her boyfriend. The parents refused permission. "No dates on school nights," they said. She argued that her classmates had no such restrictions, but her parents were unmoved. She did not speak to them for three days. She did not say mean or angry things. She said nothing at all. In this instance, silence was not golden; it was coldish. And the parents got the message—loud and clear and silent.

There are different kinds of silences; we are silent for different reasons. I am sure you can add to my list, but here are eight kinds of silences I can think of:

The Silence Of:	The Message Is:
Isolation	"I don't want to be bothered now."
Dogmatism	"I've said the last word on that subject."
Anger	"I am irritated with you."
Grief or Pain	"I'm hurt." or "I'm wounded."
Reverence	"I am in awe."
Contemplation	"I'm thinking about it."
Confusion	"I don't understand."
Compassion	"I do understand." (and words are unnecessary.)

Can you think of an illustration from your own experience for each of these kinds of silences? Can you think of instances when the message intended (or understood) by the sender was one kind of silence and the message received (or inferred) by the receiver was a different kind of silence? Wasn't that the problem between my student and me? My silence was one of contemplation; she thought it was a silence of isolation.

As you can see, not all the silences are negative. If I am silent because I wish to show reverence or respect, I intend to send a positive message. If I do not answer you immediately because I am considering what you have said, my reaction is not negative at all. And there are times when there are feelings too deep for words; the silence of compassion, an empathic silence, is as positive as any words could possibly be.

Seeing

We get messages from three kinds of things that we see: (1) object, (2) action, and (3) space.

OBJECT

Do you form ideas ("get messages") based on *objects* you see? Of course. We all do. Indeed, when you see somebody for the first time, don't you attach significance to what you see? You are viewing the person as an object, a thing, a physical or material entity. You see the person's features, physique, clothing, and jewelry. Do you make inferences about the person's hair style? And do you attach meaning to the kinds of clothes or hats or shoes a person wears? If a person wears sneakers, what does that mean to you? If a person wears loafers, what significance does it have? If a man wears patent leather shoes with tassels, what information does that "convey"?

A few years ago, I was at a university with a large ROTC program. Every male student was required to participate in the military training program. One student I know had worn a small, plain gold earring for

Seeing

several years before enrolling in the university. When he went to his first ROTC class dressed up in his uniform, the instructor (a regular army officer) reacted with fury. "You're out of uniform," he shouted. "Take off that damned earring!" The student refused. The officer insisted. The student told the officer he would take off his jewelry (the earring) if the officer, also in uniform, would remove all his jewelry—including his wedding band. The officer thought this offer outrageous and insubordinate; he thought the earring quite different from his finger ring. After all, he said, "My wedding ring means I am normal—in direct contrast with your earring!" Didn't both the student and the officer get messages (meanings) from the jewelry the other wore? Isn't that getting messages from objects?

If you see someone wearing a little American flag pin in his lapel, what message do you get? If you were to see someone with an American flag patch sewed on the seat of his or her jeans, what would you take that to mean? If you see a thirtyish man wearing a high school athletic sweater or jacket with a letter on it, what ideas do you form about that person?

I recently walked into a classroom on our campus and discovered several cigarette butts on the floor around the teacher's desk. What message do you suppose I got from those objects? Right! I said to myself, "One of our teachers is addicted to nicotine and can't get through a class period without a smoke." I also interpreted those cigarettes to mean that some instructor(s) on our campus are lawbreakers, since it is against the law to smoke anything in a classroom in New York State.

If I walked into your home and looked around—at the architecture, at the furniture, at the art objects, and at all the other things there—what messages do you think I would receive? How accurate do you think those messages would be? Or, put another way, how similar would my meanings and your meanings for those objects be?

Two other stories about object language—messages received from viewing objects: One of my former students and dear friends was driving with some college-age friends from Kentucky to New York City. They drove up in an old van painted in psychedelic colors and designs. Though they carefully obeyed all the traffic laws (including those on speed), they were stopped by police three times in a neighboring state. What message do you think the state police got from viewing that van? The other story also concerns a young male college student. He was traveling in Europe, dressed casually in bluejeans and carrying a pack on his back. He also carried a pair of handmade cowboy boots that were precious to him. Stuffed into those cowboy boots were some other items that were precious to him—four rolls of soft American toilet paper. When he got to the border, traveling from France to Italy, he had to pass customs inspection. The inspectors saw the fellow and the way he was dressed. They saw the length of his hair, the pack on his back, and the dangling cowboy boots stuffed with toilet paper. What do you think these things meant to those Italian customs inspectors? Right! A hippie smuggling drugs. To his horror, the student watched as they unrolled every inch of each roll of the precious paper. To their amazement, they found nothing—except toilet paper. What do you think the paper meant to them then?

In Shakespeare's play *As You Like It*, the Duke remarks that his forced exile in the country had brought some benefits—related to object language. He had learned that the objects of nature could "speak" to him. He said:

> *Sweet are the uses of adversity;*
> *Which, like the toad, ugly and venomous,*
> *Wears yet a precious jewel in his head:*
> *And this our life exempt from public haunt*
> *Finds tongues in trees, books in the running brooks,*
> *Sermons in stones and good in everything.*[1]

Do you get messages from Nature? What are they?

One last question regarding object language: Do you think the fact that a person wears eyeglasses means that person is intelligent, intellectual, or industrious?

---

[1] William Shakespeare, *As You Like It*, Act II, scene 1.

We not only get messages from objects we see; we also get messages from *actions* we see. Don't you form ideas (meanings) based on what people do, as well as what they say? I think we all do. According to the old saying, "Actions speak louder than words." One of the Biblical writers indicated that actions communicate more (and more honestly) than words. Isn't that what these comments of James maintain:

> My brothers, what good is it for someone to say that he has faith if his actions do not prove it? . . . Suppose there are brothers or sisters who need clothes and don't have enough to eat. What good is there in saying to them, "God bless you! Keep warm and eat well!"—if you don't give them the necessities of life? So it is with faith: if it is alone and includes no actions, then it is dead.[2]

We receivers, I think, get information from and attach meaning to two kinds of actions: those the sender consciously, intentionally uses to communicate and those the sender performs without conscious intent to communicate. Let us look at each of these briefly.

I remember a faculty member at one university who lost his position and refused to take the decision without making a reply. Carrying a sign, but without speaking, he marched back and forth in front of the administration building. He intended to use action to communicate.

Rosa Parks was not given to making speeches about inequality, injustice, discrimination. But she sent a message that was noted, understood, and reacted to. She simply sat down. Not so dramatic an act, after all—as acts themselves go. But it was a courageous and memorable act, and it helped effect great changes in the United States. That Black woman who simply sat down in the "white section" of a Montgomery, Alabama, bus communicated a powerful and revolutionary message. What was it?

We receivers also get messages from actions of other people that they do not know are communicating information to us. Do you get ideas about people by watching such everyday actions as how they walk or how they eat? If someone gobbles down his or her food as rapidly as possible, do you attach meaning to those actions? If someone uses a spoon to shovel in the peas from the plate to the mouth, do you think that significant? If so, what does it mean to you? If someone uses the salad fork to transport the meat to the mouth, do you notice and think it meaningful?

If I notice the students squirming in their seats, what message might I get? I recently came upon a couple passionately kissing just outside a classroom door. What message would you have gotten as you walked past them into class? If, on a lovely spring day, you see a professor leading his class outside to a grassy spot under a tree, what do you conclude? All of these are actions that a receiver may think expressive or meaningful.

Do we human beings get messages from *space?* Indeed we do. I am not referring to outer space right now, of course, but to the utilization of space

---

[2] James 2: 14–17, *Good News Bible* (New York: American Bible Society, 1976).

here on earth. We see and attach significance to amounts of space, arrangements in space, and distances. In the same way objects and actions "speak" to us, so also there are "languages of space." (I used the word *languages*—the plural—because different cultures attach different meanings to space.)

We make inferences and attach significance to varying amounts of space, don't we? If you see a small house sitting on an extremely small lot, crowded next to other small houses on small lots, what message do you get? If, on the other hand, you see a very large house surrounded by several acres of lawn and trees, what does that say to you? Right now, we are separating the size (or space occupied) from the object itself. The amount of space occupied by the objects tells us something. Look at the classroom of your communication class. How much space is allotted to the instructor and how much to each student? Is the space for the instructor almost as large as the entire space provided for all the students? What message do you get from those space allocations?

If you were to walk down the hall of my office/classroom building and look into the offices, you would find one office about the size of a small classroom filled with six desks, other offices 9 feet by 13 feet with two desks, other offices 9 feet by 13 feet with one larger desk, and one office 15 feet by 20 feet with one large desk. What message would you receive from those relative space allotments? Isn't the person who has the office with more space likely to be higher in rank and status and, maybe, power? Where do you think the six-in-an-office persons are in the academic pecking order?

In our college, student desks are really small tablet chairs. Teachers have real desks with separate (padded) chairs. The instructor's desk is much larger than a student desk. Is that significant? Is it significant that, in our department, many instructors do not sit at the instructor's desk, but rather sit in one of the tablet chairs that students use? What message would you get from the instructor's use of space if you were in such a class?

We get messages from spatial arrangements as well as from amounts of space. In business and government, an office on a higher floor may indicate greater importance or higher rank. The Chairman of the Board may have an office on the top floor of the company's building. He or she would literally be at the top of the company and have reached the heights!

Look at the arrangement of furniture in your classrooms. If the student chair/desks are arranged in a circle or semicircle, does that convey a message to you? What is it? If they are lined up facing the teacher's desk in neat, orderly rows, what do you interpret that arrangement to mean? In which of those classes would you expect the instructor to be more democratic? More authoritarian? More formal? More relaxed? More inclined to lecture? More open to student participation and free discussion? Did you get those messages from spatial arrangements? This insight, of course, is not new. Why did King Arthur use a round table? He did not have the benefit of modern research studies that seem to indicate that, if a rectangular table is used, the people sitting at the ends are more likely to talk and be talked to than are the people sitting on the longer sides. King Arthur knew that there could be no "head of the table" at a round table!

In one college where I taught, when my department held its meetings chairs were arranged in a semicircle. One member of the department consistently sat on a chair in back of the semicircle. There were enough chairs for all the members *in* the circle, but he sat outside the group of chairs. Do you think he was sending a message to the other department members? What was it?

Human beings, like many of the lower animals, have a sense of territoriality; they have a personal space that they believe belongs to them. Each of us marks out, in his or her own mind, a kind of invisible circle of space around us: that space is mine! If someone else invades our territory by crowding in upon us, we are offended. We feel aggressed upon. How far out from the body that personal space extends depends on the personality of the individual; we each set our own territoriality limits. As we shall see, however, there are cultural patterns involved here.

Before we examine the cultural variations in perception of appropriate distances in interpersonal communication, let us look at one other aspect of territoriality. We not only have a little space around ourselves that we think belongs to us; we also have some locations—specific places—that we think are ours. Do you have a chair that is yours? Do you resent anyone else sitting in that chair? Archie Bunker is not atypical in that regard. Haven't we all staked out some spaces that are ours alone, that we want other people to keep hands off? When you eat with your family, are there particular places for each person to sit? Not that those places are marked with placecards—far from it, but the individual places are understood.

My mother came in and complained to me one day, "Someone has been sitting on my bed!" I called her "Momma Bear" and told her it must have been Goldilocks. It did not amuse her; her territory had been invaded. I am sure you can give far more illustrations of spaces and places that people think of as their very own. I would be delighted if you would share them with me.

So far we have looked as the language of space in terms of amount and arrangement. Let us now examine distance.

What is the proper distance for conducting interpersonal communication? It depends. It depends on the relationship between the people involved, on the situation (context), and on the culture. Edward T. Hall has studied interpersonal distances, and he notes that cultures establish the meanings attached to space between persons. That means, then, that the meanings will vary from culture to culture.

How much distance do you put between yourself and other people? Well, I'm sure you are saying, even inside the same culture, that varies.

There are times, aren't there, when you are whispering secret or confidential information or ideas to someone else? The person you are talking to must have a very intimate relationship with you for you to share such information. You would operate on that kind of basis with your lover, your wife or husband, your best friend, and perhaps some members of your family—but few others. To communicate that kind of intimate information, based on an intimate relationship, you will probably position yourself at an *intimate distance.* That's very close. Just how close is it? Check it out for yourself.

There are many people with whom you are on a friendly basis, but who are not close friends. They are acquaintances. You see them at parties, at school, at work. When you converse with them, you are on a personal plane, though not an intimate one. The information you are sharing is not secret or confidential. In this case we position ourselves with more space between us and the other person(s). It is a personal distance—a normal conversational distance. Even when we talk with close friends, if we are not sharing secret or confidential information, we will use this *personal distance,* won't we?

We communicate with many people every day with whom we have only a casual relationship. We talk to salespeople, mechanics, security guards, repairers of all sorts, telephone installers, and many others. We do not not discuss personal matters with them; we certainly do not discuss intimate matters with them. More than likely, our communication is brief and businesslike. The distance we put between ourselves and such people is somewhat greater than the personal distance we use for friends and acquaintances. It is an *impersonal* or *casual distance.*

When one is speaking to a group of people, especially a large group of people, we not only speak more loudly; we also speak from a greater distance. We can call that distance a *public distance.*

How much space constitutes the appropriate personal distance or the appropriate casual distance? Just how many feet or inches are we talking about in each case? That varies with one's culture. According to Hall, most Americans find two to three feet the comfortable distance for social conversation. That is considered the "proper" personal distance. In Latin and Arab countries, however, the "proper" distance for conversation is less than two feet. Can you imagine what might happen when an American (not of Latin descent or heavily influenced by Latin culture) engages an Arab in conversation? (Or someone from France, Spain, Italy, or Brazil, for that matter.) The American would establish the "normal" personal distance of around three feet; the Arab would read this distance as casual and cold and move closer in order to be at the "proper" personal distance. The American would read this distance as either intimate or pushy and move back to create the "correct" personal distance. This little forward move and backward retreat would make a kind of dance to accompany the conversation. Both would be uncomfortable throughout; they would be reading different languages of space!

We do receive messages from space—from amounts of space, from arrangements in space, and from distances through space. We ought to be aware of what is communicated to us through the language of space, but we also must remember that the way space is interpreted varies greatly from culture to culture.

A Multisensory Type: Time

We have examined five types of nonspeech communication: touching, tasting, smelling, hearing, and seeing. But there is one important type of nonspeech communication that does not fit into this classification system. We do not perceive this particular type of communication through one of the senses. If we perceive it at all, we do so through several of the senses. Time, after all, involves relationships. How are you aware of time and differences in time? You don't touch, taste, smell, hear, or see it. How, then, do we grasp it? We construct it in our minds by using several of the senses—or more accurately, by using information received through several of the senses.

Though we may be aware of time indirectly rather than directly through one of the five senses, we are (at least in our culture) aware of time. And time variations do give us "messages."

Time

We talk about time as if it were something tangible. Have you ever said, "Give me just a little of your time," or "I want to take some time for that today," or "I don't want to waste my time," or "He lost no time in doing that"? Perhaps you "spend your time" studying or you wonder how much "time a particular assignment will consume." You may even have commented about "the ravages of time." In all these cases, we are referring to time almost as if it were an object.

In our culture, we view time as something linear; it is sequential. We can divide this sequence into points that occur one after the other. These points are combined into segments of varying duration. After all, we divide time up into millennia, centuries, years, seasons, months, weeks, days, hours, seconds, and we can even divide the seconds up into smaller units. Not all cultures look at time in this same way.

We will be influenced, of course, by the way our culture looks at time and divides it up. We will also be influenced by the way our culture values the segments and the intervals. Think about it for a moment. Do you place a high premium on punctuality? Do you think it important to be "on time"? What is "on time" to you? Is it "right on the dot"? What is "the dot"?

If you have a date with someone for 8:00 P.M., and 8:00 P.M. comes and goes, but your date does not arrive, will you get a message? Right or wrong, will you attach meaning to the fact that the person was not there at the appointed time? What if the person does not arrive at 8:30 or 9:00 or 10:00? What message, if any, would you get? Isn't the message based on *time?* The point in time came, but the person did not.

One of my students told me she had lost five jobs in one year. She had a problem arriving at work "on time." The employers expected her at the time the offices opened—9:00 A.M. She usually arrived between 9:30 and 10:00. They interpreted her tardiness as lack of interest in her work, and they lost interest in keeping her employed.

Do you think an instructor might get a message if a student consistently comes to class ten minutes after the class has begun? What message do you think the teacher would receive? Is that the only possible explanation for the student's behavior (tardiness)? You're right. We can get the wrong message from nonspeech communication—just as we can from speech communication.

Attitudes toward time vary greatly from culture to culture. I remember well my first trip to Greece. I had a ticket for a play, and I was eager to see it. My ticket said 10:00 P.M. (the regular show time in Greece—at least the regular official show time). At 9:45 P.M., I met my friend Dimitri and began walking as fast as I could. I knew we were about a half hour from the theatre and wanted to rush. He asked me why I was in such a hurry, and I noted the time of performance written on the tickets. He laughed and suggested I relax. "The play will begin at 10:30," he said confidently. "But it says 10:00 right on the ticket," I persisted. "Take my word for it," he rejoined. "We are in Athens. No one expects the play to begin when they announced. It will start at 10:30." We got to the theatre at 10:20, and the audience was still strolling in. That show started promptly—at 10:30.

I was told of an incident that occurred in Italy. An Italian family in Venice asked an American to dinner. The time given was 8:00 P.M. The American arrived at 8:00, but the family was not ready for him. They didn't expect him for another hour, and dinner was served closer to 10:00 P.M. than to 8:00. There were different cultural readings of the language of time.

What does it mean to be early or late? And how do you interpret "earliness" or "lateness"? Not only are there cultural factors involved; there are personal ones as well.

We get some messages related to points in time; we get messages also from duration in time. If I devote only a "short time" to some subject or devote a "long time" to something else, would you get a message, based on the duration of time consumed? Do you tend to think something that takes a long time is more important than something that is covered quickly? And just how long *is* "a long time" anyway?

Is "a long time" spent in the dentist's chair the same long time as that spent in your lover's arms? Or is "a short time" spent making love the same short time spent making supper?

We do get messages from an awareness of time, but the messages vary greatly from person to person and culture to culture. We must be careful not to think our interpretations of the language of time are absolute or infallible.

reminders about nonspeech communication

Perhaps it would be wise to close this chapter with a few reminders.

1. The interpretation of nonspeech communication is learned. If one divides communication into the categories *verbal* and *nonverbal,* the same principle applies. The meanings of words are learned; so are the meanings of nonword stimuli.

2. Nonspeech communication communicates primarily emotional information. When we want to stir up heavy, intellectual meanings, we turn to words.

3. Attaching meaning involves making inferences, and one can get a mistaken message from nonspeech "languages."

4. The interpretation of nonspeech communication is culturally conditioned. People from different cultures, therefore, may make quite different assumptions about nonspeech communication, may use nonspeech communication in very different ways to communicate quite different meanings, and may attach quite dissimilar meanings to the same stimuli. Nonspeech communication is not universal. Not only may people from

other cultures perceive different things from the ones we perceive; they may attach significance to things we do not attach significance to, they may not attach meaning to things we attach meaning to, and they may get different "messages" from the same things.

SUGGESTIONS FOR FURTHER READING

BIRDWHISTELL, R. L., *Introduction to Kinesics* (Louisville: University of Louisville Press, 1952).

BIRDWHISTELL, R. L., *Kinesics and Contexts* (Philadelphia: University of Pennsylvania Press, 1970).

BOSMAJIAN, HAIG A., *The Rhetoric of Nonverbal Communication* (Glenview, Ill.: Scott, Foresman, 1971).

EISENBERG, ABNÉ M., and RALPH R. SMITH, JR., *Nonverbal Communication* (Indianapolis: Bobbs-Merrill, 1971).

HALL, E. T., *The Silent Language* (New York: Doubleday, 1959).

HALL, E. T., *The Hidden Dimension* (Garden City, N.Y.: Doubleday, 1966).

HARRISON, R. P., *Beyond Words* (Englewood Cliffs, N.J.: Prentice-Hall, 1974).

KNAPP, MARK L., *Nonverbal Communication in Human Interaction* (New York: Holt, 1972).

KONEYA, MELE, and ALTON BARBOUR, *Louder Than Words: Nonverbal Communication* (Columbus, Ohio: Charles Merrill, 1976).

LEATHERS, DALE G., *Nonverbal Communication Systems* (Boston: Allyn & Bacon, 1976).

MEHRABIAN, ALBERT, *Silent Messages* (Belmont, Calif.: Wadsworth, 1971).

MONTAGU, ASHLEY, *Touching: The Significance of Skin* (New York: Columbia University Press, 1971).

ROSENFELD, LAWRENCE, and JEAN CIVIKLY, *With Words Unspoken: The Nonverbal Experience* (New York: Holt, 1976).

RUESCH, JURGEN, and WELDON KEES, *Nonverbal Communication: Notes on the Visual Perception of Human Relations* (Berkeley: University of California Press, 1956).

11
VERBAL MESSAGES: PURPOSES, TYPES, AND DELIVERY SYSTEMS

general goal:

To learn why we send verbal messages, what kinds of verbal messages we send, and how those messages are conveyed.

specific objectives:

After completing this unit, you should understand:
What messages are—and are not.
Four general purposes for which verbal messages are sent, or, put another way, four types of responses the sender tries to elicit.
Three types of messages we send and receive.
The nature and effects of the various channels and media used in human communication.

IN CHAPTER 2, we noted that one way to look at the process of human communication was to ask this series of questions:

Who?
Says what?
To whom?
In what context?
Through what channel?
With what response (effect)?

It is time to look much more closely at the *what*—the messages transmitted by the message-producer and reacted to by the message-receiver. In this chapter, I will discuss what messages are (and are not), some purposes for which messages are transmitted, three types of messages sent and received, and channels through which messages are conveyed. In the next chapter, I will discuss with you aspects related to the structure and content of messages.

what messages are (and are not)

First, let's deal with what messages are and are not. When discussing the process of human communication and the elements in that process, I pointed out that we cannot transmit ideas from person to person. Instead, we transmit messages. Ideas are electrical impulses and chemical reactions that stay locked up inside our own brains; there is no way we can *send* those to another person. Not only do we not transmit ideas from person to person; we do not *transfer* meaning when we communicate. To transfer something, you simply take it from one place to another; you load it up (like cargo on a truck, for example) and ship it to its destination, where you unload it. What you unload at the destination is the same thing (the cargo) you loaded at the beginning of the shipping process. When you move your belongings by truck, you expect the *same* belongings you put into the truck to come out at unloading time. *Transfer,* after all, denotes "to carry across." You just carry something from one place (or person) to another. But *meaning* is not tranferred in the communication process; that process is much more complicated than shipping household goods!

What we transmit is not meanings—ideas, purposes, feelings, intentions; what we transmit is messages that represent those ideas, purposes, feelings, and intentions. But what are messages? First, a general definition: *A message* is any sign (signal *or* symbol) capable of being interpreted meaningfully. All messages are made up of signs, which, you remember, stand for something else. The signs in the message may either announce what

The Message Intended

they stand for, pointing directly to the referents (signal), or the signs may remind one of what they stand for, giving clues to the referents (symbols).

In human speech communication, there are three senses in which we use the term *message*. In fact, there may be, in any human speech communication event, three distinct messages involved: the message selected and intended by the sender, the message-producer; the message transmitted by the sender, the message-producer; and the message received and interpreted by the listener, the message-receiver. Let's look at what happens and see if we can clarify those distinctions a little.

A person never deliberately sends a message unless that person has a reason for doing so; that reason is the sender's purpose or intention. We communicate in order to achieve certain intended results, to elicit certain responses from the receiver. The message-producer must decide on a message before sending it. The message selected is one that suits his or her prupose, the situation, and the intended receiver. There are many choices open to a message-producer; one can represent the same basic ideas many different ways. The first message, then, is the one created in the mind of the sender *before* it is sent.

The Message Transmitted (or Produced)

After the message-producer, the sender, has selected and organized a message mentally, he or she converts that message into code and transmits it. In this sense, the message is the actual physical product of the message-sender; it is the spoken words, vocal sounds, and visible signs produced by the sender that carry information and stimulate meaning. The transmitted message is made up of the sights and sounds transmitted; it is the communiqué transmitted by one communicator and received by another communicator. In human speech communication, this message is *behavior;* it is transmitted *in physical form*—as audible sounds and as visible action.

The concept of message as *product* is important. The message is something we human beings produce; it is something we make and do. That is true of all human communication, not just speech communication. When we paint, the picture we produce is the message; when we compose, the song we create is the message; and when we speak, speech (with all its three elements—verbal, vocal, and visible) is the message. Indeed, we may define message transmission as the production of behavioral events related to the internal states of human beings and intended to induce effects in other human beings.

Since the messages we send are intended to stimulate meaning in others, these messages could be called *transmitted stimuli*. These messages are created out of selected bits of information, transmitted in some code, and organized into some pattern or structure. If we analyze a message, we must examine its code, its content, and its structure.

A *code* can be defined as a transmittable system of signs. To be a code, it must be made up of signs—elements that signal or symbolize meanings. The gestures of the officials in football games meet that criterion, and most printed programs at football games include a translation of the various gestures for those who do not already know the code. We noted in Chapter 7 that languages are codes and that the code we are using is American English.

All codes are made up of elements (signs) that can be transmitted. We transmit the 42 sounds of American English with our speech mechanisms; the Navy had a code that used lights; and the Native Americans transmitted messages using a code of smoke signals. For a code to work, it obviously must be transmittable.

All codes have a system. They have patterns; they have structure; they have predictability (if one knows the patterns). There is an organization or method basic to each code. Of course, it is a secret code unless one knows it! Some codes have a more complicated system than others, and those are more difficult to break. I am told that the Japanese were never able to break the Navajo code in World War II, when Americans used speakers of Navajo to transmit and receive radio messages containing American plans and orders. The Navajo language is a difficult system to master. American English is much easier.

The coded messages that we send contain bits of information; these bits of information are the message's *content*. It is easier to tell you what information *does* than to tell you what it *is*. Information asserts, and by asserting something, it eliminates other possibilities. Information reduces ambiguity and uncertainty. It narrows choices. At the very least, any bit of information makes an assertion and excludes the possibility of its opposite. If I say, "It is raining," the information provided excludes the possibility of the sky being completely clear. What if I say, "I have hurt myself"? Hasn't that information eliminated the option of "I am unhurt"? But note that I can eliminate other possibilities by providing more specific information. I can tell you, "I have hurt my arm." That information will narrow the search for my injury; you can forget about the rest of my body for the moment. Of course, I could have been even more specific had I given you this bit of information: "I have dislocated my right elbow."

We must remember that the information we transmit is sent out in signs. For that reason, it has been called *symbolic information*. But we cannot forget that messages contain content, because the signs are expressions (representatives) of ideas.

To analyze a message, we must not only analyze its code and its content; we must also analyze its *structure*. Every message is organized in some particular way. (Remember we are not talking about speeches, but messages, which may be only one sentence long.) It is impossible *not* to structure messages; in other words, it is impossible for a message *not* to have structure. It will have some form. What that form will be is up to the message-producer/sender. There are multitudes of choices open; how one puts the message together is a very personal matter.

We have looked at the language code in some detail in Chapter 7. We will examine structure and content of messages in Chapter 12. It is enough for now to remember that the messages transmitted contain coded bits of information arranged in some kind of structure.

The Message Received

Some time back in this chapter, I said that there were three distinct messages in one speech communication event. Thus far, we have examined two of them: the message the sender intended and the message the sender actually transmitted. The third message is the message the receiver gets and interprets. What the receiver actually gets is sensory intakes. The sights and sounds picked up go through the perception process (back to Chapter 3!) and are interpreted as meaning something. The meaning(s) attached to the signals and symbols received by the receiver are the message—as far as the receiver is concerned. The receiver has picked up (taken in) a coded message that must be *decoded*, *organized into symbols and patterns*, and *interpreted*. The result of that decoding, organizing, and interpreting is the listener's message. It is hoped that the receiver's message and the sender's message will have more than a faint resemblance to each other!

purposes of messages

Messages are *what* we transmit. But *why* do we transmit them? We produce messages in order to accomplish certain goals, to elicit certain responses in our receivers. Messages may be classified, then, according to the *purpose* or intention of the message-producer. Traditionally, writers have listed four purposes (or general goals) of message-producers. Although there are writers who have disputed this classification system, it does seem to serve a useful purpose if we focus on the kinds of responses the sender hopes to elicit from the receiver(s).

No one intentionally sends a message to another human being without attempting to induce a response. (Of course, we send out unintentional messages all the time, but here we are concerned only with conscious, intentional messages.) That means the sender has some goal to reach or purpose to achieve. What are the four purposes that motivate our message-sending? We send messages to inform, messages to persuade, messages to inspire, and messages to entertain.

Sender's Goal:	Response Desired From the Receiver:
To *inform*	Understanding; learning
To *persuade*	Changed beliefs or behavior; agreement or action
To *inspire*	Intensified emotions; heightened feelings
To *entertain*	Amusement and enjoyment

If my goal is to inform you, what kind of response do I hope to get from my receiver(s)? I want you to understand what I am explaining to you, to get a clear picture of what I am trying to show you. I may want you to learn something new—to add to your store of concepts and categories, to expand your mental card-file of knowledge. When I finish my message, I do not want you to *do* something or *believe* something; I want you to *know* something.

**One purpose of messages:
Informing**

If my goal is to persuade you, what kind of response am I seeking? I want you to accept my views on some subject. I want you to change your belief system or behavior patterns to fit my world view. I want you to conform to *my* beliefs, values, and attitudes, no matter what your previous beliefs, values, and attitudes were. I want you to agree with me; perhaps I want you to act in conformity with my suggestions. I am clearly trying to exert influence on you; that is what persuasion is all about. *Persuasion* comes from two Latin words meaning "through sweetness." Maybe the old Romans heard my mother say, "You get more flies with sugar than with salt!" Persuasion is the attempt to attract folks over to your side of the opinion fence.

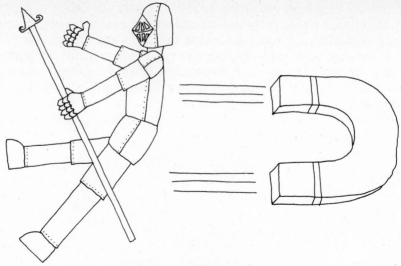

One purpose of messages: Persuading

Inspire

If my goal is to inspire you, what response do I try to get? I am not trying to increase your store of knowledge; I am not trying to change your opinions on some subject. Rather, I am simply trying to take the feelings you already have and stir them up or charge them up a little. I am trying to stimulate you by touching your emotions, deepening your loyalties, and strengthening your sentiments. *Inspire*, in Latin, means "to breathe into," and the message-producer's goal is to breathe life (and maybe a little fire) into the listener's emotions.

One purpose of messages: Inspiring

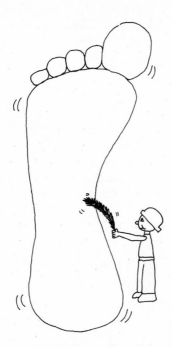

It should be clear that, if my purpose is to entertain you, the response I hope to achieve is enjoyment—not laughter, necessarily, but amusement certainly. This kind of message is sent just for fun, and the reaction desired is pure pleasure. Or maybe sometimes impure pleasure. But pleasure for sure.

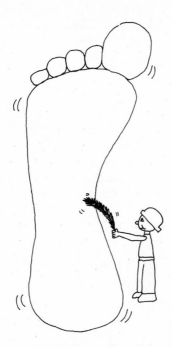

One purpose of messages:
Entertaining

Those are the four goals or purposes for which messages are produced. Here are some examples of short messages (not speeches—messages). Identify the goal or purpose of each:

In the blank, write whether the speaker's purpose is to inform, to persuade, to inspire, or to entertain:

_____ 1. "There are two kinds of opinions: inferences and value-judgments. Neither one can be 'proved' to the same degree of certainty that facts can be. Both are messages about what a person believes." —Professor Artie Craft

_____ 2. "When two Greeks get together, they either start a restaurant or an argument." —Les Sensible

_____ 3. "What this country needs today, brothers and sisters, are men and women who are not ashamed to put on the whole armor of God, who are not ashamed to fight for

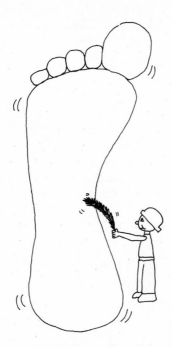
Entertain

281

the cause of righteousness openly and publicly, who are not ashamed to march forward to the martial strains of 'Onward Christian Soldiers!'" —Reverand Hal E. Luyah

_____ 4. "There are two compelling reasons why capital punishment should be forever abolished. First, there is absolutely no proof that it reduces or inhibits crime. Second, all killing is wrong, and the state has no more business killing folks than anybody else does." —Rosetta Stone

types of messages

Not only can we classify messages according to purpose (or goal); we can classify them according to *type*: what *kind* of message is it? I am not talking about content (what information does the message contain?), but about the nature of the message itself. Messages are of three different kinds. One is a fact kind of message, and there are two opinion kinds of messages.

Fact Kind of Messages

Look at these sentences. If you had to label them in terms of fact or opinion messages, which would you call facts?

> New York City is a big city.
> Wilt Chamberlain is tall.
> Farrah Fawcett-Majors is beautiful.
> There is a God who created the universe(s).
> The sun will "rise" tomorrow at 6:38 A.M.

If you called any of these statements fact kind of messages, we need to look at the three types of messages much more closely. None of these sentences is a fact kind of message. Whether you agree with the sentences or not is irrelevant. Even if everyone in the world agreed with these sentences (and that is a doubtful assumption), they still would not be fact kind of messages.

What *is* a fact kind of message? What distinctive properties does it have? How can we recognize it? A fact kind of message relates (or reports) empirical observations; it states information about events in the physical world. It does not evaluate those events; it does not offer interpretations of those events; it does not reach conclusions about those events. It just says: This is the way it is, and the way it is can be checked.

Checking. That is the clue. Verification. Fact kinds of messages can be verified to relative certainty. (I have to be careful about claiming absolute certainty—even for "facts"!) But I can almost hear you saying, "But I can *prove* it. New York *is* a big city, and anybody with eyes can *see* that Wilt Chamberlain is tall. Isn't that verification? Doesn't that make them fact types of messages?" Sorry. No. When I am talking about verification here, I am talking about sense perception—using direct observation by the five senses to check on the accuracy of the message. The argument is probably continuing: "But seeing is one of the senses. So if I *see* that Wilt Chamberlain is tall or Farrah Fawcett-Majors is pretty, that is direct observation by one of the senses." But think a moment. Do we really *see* tallness or prettiness? No, tallness, like beauty, is in the eye of the beholder; both statements contain evaluations of what we see.

If you are still not convinced or if I have not made the concept clear to you, let me try another route. A fact kind of message is clearly either true or false. We can check to find out whether any fact kind of statement is true or not true. There is no point in arguing about facts. Check them out. Anyone with all his or her senses (or access to the information provided by people who were in a position to make the direct observation and had all their senses) should come to the same conclusions. Fact kinds of messages—and only fact kinds of messages—can be labeled "right" or "wrong," "true" or "false."

Can you prove to absolute (or almost) certainty that Wilt the Stilt is tall? Would everyone agree? "Well," someone says, "he sure looks tall to me!" That is the point. It is your evaluation. Would he also look tall to Kareem Abdul-Jabbar? Jabbar's basis for evaluation is different from mine (by over a foot), so what he considers tall may differ a great deal from what I consider tall. To a tribe of pygmies, even I may seem tall! Their basis for evaluation, like mine, is relative. But fact-type messages do not vary with relative criteria. They are statements of what *is* rather than of what it *seems to me.*

If I said, "Wilt Chamberlain is five feet four inches tall," is *that* a fact kind of message? Yes, it is. "But," someone is sure to note, "it is not true. It is a lie!" Right again. The fact kind of message may be either true or false. People can make statements about what is without stating accurately what is. We human beings can be mistaken, and we can (occasionally) lie. The test of a fact *type* of message is not whether it is true or false, but whether it can be established whether it is true or false.

If someone tells me, "Farrah has green eyes," that is a fact kind of message because it can be verified; we can check it out for sure. I do not know whether it is true or false, but I do know we could find out. That makes it a fact type of message.

Since fact statements can be made only about what can be directly observed, fact statements can speak only about the past or the present. We can talk about what *was* or what *is,* but we cannot make factual statements about *what will be.* Until something happens, it is not observable; if it is not observable, it cannot be a fact. Facts are statements we can be certain about, and who can be *absolutely* certain about the future? Not even the greatest meteorologist would claim that his or her predictions are facts. It is hoped that those predictions are based on facts, but the predictions themselves are not fact-type messages.

Let's check again. Here are some sentences. Which of them is a fact kind of message?

New York City has a population of 8.3 million people.
A. Kidney Beane is mayor of the city of New York.
Columbus sighted the island of Hispaniola first in 1789.
There are 26 letters in the English alphabet.
Spiro Vlaka Malaka holds dual citizenship—in both the United States and Greece—and carries two passports.

Did you recognize all the fact kind of messages? That's right. All five sentences are fact-type messages. One could check each of them out for accuracy and find out if what they report is true or not.

Since the word *fact* is used generally to mean what is so, what *is,* how can we talk sensibly about fact kind of messages being either true or false? A *fact*, after all, is not true or false; it just *is.* We must distinguish between the facts, which exist in the physical world, and statements about facts. It is the statements (the attempts to report facts) that can be either true or false. And you will notice that all the way through this discussion I have been careful to talk about "fact *kind* of messages" or fact-*type* messages." It is these messages that can be either true or false, depending on whether they conform to the facts themselves.

I hope that, after all this discussion, if some investigator (or attorney) asks you to "just give us the facts," you will be able to report accurately and factually, without slipping into evaluations, interpretations, and conclusions. Well, you might try *reporting* (using fact-type messages only) the nature of the room you are in right now. Try it. Can you stick to stating facts? Difficult, isn't it? But possible.

Value-Judgment Kind of Messages

There are two kinds of messages that are opinions: value-judgments and inferences. Both are kinds of beliefs, and perfectly rational people with full command of all their senses can disagree about them. They are not statements about physical reality (what is), but about our views of reality (how we see things). Neither value-judgments nor inferences can be called true or false, because we cannot verify them empirically (through direct observation of sense data). Therefore, we cannot be as certain about value-judgments and inferences as we can be about facts.

The trouble is that many people think their opinions are facts and hold to them with dogmatic certainty. Much of the trouble in the world can be attributed to this confusion about kinds of messages! If I am absolutely *sure* that my opinion is a fact (and therefore certain), how can I respect—or perhaps even tolerate—anyone who believes something patently *false*? If my social reality is the only *real* reality, how can you expect me to be patient with people whose view of the world is *wrong*?

Fact messages are not superior (or inferior) to value-judgment and inference messages. Human beings do make evaluations and reach conclusions, and we must send messages about those opinions we hold. But serious communication problems result from thinking those messages are statements of fact. If I send an opinion message (of either opinion kind), thinking it a fact kind of message, and you (my receiver) recognize it as an opinion and disagree with it (responding differently from the way I expected and intended), we will have a communication breakdown. On the other hand, if I send an opinion message, recognizing it as an opinion (and therefore to be held tentatively rather than tenaciously!), and you (my receiver) think it a fact kind of message and accept it as fact, we still have an inefficient communication event (transaction). Both sender and receiver must be able to recognize kinds of messages so they will both be able to assess them and respond to them appropriately.

Value-judgment-type messages state a rating of something based on one's own personal scales of values. They state assessments and attitudes; they evaluate (note the word *value* built in) something.

We have already talked about the many groups that have affected us and about the norms and values we have learned from those groups. Each of us has put together a view of the world—a system of beliefs, values, and attitudes—that is our own. It is on the basis of those values we have incorporated into our world view that we judge ourselves, other people, and anything else in the world we decide to rate. Those values provide the criteria, the standards, for our judgments. They are something like yardsticks; we use them to measure things. These value-measuring devices each have a scale of degrees, ranging from very positive to very negative. The concept may be easier to illustrate than to explain. If I judge Lily Tomlin to be beautiful, what scale of values am I using? The beauty scale, you say, and that's right. And what are the various degrees on the beauty scale? That particular value yardstick would look something like this:

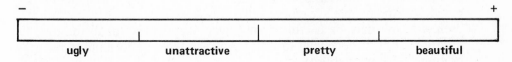

Look at these statements. Are all of them value-judgments? Do all of them rate something? And what kind of scale does one apply in each sentence?

> Compromise is cowardly.
> Algebra and geometry are useless to most people.
> Present income tax laws are unjust.
> Religion is extremely harmful to human beings.
> Religion is extremely beneficial to human beings.
> Hitler was an honorable man.
> Willie Copout is quite lazy.
> Drinking alcoholic beverages (or using any other drugs) is immoral.
> The Affirmative Action program at this college is a failure.
> Speech courses are valuable and relevant.

Did you recognize all ten of these statements as value-judgments? Did you look for (and find) the rating word(s) in each statement? Judgments usually use adjectives or adverbs to express the judgments. In contrast with fact-type statements, which emphasize denotative meanings, value-judgment-type messages emphasize connotative meanings. Where fact-type statements are rather objective (focusing on the object of the message rather than the source), value-judgments are, by their very nature, subjective (focusing on the sender's attitudes and leanings).

Look at the evaluative words: *cowardly, useless, unjust, harmful, beneficial, honorable, lazy, immoral, failure* (not all evaluative words are adjectives and adverbs!), *valuable,* and *relevant.* Each of them states the message-producer's assessment of something's worth (value) or lack of worth. They show the sender's approval or disapproval. They are I-like-it or I-don't-like-it, I'm-for-it or I'm-against-it, I-think-it-worth-something or I-think-it-worthless kinds of messages.

Do you agree that the value-yardsticks for the sentences above use these scales, running from positive to negative evaluations:

—	+
cowardly	brave
useless	useful
unjust	just
harmful	beneficial
dishonorable	honorable
lazy	energetic (maybe tireless)
immoral	moral
failure	success
valueless	valuable
irrelevant	relevant

Unlike fact-type messages, which attempt to report, value-judgments state reactions. And people's reactions differ, because their values differ. What is useless to me may be useful to you; what seems harmful to me may be harmless or even beneficial to you; what may feel comfortable to me may be quite uncomfortable to you.

Two brief stories may serve to underscore the point. A few years ago, I received a telephone call from a worried mother. She knew that I knew both her daughter and the young man with whom the daughter was going out. She did not know the young man well, she said, and wanted to ask me a delicate question. "Would he ever do anything—immoral?" she asked. I was taken aback and told her I did not know what she meant by "immoral." "Of course you do," she persisted. "Everyone knows what's immoral. Would he ever do anything *immoral?*" I was just as insistent that the word *immoral* meant different things to different people, though she maintained that morals were absolute and clear-cut. Knowing something about the young woman's background, I said to the lady, "You're a minister's wife, aren't you?" She was. "And," I deviously continued, "I've heard you are a very gracious hostess. Do you ever serve wine with your meals?" This good Lutheran pastor's wife seemed a little shocked that I would even doubt it. "Of course," she replied, "we have wine with every evening meal." I then informed her that my mother's pastor would very quickly tell her that she and her husband were immoral, because they drank alcoholic beverages. "Drinking wine is not immoral," she rejoined. "That's nonsense!" "To you," I said, "it is not immoral. To him it is very immoral. Morality is different things to different people. Concepts of morality are relative to the culture; they are not universal or absolute. What you judge to be immoral, someone else might judge to be quite moral. I cannot answer your question about your daughter's friend." The conversation ended with an impasse.

In the not too distant past, one of my relatives wrote me in despair about her son. He was, she said, a dismal failure. And even worse, he seemed happy with his life and thought himself a success! The parents were quite distressed, because they had helped the young man get a good education, and he preferred to work in a garage instead of at a profession. I did the best I could to help this perplexed parent see the value system of her son. I am not sure I convinced her that what she thought to be failure could be viewed as success and that what she thought was a "wasted life" could be viewed as a "useful, productive" one. But I certainly tried.

We cannot (and should not try to) impose our personal values on other people. We can state our judgments; we can explain the rationale for our judgments. But other people have as much right to their scales of values as we do to ours. The best we can hope for, really, is to compare judgments with them and try to understand the basis on which they made evaluations so divergent from our own.

Inference Kind of Messages

The other kind of opinion messages is called inferences. Inferences are conclusions reached by logical means. We make guesses about the unknown, based on what we know and believe; those guesses are inferences. We "prove" inferences with the reasons we believe them to be valid. But we cannot prove inferences to certainty—even relative certainty; we can, at most, establish a high degree of probability for them.

So far, we have clarified what fact-type messages and value-judgment-type messages are. Inferences are any opinions that are not value-judgments (ratings, assessments, evaluations). Will that hint help in identifying them? Let's try. Look at these statements. Which of them are inferences:

1. Gerald Chevrolet was once President of the United States.
2. Gerald Chevrolet is brilliant.
3. Gerald Chevrolet should be returned to office.
4. The U.S. Bureau of Labor Statistics reported that the unemployment rate rose by 1 per cent in August.

5. The rate of unemployment in the United States is too high.
6. The United States is going through a period of recession.
7. Four of the ten magazines with the greatest circulation in the United States are sex-oriented magazines.
8. Viewing pornography is personally and socially harmless.
9. Pornography (sexually explicit materials) should be kept out of the hands of children under the age of 21.

I am sure you recognized the pattern to the statements. 1, 4, and 7 were fact-type messages; 2, 5, and 8 were value-judgment-type messages; and 3, 6, and 9 were inferences. "But I can give you facts to back up statements 3, 6, and 9," I can hear someone saying. Perhaps, but the statements *themselves* are not facts; they are conclusions one may (or may not) come to, based on facts, value-judgments, and other inferences.

Inferences are not reports of events, but interpretations of events; we reach generalizations about past or present events, and we can make predictions about future events. Through reasoning, we reach conclusions; those conclusions (or claims) are inferences. Inferences, then, are the final link in a chain of reasoning. But what is reasoning? It is moving from one statement to another on the assumption that the first statement makes the second statement either *inevitable* or *highly probable.* There are three links in that reasoning chain: the first statement (a premise—something known or believed), an assumption (a belief, often unstated and unarticulated, that seems to warrant or justify moving to the conclusion), and the concluding statement (the conclusion, the claim, the inference).

We make inferences all the time. Reasoning forms the basis of what we believe and do throughout our life. And underlying every chain of reasoning is some assumption—often an inference or conclusion that we arrived at earlier. Think about a simple example of the reasoning process for a moment. You must decide whether to sit down on a chair or not. You know that you have sat on other chairs and they have held you up (your premise); you *assume* that this chair is like the other chairs you have sat on and will hold you up also (your assumption); so you decide you can trust this chair to support the weight of your body (your inference), and you sit down. Of course, the assumptions on which we proceed can sometimes be mistaken. The chair could have been broken or weak, and it could have collapsed when we sat down. Inferences are guesses, a kind of gambling, and we operate on the principle of probability (or, in gambling terms, we figure the odds). Usually, the chairs *do* support our weight.

Take another simple example of the reasoning process we use in everday life. Your spouse has cooked a new main dish for dinner; you have never tasted it before. You know that almost everything your spouse has ever cooked has been quite good (your premise—a value judgment, by the way); you assume that this new dish will be just as good as all the others he or she has prepared (your assumption); so you conclude it is safe to eat this new entree (your inference). What if the new dish turns out to be a disaster and tastes terrible? Well, you guessed wrong. Tough luck. But there was no way of *knowing* until you tried it. You had to make some inference about how to act; you could not do anything (and refusing to try it is doing something) without using the reasoning process and drawing a conclusion (making an inference).

Of course, we must be careful about the assumptions we make. Those assumptions (so thoroughly *assumed* that we rarely examine them closely or question their validity) are the essential link in the reasoning chain. Even if the premise is quite solid fact, if the assumption is mistaken, the conclusion will be awry. It is important that we know we are making assumptions when we jump to a conclusion. (And every conclusion *does* require a jump—what the philosopher Kierkegaard called "the leap of faith.") It serves to remind us that, even though the conclusion is *probable*, other conclusions are *possible*; it reminds us that there is a margin of error in the process.

Perhaps some natural science major is saying, "That all may be true of reasoning in everyday life, but in science our system is different." Kierkegaard and Einstein would reply that that is not so; rather, they would say, scientists use the same system of logic as everyone else, and they too must jump to conclusions. True, they tend to look before they leap, but they must make inferences too, and their inferences also require a leap of faith. Think of another simple example: You go to your physician because you have some red splotches on your body and you want whatever it is cured. Your doctor looks at you and sees the red splotches. He or she may or may not say, "Aha! I see red splotches on your body," but the doctor will note those facts (his or her premise). The physician will, perhaps, assume that those splotches on your body are symptoms of an illness because they resemble other splotches he or she has seen (the doctor's assumption). The physician will then say, "I think you have measles"—or an allergy or syphylis or hives or acne or whatever the physician guesses the problem is (the doctor's inference). True, the doctor's guess is an educated guess; her or his inference is a trained, thought-through inference. But it is an inference, a guess, just the same! And that inference is based on *assumptions*—unproved and often unknowable!

When I offered a definition of reasoning earlier, I said that it is "moving from one statement to another on the assumption that the first statement makes the second statement [the inference] either [logically] inevitable or highly probable." That definition implies that making inferences involves analyzing relationships between sentences (or among sentences, if you include the often-unstated, but important, assumption). Reasoning is involved with two kinds of relationships: inevitability and probability.

The principle of *inevitability* notes that once we have posited one sentence, other sentences may be necessarily implied by it. The premise(s) almost *require* the conclusion. Once we grant the premise(s), we must, of necessity, grant the inference. Such inferences are attempts to eliminate uncertainty. We must remember, however, that they would produce absolute certainty only if all the premises were absolutely certain (facts), and that is rarely if ever so.

Inevitability

Let us look at a chain of reasoning that relies on the principle of inevitability. "All of the students at this college are brilliant. *I* am a student at this college. *So*: I must be brilliant." If you grant the two premises, isn't the conclusion inevitable? The real question, then, in reasoning on the principle of inevitability, is this: Are the premises (and the unstated assumptions, if any) *really* sound? Because the premises, once conceded, will lead us inevitably to the conclusion (inference).

Let's look at one more example of the principle of inevitability. You have just been introduced to another student on campus, and in the course of the conversation, you say, "All college athletes are stupid freeloaders." The person to whom you have just been introduced replies, "I'm an athlete and I'm going to this college." Both of you will probably be a little embarrassed. What conclusion is *inevitable* if we grant both your statement and the other student's statement? If what you say is so and what he or she says is so, that person is a stupid freeloader. No way around it! When we send messages, we need to be sure we really mean to imply what our sentences imply *of necessity*. Watch out for those necessary implications!

The other kind of relationship that may be involved in reasoning is *probability*. The principle of probability notes that once we have posited one (or more) sentence(s), other sentences might be posited with a high degree of probable accuracy. In this case, the premise(s) do not require the conclusion, but they do make the conclusion highly probable. The odds on the conclusion are pretty good. Any time you are making guesses about the future, you are dealing with probabilities. Until something happens, it is not directly observable; until something happens, it is not a fact; until something happens, it is not absolutely certain—no matter *how* highly probable. Anything in the future is in the realm of the possible/plausible/probable—never in the realm of the certain.

Probability

Now it is true that some people *feel* certain about future events, but we must recognize that those events are not certainties until they occur. Otherwise, we become dogmatic and intolerant of those who have reasoned to different conclusions from our own. "Well," said a member of the Seekers Club when we came to this point in the course, "you are not going to shake my belief in the Second Coming of Christ or in the surety of a Last Judgment!" I assured her I was not trying to shake her *faith*, but those matters *were* matters of faith rather than certainty. Indeed, certainty makes faith unnecessary. People of faith live as if the future were sure—without requiring sense verification for assurance; they "walk by faith and not by sight." If you are absolutely *sure* of something, what do you need faith, and trust, and hope for? Faith is feeling and living assured—without asking for direct, sense proof.

Inferences cannot be verified in the way that fact kind of messages can be verified. I would hesitate to use the word *true* of inferences, because (unlike fact kind of messages) we cannot establish the truth or falseness of inference-type messages. Inferences may be valid or invalid, but they are not either true or lies.

Let us look at a chain of reasoning based on the principle of probability. The weatherman on the TV Evening News says: "It is now raining thirty miles to the west of us. The rain should reach us within three hours. You can expect heavy showers about 10 P.M." The meteorologist is an "expert" and has access to a great deal of factual data. "It is now raining thirty miles to the west of us" is a fact kind of message, and the meteorologist knows the wind direction and wind velocity. On the basis of the known facts, the weatherman predicts our weather report by weighing probabilities and making inferences. Sometimes, the meteorologists will tell us the "odds," like when they say, "There is a 40 per cent chance of rain this evening." At other times, they do not state their report in terms of the probabilities, but their inferences are based on the principle of probability just the same.

We do not stop at *making* inferences, we *act* on the basis of these guesses. If we do not recognize inferences for what they are but instead mistake them for facts, we may act in a mistaken, misguided, unfortunate, or perhaps even dangerous way. If we do not treat inferences as the guesses they are, if we act on them as if they were certainties, we will not calculate the margin of error; we will not do the necessary monitoring (checking). The results may be costly to us and to others.

So far in this chapter, we have examined what messages are and what they are not; the three senses in which we use the term *message*, the three components of any message (the code, the content, and the construction), the four purposes for which we send messages; and the three types of messages we send and receive. We are now ready to turn our attention to the delivery system through which we send messages.

delivery system

In Chapter 2, I discussed the current confusion of terms related to the delivery system through which we send and receive messages. (See pp. 52-53.) This section, then, will be a review and slight amplification. As you will remember, I offered a suggestion for making our terminology more consistent.

At present, scholars in communication theory use two words to refer to the various means we use to get our messages back and forth between human beings: *channels* and *media*. Both the words *channel* and *medium* (the singular of *channels* and *media*) are metaphors (words containing images); they picture ideas for us.

What is a channel? Well, what is the English Channel? What does it do? It is not a sea or an ocean; instead, it is a small body of water between a sea and an ocean that serves to connect them. You can get from the Atlantic Ocean to the North Sea *through* the English Channel. Another water channel closer to home (at least to *my* home) is the misnamed Harlem River, which is not a river at all, but a channel. It connects the East River with the Hudson River; indeed, the Circle Line sightseeing boats sail from the East River to the Hudson River *through* (or by means of) this channel regularly.

And what about the word *medium*? Its basic meaning is "in the middle," something in between. Do you like your steaks well done, rare, or medium? You probably don't believe in them, but did you ever go to a medium? Mediums are the folks who claim to be able to stand in the middle between the physical world and the "spirit world" and communicate messages back and forth. They claim to be Mr.-or-Ms.-In-Between. (Maybe you know Gian-Carlo Menotti's opera *The Medium*, and that helps clarify the picture.)

All right, you are doubtless saying, a channel is something that provides a connection, and a medium is something in the middle. So? As I said in Chapter 2, we can't have communication without some delivery system. We must have some method of getting the message from the message-producer (the source or sender) *to* the message-receiver. The delivery system is what the message goes *through*. Both *channel* and *medium* are apt metaphors, because whatever the delivery system, it serves as a passageway or connection (a channel), and it is in between the sender and the receiver (a medium).

The problem is that the two terms have been used interchangeably and both have been used to designate several different kinds of things. There have been at least two distinct senses in which the terms *channel* and *medium* have been used. Channels or media are, it is agreed, conveyors; they are carriers. But what do they convey? The terms have been applied both to message-conveyors *and* conveyors of message-conveyors!

First, let me use an analogy and then apply it to human communication. I wish to send a package from my house in the city to my cabin in the country. I decide to use United Parcel Service to take the package from one place to the other; United Parcel Service carries packages from place to place on trucks, and trucks travel over roads. Now, the application: What *means* or *method* did I use to convey my package? The truck was the conveyor, you say. No question about it. And I agree. But that leaves me with the question: What is the road? Isn't it also *between* my house and my cabin (a medium)? Isn't the road also used to convey the package from one place to another? Doesn't the road play a necessary part in the transporting (*conveying*) of the package? Doesn't the road *connect* my house with the cabin?

All right, let's leave the analogy for a moment and look at real-life human speech communication. My friend Tony and I are talking in a face-to-face situation. The messages I send are speech communication messages (with verbal, vocal, and visual components). How are those messages conveyed? Easy, you say. Sound waves and light waves carry the messages. So sound waves and light waves are the channels (media) of communication we are using, right? Right. It is through those vehicles that the message is carried. But does anything support or carry those sound waves? Yes, you say: air. Can the air between us, through which we send the sound waves, also be called a channel? Clearly, it stands in a different relation to the message from that of the sound and light waves. The sound and light waves are message carriers, whereas the air is a conveyor of message carriers. We are back to the truck and road problem—labeling two different kinds of things with the same name.

Another example from real life: Tony and I are talking again, but this time by telephone. What is the channel we are using to convey our messages to each other? Again we are using sound waves; it is the auditory channel, you say, and rightly so. But is the telephone a channel or medium for our communication? Yes, you say, it *is* a means of getting your messages back and forth to each other; it has to be called a channel or medium of communication. But the telephone is the means of conveying the message-conveyor (sound waves). True, but it is clearly a carrier, carrying messages from the source to the receiver. Here again, the words *channel* and *medium* are being used in two different ways: for the message vehicle and for the vehicle carrier.

I am more and more convinced that we must use different terms for the functions of message vehicle and for vehicle carrier. That would solve a great many of our semantic problems in this area. If we could agree to call the message vehicles *channels* and the vehicle carriers *media*, we might help end the confusion. In that case, the channels would almost always be sensory: visual, auditory, gustatory, tactile, and olfactory. The media would be quite varied (and sure to increase with the human race's inventive genius!).

Channels: Message Carriers

Messages are coded into physical stimuli, and we receive those physical stimuli through the five senses. The five senses are really the channels *through* which messages reach us. When you speak to me, I take in light waves through the visual channel and sound waves through the auditory channel. When you send me a letter, I take information in through the visual channel. If you put on an especially enticing perfume or cologne, I can get a message through the olfactory channel. Hug me, pat me, or slap my face; I will get the message through the tactile channel. Welcome me home with a sumptuous meal. That message will be gratefully received through the gustatory channel.

Channels are the means by which messages are conveyed to us receivers. *Channels,* then, are message carriers.

Media: Carrier Conveyors

If we use the distinction in terms I am advocating here, *media* are the means by which channels (the actual message carriers) are conveyed. Media are vehicles for conveying the physical stimuli to the receiver(s).

Many people use the word *media* to refer to the mass media of communication, especially the electronic media of radio and television. As we are using it here, however, the word *media* is a much broader term. It refers to any method of getting the physical stimuli from a message-producer to a message-receiver. Air is a medium for carrying sound waves; a letter is a medium also. Telephones, teletype, television, newspapers, billboards—all are media of communication, though all are not *mass* media, and certainly all are not electronic media.

Perhaps it would be useful to subdivide media into personal media, public media, and mass media. Personal media would be open ones; they would permit immediate feedback. Personal media permit interaction between message-producer and message-receiver(s). Unlike personal media of communication, public media and mass media are closed; they provide primarily for one-way communication. They certainly provide limited opportunity for significant feedback.

If we tried to use this classification system, would you classify the following under personal media:

> A personal letter?
> A phone call?

Would you classify the following as involving public media:

> A public speech to an audience of 500 persons?
> The principal's morning message sent over the intercom to the entire school?
> A form letter sent to every student at your college?

Would you classify the following as involving mass media:

> A radio broadcast over your local station?
> An article in *NAI* magazine?
> A *Sixty Minutes* telecast?
> A billboard advertising Terminal cigarettes?

Much of the literature has concentrated on the mass media of communication, which can reach a vast audience with the same message, often simultaneously. Both print and electronic mass media make it possible to reach an audience that is at a long distance from the message-producer and from other members of the audience. Television, particularly, seems to have become increasingly important as a source of news, entertainment, norms, social practices, ideas, and advertising. (A recent study in Germany indicated that people can become addicted to television and that depriving those people of TV can result in significant withdrawal symptoms! And a recent poll in Japan revealed that the typical television viewer would give up telephone, refrigerator, and even car before parting with his or her color television set.)

Your instructor may ask you to keep a log of your contacts with mass media for a day or two. It is an interesting experiment. You may be shocked at just how much contact you have each day with various mass media of communication. And the experiment may make you more aware of just how much we all are influenced by the mass media and what those media bring to us receivers.

SUGGESTIONS FOR FURTHER READING

BERLO, DAVID K., *The Process of Communication* (New York.: Holt, 1960).

BITTNER, JOHN R., *Mass Communication: An Introduction* (Englewood Cliffs, N.J.: Prentice-Hall, 1977).

FREELEY, AUSTIN, *Argumentation and Debate,* 4th ed. (Belmont, Calif.: Wadsworth, 1976).

GILMAN, WILBUR, BOWER ALY, and HOLLIS WHITE, *The Fundamentals of Speaking,* 2nd ed. (New York.: Macmillan, 1964).

MCCROSKEY, JAMES C., *An Introduction to Rhetorical Communication,* 2nd ed. (Englewood Cliffs, N.J.: Prentice-Hall, 1972).

PACE, R. WAYNE, and ROBERT R. BOREN, *The Human Transaction: Facets, Functions, and Forms of Interpersonal Communication* (Glenview, Ill.: Scott, Foresman, 1973), Chapters 5 and 6.

PEMBER, DON R., *Mass Media in America* (Palo Alto, Calif.: Science Research Associates, 1974).

SCHRAMM, WILBUR, *Men, Messages, and Media: A Look at Human Communication* New York.: Harper & Row, 1973).

SCHRAMM, WILBUR, and D. F. ROBERTS, eds., *The Process and Effects of Mass Communication,* rev. ed. (Urbana, Ill.: University of Illinois Press, 1971).

12
VERBAL MESSAGES: STRUCTURE AND CONTENT

general goal:

To learn how to examine and evaluate the structure and content of verbal messages.

specific objectives:

After completing this unit, you should be able to:

Recognize the structure of verbal messages.

Structure your own messages more effectively.

Pick out the central idea of a verbal message.

Identify the kinds of supporting material (where they exist).

Test the validity of supporting materials.

Select appropriate supporting material for your own verbal messages.

Recognize the types of reasoning used for support in verbal messages (if they are used).

Test the validity of the various kinds of reasoning.

Use the various forms of reasoning more validly and effectively in your own verbal messages.

structure of messages

WHEN DISCUSSING the nature of messages in Chapter 11, we looked at the three components of messages: code, content, and construction. Three chapters of this book are devoted to the language code, and one chapter is devoted to wordless (nonverbal) codes. This chapter will focus on the content and structure of messages.

First, let's look at structure: how messages are constructed. "Well," you may say, "if we are talking about everyday, spontaneous communication (and we are), I do not *construct* messages. I just talk. They just come out. 'Construction' sounds like messages are architecturally planned and built according to those plans. I certainly don't do that!" Don't you? Let's see.

***The
Inevitability
of Pattern***

First of all, *anything that exists has some kind of structure; everything that exists exists in some form.* Take something as simple as a piece of paper. Look at it. Does it have some form? Yes, I'm sure you agree, it does. Now wad it up. Does it still have some form to it—even if the form is changed from what it was before? Or, instead of wadding it up, tear it up into pieces, or punch holes in it. Does it still exist in some *form?* We may think it a messed-up structure, but it is a structure nonetheless.

I think of the old answer to the surprised question, "What are you doing here?": "Everybody's got to be someplace!" Yes, anything that exists physically will exist *someplace,* and *anything* that exists will exist in some form—structured in some way. There is no question about *whether* it will have structure; the only question is: *what kind* of structure does it have? If we want a fancy phrase to remember this principle, we can call it "the inevitability of structure."

Structure involves the ways in which various elements are put together; structure involves patterns or forms. "But," objects Thomas Thomas, "we are not talking about pieces of paper. We are talking about messages spoken and heard and seen by human beings. Something *physical*—like a piece of paper or a table or a house—will have structure, but a spoken message?" Yes, spoken messages all have structure too.

For one thing, our messages are coded. And codes are systems of signs. Systems require structure. We looked at the patterns inherent in language and some of the distinctive patterns of American English in Chapter 7. When we send a message, we select a particular code (American English or Mexican Spanish, for example); we select specific elements of that code to use (remember Chapter 8 on choosing words); and we decide how we will put together the elements of the code we have chosen. Picking out parts and putting them together is *construction.* Already we are in the message-construction business!

Not only is there structure (construction) involved related to the code of the message; there is also structure involved in the content of the message. We select material to express our purposes. The material we select must be put together in some way. Content is made out of bits of information, and these bits of information must be ordered, arranged, structured—to make a message. Content structure (on which we are going to focus now) also forces us into the message-construction business.

Yes, Thomas, we are not talking about pieces of paper or tables or houses, but I hope I have convinced you that the messages we human beings send and receive have structure too.

The Analysis of Structure

To analyze any message structure, we must examine three things: the parts, their positioning, and their proportion. The parts are the elements selected; the positioning refers to the arrangement and order of the parts; and the proportion(s) relate to the amount of emphasis or prominence given to the various parts. Let's look at each of these briefly.

PARTS

First, to construct any message, one must select the elements that will go into that message. Messages are made up of bits of information, which, of course, are transmitted in code. If you are going to analyze *anything* that has been created, you have to take into account the materials chosen to make it. We human beings have multitudes of materials available to us, out of which we can create our messages.

We must look at the concept *bit of information.* That concept is based on the idea that any message is made by putting pieces ("bits") of information together. But what *are* these bits, these building blocks of messages? Well, again, it is easier to tell you what they *do* than to tell you what they *are.* Each bit of information reduces ambiguity by one-half; each bit cuts the receiver's choices in half by eliminating other choices. If each bit affirms (or asserts) something, it (presumably) negates the opposite—thus reducing the receiver's alternatives by half.[1]

Maybe an example will make the concept clearer. If I send the message, "I dislike goats," at least I have eliminated the possibility of liking goats. "Dislike" would be one bit of information. What if I added to the message and said, "I dislike goats and sheep"? Is the addition of *sheep* a bit of information, and did it further reduce ambiguity by another half? Yes, to both questions. You know twice as many of my dislikes as you did before I tacked on the *sheep.* Bits of information, then, do not add up; they multiply. Or, put another way, each bit does not subtract from the receiver's choices; each divides the receiver's choices by another half.

[1] Gregory Bateson and Jurgen Ruesch, *Communication: The Social Matrix of Psychiatry* (New York: Norton, 1951), p. 175.

If I am going to analyze any message, I have to examine the materials out of which it is made: the words chosen to express the ideas (in terms of the verbal component of the message). What did the message-producer *select* for inclusion in the message, and conversely, what did the message-producer select for exclusion from the message? Those are the message *parts,* and they are an integral component of the message structure.

POSITIONING

The message-producer must not only select the parts (elements) of the message to be sent; the message-producer must also decide how to arrange those elements. What kind of order will be used in the message?

Grammatical patterns are given by the language, of course, as we noted in Chapter 7. Word structure and sentence structure follow certain patterns in each language, although it is true that a message-producer can violate those patterns (either through choice or ignorance).

Even in a message as short as a sentence, however, we have many possible, grammatically acceptable choices for arranging our materials. Whether you say, "It is I" or "It's me" is a matter of choosing parts. But whether you say "It is I" or "I'm the one" is a matter of positioning. The crucial bit of information is carried by the word "I" in both versions of the message. The "I" comes last in one version and first in the other. Which order you choose to use is up to you. Which do you prefer?

Do you prefer "Jerry flunked the test" or "The test was flunked by Jerry" or "Flunking the test was Jerry's fate"? The pieces of the message are essentially the same, but the order in which the material is presented to the receiver is different each time.

Longer messages give us even more alternatives as far as organizing the materials is concerned. Will you put the most important information first and last, where it will get the most attention and perhaps be best remembered? Will you start with the least important pieces of information and build to a climax? Will you put your major idea first and use the rest of the message to back it up? These are questions related to positioning. And there are no right answers to them. You must decide on the order of materials based on your own purpose, your listener's concepts of what is well organized and your listener's needs and attitudes, the nature of the information contained in the message, and the communication context. You may organize the same message differently when transmitting it to different receivers in differing contexts. Indeed, positioning message parts is closely related to the interaction between the communicators, and message-producers must be flexible in organizing their messages so they can adapt to the changing dynamics of the communication interaction.

PROPORTION

When we send messages, we not only have choices to make about what to include and exclude from the message (parts) and what orderly arrangements we will put these parts into (positioning); we must also decide what to emphasize and what to deemphasize in the message. That is the element of proportion. On which parts of the message will we try to focus most attention? Which elements in the message will be played down?

What we are dealing with is the amount of prominence given the various parts of the message. What do we fashion in such a way that it will stand out? Recently, some students were talking to me about a professor's "lecture." In that fifty-minute period, the professor had discussed the announced topic for ten minutes and his personal problems for almost forty minutes. The students got the impression somehow that the professor considered his personal affairs more important than the subject matter he was supposed to be teaching. They got this impression from the proportion of time given to each part of the lecture.

In this book, we are focusing primarily on human speech communication, but many of the principles apply also to written communication. All the principles related to messages apply both to spoken/heard and written/read messages. For example, think of the principle of proportion. How does the newspaper apportion space in its message-sending? What stories are placed on page one, and which ones on page twenty? What stories get half a page of coverage, and what stories get only one column inch? Which stories receive the biggest headlines or are set in the boldest type? Check your favorite newspaper to see how it deals with the principle of proportion (or prominence). Then focus on a few news stories and compare the coverage (in terms of proportion) in two different newspapers. Did each paper give a different amount of emphasis to the same story? (We could also have made the same kind of comparison examining the parts (elements—the bits of information) included and excluded and the positioning of the materials in the stories (the arrangement, the organization, of the parts) of the stories.

As message-producers, we should pay careful attention to our message construction. We should carefully select the materials, organize those materials in a way our receiver(s) can understand and follow, and so apportion the materials that the most important elements of the message are the most prominent. As message-receivers, we should recognize that we too will impose a structure on the message as we receive it; we will select what materials to notice, organize those materials into some form in our own minds, and give most prominence to those elements we consider most important. Both sender and receiver create structures; it is hoped that those structures will be somewhat similar.

content of messages

Let us turn now to the analysis of message *content*. Someone is sure to say, "I thought you talked about that in the last chapter when you discussed types of messages. Fact-kind, value-judgment-kind, and inference-kind—doesn't that have to do with content?" Good thinking. But I want to draw a distinction between the type or nature of the message (what kind is it?) and the content of the message (what is in it?) Types of messages differ in the ways we use to check them out; messages differ in content in terms of what they state (or what they say).

Twenty-five hundred years ago, a speech communication scholar said that there are only two content elements to a message: the point you are trying to make and the proof you use to back that point up. Everything else, he said, is embellishment. I think he was right, so in this section on content analysis of messages we will examine the point of a message (we'll call it a central idea) and two kinds of supporting proof (evidence or supporting material and reasoning).

Central Idea

Every message sent and received has a major theme. We call that major theme the thesis or central idea. Every message? Every message—whether it is one sentence, a speech, a paragraph, an article, a book, a telecast, a film. Every message can be summarized in terms of its central idea or theme.

The message-producer must formulate in his or her mind the central idea of the message, although that summary statement may not be transmitted to the receiver explicitly. And the message-receiver must reconstruct that central idea in his or her own mind (asking, "What is the main point of all this?") even though the sender may not have said the thesis in a straightforward, word-for-word way.

The central idea is a total summary of the content of the message. Whatever the message, you should be able to state the central idea in one sentence. Message-sender, if the message-receiver cannot reconstruct your central idea, then it is likely your message was faultily constructed. Your instructor may want some of you to send brief (maybe one-minute) messages to another class member to see if the message-receiver can reconstruct your central idea. It sounds easy enough, but is it?

I said that *any* message has a central idea. If one views a 30-minute telecast as a total message, then it should have a central theme or idea. Right. I read recently that one script for an episode of the TV program *Maude* went through ten complete rewritings. Those responsible for the program were concerned that the program's central idea be unmistakably clear. The episode was concerned with alcoholism, and though the program was "entertainment," its central idea was a very serious one: "We Americans are drinking too much, and it has gotten out of hand." That was the central idea as conceived by the producers and writers, at least. It would be interesting to know if that is the central idea as perceived by the majority of those who viewed the episode, the message-receivers.

Sometimes message-producers do not make their point directly. Sometimes they use such techniques as irony (saying one thing but meaning the opposite) to make a point. At other times, they may use wild exaggeration (hyperbole) to stress an idea. The receiver must understand the technique being used by the sender if he or she is to get the central idea correctly. What is the central idea of the following comments on professional boxing?

> I certainly do not believe professional boxing should be abolished. Quite the contrary! I am in favor of following the principles of professional boxing to their logical conclusion and bringing back gladiatorial combat. I think we should not let the gladiators use gloves to protect their hands, as they do now. (The gloves do not reduce damage to the opponents, you know, but to the gladiator himself.) Instead of gloves *on* the hands, there should be weapons *in* them! Knives, spears, tridents, nets. We in the audience would get to see more blood, and we wouldn't have to wait so long for the blood to start flowing. Of course, some of the gladiators might get killed in the ring, but that happens now too, and anyway, those who went into it would know the risks. Besides, there are risks in any contact sport. Gladiatorial combat we have now, but in a less exciting, interesting, athletically challenging form. I say: bring in the real thing. And no more of this talk about abolishing the sugar-coated gladiatorial substitute we have now; better a little blood than none at all!

Is the speaker really in favor of bringing back the arenas of the Roman era? What is his message about professional boxing? Can you state it in one sentence? Was the central idea you reconstructed something like: "Professional boxing is barbaric," or "Professional boxing is as unacceptable as gladiatorial combat," or "Professional boxing is gladiatorial combat in another form and under another name"? I think you are right. I. C. Redd, the speaker, was not in favor of boxing, although it would have been easier for you to get the central idea, admittedly, if you could also have heard the paralanguage and seen the kinesics. The message's central idea was never stated directly in the words of the message. Quite the opposite. The receiver had to formulate the statement of the central idea herself or himself.

Last year I was taking part in a discussion about the usefulness of violence as a method of settling disputes. A student who considered himself a devout Christian advocated violence—at least for self-defense and revenge for oppression. I mentioned that I had read in a book about some foolish, naive man who opposed not only violence but any resistance to evil, aggressive people; I referred to that man's statements about turning the other cheek after someone strikes you on one cheek and about walking a second mile if an oppressor commands you to walk one. What was the central idea of the message I was intending to send? What was the central idea you would expect my receiver to get? Well, I was certainly surprised. The message I was trying to convey was: Jesus, whom you claim to follow, opposed violence. The only message the man received was: He believes Jesus is a fool. I was not just surprised; I was dismayed when I learned later (by accident really) what the student thought the central idea of that message was! He missed *my* central idea completely!

Look at these brief messages, and formulate the central idea for each:

Did you see Dr. Ira Flect today? His shirt was askew, the buttons in the wrong buttonholes; his socks didn't match, and one of his shoes had a big hole in the sole. Isn't that just like a professor?

H. L. Seeke began without a penny and became a millionaire. And some people doubt or deny that America is the land of opportunity!

Look at the employment patterns in America's television stations. Members of racial minorities—Blacks, Orientals, Hispanics, or Native Americans—are not employed as professionals at 50 per cent of the stations, as technicians at 55 per cent of the stations, or as sales personnel at 81 per cent of the stations. Now tell me no affirmative action is needed!

How did you, the receiver of these messages, reconstruct their central ideas? You might compare your reconstructions with mine: (1) Ira Flect is typical of professors—carelessly dressed. (2) H. L. Seeke's experience demonstrates that America *is* the land of opportunity. (3) Too few members of racial minorities are employed in American television stations in top-level jobs, and affirmative action is needed to correct the situation. Did we get essentially the same central ideas from the messages?

Supporting Material

We back up the central ideas of our messages with different kinds of supporting material. In a sense, we use these devices to prop up our main points, to undergird our main ideas so they will stand up under close scrutiny. To use another metaphor, we fortify our ideas with supporting materials—to strengthen the main themes of our messages and make them more defensible.

Remember that this is not a textbook on public (or platform) speaking. We are concentrating on principles of human communication that apply more universally than that. When we talk about supporting materials, then, we are focusing on their use in everyday, spontaneous communication. It is true, however, that these same kinds of materials are used to support the main points in speeches, and you may want to use the information you gain in this section to help you listen critically to public speeches as well as to analyze everyday messages you send and receive.

There are seven principal types of supporting materials: authority, examples, illustrations, facts, statistics, descriptions, and explanations. We will look at each of these kinds of supporting materials, because understanding them will make you both a better sender and a better receiver of messages.

AUTHORITY

If you back up your idea with an authority who agrees with you, you are hoping that authority's say-so will convince the listener that the point is a good one. You are backing up your point with "expert testimony." You may quote this expert, you may paraphrase the expert, or you may only cite the expert's agreement with your position. In any case, you trot out an authority on the subject to bolster your case. "It is true, and Sarah Brate says it is true!" Now, of course, the proof you are offering your listener is the *opinion* of someone else. You are using it as evidence because (1) that opinion agrees with yours and (2) you believe your receiver will respect the opinion of that authority.

**One type of supporting
material: Authority**

We call this type of supporting material *use of authority* no matter who or what is cited as the authority. But we (especially we receivers) must look at the authority used to decide if that authority is really an expert on this subject or not. No one is an authority on everything, and people may have great expertise in one field but be relatively uninformed about other areas of knowledge. Actually, whether this type of support is effective or not really depends on the receiver's attitudes toward, or acceptance of, the person or thing as an expert. If your receiver views the authority you cite as authoritative, this kind of supporting material will strengthen your point.

Look at each of these brief messages. First, identify the central idea of the message (the point); then note the supporting material. Does each message use authority to prop up its main point? If so, is that authority really qualified to offer an expert opinion on that point?

Every soldier in every army who kills one of the "enemy" and every executioner for the state who puts a person to death *is a murderer.* As it says in the Bible, "Thou shalt not kill!"

Take Joe Namath's word for it: Hamilton Beach makes the world's best panty hose.

Some people still question the findings of the Warren Commission that Lee Harvey Oswald was the lone assassin of President John Kennedy. In spite of the Commission's lengthy report, these people believe that there was a conspiracy—that other people were involved and that Oswald may have been set up. These conspiracy theories are unfounded. Former President Ford served on the Warren Commission and was in a position to look at all the evidence. He has stated that no evidence has appeared to change his agreement with the Commission's conclusions.

If you use Vitamin C in sufficient amounts, you can avoid catching colds. Linus Pauling, the Nobel-prize-winning scientist, says it works.

Examples are specific, typical instances named to support your point. If you offer an example as support, you do not give details about the instance; you merely point the instance out. It is important, then, to pick instances that will be so familiar to your receiver(s) that merely naming them is enough to strengthen the point. You remind your listener of the instance(s), or you inform your listener of the instance(s), but you do not have to explain the instances. Just citing them is sufficient.

EXAMPLES

One type of supporting material: Example

If you use examples to support your point, of course, you must be careful to chose instances that are truly typical of the point being made. If you are a receiver, and the message-producer is using this form of supporting material, ask yourself (after you identify the type of support used), "Are these examples really typical, or are they unusual (atypical) instances instead?"

Again, look at each of these brief messages. First, identify the central idea of the message (the point); then note the supporting material. Does each message use example(s) to prop up its major point? If so, are the examples really typical? Are any facts alleged true?

Teachers at this college are very lenient in their grades. Just look at Professor Ellie Mentry, Professor Ewell Passit, and Professor E. Z. Mark.

TV producers take an idea and run it into the ground. If a formula works, they use it over and over. First there was a bionic man, then a bionic woman, and now a bionic dog!

Many people have said that it is impossible to restore democracy once a dictatorship takes over a country. I do not believe this is so. In fact, there is convincing evidence to the contrary. Look at what has happened in both Greece and Spain. Hallelujah!

<table>
<tr><td>ILLUSTRATION</td><td>

An illustration is one instance with details. Often, the illustration is a story, either fictional (hypothetical) or true. These anecdotes are sort of expanded examples. Examples remind us of specific instances; illustrations relate the stories of specific instances. When an illustration is used as supporting material for a point, the story and its details, taken as a whole, should confirm the point being made. And only really necessary details should be included. If the story goes on too long, your listener may forget the point you are trying to make! An honest communicator will make it clear to his or her receiver whether the illustration comes from real life or the sender's imagination.

</td></tr>
</table>

One type of supporting material: Illustration

As with examples, the crucial question (both for the sender and the receiver) is this: Is this instance really typical?

I am going to present a couple of brief messages to you. First, identify the central idea. That is very important. As soon as you have read the message, formulate in one sentence a complete summary of the message (the point the sender is trying to establish). After you have determined the point, then examine the message to see if there is any proof (supporting material), and if so, what kind of supporting material it is. Then, if the support is an illustration, examine that illustration to determine if it is typical of what it purports to prove.

This college is fortunate to have so many outstanding, dedicated, and highly qualified faculty members. A typical one who comes to my mind is Professor Francoise, a distinguished member of the French Department. She lived in France and Switzerland for her first twenty-five years. She studied at the Sorbonne. She earned her doctorate in France, where it is very difficult—especially for a woman. And she has loyally remained at this college, though she has been sought by Harvard and Berkeley to join their faculties.

Union leaders are all crooked. The head of Local 69, Willie Cheatem, is typical. He has a salary of $25,000 a year plus a $10,000-a-year expense account. Although he has been president of the union only three years, in that time (with no visible outside income) he has paid off a $100,000 house, bought a $75,000 yacht, acquired a winter home in the Bahamas, and increased his stock investments from zero to $250,000. Cheatem and his ilk are all on the take!

FACTS

One way to undergird major points is to provide facts to back them up. Facts are concrete, specific, verifiable data. Facts are first-hand observations that can be checked out by sense perception to relative certainty. We still have to say *relative* certainty rather than absolute certainty, because our senses, though they are the best sources of information we have, may mislead us. Of course, we can check out our own observations against other people's observations in an effort to avoid being fooled.

One type of supporting material: Facts

Thanks to spoken language, we can know the facts that other people have observed and reported to us, and thanks to written language, we can even know about facts observed by people centuries—or even millennia—ago. Statements of fact, if accurate (there's the rub!), are a great way of supporting major ideas. An ethical message-producer will try to be certain his or her statements about facts are correct, and message-receivers will have to ask: are those assertions about facts really true?

Here are some brief messages. As before, after reading the message, identify the central idea of the message. Then look for supporting material. Is there a statement of fact (or several facts) used to back up the main point? If so, can you determine whether those statements are true or false?

In 1940, there were 7000 policemen working for our city. In 1950, there were 10,000 policemen at work here. Now—this year—there are only 9500 policemen employed by this city. We are not making progress in our efforts at law enforcement, but instead are going backwards!

Taxes—income taxes—on single people are outrageous. I just got a raise of $212 a month. This month I looked for that $212 in my paycheck. Some joke! Out of that $212 increase in salary per month, after taxes I took home only $78. Surely no married person would be taxed that heavily!

How about a historical footnote? Cassius Marcellus Clay, a cousin of Henry Clay, advocated the aboliton of slavery and helped to found the Republican Party. He freed all the many slaves he inherited. Noted as one of the greatest orators of the nineteenth century, he spoke publicly many times against slavery. It is ironic that this man—one of the greatest Kentuckians of all time—is so little known today.

STATISTICS

Statistics are numbers—but not just any numbers. They are a special kind of numbers. Rather than specific, absolute, verifiable numbers (which would make them fact kinds of assertions), they are generalized, relative numbers, usually based on a sampling or a survey. Statistics, at least in the sense that I am using the word, are not facts. They are interpretations; they are based on unprovable assumptions; they are inferences. Like any other educated guesses, they should be examined, carefully, both by the message-producer and the message-receiver.

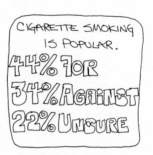

**One type of supporting
material: Statistics**

I said that statistics are not absolute numbers. Instead, they are either relative or generalized numbers. Let's look at the concept of relative numbers first. If I am going to give you an accurate, factual count of something, I would give you a concrete number that could be checked out by counting. Anybody else who did the same counting should come up with the same number I did. If I tell you there are four chairs in my office, that report could be checked out. The number is an absolute number, and we can find out if the report is true or false. Statistics are not that kind of numbers. They are *relative* numbers; they are numbers related (that's what *relative* means, after all) to some other (usually unknown) numbers. They are proportions or ratios or percentages. Let's go back to the chairs in my office. If I tell you, "Three-quarters of the chairs in my office have broken legs," you know a proportion—a relationship—but do you know how many chairs have broken legs? No, not unless I give you the concrete number of chairs in the room. You won't find out from the statistics themselves. If some product claims, "Three out of four doctors surveyed recommend the ingredients in Schmaltz," do you know (1) how many doctors were surveyed, and (2) the concrete number recommending those ingredients? (I hope you noted that the product did not claim the doctors endorsed the *product* but only ingredients contained in the product!) No, we cannot find out from the statistics how many doctors are involved or how many specific doctors made the recommendation. We only know that, of the total number asked, 75 per cent (three out of four) responded in a certain way. Statistics told us the *relationship,* but not the actual numbers.

Now, let's look at the concept of generalized numbers. That is a little tricky and could easily mislead people. These numbers may be stated as absolute numbers, but they are estimates rather than actual counts. *Estimate* is another word for "guess." And guesses (remember our long discussion of inferences) are not sure things!

A good example of generalized numbers might come from reports about the audiences for TV programs. TV programs live or die on the basis of ratings. Indeed, even the news programs vie for those statistical standings. Sometimes the ratings are expressed as percentages of the viewing audience (relative numbers), but sometimes the audience reports are also expressed as specific numbers. You might read, for example, that last week thirty million people watched the TV show *All in the Family.* Or you might read that fifty million were in the viewing audience when the President participated in some important ceremony. Those numbers certainly *sound* definite. Sounds like factual reporting, doesn't it? Well, it is not. Nobody actually went around and counted every member of that mass audience; those numbers are not based on direct observation. Those are generalized numbers—estimates based on the relative numbers (the percentages), which in turn are based on a *sampling* technique. Let's look at the sample used in the TV ratings for a moment.

There are over two hundred million people in the United States now, according to the Census Bureau. According to estimates, there are more than one hundred million television sets in the country. The prestigious Nielson ratings are based on records of what channels are on at what times on a selected number of TV sets scattered across the country. There is a device attached to the TV sets to keep a record of when the set is on and what station the set is tuned to. The results mean life or death for programs, based on what percentage of the participating sets were tuned in or were not tuned in. Now, how many families would you expect to be participating in this sampling process? How many sets would be equipped with this recording device? I wish I could find out your guess on what would be a reasonable number. Of course, you may already know that the actual number is 1200. That is not a printing error. I did not mean 12,000. The number is a little over a thousand! If 800 of the sets are turned on at a given time, how many would it take to make up one-fourth of the surveyed sets in use? That's right, math majors. 200! On the assumption that the surveyed sets are representative of the total number of sets in the country, the estimates would be projected. In this case, for example, if there were thought to be a total of one million sets in the United States, it could be projected that 667,000 of them were on at that time (the same ratio as 800 out of 1200) and that 166,750 of those sets (the same ratio as 200 out of 800) were tuned in to a particular program. This may be a slight oversimplification of the system—but not much! The resulting numbers, however hard and fast they may sound, are *generalized* numbers. They are statistics and not facts.

You might look at Darrell Huff's book *How to Lie with Statistics.* Though over twenty years old, that book is certainly not out of date! A cynic has said that a statistician is one who can tell you everything about the Sahara Desert by looking in a sandbox. That barb is unfair, but it does remind us to examine carefully statistical supporting materials.

Check out the following brief messages. As before, be sure to identify the central idea of the message first. Then look for supporting material. If there is supporting material, is it statistical in nature? Then, if possible, check out the statistics by asking: Is the source of the statistics unbiased? Were those sampled (or surveyed) typical of the whole? Were the sampling techniques or instruments (questionnaires, for example) unbiased? Was the sample that was taken sufficiently large to yield reliable results? Do the statistics actually, clearly, logically support the point being made? Do the statistics conform to other available evidence? Here are the messages:

It is clear that Blacks and Puerto Ricans are not sharing equally with other New York City residents in income gains. Just look at the figures: In 1970, one quarter of the Blacks and 35 per cent of the Puerto Ricans were below the poverty level. The contrast with whites is staggering; in 1970, only 8.9 per cent of the whites were below the poverty level.

Blacks and Puerto Ricans made great economic strides in the decade from 1960 to 1970. During the 1960s, the median family income of Blacks increased by 61 per cent, and the median family income of Puerto Ricans increased by 46 per cent. These gains are impressive and gratifying.

(*Median* means "in the middle." Hence, "median family income" means that half of the families were above a particular figure and the other half below that figure.)

In a survey taken at Old Pugh University, three out of five respondents said they were not satisfied with the courses they were taking. Most college students today are displeased with their classes.

Most people will like Maxwell House instant coffee better than freeze-dried coffee if they make a real test. An independent survey showed that 40 per cent of those who answered liked Maxwell House better if they really compared the two in a taste test.

When we describe something, we provide the details needed to stir the receiver's imagination. We use sensory imagery to help the receiver imagine what something is (or was) like. The more senses you can utilize, the better. Try to get your listener to imagine what something looks like, tastes like, sounds like, feels like, moves like, or smells like. We employ this form of supporting material to help make our general statements more vivid.

One type of supporting material: Description

From the following brief messages, reconstruct the central idea and note the use of description to support that idea.

She is not just beautiful; she is stunning! She has deep blue eyes, long, silky blonde hair, classic features, a petite but shapely body. She's exquisite.

I do not know why you would call him sexist. What's so unusual about leering at every girl you pass, pawing every girl you date, smacking your lips, drooling a little, and panting hard over especially provocative broads? I do admit he also whistles occasionally or sucks air through his teeth to attract a dame's attention, but he only does that when she is too far away to get with his breezy greeting, "Let's get it on, gorgeous," growled out in that gutteral voice of his.

The room was a mess. Dirty dishes were piled high in the sink; there were clothes thrown all over the floor and the furniture. The sofa, minus two legs, tilted at a wild angle. The sofa's dirty, torn upholstery let the ticking show through in places, and a couple of springs protruded menacingly. It was difficult to tell the original color of the upholstery because of the coffee stains and the cigarette burns. In one corner of the room lay a pile of newspapers and magazines; in another was a reeking box of kitty litter. The stench was almost unbearable. There were ashtrays on the plastic tables—all filled to overflowing with half-smoked cigarettes and well-chewed wads of chewing gum. I couldn't believe my eyes and nose!

When we support a generalization with descriptive statements, we provide details that stimulate the receiver's imagination. When we support a

generalization—a main point—with an explanation, we provide details that
will make the point clearer or more understandable. Sometimes this form
of supporting material is called exposition or explication. These details
usually tell why or how or what. That is, they back up the point with some
kind of analysis or definition, explaining why something is, how something
works, or what something is. The message-producer is supplying background information to aid the receiver in understanding the main point of
the message.

**One type of supporting
material: Explanation**

Let us look at a few brief messages in which the central idea is supported
with explanation. Note what kind of details are provided to enhance the
receiver's comprehension. Was the supporting material necessary? Was it
helpful or useful? Was it well selected?

> Why do I maintain that the federal government is giving special treatment
> to the Southern states? Because those states pay into the federal treasury far
> less in taxes than do the Northern and Western states, but they get back in
> federal contributions far more per capita than the Northern and Western
> states. And look at where the federal government has placed the most defense
> establishments, which greatly benefit the local economies—in the South.

> Children learn to speak by progressing through a three-step process. First,
> they go through a period of babbling—just making all kinds of noises at
> random. Second, they have a period of lalling—repeating some sounds and
> syllables they like, just for the fun of it. The third stage is called echolalia, a
> period in which they mimic (echoing) the words pronounced to them by
> those around them. After they are able to say words back, it is an easy step to
> meaningful speech.

Here is a brief review of the seven kinds of supporting material we have
studied. The chart gives only the names of each and a short definition.
It is not enough to be able to recite the definitions, however. We must
be able to recognize these forms of support when we use them and when
others use them, and we must be able to evaluate each type of support
systematically.

Supporting Materials

AUTHORITY | "Expert" testimony; some "authority" on the subject cited, quoted, or paraphrased

EXAMPLES | Specific, typical instances named or pointed out

ILLUSTRATION | One instance with details; often a story—either fictional or true

FACTS | Concrete, specific data that can be checked out by sense perception or records of direct observation

STATISTICS | Generalized, relative numbers, usually based on a sampling or survey

DESCRIPTION | Details that stir up the imagination (using sensory imagery)

EXPLANATION | Details that make something clear; details that tell why or how or what—providing analysis, exposition, or definition

Not only do we back up or central ideas, our main points, with different kinds of supporting materials; we also use reasoning to undergird the points we are trying to make. I defined reasoning in the preceding chapter when discussing inferences. If we make an inference (draw a conclusion from premises), we have "reasoned." Reasoning, you remember, was defined as moving from one statement to another on the assumption that the first statement makes the second statement either inevitable or highly probable. The first statement is called a premise; the second statement is what we conclude or claim to have proved. We move from the premise to the conclusion on the assumption that that move is warranted, that it is

Reasoning

justified. (Indeed, in his analysis of the reasoning process, Stephen Toulmin calls the assumption the *warrant*.)

Each three-link chain of reasoning

is called an argument. An argument is a unit made up of a premise, an assumption, and a conclusion—but the assumption often goes unstated. If the assumption is taken for granted, the message-receiver should note *what* the underlying assumption is and whether he or she *does* grant that assumption. One should ask: Does that assumption really justify (warrant) jumping to that conclusion? And we *do* jump to conclusions—all conclusions!

Let's look at *premises* first. They are the jumping-off places of any argument (a three-link chain of reasoning). Purists, I am sure, will object to my mixing metaphors here—a chain does not have places to jump from or jump to—but the two separate images *do* convey important aspects of the reasoning process. In any case, let us look at premises, the first step in that process.

A premise is a statement of something known or believed. Some writers call that statement the *evidence* statement. I do not like the term, but it might serve to remind us that the message-producer thinks the statement reports or affirms something that is quite evident or apparent (to him or her). These premises *may* be fact-kind of statements, but they are just as likely to be value-judgments or inferences. If they are fact-kind of statements, the statements may or may not be true. If they are value-judgments or inferences, they may or may not be supportable and they may or may not be shared by the receiver.

Note the premises in the following arguments:

> There are no two-year vocational programs offered at this college. It is clear we should institute several such programs at once.
>
> Offering a course in Sanscrit at this college was a foolish mistake. We should take that course out of the curriculum.
>
> A college should not teach courses with a practical application. All vocational courses and curricula should be abolished.

Is each of the three premises different? If you were listening to some professor stating these arguments, would you carefully examine the premises? Or would you simply swallow the premises whole? Too many receivers look for flaws in the argument only in the conclusion. We all need to be reminded that we must look at all three links in the chain. A weakness in the premise or the assumption renders the reasoning just as invalid as a weakness in the final conclusion. Indeed, if the argument is constructed properly (its form is correct), the conclusion will be either inevitable or highly probable. So we *must* look at the premise and assumption!

Examine this line of reasoning:

> Germans are the Master Race.
> Since the Master Race should rule the world,
> Germans should rule the world.

Is that line of reasoning properly constructed? Does it have a clearly stated premise, even a clearly stated assumption, and a conclusion that logically follows from the premise and the conclusion? The answer, of course, is *yes*. There is nothing wrong with the construction (form) of that argument. If you grant the premise and assumption (whether the assumption is articulated or not), then the conclusion is inevitable; it necessarily follows. But *do* you grant the premise? It is as much an inference (based on reasoning) as the conclusion of this argument itself. And that assertion (the premise) is no more absolute and certain than any other inference (remember that inferences are opinions—not fact kind of statements).

If we message-senders do not want to use shaky, invalid arguments to back up our main points, and if we message-receivers do not want to be taken in by shaky, invalid arguments, then we must examine the premises (the starting statements) of those arguments carefully and critically.

We must analyze *assumptions* just as carefully and critically as we do premises. Perhaps we should be even *more* suspicious in our examination of assumptions in lines of reasoning. Since they often go unstated, they often get overlooked. All the more reason to see if they can stand the light of day and thorough scrutiny. In the following chains of reasoning (arguments), the underlying assumption (that presumably warrants jumping to the conclusion) is not stated. What is that assumption in each case? Be certain that you can formulate it.

Since light-skinned people are intellectually inferior,

_____

light-skinned people should not be allowed to vote.

X. Kahn has been convicted of four felonies,

_____

and he should therefore be put to death.

If patients get to choose all their physicians,

_____

students should get to choose all their professors.

Left-handed people are abnormal,

_____

so left-handed people should not be allowed to teach school.

Drinking alcohol and smoking cigarettes are harmful to the health of human beings,

_____

so drinking alcohol and smoking cigarettes should be prohibited by law.

Can you fill in the blanks? What did the message-producer assume (and expect the message-receiver to assume)? Go back and look at each of the five arguments and the missing assumption you have formulated. Do you agree that these are the five underlying assumptions?

1. People who are intellectually inferior should not be allowed to vote.
2. Anyone who has been convicted of four felonies should be put to death.
3. The patient-physician relationship is comparable to the student-professor relationship, and whatever applies in the first will also apply in the second.
4. People who are abnormal should not be allowed to teach school.
5. Anything that is harmful to the health of human beings should be prohibited by law.

If those *are* the underlying assumptions, are they what *you* assume? Are they part of *your* belief system? Do they fit into your world view—the way you see things? Frankly, I do not agree with all those five assumptions, and I would have serious reservations about a conclusion based on those assumptions. Would you have been more likely to accept the arguments *before* this examination of the assumptions that are an essential part of those arguments? If so, isn't that a good indication that you should look for every argument's underlying assumption?

Every link in a chain must be sound in order for the chain to hold, so we must examine an argument's *conclusion* also. If, as I said earlier, we all must jump to our conclusions, then the old advice is wise: look before you leap! What should we look at, and what should we look for? The conclusion is an inference; it is what we *claim* to have established with our chain of reasoning. The question, then, is this: Is that claim justified (warranted)?

There are, you remember, two kinds of inferences: those that, on the basis of the premise and the assumption, are *inevitable;* and those that, on the basis of the premise and the assumption, are highly *probable.* There are, therefore, two basic questions to ask about any conclusion: (1) does this claim necessarily (inevitably) follow, if one grants the premise and the assumption? and (2) does this claim have a high probability of being so, if one grants the premise and the assumption? If the claim (or conclusion) does not pass one of these two tests, reject it.

Another way of looking at the same tests: (1) from the premise and assumption, what statement(s) inevitably (necessarily) must be drawn? and (2) from the premise and assumption, what statement(s) would have a high probability of being so? A statement that results from asking those two questions is a valid claim.

At this point, we are not looking at the basic premise or the assumption. Presumably, you have already examined those two links in the chain and they are sound. Now, we are looking only at the conclusion itself. And that conclusion must pass one of the two tests: inevitability or high probability.

Be careful. People can *claim* to have established more than the premise and the assumption warrant. Unwarranted conclusions are claims that are neither inevitable or highly probable. Surely we all want to be ethical message-producers. If so, we will strive to draw valid conclusions (to make valid claims). Certainly we need to be able to analyze conclusions if we, as message-receivers, are not to be hoodwinked.

Let's look at a few chains of reasoning and examine the conclusions. Can they pass the two tests we have established?

> Professor Sy Kopath teaches psychology.
> All psych professors are a little crazy.
> Professor Kopath must be a little crazy.

> All qualified citizens should vote.
> I am a qualified citizen.
> I should vote.

> Pacifists will not fight in wars—even to defend the country.
> Traitors will not fight for their country.
> All pacifists are traitors.

> My friend Helen Bach has just died.
> Everything that happens has a purpose and is for the best.
> Helen's death has a purpose and is for the best.

> The laws of the ancient Hebrews, recorded in Leviticus, forbade planting two kinds of seed in the same field and wearing clothes made of two kinds of material.
> All laws of the ancient Hebrews recorded in Leviticus should be enforced, by law, in the United States.
> It should be against the law in the United States to plant two kinds of seed in the same field and to wear clothes made of two kinds of material.

> C. Z. Leight is for the Equal Rights Amendment.
> The Communist Party is for the Equal Rights Amendment.
> C. Z. Leight is a member of the Communist Party.

> I studied very hard for this exam.
> Everyone who studies very hard has a good chance of passing.
> I have a good chance of passing this exam.

> Mike Rophone is a major network announcer.
> Most major network announcers make over $100,000 a year.
> Mike Rophone probably makes over $100,000 a year.

If you grant the premises and assumptions (and those are *very* big *if*s), are all of the conclusions valid? Do they all follow inevitably or probably? No. Did you catch the two instances where the claim was unwarranted? In these examples, the conclusions about pacifists and C. Z. Leight were not justified. The premise and assumption, in each case, did not lead inevitably or even probably to that conclusion. In both cases, the form of the reasoning was the same as that employed in this wild chain:

> United States money is green.
> Grass is green.
> United States money is grass.

Just remember: Conclusions, like police search and seizure, must be warranted. Examine them carefully.

After this brief introduction to reasoning, we are going to study the six different kinds of reasoning we use to back up our central ideas: deduction, induction, literal analogy, figurative analogy, sign, and causation.

When we reason, we draw a conclusion (or make a claim) about the unknown on the basis of what we know or believe. That is, we move from a statement of what we know or believe to a statement (conclusion) of what we do not know (but guess) on the assumption that the first statement leads logically to the second one. The conclusions are called *inferences*. They are, as I just noted, really guesses. Hopefully, they are educated guesses. But they are guesses nonetheless.

The six kinds of reasoning are distinguished by the kinds of relationships that the first statement may have to the second statement. We jump to our conclusions. We classify the kinds of jumps we make—where we jump from and where we jump to. In *deduction*, we move from a general statement to a more specific conclusion. In *induction*, we move from a specific instance or example to a general conclusion. In the two kinds of *analogies*, we move from a comparison to a conclusion. In reasoning from *sign*, we move from some indication(s) to a conclusion. And in *causal* reasoning, we move either from cause to effect or from effect to cause.

To help you remember the six kinds of reasoning, here is a chart with key words for each type. You may think these key words are crutches, but they help *me* keep the distinctions in mind!

TYPES OF REASONING: DEFINITIONS

I NDUCTION
NSTANCE

Reasoning from specific *instances* to general conclusions.

BROA **D** EDUCTION

Reasoning from *broad* general principles to specific conclusions.

A **L** ITERAL
IKE

Reasoning based on *likenesses* in two things of the *same* category.

DIF **F** IGURATIVE
ERENT

Reasoning based on *similarities* in two things from *different* categories.

S IGN
ENSES

Reasoning from *indications* gathered by one of the *senses* to a conclusion.

BE **C** AUSE
AUSE

Reasoning based on the assumption that one thing has *caused* or will cause another.

Let's look at each of these types of reasoning a little more closely.

Deduction is reasoning from broad, general principles to specific conclusions. We start with a statement of a general belief. We conclude with a specific inference. Note these examples of deductive reasoning:

> All politicians are crooked.
> Therefore, since Howie Gaines is a politician, he must be crooked too.
>
> College professors are part of the Establishment.
> Since all in the Establishment are against change, college professors will be conservative and against change.
>
> The Unohu Tribe is inferior in mental ability to the rest of the human race.
> Ben D. Neid is a member of that tribe, so he must be dumb.
>
> If a person feels threatened, that person will likely become aggressive.
> O. Shaw feels threatened, so he will probably become aggressive.
>
> Either the federal government must reduce expenditures or increase taxes.
> The government is not going to reduce expenditures, so it must raise taxes.

Did all of these chains of reasoning begin with a statement of a general principle—a belief that formed the basis of the argument? Did all of them apply that general principle and come to a specific conclusion? You're right. They did. They are all examples of deductive reasoning.

Although we will not go into depth in analyzing deductive reasoning, we should look at some of the basic principles of deductive logic. We need to be able to use them properly in our daily communication. We can test deductive reasoning by applying these logical principles. The formal structures called the *syllogism* and the *enthymeme* give us a framework for analyzing deductions.

A syllogism is a three-step deduction made up of two premises and a conclusion. The first, or *major,* premise states a generalization; the second, or *minor,* premise makes a statement related to the generalization; and the conclusion necessarily follows from these premises. The reasoning is said to be *valid* when the conclusion is truly inevitable if one grants the two premises.

There are three kinds of syllogisms: the categorical, the conditional (or hypothetical), and the disjunctive (or the alternative). Let us look at each briefly. You will recognize that we all use them in reasoning quite often. The kinds of syllogisms are so named because the major premise in each case uses a particular kind of grammatical construction. Either the syllogism starts with a categorical statement (about some category or class of things), or with a conditional (if) clause, or with the statement of two alternatives (either-or). Note these three chains of reasoning. Look closely at the major premise in each case.

> All Communists are atheists.
> Karl is a Communist.
> Karl must be an atheist.

If Father O'Neel marries, he will be excommunicated.
Father O'Neel is getting married.
He will certainly be excommunicated.

Either the referee is partial or blind.
The referee is not blind.
Therefore, he must be partial.

Categorical syllogisms, as I said, begin with a categorical statement. That proposition usually contains a word such as *all, every, each, any, some,* or *most*. Sometimes that word is not stated explicitly; it is only implied. If someone says, "Communists are atheists," the person means "*all* Communists are atheists"—even if the "all" is left unsaid. And notice that we are making a statement about a class or category or group in that premise; that is a categorical statement!

Categorical syllogisms may begin with any one of six kinds of statements:

All A is/are B.
No A is/are B.
Some A is/are B.
Some A is not/are not B.
Most A is/are B.
Most A is not/are not B.

Many authors have used diagrams of circles to make the concepts clearer.

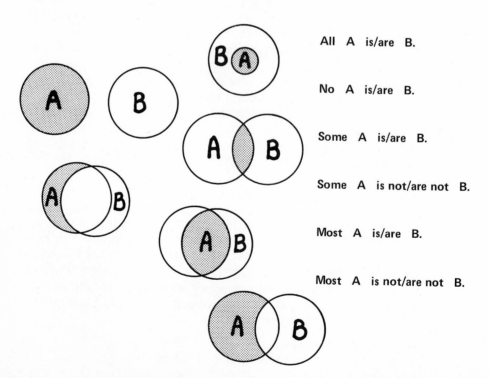

In each case, we are dealing with the relationship between two things. We are interested in this: To what extent, if any, is A (whatever A is) included in the category B (whatever B is)? Look at these statements. Each illustrates one of the six kinds of categorical statements. Can you identify which is which?

> Most New Yorkers are crazy.
> Americans are rich.
> American teachers cannot get rich teaching.
> Most textbooks are not interesting.
> Some athletes are intelligent.
> Some intellectuals are not snobs.

You can test a categorical syllogism to see if it is valid. There are six rules governing the validity of categorical syllogisms:

1. The syllogism must contain three (and only three) terms: A, B, and C—also called first term, middle term, and third term.
   Note this example:

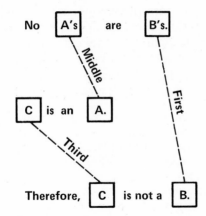

2. Each term must be used twice in the syllogism, but only once in each premise or the conclusion.
3. The middle term (which does not appear in the conclusion) must be used in a universal, unqualified sense in at least one premise.
4. If one of the premises contains a qualifier (negative or partial), the conclusion must contain a qualifier (negative or partial).
5. At least one premise must be affirmative (positive).
6. Any term used in a universal sense in the conclusion must be used in a universal sense in one of the premises.

Check the validity of these syllogisms. Do each of these syllogisms meet the six requirements? If they violate any rule, they are invalid.

> No student will register for CMS 110.
> Sally Forth is not a student.
> Therefore, Sally Forth will not register for CMS 110.

Most psychologists do not believe homosexuality is a mental illness.
Ima Freud is a psychologist.
Therefore, Ima Freud does not believe homosexuality is a mental illness.
Most human beings have some kind of faith or beliefs.
Ira Flect is a human being.
Therefore, Ira Flect cannot be an atheist.

You are right, of course. None of these are valid categorical syllogisms. Were you able to identify which rule each one violated? Invalid structure in logic results in unwarranted (unjustified) conclusions.

Conditional syllogisms are also called hypothetical syllogisms. They begin with a hypothesis, such as "if this exists" or "if this happens." The basic structure of the conditional syllogism is *if-then.* The basic premise, then, takes for granted something that is uncertain; it asks the receiver to "grant this for the sake of argument." Usually, there are conditional words to note the hypothesis, such as *if, supposing, just suppose, assuming,* or *if you grant.* Sometimes the conditional nature of the status or event is not explicitly stated, but only implied. Watch out for such supposing!

In conditional syllogisms, the major premise will state the if-then relationship, and the minor premise will either affirm the antecedent (the *if* clause) or deny the consequent (the *then* clause—the result). The antecedent clause states the condition, and the consequent clause states what necessarily follows from that condition (the consequences).

There are two rules governing the validity of conditional syllogisms:

1. The minor premise must affirm the antecedent or deny the consequent.
   a. If the minor premise affirms (upholds) the antecedent, the conclusion must affirm the consequent.
   b. If the minor premise denies the consequent, the conclusion must deny the antecedent.
2. No valid conclusion can be drawn if the minor premise denies the antecedent or affirms the consequent.

Here are a few conditional syllogisms. Check their validity by applying the two basic rules.

If Shirley Knott doesn't quit smoking three packs of cigarettes a day, she will probably get lung cancer.
Shirley will not stop smoking.
Therefore, she will probably get lung cancer.

If Shirley Knott doesn't quit smoking three packs of cigarettes a day, she will probably get lung cancer.
Shirley will stop smoking.
Therefore, she will probably not get lung cancer.

If Senator Haydn owns oil stocks, he will vote to increase oil company profits.
Senator Haydn will vote to increase oil company profits.
Therefore, Senator Haydn owns oil stocks.

If the United States increases its contributions to the United Nations, other nations will decrease their contributions.
Other nations will not decrease their contributions to the United Nations.
Therefore, the United States will not increase its contributions.

Examples one and four are valid. The second syllogism violates rule 2 because the minor premise denies the antecedent. The third syllogism violates rule 2 because the minor premise affirms the consequent.

Alternative syllogisms present two mutually exclusive alternatives in the major premise. The major premise states a clear, discreet choice: either this or that. Sometimes these syllogisms are called disjunctive syllogisms. (The main disjunctive conjunction is *but*. The disjunctive formula for this kind of syllogism is: this but not that. The idea is the same—two clearly contrasting choices are offered.)

There are three rules governing the alternative or disjunctive syllogism's validity:

1. The major premise must contain all the possible alternatives.
2. The two alternatives presented in the major premise must be discreet (mutually exclusive).
3. The minor premise must either affirm (uphold) or contradict one of the alternatives presented in the major premise.

Check the validity of the following alternative syllogisms by applying the three rules:

Psychosis results either from genetic factors or chemical disturbances in the brain.
Psychosis does not result from genetic factors.
Therefore, it results from chemical disturbances in the brain.

No one can be both American and poor.
Mark Itwell is an American.
Therefore, he cannot be poor.

The college must either increase the size of the student body or decrease the size of the faculty.
The college will not increase the size of the student body.
Therefore, it must decrease the size of the faculty.

Unless our employees form a union, they will be dissatisfied.
Unions exploit employees as much as employers do.
Therefore, our employees will not form a union.

The first example did not exhaust all the possible alternatives, did it? Are there any other possible causes of psychosis? Then the syllogism did not give you all the available choices. It is invalid. In the second example, are the two alternatives (being American or being poor) mutually exclusive? Not if one can be *both!* Then that syllogism is not valid either. The fourth example is invalid because the minor premise does not affirm or deny one of the alternatives. It goes off on a tangent and thus destroys the syllogism's structure (and validity).

Now, I can just hear you saying: "But we don't talk in syllogisms! They may be a useful way of analyzing chains of reasoning, but we don't use them directly in our everyday communication." And, of course, you would be quite right. They form a way of stating our reasoning clearly and of checking that reasoning out, but in real life we reason using *enthymemes.* Enthymemes are abbreviated syllogisms with one of the premises assumed rather than stated. That omitted premise is the assumption (discussed earlier). If you examine an enthymeme, you must drag that assumption out into the open, examine it, and test the resulting syllogism for validity. That is why it is important to be able to analyze syllogisms. Enthymemes are syllogisms with one of the vital parts missing. To check out that enthymeme, you must find the missing part and then apply the appropriate tests to see if the reasoning is valid.

Look at this enthymeme:

> Federal health insurance will lead to federal control of hospitals.
> Therefore, federal health insurance is undesirable.

What is the missing assumption? What statement (premise) would complete this syllogism? I hope you said: "Federal control of hospitals is undesirable." Now, is the resulting syllogism valid? What kind of syllogism is it? What tests must you apply to test for validity? The questions about validity will tell you only if the structure is acceptable. Now about the material the syllogism is made of: Do you grant both premises? Are they opinions (and they *are* opinions!) you agree with?

You may disagree with a line of reasoning either because there is faulty construction (validity) or because it used faulty materials (premises). Structure we can test rather objectively, but materials must be evaluated personally. To be persuasive with a receiver, your deduction must be accepted as valid (built according to specifications) and materially sound (made of acceptable materials).

INDUCTION

Induction is reasoning from specific instances (examples) to generalizations. We draw general conclusions from typical examples. When we reason inductively, we make an inference that what is true of some members of a group (class or category) will be true of all members of that group. Since we cannot observe or examine the entire group, we examine some and then guess that the rest will be like the ones we have observed. From the cases we know, we make inferences (guesses) about the cases (in the same category) we do not know.

You can see that there are dangers in using inductive reasoning. Of course, there are dangers any time we reason, because reasoning (by definition) is guessing about the unknown and coming to conclusions about matters we cannot be certain about. There are some tests, however, by which we can check inductive reasoning. If the reasoning meets these four tests, it should be relatively sound:

1. Is/are the case(s) cited relevant to the conclusion drawn?
2. Is/are the case(s) cited typical (truly representative of the group)?
3. Do(es) the instance(s) cited provide a sufficient sample (enough cases)?
4. Is there an absence of critical conflicting instances?

These four tests are simply good common sense. You should not offer or accept a generalization (inductive reasoning) if: (1) the examples used are irrelevant to the issue, (2) the examples used are exceptions rather than typical, (3) the number of instances used is insufficient to make a sensible judgment about the entire class or category, or (4) there is contrary or contradictory evidence—conflicting examples.

Note these examples of inductive reasoning. Would you accept all of them as being sound? Do they measure up to the four tests?

Willie Steele is a crooked politician.
Therefore, all politicians must be crooked.

H. L. Seek began without a penny and became a millionaire.
Everyone in this country has a chance to become a millionaire.

CMS 11 is an interesting class.
All courses in Communication must be interesting.

I have four education majors in my classes this term, and they are all dumb.
Education majors are a dumb bunch!

I have known several professional musicians, and they were all very moody.
Musicians, artists, and actors are temperamental.

When we reason by *analogy,* we base our reasoning on some comparison. We compare what we don't know to what we do know, and we guess that what is true of what we know will be true of something similar (or comparable) we don't know. There are two kinds of analogies: literal and figurative.

LITERAL ANALOGY

Literal analogy is reasoning based on similarities in two things of the same category. We reason that whatever is true in one situation will be true in another situation if the two situations are sufficiently similar. To be a literal analogy, the two things compared must fit into the same classification. They must both be colleges, or states, or countries, or hospitals, or rivers, or companies—or something. Some *same* thing.

Note these examples of literal analogies:

Since they have a successful course in Sanscrit at Queens College, we should institute such a course here at O.P.U.

My religion of Zoroastrianism has been very beneficial to me. I don't know anything about the religion of Seven-Day Hedonism, but I am sure it is very good and beneficial to her.

Great Britain has national medical insurance for its citizens. The United States should also provide health insurance for all United States citizens.

No Rhodesians fought in the American Civil War; no Americans should fight in any Rhodesian civil war.

New York State permits drinking alcoholic beverages at 18. Connecticut should lower its drinking age to 18 also.

To have a chance of being sound, a literal analogy must pass the following three tests:

1. Are the two things being compared significantly similar in matters critical to the issue being discussed?
2. Are the differences between the two things being compared noncritical (unimportant to the issue being discussed)?
3. Are the statements alleged about the things compared actually so (or granted)?

These tests make sense, don't they? If your reasoning is based on a comparison of two things—that is, based on the assumption that the two things are essentially alike—then you want to be sure that (1) the two things are really alike in essential respects, (2) any differences between the two things are irrelevant, and (3) any statements (or assumptions) made about the thing known are really established and realistically represented. Now go back and examine the five literal analogies. How do they match up to the tests? Would you grant all of them as sound?

FIGURATIVE ANALOGY

Figurative analogy is reasoning based on similarities in two things from different categories. Many writers do not accept figurative analogies as a legitimate form of reasoning. They believe all figurative analogies are necessarily specious. I grant that figurative analogies run great risks of coming to mistaken conclusions, but I recognize that we human beings use this form of reasoning all the time. It may be inherently flawed, but it is a form of reasoning, and we must examine it.

If one uses a figurative analogy, that person assumes there are important, significant similarities between two things (or situations) from different categories. We are no longer comparing two colleges or two countries, for example. Instead, we may compare a college to a human body or compare the relationship between two countries to the relationship between two neighboring families who live on the same street. Such comparisons may form the basis for an inference; that reasoning is figurative analogy.

Look at these examples of figurative analogy. In each case, what comparisons are being made?

If a person is drowning and you are trying to save that person, sometimes you have to hit them and knock them unconscious in order to save their life. It's like that when you turn in people who are addicted to drugs. Sometimes you have to force addicts to get treatment against their will.

When a fire department has a limited supply of water and fire-fighting equipment, it cannot put out all the fires in town. It must concentrate on the important fires—the ones that will do the most damage. Just so, the United

States cannot solve all the troubles and crises in the world; it does not have the resources to do that. So it must concentrate its efforts on solving the important problems and conflicts around the world.

If a person is so fat that his or her health is in danger and that person is still gaining weight, any good doctor would tell that person to stop gaining weight and try to cut the weight down. Now, the earth is so overpopulated that the future of the planet is in doubt. Anybody with common sense knows we have to not only stop the increase in population, but we must also work to decrease the number of people on Earth.

Spiders spin a beautiful web, but their purpose is to trap unsuspecting flies and kill them. The Commies give out a beautiful line of talk filled with noble words, but their purpose is to trap unsuspecting fools and destroy them.

Pentagon lobbyists have maintained that defense spending should increase as the gross national product and the population climb. That is like saying a man should buy a new shotgun for self-defense every time his income or his family increases!

Analogies rest on perceived similarities. To be sound, the similarities must outweigh the differences in all essential regards. Look at the five figurative analogies again. Are the situations being compared in each case really similar? And, if so, do those similarities justify the inferences made?

SIGN

When we use *sign* reasoning, we reason from observed indicators to unobserved conclusions. As with any inferences, we are making guesses about the unknown. In sign reasoning, we make those guesses based on sense data—something seen, something heard, something tasted, something smelled, something felt.

Sign reasoning is based on the assumption that there is a necessary relationship between two variables. That is, the presence of one thing will indicate the presence of another, or the absence of one thing will indicate the absence of another. "Where there's smoke, there's fire" is a good example of sign reasoning. You may not be able to see the fire itself, but you assume there *is* a fire if you can detect the smoke. Smoke, then, is taken as a *sign* of fire.

Abstract concepts cannot be grasped by the senses. We cannot see spring or fall; those are abstract ideas in our heads. We can, however, see *signs* of spring and *signs* of fall. We are using sign reasoning when we say, "The trees are budding. Spring is on the way." Or when we say, "The leaves are turning to gold and crimson. Fall is here."

We can, of course, make incorrect inferences based on our observations. I know a young woman who was mortified when an acquaintance was misled by sign reasoning. She had not seen the acquaintance for months and, in the interval, she had gained a great deal of weight. At the pool last summer, the acquaintance asked, "When is the baby due?" The acquaintance had taken the increased weight as a sign of pregnancy. The young woman was not pregnant. You can see why she was upset! Signs *can* lead us astray. There are some tests we can apply to sign reasoning to try to guard against such mistakes:

1. Is the indicator a necessary sign or only a possible sign? That is, can this sign indicate *only* one thing or can it indicate several different things?
2. Does this sign agree with other available evidence?

These two tests remind us to check out sign reasoning and not to jump to conclusions based on perceived signs. Sometimes we do not think of other inferences that can be made from the same sense data and are therefore misled. Remember the nonpregnant young lady!

Look at these examples of sign reasoning. How would you evaluate them? Do you think they are probably sound? Why?

His nose is red. He must be an alcoholic.

U. R. Schick has a rattling chest cough. He probably has pneumonia.

Mary's wearing a wedding band. When did she get married?

I saw Sophie Glutz sleeping during class. I figured she was bored.

I heard the sirens last night. I guess there was another fire in the neighborhood.

Those glands are really swollen. You must have mumps!

You see how the Soviets pulled out those missiles from Cuba when Kennedy stood up to them? The USSR is afraid of us!

This meat tastes funny. It must be spoiled.

Look! The police are arresting that man. He must have committed a crime.

Look at that long hair, those beads, and that earring. He must be a radical, for sure!

CAUSATION

Causal reasoning is the process of making inferences that one factor has caused or will cause something else. This process may move in either of two directions: we may reason from the known results (effect) back to the unknown cause(s) or we may reason from a known factor (cause) forward to what will probably result (the effect). We might use these diagrams to make the variations in the process clear:

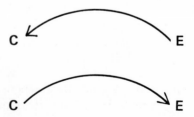

The first is an inference (guess) about *why* some condition occurred; the second is a prediction of what will happen if a particular state of affairs exists.

Cause-effect relationships are different from other relationships in that a time sequence is involved. Presumably, the cause always precedes the effect. Now, beware. Just because one event follows another in time does not mean that the first caused the second. The essential question is this: Did the second event necessarily follow the first? Or would the second event necessarily follow the first? *Necessarily* is the key word. If the first were not present, would the second occur? If the first *is* present, will the second inevitably follow? There must be an inevitable relationship, a constant relationship, for it to be a cause-effect situation.

There are real hazards in using causal reasoning. I have already mentioned one of them—the assumption that whatever comes after was caused by whatever came before. That fallacy is so old it has a Latin name (*post hoc ergo propter hoc*—"after this, therefore because of this"). The other great danger, of course, is oversimplification: assuming one factor, and one factor only, to be *the* cause, when there may in fact be many factors required to produce the result.

There are four tests we can apply to causal reasoning in an effort to reduce the dangers of being misled:

1. Is there a necessary (inevitable) relationship between the alleged cause and effect?
2. Is this the sole or essential cause?
3. Could any other circumstances follow from this alleged cause?
4. Are there other conditions present that will (or might) counteract the cause and prevent (or hinder) the result? (This test is appropriate when reasoning from cause *to* effect.)

Examine these examples of causal reasoning. How well do they pass the four tests? Would you grant them as probably sound?

When the Japanese people started to eat Western foods, including animal fat, the amount of cancer in Japan went up sharply. Eating animal fat produces cancer.

Why did Ima Laster live to the age of 103? She never smoked tobacco, drank liquor, or chewed gum.

Of course Willie Settle is going to pass CMS 11. He studies for that class three hours every day! (Since studying results in passing . . . .)

Most pillheads started with aspirin. Taking aspirin leads inevitably to using harder drugs.

I'm not surprised he went blind! He watched TV ten hours every day.

Vera Little is drinking five milkshakes a day. She's bound to gain weight!

Did you grant the assumptions on which these instances of causal reasoning were based? Did any of these chains of reasoning from cause to effect or from effect to cause meet the criteria for sound causal reasoning?

We have now looked at six types of reasoning that we use to back up our main ideas—deduction, induction, literal analogy, figurative analogy, sign, and causation. Try this little review and see if you can identify each of the types of reasoning used. After you have identified the *type* of reasoning, you should then apply the appropriate tests to see if the reasoning is sound.

Identify the type of reasoning—simple induction, simple deduction, literal analogy, figurative analogy, sign, or cause-effect:

_____ 1. I see Buster Chopps has a black eye. He must have been fighting with his wife again.

_____ 2. The U.S.A. hasn't honored any of its treaties with the American Indians. If it makes a new agreement with the Sioux, it won't keep that treaty either.

_____ 3. Sweden cut the accident rate on its highways by rigidly enforcing the laws against drinking alcoholic beverages and driving. The United States could cut its accident rate by doing the same thing.

_____ 4. Dr. Mark E. D. Sade is a very strict teacher. All professors with Ph.D.s are tough.

_____ 5. After the Dairy Association contributed to the President's reelection campaign funds, the government permitted the price of milk to rise. The dairymen found that it pays to be generous!

_____ 6. The ancient worshippers of Moloch sacrificed their own children in the fiery arms of that god. But isn't it the same thing we do when we send our children off to war?

_____ 7. All politicians are on the take. Hugh Briss must be making a fortune.

_____ 8. Studying mathematics makes a person more logical. If you take Math 101, you should think more clearly than you do now.

SUGGESTIONS FOR FURTHER READING

GRAVES, HAROLD F., and BERNARD S. OLDSEY, *From Fact to Judgment* (New York: Macmillan, 1957).

HUFF, DARRELL, *How to Lie with Statistics* (New York: Norton, 1954).

HUGHEY, JIM D., and ARLEE W. JOHNSON, *Speech Communication: Foundations and Challenges* (New York: Macmillan, 1975).

TOULMIN, STEPHEN, *The Uses of Argument* (Cambridge, England: Cambridge University Press, 1958).

TOULMIN, STEPHEN, RICHARD RIEKE, and ALLAN JANIK, *An Introduction to Reasoning* (New York: Macmillan, 1979).

13
RECEIVING MESSAGES: OBSERVING AND LISTENING

general goal:

To learn to listen and observe more accurately, more critically (when that is appropriate), and more empathically.

specific objectives:

After completing this unit, you should understand:
Some common problems in accurate observing and listening.
How to improve your own listening habits in terms of accuracy.
How to examine what you observe and listen to more critically.
Some common verbal tricks for which a receiver should be on guard.
The importance and difficulty of deferring evaluation in observing and listening (empathic listening).

IN CHAPTER 1, I said that our view of human communication is receiver-oriented. Without a receiver, communication does not take place. In this chapter, we focus on receiving of messages—a crucial element in the communication process. Before reading this chapter, it might be wise to go back and review the material on reception in Chapter 2 (pp. 53-58) and that on perception in Chapter 3 (pp. 61-71, 93-97).

According to various studies, we spend about 70 per cent of the time we are awake involved in communication activities. Paul T. Rankin's 1926 doctoral dissertation provided some interesting statistics, which have been tested and generally supported since. He reported that, of that 70 per cent of our waking time, we spend 30 per cent speaking, 45 per cent listening, 9 per cent writing, and 16 per cent reading. Writing and reading, then, consume only 25 per cent of our communication efforts, while speaking and listening account for 75 per cent of our time expended in communication.[1] And, according to this data, we spend more time listening than speaking! Do you think the advent of television has increased the amount of time spent listening? What would a log of one of your typical days indicate in terms of the time spent on each of the activities of speaking, listening, writing, and reading? You might try it and see.

Think about what you know about the world, about life, about anything. How much of that did you learn through reading? How much through first-hand experience? How much through listening to other people? There are estimates that we learn about 85 per cent of all we know through listening! If that is true, you can see how important it is.

Already I have been using the word *listening* without defining it. What do you think about when you hear the word *listening*? It is more than hearing, isn't it? Indeed, it is much more. Listening involves hearing, but it certainly does not stop there.

Speech, you remember, involved three component parts: verbal, vocal, and visual elements. If I listen to you speak, must I not receive all three components? That's right. I must. At least in the face-to-face situation. And just as there were three activities involved in transmission (mental, vocal, and physical activity), so there are several activities involved in the reception of messages we combine in the term *listening*.

Listening is a combination of what we hear and see, what we understand, and what we remember. We take information in through the senses of both hearing and seeing. We hear the speech sounds and the vocal variations, and we see the bodily activity of the sender. Going through the perception process, we arrive at an interpretation; we attribute meaning to the words we have reconstructed in our minds and to the variations in voice and physical activity we have noted. We get a message and we store it. Maybe.

---

[1] Paul T. Rankin, "Measurement of the Ability to Understand the Spoken Language," unpublished doctoral dissertation, The University of Michigan, 1926.

Ralph Nichols and his associates at the University of Minnesota have provided us with some shocking data on the results of listening. Their studies demonstrate that we human beings (at least American human beings) are not very efficient listeners—if remembering information is the test of efficiency. Their studies indicated that people remembered only half of what they "listened to"—when tested immediately after listening.[2] Their studies, which have been confirmed by other studies at Michigan State and Florida State,[3] indicated that after a lapse of two months, people remembered only one-fourth of what they had "listened to."

Of course, just as we cannot pay attention to every stimulus that comes to us, so we cannot remember every piece of data we collect. These studies should not frighten or dismay us. But they may encourage us to work on our listening skill(s). (There is no universal agreement on whether listening is a unitary skill or a combination of skills. There is a lot more we don't know about listening than we do know.)

At least as I am using the term, I am speaking of the receiving of spoken messages. This reception involves more than just the sense of hearing. And it involves more than just verbal communication, since speech communication (which is what is being received) involves both verbal and nonverbal aspects. These verbal and nonverbal aspects are transmitted together, and they are received together. The entire received package ("message") is the result of "listening."

We will look at three facets of receiving messages: (1) accuracy in observing and listening, (2) critical judgment in observing and listening, and (3) the deferral of evaluation in observing and listening.

accuracy in observing and listening

Look at the picture on page 337. Then answer the questions. You are to mark *T* (for *true*) if, from direct observation, you know the statement to be true, *F* (for *false*) if, from direct observation, you know the statement to be false, and *?* (for *don't know*) if, from direct observation, you cannot determine whether the statement is true or false. Do not check your answers until you have completed the entire list of questions. In fact, wait a little longer and try the next exercise before checking both sets of answers.

In my classes at this point, I read a story and have my students write their answers on an answer sheet immediately after listening to the story. We are, of course, checking for accuracy—getting the story right. As they used to say on TV's *Dragnet*, "All we want is the facts"—no additions, no deletions, no distortions or changes. Since I cannot read you a story, I will

---

[2] Ralph Nichols and Leonard Stevens, "Listening to People," *Harvard Business Review*, **35**:5 (1957), pp. 85–92.

[3] J. J. Kramer and T. R. Lewis, "Comparison of Visual and Non-Visual Listening," *Journal of Communication*, **1** (1951), p. 16.

IN THE BLANK, WRITE "T," "F," or "?"

Write T if, according to what you can directly observe in the picture, the statement is definitely, completely true and accurate.

Write F if, according to what you can directly observe in the picture, the statement is definitely false.

Write ? if, from what you can directly observe in the picture, you cannot be definitely certain about the statement.

_____ 1. There are four people in the room.

_____ 2. The Gibson family subscribes to *Time, Newsweek,* and *New York* magazines.

_____ 3. The Gibson family consists of a father, mother, baby, and grandmother.

_____ 4. The Gibsons own a television set.

_____ 5. Mr. Gibson is a student.

_____ 6. The grandmother is making an afghan.

_____ 7. The Gibsons are a happy family.

have to let you read it instead. If you can get a friend to read it to you, all the better. Then try answering the questions after the story.

Here's the story:

> Chris Martin began taking drugs in 1966. Two years later, his daily intake of drugs was greatly increased. In November 1970, Chris Martin was found dead, along with several friends, at 1280 Broadway. The body was discovered by Pat Downs, an officer in the New York City Police Department.

Here are the questions (and the instructions again):
In the blank, write T, F, *or* ?.

Write *T* if, according to the story, the statement is definitely, completely true and accurate.

Write *F* if, according to the story, the statement is definitely false.

Write *?* if, from the information presented in the story, you cannot be definitely certain. If any part of the statement is doubtful, write *?*.

_____ 1. Chris Martin was addicted to drugs.
_____ 2. Chris Martin died in November 1970.
_____ 3. Mr. Downs himself discovered the body.
_____ 4. Chris Martin was found dead at 1820 Broadway.
_____ 5. The man who discovered the body was an officer in the New York City Police Department.

If you managed to get someone to read the story to you, and you listened to the story only one time, you were putting yourself to a more real-life test. When we listen, we usually do not get instant replays. We hear it once and it is gone. We must pay special attention, then, when we listen. On the other hand, if you read the material to yourself from the book, you had the chance to go back and check on details. That makes the task a little easier. Now check on the answers. They are found on page 357.

How accurate were you at observing what was there in the picture? What questions did you miss? What problems did you encounter? Do you understand why the answers are what they are? Did you make inferences about the picture and assume the conclusions were in the picture rather than in your mind? Then you added information that was not in the picture you saw at all. Did you omit information that was there or get some information mixed up?

What about the story? Did you get all the questions right? If not, what was the reason for each one you missed? Again, did you add in information that was not in the story and assume it had been there? We must learn to separate the information we take in from the inferences we make about that information. Did you forget information or get some information confused?

Just how accurate a listener do you think you are? Or perhaps I should ask, just how accurate a listener and observer do these little tests reveal you to be? Do you need to work at accurate reception of messages? Take heart. We all do!

We must work to sharpen our perceptions. Our purpose is to be able to observe things more nearly as they are, to listen for what a speaker is saying and what he or she intends to mean—in short, to gather information that is as accurate, complete, and undistorted as we can.

What can we do to improve our listening (and observing) for accuracy? Here are thirteen suggestions:

1. *Pay attention.* We cannot listen if we do not pay attention. That is almost self-evident. We are literally bombarded by stimuli competing for our attention. We must select stimuli to focus our attention on. Some of the stimuli we notice eventually get stored (remembered) for future use; some do not. But no information (perhaps I had better say *little* information) gets stored that does not get attended to. Go back and read the material on perception (pp. 63–65, 88–90) in relation to selection and attention.

Do you think you can pay attention to several different stimuli at the same time? That is, can you divide your attention energy up among several stimuli? Right, you can. But when you do, of course, you give less attention to each of the stimuli than if you concentrated your energy on one stimulus alone.

Just deciding to concentrate on a stimulus by "paying attention" does not mean that you can focus on that stimulus indefinitely. It certainly does not mean you can give maximum attention energy to that stimulus till you decide to quit. Our attention energy fluctuates; it crests and ebbs quite apart from our will. The trick, of course, is to try to catch the crests!

Even at the crest of attention intensity, there are limits on what we can attend to. We cannot notice *everything.* If we really tried, we would overload our mental circuits. That is why we *must* select certain stimuli for attention and screen out others. Effective listening depends on this process of proper selection.

2. *Distinguish between your assumptions and your inferences* and *what you hear and observe.* The incoming data and what you think about the incoming data are two different things—as we may have discovered with our little exercises. It is important that we not get the two confused.

Some writers assert that we can think much faster than we speak. If so, that poses an opportunity, a challenge, and a danger for the listener. It is an *opportunity* because the listener can use the extra time to think about what is being said, a *challenge* because one can, but need not, use the time constructively to examine what is being said, and a *danger* because one may use the time to think about other things or to daydream.

Most of us talk at the rate of about 125 to 150 words per minute. It is thought that we can handle words much faster than that—maybe four or five times as fast. There have been some studies in which recorded material was speeded up and listeners' comprehension tested. Although such tests have produced varied results, David B. Orr has concluded that maximum comprehension can be achieved at a rate of 275 to 300 words per minute.[4] He notes, however, that factors such as the difficulty of the subject, the familiarity (or strangeness) of the subject, the complexity of the language used, and the intelligence of the listener affect the relationship between optimum possible rate and maximum comprehension.

If there is extra time for the listener to think about what is being said, and if the listener uses that time to make inferences based on assumptions about what is being said, then it is important that the listener keep those assumptions and inferences separated in his or her mind from what was actually said. There is nothing necessarily wrong about making inferences; quite the contrary. But we must not get it in our heads that the speaker *said* what we guessed (inferred). The inferences may be valid or invalid; that is not the point I am making. The point is that the inferences are *added* to what was said; they are not part of what was said. In other words, they are part of the mixing step of the perception process rather than part of the gathering step of that process.

It is important that the listener keep this distinction in mind; it will help avoid serious misunderstandings. Have you ever been in the position of saying either "But you *said* . . ." or "I didn't say that; what I *said* was . . ."? A few years ago, I had the unpleasant task of giving a rating to an employee whose work had not been satisfactory. I said to that person, "I must tell you that your work this year has not been satisfactory." The person later was furious and reported that I had said *he* was "inferior." What was the basis of the misunderstanding? Hadn't the person made an inference and then decided I had *said* what he inferred? You can doubtless think of many instances in which you have observed this same problem.

3. *Identify the speaker's central idea.* We have talked about the central idea before. (See pp. 303–305.) There must be a point to any transmitted message. Try to figure out what that point is. In sum, what is the speaker saying?

4. *Identify the speaker's main points.* Don't try to hold on to each little detail. The person talking will have a few important points to make. Hang on to those.

5. *Identify the structure of the message.* Every message will have some kind of structure. (See pp. 300–302.) You may discover the structure is orderly, or you may discover it is a hodgepodge. In any case, try to figure out what kind of organization the message has. Is it arranged in chronological order, space order, topical order, problem-solution order, cause-effect order, a list order, or what?

6. *Identify the forms of support used.* We have discussed the various kinds of supporting material that speakers use in their messages. (See pp. 305–315.) Which, of the different kinds of evidence, is the speaker using to back up his or her points? Indeed, is the speaker using *any* supporting material to back up what is being said?

---

[4] David B. Orr, "Time Compressed Speech—a Perspective," *Journal of Communication,* **18** (1968), p. 288.

7. *Identify the forms of reasoning used.* Review the six types of reasoning we discussed. (See pp. 315–332.) The people who talk to us every day use each of these forms of reasoning. As we listen, we should note the kinds of reasoning used to back up the main points. Later we can evaluate those lines of reasoning to see if they are valid.

8. *Identify emotional appeals.* People who talk to us may try to influence us (indeed, they *will* try to influence us) based on our drives (needs), motives (concerns), and emotions (feelings). They will try to move us through the use of emotional appeals. We should note the appeals made; later we can evaluate them.

9. *Organize as you go along.* Make internal summaries. Try to pull the message together into some organized system. At the end, of course, you can make a more complete summary, but all the way along you can keep tabs on where the message seems to be going.

10. *Infer the speaker's purpose.* I probably should have put this suggestion earlier in the list. Perhaps just after number 3, "Identify the central idea." Sometimes, however, it is not easy to guess the speaker's purpose early in the message. The speaker may ramble, may not get to the point directly or quickly, or may deliberately avoid revealing the purpose at the outset of the message. It is important that we try to guess the speaker's intention (purpose) or objective, but it is equally important that we keep in mind that we are making an inference. We usually must *guess* what response the speaker is aiming for. And we must leave room for that guess to be revised or corrected.

11. *Take your own biases into account.* We are all biased. (See pp. 76–80, 93–94.) We each have a world view (a set of beliefs, values, and attitudes). And, as we have noted earlier, we tend to expose ourselves only to those persons and those views that fit in with our present view of the world. We try to maintain those world views; we try to keep them integrated and consistent and stable. Even if we are exposed to other, conflicting views, we are likely to edit them out by using selective attention. We protect ourselves from views that might upset our intellectual and philosophical applecarts!

Knowing this tendency may help guard us against it. After all, there may be some new, different information of worth trying to break through to us. If one knows his or her own world view—recognizes his or her biases—and faces where that mind-set might pose listening problems, then one can compensate for the bias.

The point is that we listen with our biases or through our biases—if our biases let us listen at all—and we will listen more accurately and carefully and objectively if we take those predilections into account. We must be aware of those leanings if we are to have a chance of neutralizing them.

12. *Control your emotions.* This suggestion, of course, is related to the previous one. If we hear something contrary or contradictory to our biases, we may react immediately and emotionally. We may get quite angry or even hostile. We may spend our extra thinking time arguing with the message rather than examining it. We may become preoccupied with

countering the message rather than considering it. Fear, hate, and anger short-circuit logical analysis. If we are to get the message right and give it a fair hearing, we must keep our emotions in check. We will want, eventually, to judge the message, to evaluate it. But we must *get* the message first. If we get too excited in midmessage, we may miss what the speaker's message really was intended to be.

13. *Tune out distractions.* This advice is easier to propose than to practice. Of course, we will all listen better if we are not distracted. Attention is hard to maintain at best, and distractions are an added curse. There are three kinds of (or sources of) distractions that we must guard against: (1) those related to the speaker, (2) those related to the physical environment, and (3) those related to our own selves. Let us look at each of these sources of distractions briefly.

Are there some kinds of people you just don't want to listen to? Now be honest. Are there some people that turn you off and you tend to tune out? Then something about the person is distracting you from that person's message.

Maybe a speaker's personality is distracting. What kinds of personalities offend you—to the point that you don't want to bother listening to anything the person says? Do you know some people who dislike certain kinds of personality traits so much that they ignore messages coming from people with such traits?

Some people are distracted by a speaker's character. They do not pay attention to what is said if it comes from a "bad person." Each person's idea of what a bad person is may differ, but the distraction is a real one. Do you believe a bad person can have a good idea? If so, are you willing to listen and give that idea a fair hearing?

Are you distracted by some speakers' appearance? If so, what kinds of appearance sidetrack your attention? Aren't there still some people who will not listen to a male with long hair? Or a female with short hair? What about clothes? Can't the way a person is dressed turn off a potential listener? What do you look for in clothing? What might distract you from a speaker's message? What do you consider eccentric or bizarre clothes? Are you more inclined to listen to a thin person than a fat one? One with teeth than one without any teeth?

Every person has distinctive mannerisms. We all have idiosyncrasies, don't we? Ticks or unusual bodily activity may be distractions. So too may nervous habits such as drumming the fingers or rattling change or keys. Do such distractions take your attention away from what the person is saying?

What about a speaker's speech patterns? What kinds of voices irritate you? Are you bothered by accents or regional or social dialects? Do you quit listening as soon as you detect a Southern drawl or a Midwestern twang or Brooklynese? Are you distracted by unusually high- (or low-) pitched voices? Isn't what someone says more important than the way that person says it? Then we must guard against this kind of distraction, mustn't we?

Are you easily distracted by language—that is, by the words a speaker uses? Are you easily offended by certain taboo words? (See pp. 225–226.) Isn't the language of the speaker a very common turnoff? And it is not always taboo words that serve as the distractions. Some people are put off by large words and involved sentences. Others are put off by slang or jargon. What kinds of language tend to distract you?

We have already noted that some people are unwilling to listen if the speaker puts forth new or different views, but there is one other distraction connected with the speaker that we might note. That is the speaker's group memberships. Have you ever heard someone say, "I have no intention of listening to _____" (here you can fill in some category or group). Are there people in any category *you* don't wish to listen to? We are facing the problem of stereotyping and prejudice, aren't we?

Sometimes there are distractions imposed by the physical environment. If you find that something is disturbing your ability to listen, try to correct the situation. Open the window, close the door, turn off the noisy fan, move closer to the speaker, turn down the thermostat, turn off the television set (or at least turn off the sound!), or turn down the volume on the stereo. You can, to a large extent, control the physical environment. Do what you can to eliminate the distractions.

Some distractions are neither in the speaker nor in the physical environment. Some distractions are in our own selves. A common excuse for poor listening or inattention is boredom. If you are bored, the feeling is internal; the problem is yours. Deal with it. You may be surprised to find, if you genuinely listen, that the speaker has something interesting to say.

Another internal distraction is fatigue. I know I cannot listen as well when I am tired. I do not have a quick cure for this distraction, I am sorry to say.

I have already mentioned the problem of daydreaming. Does your mind wander when you are supposed to be listening? The daydreams may be pleasant, but the time might be better spent examining what the speaker has said.

Related to daydreaming but different from it is the problem of preoccupation. If your mind is on other subjects, you may find it difficult to listen—to give full attention to the message the speaker is trying to convey.

I hesitate to mention another distraction, but I must. Some of us (not you and I, of course) are lazy. Listening is work. It requires effort—a real expenditure of energy. And the more difficult the material being transmitted, the harder is the listener's task. There may be people who would rather avoid exerting themselves enough to listen, especially to "hard subjects." If so, then laziness is a real distraction.

The last distraction that may be within the listener himself or herself is insecurity. We have referred to this problem in other ways, but it bears repeating. Charles M. Kelly has found that good listeners (those who are better at accurate listening) were emotionally stable, secure, mature, sophisticated, and willing to take risks. Poor listeners, on the other hand, were tense, timid, emotional, simple, and insecure.[5] Kelly's findings indicate that those people we would label mature or well adjusted because they are more able to cope with change and uncertainty are the best at listening. Isn't that what you would expect? The more open a person is to new ideas, the better listener that person will be. And the less open to new ideas and the more frightened of change a person is, the more the person's internal fears will detract from incoming messages.

So far, we have looked at some problems in acccurate listening and examined thirteen suggestions for improving accuracy in listening and observing. We are now ready to turn to critical listening.

critical judgment in observing and listening

After we observe as accurately as we can what exists or we listen as accurately as we can to what a speaker is saying, we must often subject what we have observed and what we have listened to to critical analysis. This thoughtful (perhaps even suspicious and skeptical) approach is necessary. What we observe and listen to must be examined to see if what it appears to be or purports to be will stand up under this kind of examination. Such an examination process should make us more immune to devious appeals from advertisers, con artists, and some politicians.

Three Suggestions for Critical Listening

Our task in critical listening is to go beyond understanding what the speaker said and what the speaker meant; we must evaluate the speaker's message. We must decide about the validity and acceptability of the message—both the message as a whole and the parts of the message. The question now is not "What did the speaker say and mean?" but "How does what the speaker said stand up?"

I have three suggestions for critical listening.

1. EVALUATE THE SUPPORTING MATERIAL

There is no point in repeating here the tests of each kind of supporting material. Review that information on pp. 305–315. In Chapter 12, we looked at supporting material from the point of view of the message-sender. Now we are examining supporting material from the listener's viewpoint. After all, it is the listener who must decide if the evidence is sufficient and acceptable.

---

[5] Charles M. Kelly, "Mental Ability and Personality Factors in Listening," *Quarterly Journal of Speech,* **49** (1963), p. 152.

Again, review the information on reasoning found on pp. 315–332. For each type of reasoning, there are tests for validity. Be sure, as you listen, that a speaker constructs valid arguments of solid material. Apply the appropriate test to each line of reasoning offered. And remember to examine the premises and assumptions as well as the conclusions!

There are five categories, or kinds, of word tricks that we will examine: (1) dismissal, (2) derision, (3) distractions, (4) distortions, and (5) defective reasoning.

Dismissal. This is an easy trick to understand—and to spot. The speaker simply refuses to discuss something; instead, he or she dismisses the subject as being of no importance. Have you ever heard someone say, "I won't even honor (or dignify) that statement with a reply"? Or "That charge is not worthy of an answer"? Or "That is ridiculous on the face of it, and I won't waste time talking about it"? All of these are statements of dismissal.

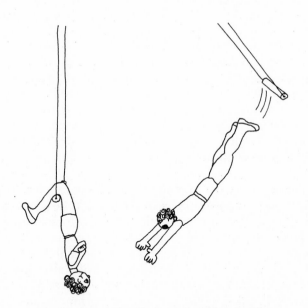

One kind of verbal trick: Dismissal

Now there may be some subjects that are not worth talking about and some charges that are not worth answering. On the other hand, I think you should be suspicious if a speaker just dismisses a subject out of hand. It may well be that the speaker cannot answer. *You* must decide whether the subject being dismissed so lightly really deserved a hearing.

Derision. This trick, of course, involves the use of ridicule to "put down" an idea or an argument. Again, some ideas may be ridiculous (to you or to me), but we had better remember all the great thinkers whose ideas were laughed at by their contemporaries before we lead the guffaws.

**One kind of verbal trick:
Derision**

I remember an incident at a press conference when one of the few women in the Washington press corps covering the White House asked President John Kennedy a question related to women's rights. He answered, his voice dripping sarcasm, that he thought women ought to get everything they wanted. The men of the press corps roared with laughter. He did not wish to deal with the serious issue she raised, so he treated it as a joke—with derision. The trick worked at that moment with that audience—which, I think, says more about the listeners than it does about the issue.

At this writing, the question of the rights of homosexual citizens to jobs and housing is being debated in New York City. Opponents of the anti-discrimination ordinance are especially opposed to acknowledged homosexuals serving as teachers, firefighters, and police officers. One wag recently commented, "If you let them in, there'll be no room in the firehouse dorms. As soon as they move in with all their makeup kits, countless pairs of high heels, evening gowns, and feather boas, there'll be no space left at all!" That's derision; it is an attempt to make the opposing case appear absurd and stupid; it assumes that the opposing view is ludicrous.

"Sure, Copernicus, the world is a revolving sphere! Of course it is. And we are standing on our heads half the time, right?"

"O.K., Galileo, you may doubt the three-layered universe *now*. But we know there is a heaven above and a hell below the earth. God says so. We'll just wait till you die, see which direction you go, and see how long you hold onto those crazy theories *then*!"

"Orville and Wilbur think that thing is going to fly. That's because they have bird-brains!"

If someone tries to use derision on some viewpoint he or she disagrees with, withhold your laughter long enough to find out if the ridiculed ideas have some merit. After all, the one who laughs last . . . .

Distractions. Distractions are diversionary maneuvers. They are attempts to divert attention away from the real issues. They are sleight-of-mouth tricks. Just as magicians are able to pull off their tricks right in front of our eyes by diverting our attention, so verbal tricksters also attempt to put something over on us listeners. If they get us to focus on something other than the real subject, we can be fooled.

**One kind of verbal trick:
Distraction**

There are five such tricks one should be aware of and on guard against: (1) attacking opponents personally, (2) loaded words, (3) appeals to base emotions, (4) red herrings, and (5) straw man. I will define each of these tricks and give a few examples to show you how they work.

attacking opponents personally.   This trick diverts attention from what a person is saying and shifts the attention to the person himself or herself. If a speaker can get us to concentrate on the person rather than on the message of the person, we will not listen well to the person thus attacked. Therefore, be leery of those who use this trick.

Here are three examples:

Willie Neel, a prisoner at Attica, asked a grand jury to investigate brutality by guards at the prison. One member of the grand jury said, "That's not even worth discussing. He's a convicted criminal!"

Howie Lost was running for Congress and said he was for cutting military spending. Howie's opponent, Sandy Shore, refused to talk about the budget but commented, "Are you going to send a man like that to Congress? His wife even left him! And the voters will divorce him at the ballot box too!"

Elaine Noble (a real person) ran for the State Legislature in Massachusetts in 1974. She ran on a platform of improved housing and better care for the elderly. Her opponent's main theme was: "Don't put a lesbian in the Legislature!"

loaded words.   There are some words that carry such emotional charges (at least for many people) that they can short-circuit thinking. Bring up those words, and you push an emotional button. These words seem to trigger signal responses. (See pp. 17–18.)

Here are some examples:

John Wilson, attorney, called Senator Inouye from Hawaii "that little Jap."

One recent candidate for mayor of my city said he was going to rid the city of "punks, pushers, and perverts."

One fictional citizen, D. Ranged, said: "Our precious heritage is being attacked by those dirty, worthless, fuzzy-headed and fuzzy-minded radicals!"

One student (not fictional) at a college I know well recently said to a dean, "You are a f—ing racist pig."

appeals to base emotions.   Emotional appeals are powerful tools and should be used in a responsible way by speakers. Like any instruments, these may be abused. Beware of those speakers who attempt to divert your attention from real issues or significant problems by stirring up (or attempting to stir up) hate, hysterical fear, racist bigotry, religious prejudice, or national animosities. Base (low-down) emotions, such as hate and fear, are easy to turn on, but they are difficult to turn off. We must guard against those unethical speakers who attempt to use our feelings against our best judgment.

Here are three examples:

I. B. Lieve recently commented, "We know where those people get their funds. They parade as patriots, as loyal Americans, but we know who they really work for. We know who is behind them. And we know what they are trying to do to our precious system of government. That is why we are exposing their sly deeds."

Ima Frayed recently told a friend, "If you let those people in, they take over. Your job is not safe, your house is not safe, your family is not safe. It's us or them. We've got to keep them out."

A self-styled "revolutionary," May Day, said: "Whoever is not in the revolution, whoever does not work actively for the revolution, whoever does not openly support the revolution is an enemy of the people—an animal rather than a human being—and should be exterminated."

red herrings.   Red herrings are false issues dragged in to divert attention from the real issues. They are other subjects completely, introduced for the purpose of leading you off the trail of the main idea, which may be too shaky to stand careful scrutiny.

Here are three examples:

> Moe and Les were arguing about whether students ought to give them-selves grades or whether teachers should do the grading. Les said, "Just look at how much money the teachers are making!"

> In a recent debate over whether women should be able to get legal abortions if they want them, Seymour Kleerly commented: "I remember the Nazis with their experiments on human beings; I remember how they tortured and killed millions of innocent human beings!"

> When Social Security was proposed in the 1930s in the United States, the American Medical Association opposed it (as they did Medicare and Medic-aid years later) because, they said, "Socialism is an evil system."

straw man. Have you ever seen a scarecrow? What is it? A dummy, right? A fake person set up out in the field to scare away crows. The assumption is that crows are so dumb they will be fooled into thinking the dummy is a real person and not come and eat the seed corn. This verbal trick is called *straw man* because it too is a dummy. It involves creating a fictitious opposing position and then knocking that position down.

It is an interesting verbal trick and too often effective. It is intended, of course, to take the listener's mind off the position of the speaker. By thus distracting the listener, the speaker may be able to get a weak point or argument accepted with little critical examination.

If I say, "Jerry Mander is in favor of changing the Congressional district lines," Jerry can answer me—if that is not her position. If I say, "The A.C.L.U. is in favor of government censorship of plays," a spokesperson for that organized group can issue a statement correcting my misrepresen-tation of their position. But if I do not say exactly who believes the things I attribute to "some people," or if I make up a name for some group I have created in my own mind and talk about what this "group" believes, who can answer me? The group is a dummy; it is my own creation. I can call it what I please, and I can attribute to it any beliefs I choose. And there is no one who can refute my statement of "their" position, because there is no real "they."

Here are some examples:

> There are some people who think we should close all the schools of the country, who want to keep our little children in ignorance, who want to suppress all the teachers and destroy all the textbooks. Beware of the antieducationists, my friends. Reject their foolish attacks on our great system of free education.

> I am here today to oppose the growing cult of scientism. This simple-minded, naive faith that parades as knowledge worships science. Its followers believe that science has all the answers to all of our problems. They ask us to put our fate and the fate of the whole human race into the hands of the scientists alone. But the truly wise will refuse to be fooled by this new *ism,* scientism.

> General I. C. Redd is reported to have said, "There are those who want the United States to destroy all its arms and to do away with every means of

protecting itself. Those who attack the Pentagon and the armed forces daily do so because they want to see America weak and helpless before its enemies. They want to see America fall into the hands of godless foreign conquerors. Those who work against the Defense budget requests are speaking for one-sided disarmament and surrender. No one but a fool would heed them!"

Distortions. The trick in distortions is not to get the listener's mind off the issue at hand and on to something else (those are distractions); rather, the trick lies in an attempt to present the real issue inaccurately.

**One kind of verbal
trick: Distortion**

Distortions are attempts to deceive by twisting the material presented in some way. Let us look at five such tricks: (1) careless exaggeration, (2) unwarranted conclusion, (3) misrepresentation of facts, (4) misinterpretation of another's position, and (5) withholding of evidence. I will define each of these tricks and offer a few examples for you to examine.

careless exaggeration. Careless exaggerations are wild, sweeping generalizations. They exceed hyperbole, which is, after all, used only for effect; everyone understands that hyperbole is not to be taken literally. These statements are bald, bold assertions so broadly stated that they leave no room for exceptions. Although the "all" is not always expressed, it is often assumed in these sweeping generalizations.

Here are some horrible, but recognizable, examples:

Miss Fitt told Sophie Glutz that: "All those Indians are lazy, ignorant drunks. There's not a sober, dependable working person among them."

Ima Little Dumm said: "Men in the United States believe women are maids, nurses, mistresses, and slaves. The United States male is not capable of looking on a woman as a human being."

One "student leader" at an urban college said: "The teachers at this school are racists. They don't like students unless they are white. They want everyone else to fail."

C. Z. Leight recently commented: "Bigotry is built into the white man in this country."

Rob Nichols said: "Poverty is the cause of crime in the United States."

The mother of Tony, a young man with hyperkinesis, offered this explanation: "Tony's problem is that he is filled with the devil. Everything would be perfect if he would give his heart to Jesus."

Andy Howles has a simple, but consistent view of women; he says, "Women prefer to be dominated by men, since they are the weaker sex."

unwarranted conclusion. If I claim to have proved more than I have really established with the evidence I've offered, then I have presented an unwarranted conclusion. A warrant is something that justifies an action, isn't it? If a conclusion is unwarranted, then it is unjustified. The evidence does not prove what I have claimed it proved. This is a somewhat subtle trick, because some evidence is offered after all. The trick lies in going well beyond the proof when I get to the conclusion. We must listen carefully to check the stated conclusions to see if they are justified by the proof.

Here are three examples of this trick:

Cliff Hanger said: "Two semesters ago, three people in that teacher's Communication class failed; last semester, six people in that teacher's class failed. Next semester, everybody will fail."

Y. Schorr thought this argument persuasive: "One out of every five people living in New York City is on some kind of welfare. That proves there are more on welfare than really need it."

Betty Wood provided this example: "I knew a preacher once who preached against adultery but slept with every woman in the choir. That shows that preachers are all hypocrites."

misrepresentation of facts. Fact kind of statements, you remember, are statements that can be checked out. We can find out with relative certainty whether they are true or not. If I state something as a fact, and in truth it is not so, I have lied. That is a pretty plain distortion, isn't it? I am sure you can think of much better examples than I can. Do you listen critically and carefully and consistently and conscientiously enough to know when a speaker is telling an untruth?

A student at my college recently "informed" me: "The president of the college gets a salary of $100,000 a year plus fringe benefits." This student should check his "fact."

On an application, Rob Banks said he had worked for the New York Telephone Company for five years (from 1970 to 1975). Actually, according to the company, he worked for them for five months in 1975.

misinterpretation of another's position. There are three ways to distort the position of someone else. You can deliberately misquote the person—adding words, omitting words, changing words; you can quote the person word for word, but lift the quote out of its context, thus giving an incomplete and inaccurate impression of the person's stand; or you can twist the meaning of statements attributed to the person by paraphrasing and summarizing distortions of the person's viewpoint. We must listen carefully to detect this trick, and we must have a great deal of knowledge about the real viewpoints of the people being cited as authorities.

Here are three examples:

One day, a teacher said jokingly, "*A* is for God, who is perfect; *B* is for me, since I'm almost perfect; and that leaves *C, D,* and *F* for the rest of you folks!" After class, one student told a friend that the instructor had told the class they were all going to fail the course.

When asked if he were in favor of doing away with criminal penalties for possession of marijuana, former Senator Eugene McCarthy said, "Not unless they print on every pack of marijuana cigarettes '*does not cause liver disease, heart disease, or cancer!*'" One of the reporters who heard the former Senator speak reported that Senator McCarthy was against making marijuana legal.

Ms. Oma Goodness was one of the leaders who fought against using money from the state treasury to help finance church-related schools. She believed, she said, in "separation of church and state." In a speech in a public speaking class, Faith Fuller spoke in favor of giving state aid to church-related schools and commented that Ms. Goodness was against God and the church. "Her unbelief," Faith opined, "like that of all atheists, is a terrible mistake!"

withholding of evidence. A speaker can deceive us listeners without telling us a direct lie. He or she can simply hold back vital information from us. We are as misled by that technique (or at least we *can* be) as if the speaker had explicitly stated an untruth. Whatever the technical legalities are, the trick is unethical. But it is up to us listeners to try to detect such deception, and it is not an easy trick to detect.

Here are three examples:

The police arrived at the door and asked Mrs. Conn about the whereabouts of her husband, X. Conn. Mrs. Conn said nothing. X was hiding behind the sofa in the living room. One of the police officers said (pointing to the bedroom door): "He's in there, isn't he?" "Certainly not," said Mrs. Conn.

After a medical examination in which the physician found the patient had an incurable kidney disease, the patient asked the doctor if she had cancer. "No," said the kindly doctor. "Put your mind perfectly at ease on that score."

Nita Blessing was afraid there was going to be an exam in her Religion class. As soon as she came into the classroom, she asked the instructor if he planned to give an exam in class that day. He simply answered, "No." He did not tell her that he was planning to distribute a take-home exam at the end of the period.

Defective Reasoning. I have already suggested that you check the lines of reasoning offered by any speaker. Why then include this category at all? Well, there are a few common tricks that we listeners should be especially wary of, and these tricks are related to or pass themselves off as *reasoning*.

One kind of verbal trick: Defective reasoning

It seems appropriate here to give these tricks a little special attention, because we listeners need to be able to defend ourselves against these tactics. I shall explain and illustrate five such tricks: (1) the false choice (either-or) trick, (2) *post hoc ergo propter hoc,* (3) reasoning in a circle, (4) extension, and (5) sophistry.

the false choice (either-or) trick. It is possible to set up a valid line of reasoning based on two contradictory choices. (Review the material on disjunctive syllogisms on pp. 325–326.) Two clearly contrasting choices are offered, and then one of the choices is confirmed or denied. That leaves us with the other choice eliminated or affirmed. This trick is a clever misuse of that form of deductive reasoning.

The trick lies in setting up two choices that are assumed to be discreet (mutually exclusive) and *all the choices possible* when they are not. Then one of the choices is confirmed or denied, and the "logical" conclusion is drawn.

If a speaker gives us only two choices ("It's either this or that") and tries to force us to pick one, when there are many other choices open to us, the speaker is resorting to this trick. If the listener is to prevent being fooled by this device, that listener must ask himself or herself the question, "Are those really the only two alternatives?" and "Are those alternatives really complete opposites?"

Here are three examples:

Helen Bach, in a recent conversation with a friend, stated: "Either a person will be a committed theist or a committed atheist. Ira Flect is not a committed theist, because he is not absolutely convinced there is a God. So he must be an atheist."

M. I. Hipp believed he was being logical when he told Heidi Ho: "If a person is not totally heterosexual, he is homosexual. Now you know that Jamie Ladd is not totally heterosexual, so what does that make him?"

In a controversy about whether to expand the course offerings in the Department of Communication at O.P.U. recently, Professor Art Nouveau argued: "The college must either add more courses in communication or abolish the department. Which are we going to do?"

post hoc ergo propter hoc.   I have already mentioned this trick when we discussed cause-effect reasoning. (See pp. 330–331.) The Latin phrase "after this, therefore because of this" explains this misapplication of causal reasoning. Just because one thing follows another in time does not prove that the first caused the second! That should be obvious. But this is a very common fallacy, and a listener must be careful not to be taken in by it.

Here are three examples:

"Herbert Hoover," said Willie Feight, an ardent Democrat, "was inaugurated President in March 1929, and the stock market crashed in October 1929. It only took Hoover eight months to cause the Great Depression!"

Izzy Wright, a lifelong Republican, presented this version of history: "Americans put Wilson in the White House, and World War I came; they elected Franklin Roosevelt President, and we entered World War II; Harry Truman got in the White House and brought us the Korean War; the next Democrat elected was John Kennedy, and we got involved in the Vietnam War. That is proof positive. History doesn't lie. Elect a Democrat President, and you will get a war every time!"

One evening, watching TV, Shirley Knott ate a large number of chocolate-chip cookies. In the night, a 24-hour virus struck her, and she was very ill. "I knew I should never have eaten those cookies," said Shirley. "Just look at what they did to me!"

reasoning in a circle.   If you offer two unsupported assertions to "prove" each other, you have reasoned in a circle. We listeners must not let speakers get away with this trick. But we must listen critically if we are to catch it. The trick lies in offering one statement that supposedly proves the conclusion and then using the conclusion to support the original statement. We have, as you can see, gone in a circle.

Here are three examples:

Terry Feid said: "Murder should be prohibited by law because it is morally wrong. We know it is morally wrong because it is prohibited by law." Terry's brother, Mortie Feid, gave this variation on the same circular route: "Marijuana should not be legal because it is not respectable. The fact that it is not legal proves it is not respectable."

Father O'Neal, a parish priest, told his devout parishoner Jenny Flect that "the Church should not permit women to be priests because it is contrary to the will of God. It is clearly against the will of God because the Church does not permit it."

Dusty Field is reputed to have said: "The Palestine Liberation Organization is not a member of the United Nations because it is not respected by peace-loving nations. That the PLO does not have the respect of peace-loving nations is proved by the fact it is not a member of the U.N."

extension.   This trick involves attacking an argument or a proposal because it does not extend to the lengths—unreasonable lengths—expected or demanded by the speaker. For example, if some plan has been proposed to solve some problem, a speaker might attack the plan for not solving other problems that it was not designed to solve. Extension carries an argument or an objection beyond its reasonable limits. As listeners, we must be wary of being taken in by this device.

Here are three examples:

"That plan to redevelop sections of the South Bronx is worthless," said Curt Ale. "It doesn't address the real problems of New York City's fiscal crisis."

"I am opposed to Carter's plan to set up a separate Department of Education," announced Congressman Victor Spoils, "because it couldn't possibly correct what's wrong with education in this country."

Bea A. Freud refused to take a drug to relieve her pain, because, she said, "It won't touch the underlying cause of the disease."

sophistry.   Sophistry is deliberately tricky reasoning. The reasoning may sound good, may (on first hearing) sound valid and reasonable, but it hinges on a trick. It is based on deliberately deceptive arguments. The "reasoning" is clever, slick, and fallacious. Sophistry is cleverly constructed, so it takes a critical, informed, and intelligent listener to detect it. Often the trick relies on ambiguity or a quick but unstated switch in definitions. Or it may be based on a trick definition or a premise that would not stand careful examination.

Here are three examples:

A. Postate recently said he could prove that the god of the Christians was sinful. He "reasoned": "The Christians' god is called 'Our Father.' A father must be a male. If God is a male, then he has sex. If he has sex, which everybody knows is sinful, then he must logically be sinful too."

Billie Saltine "reasoned": "America is a Christian country. If it is a Christian country, then its acts are Christian acts. One of its acts was the attempt to wipe out the Native Americans—the Indians, so obviously the wars against the Indians were acts of Christian charity."

Hope Knott denied that America is a racist country. "A racist country," she reasoned, "is one that treats one race of people unfairly. America treats Blacks, Native Americans, Puerto Ricans, Mexican-Americans, and many other groups unfairly. Therefore, since America does not treat *one* group unfairly, America is not a racist country."

deferring evaluation in observing and listening

In discussing accurate listening, I have already pointed out the need to take one's own biases into account. (See pp. 77–78, 341.) The danger, of course, is that we will start evaluating and refuting incoming messages before we have really considered them.

Early in this text, I discussed with you the concept of empathy. (See pp. 152–157.) That, you remember, is the attempt to see the world from the other person's viewpoint. Empathy is important in listening, because it helps us defer making judgments until we have looked at the message from the standpoint of the speaker.

Carl Rogers calls this kind of listening *active listening*.[6] One must participate with the speaker by imagining how it would make sense to say what the speaker is saying. It requires an acceptance of the speaker as a human being, as a person of worth, and a willingness to give attention, energy, time, and thoughtful consideration to what the speaker is saying.

Charles M. Kelly calls critical listening *deliberative listening,* and he calls the kind of listening that we are considering now *empathic listening*.[7] Personally, I prefer this term; it is the one I have always used, in addition to *nonevaluative responding*. Kelly points out that the term *empathic listening* is something of a redundancy, because all listening, if we are to listen for the maximum possible accuracy (from the other person's point of view), requires empathy. The listener cannot truly understand what the speaker means by what the speaker says unless that listener genuinely attempts to get inside the speaker's thoughts and feelings.

Are you willing to give the other person a full hearing? Are you willing to hear the speaker out without interrupting him or her—either out loud or in your own mind? Are you willing to listen to a speaker step by step rather than assuming that you know what they are going to say from now on and, thus, tuning out? That is anything but empathic listening.

Finally, as a kind of self-inventory, why not make out a list of people and of kinds (or categories) of people you do not want to listen to. Think of all the people (or kinds of people) you would have trouble listening to with an open mind. Then look over your list, find someone in one of those categories, and put yourself to a test. Get in a situation where you must listen to what that person says, and consciously work at getting what that person is saying and feeling—from the person's point of view. That is empathic listening.

[6] Carl Rogers, "Communication: Its Blocking and Facilitating," *Northwestern University Information,* **20** (1952), pp. 9–15.

[7] Charles M. Kelly, "Empathic Listening," *Small Group Communication: A Reader,* Robert S. Cathcart and Larry A. Samovar, eds. (Dubuque, Iowa: William C. Brown, 1970), pp. 340–347.

BARKER, LARRY L., *Listening Behavior* (Englewood Cliffs, N.J.: Prentice-Hall, 1971).

FEARNSIDE, W. WARD, and WILLIAM B. HOLTHER, *Fallacy: The Counterfeit of Argument* (Englewood Cliffs, N.J.: Prentice-Hall, 1959).

MORAY, NEVILLE, *Listening and Attention* (Baltimore: Penguin, 1969).

NICHOLS, R. G., "Do We Know How to Listen? Practical Helps in a Modern Age," *Speech Teacher*, **10** (1961), pp. 118–124.

NICHOLS, R. G., and L. A. STEVENS, *Are You Listening?* (New York: McGraw-Hill, 1957).

WEAVER, CARL, *Human Listening: Processes and Behavior* (Indianapolis: Bobbs-Merrill, 1972).

ANSWERS TO THE QUESTIONS ON P. 337

The correct answer is the same for all of the questions. The answer is *?* The seven statements cannot be known from observing the picture. The first six statements are inferences, and the seventh statement is a value-judgment.

You may insist that you can *see* four people in the picture, so the first statement must be true. But can you see the entire room in the picture? Are you not inferring that the rest of the room has no people in it—if you say that the statement is true? Right. It is a *?* too.

ANSWERS TO THE QUESTIONS ON P. 338

   1. *?*
   2. *?*
   3. *?*
   4. *F*
   5. *?*

Can you figure out what inferences you made or what information you added to the story if you believed any of the unknowable statements to be true?

GLOSSARY

Abstracting Considering a quality apart from the object of which it is a part; separating a quality or aspect of a thing from the thing itself.

Affinity A personal attraction to another person; a feeling of kinship.

Allomorph A variation (variant form) of a morpheme.

Allophone A variant form of a phoneme; there are two kinds of allophones of a phoneme: those that appear only in particular sound contexts and those that can be used interchangeably without affecting the meaning of the word.

Ambiguities Capable of being interpreted in more than one way; words or constructions having at least two possible meanings.

Articulation The process by which the outgoing air stream is divided into distinguishable speech sounds.

Attitudes Orientations: inclinations, biases, or leanings toward or away from something; a tendency or predisposition to react favorably or unfavorably to something.

Attraction A force that tends to draw another person. (See *Affinity* and *Homophily*.)

Audibility Capability of being heard.

Authority A type of supporting material based on "expert" testimony.

Barriers Obstacles to efficient or effective communication.

Beliefs Propositions or statements of principle that one holds to be true or valid; convictions about what is possible, probable, or certain.

Bias An inclination (leaning) toward or away from something; a predisposition in favor of or in opposition to something. (See *Attitude.*)

Black vernacular A nonstandard dialect spoken by economically disadvantaged Black people in the United States.

Breakdowns Malfunctions in communication (from the point of view of the sender); breakdowns are of two kinds: either the receiver did not understand the message as the sender intended it, or the receiver did not comply with the sender's intention and give the intended response. (See *Effective communication* and *Efficient communication.*)

Cause-effect reasoning The process of making inferences that one factor has caused or will cause something else. (Also called *causal reasoning.*)

Central idea (theme) The major theme, thesis, or point of a message; the principal idea represented in a message.

Channel A means by which a message is delivered (conveyed or transmitted) from a sender to a receiver; a vehicle for conveying messages—usually one of the five senses.

Clichés Old, worn-out words and phrases; trite words and phrases that have lost their effectiveness from overuse.

Code A system of signs. (See *Sign, Signal,* and *Symbol.*)

Cognitive dissonance Disagreement or inconsistency between ideas; the situation in which ideas that do not fit together are held at the same time.

Communication A process in which a response is evoked (elicited or induced) by a message sent and received.

Conceptualizing Organizing ideas into categories—either categories of attributes (abstract concepts), such as "laziness," or categories of classes (general concepts), such as "a human being" or "a lazy person"; the process of forming categories out of many separate perceptions.

Concord Interpersonal harmony.

Conflict Interpersonal clash, involving either substantive positions or the individuals' personalities.

Connotation Personal meaning, based on one's experiences, feelings, and attitudes.

Context The physical, social, and cultural environment in which communication occurs.

Cultural conditioning The process by which a group inculcates its norms in a group member.

Culture A group's standardized ways of thinking, feeling, and acting; a group's customary ways of looking at the world and judging behavior; a group's common perspectives and practices.

Decoding The process of translating incoming stimuli into elements of a code; for example, in speech communication, translating received vibrations into speech sounds of a language.

Defensiveness Excessive concentration on protecting oneself from expressed, implied, or imagined criticism or attack.

Denotation Relatively objective meaning.

Description A form of supporting material that involves providing details needed to stir up the receiver's imagination; the use of sensory imagery to support an idea.

Diachronic linguistics The study of language development over a period of time.

Diachronic semantics The study of changes in meaning of words over a period of time.

Dialect A variation of a language spoken by a regional or social group.

Dictionary A book containing words of a given language (usually in alphabetical order), with reports on the common spellings, common pronunciations, and commonly used meanings for the words.

Dyad A two-person group.

Effective communication Communication in which the response desired by the sender is elicited from the receiver.

Efficient communication Communication in which the message intended by the sender is understood by the receiver.

Ego ideal One's picture of what he or she should be.

Empathy The vicarious experiencing of the thoughts, feelings, values, and attitudes of another person.

Enunciation Precision in articulation; how clear and understandable one's speech is.

Environment The physical, social, and cultural situation in which the communication takes place. (See *Context.*)

Epithets Negative labels for categories of people.

Examples A form of supporting material that relies on citing specific typical instances.

Explanation A form of supporting material that provides details to make something clear; details that tell why or how or what—providing analysis, exposition, or definition.

Fact kind of messages Messages that report empirical observations (observations that can be verified by sense perception) and that state directly verifiable information.

Facts Concrete, specific data that can be checked out by sense perception or records of direct observation.

Feedback A response from the receiver(s) that affects the outgoing message of the sender.

Figurative analogy A form of reasoning based on similarities in two things from different categories.

Filters Perceptual screens, the result of conditioning, that help determine what stimuli we select to respond to and how we respond.

Frame of reference A metaphor borrowed from physics. The framework (or general structure) of one's concepts, beliefs, values, and attitudes, by which other ideas are interpreted and evaluated; one's perspective or general outlook; the vantage point from which one views the world ("reality"). (See *World view.*)

Functional varieties of a language Varieties of an idiolect that differ in degree of formality and informality.

Generalizing The process of seeing common attributes in a number of different, individual things. (See *Abstracting* and *Conceptualizing.*)

Gobbledygook (verbosity) Doubletalk; piling up words on top of words for their own sake.

Grammar The descriptive, not prescriptive, study of the patterns used in forming words and sentences in a language.

Hearing Perceiving sound waves primarily by the sensory apparatus of the inner ear.

Heterophily Differences between persons.

Homophily Similarity between persons.

Hostility Tendency to feel anger toward, and to seek to inflict harm upon, some person or group of people.

Human communication Communication in which a human being is involved—as sender, receiver, or both.

Human speech communication Communication through the production and reception of audible, visible, and verbal symbols.

Hyperbole An exaggeration used as a figure of speech; an overstatement used for effect.

Idiolect An individual's own personal variety of a language.

Illustration A form of supporting material that provides one instance with details—often a story, either fictional or true.

Inferences Conclusions reached by logical means; guesses about the unknown, based on what one knows and believes.

Intelligibility Capability of being understood. (See *Enunciation*.)

Interpersonal communication Communication between persons. (The term is often used to include small-group communication as well as dyadic communication.)

Intolerance The inability, or unwillingness, to endure another's existence or being.

Intrapersonal communication Communication within a human being.

Jargon Professional in-group language; shop talk; a kind of professional spoken shorthand.

Kinesics The study of bodily movement in human communication.

A language A specific verbal code; a conventionalized system of arbitrary vocal signs.

Language The use of words to stand for things, actions, relationships, ideas, and feelings.

Listening A popular term for the process of receiving human speech communication from message intake (seeing and hearing) through information storage (remembering).

Literal analogy A form of reasoning based on similarities in two things from the same category (class).

Meaning Significance attached or attributed to a sign (especially a symbol); associations made in the mind of a human being with a symbol. (See *Denotation* and *Connotation*.)

Medium A means of conveying message vehicles (channels) to receivers. (See *Channel*.)

Message Any sign (signal or symbol) capable of being interpreted meaningfully.

Metacommunication Secondary messages, either verbal or nonverbal, that give information about how to interpret the primary message.

Metaphor A figure of speech in which a term is used for something to which it does not usually refer, in order to imply a comparison; figurative language.

Mores Customs of a group that are considered so important to the group that conformity is rewarded and violations are condemned or punished.

Morpheme The smallest meaningful unit in a language; a meaning unit from which words are made; a root, a suffix, or a prefix.

Morphology The study of word formation. (See *Morpheme*.)

Nonspeech communication The attribution of meaning to messages received in some way other than through human speech communication.

Nonstandard dialect A variety of a language that differs from the variety (dialect) spoken by those in positions of prestige and power.

Nonverbal Without words; not in words.

Norms Standards, accepted by a group, for judging behavior; guidelines used by a group that specify appropriate or inappropriate behavior, approvable or unapprovable behavior.

Oral Made by, or related to, the mouth; spoken.

Paralanguage The vocal, but not verbal, aspects of human speech communication, including voice characteristics (variations in pitch, rate, loudness, and quality); vocal holders (nonfluencies meant to hold the listener's attention, such as *um, uh,* and *er* or *er ah*); vocal signals (such as *sh* for "silence," *ssss* for disapproval, *sssst* for "come here," *unh-unh* for "no," and *un-huh* for "yes"); and vocal reflectors (such as groans, moans, sighs, yawns, belchs, whines, throat clearings, and snoring).

Perception Awareness; the process by which a human being attempts to make sense out of incoming stimuli.

Phonation The vibratory process by which sound is produced at the vocal folds.

Phoneme A sound that may distinguish one word from another word; a group of related or similar sounds (phones) that functions as one significant sound in a given language.

Phonetics The study of speech sounds.

Phonology The study of the phonemes (significant sounds) of a language. (See *Phoneme.*)

Pitch The attribute of voice related to highness and lowness, which is based on the number of vibrations per second of the vocal folds.

Prejudice Prejudging; judging something before having sufficient information to use as a sound basis for judgment.

Process An integrated system involving interdependent variables (or elements).

Projection The process of unwittingly attributing one's own traits, attitudes, and feelings to other people.

Pronunciation The uttering of words, including the production of speech sounds and selection of syllables to stress.

Purpose The communicator's goal.

Quality The character of the sound of one's voice; vocal timbre, determined largely by resonance.

Rate Tempo; the number of words one speaks per minute; speaking speed.

Reasoning Moving from one statement to another statement on the assumption that the first statement makes the second statement either inevitable or highly probable.

Receiver Who or what takes in a message.

Reference group Any group with which a person identifies and which exerts an influence on his or her beliefs, values, attitudes, and behaviors.

Referent What a sign stands for (refers to).

Regional dialect A variation of a language spoken by people in a particular region.

Resonation The process by which sound produced at the vocal folds is amplified in the cavities of the head and chest.

Respiration The process of breathing, which forms the motor force behind speech, since we speak on the exhaled air stream.

Response Reaction.

Role The function performed by an individual in a group, including two-person groups (dyads); also, the behaviors characteristic and expected of persons in a defined position in the group.

Selective exposure The process by which one attempts to avoid coming in contact with unacceptable stimuli.

Self-esteem One's feeling of self-worth; self-respect; one's set of attitudes toward one's self.

Self-image What (or who) one thinks oneself to be.

Semantics The study of meaning in language.

Sender The message-producer.

Sign Something that stands for something else.

Sign reasoning Reasoning from observed indicators to unobserved conclusions.

Signal A sign that stands in a one-to-one relationship with the thing represented.

Signal response Reflexive reactions to signs; almost instantaneous, nonthinking responses to signs.

Significant others People who matter to you and who are likely to influence you.

Simple deduction Reasoning from a broad, general principle to a more specific conclusion.

Simple induction Reasoning from a specific instance or example to a general conclusion.

Slang Informal, in-group language.

Social dialect A variation of a language spoken by a social group (such as an ethnic group or a socioeconomic class).

Standard dialect The variety of a language spoken by the people in positions of power and prestige. (Also called *status dialect* or *prestige dialect*.)

Statistics Generalized, relative numbers—usually based on a sampling or survey.

Status Social standing, prestige, power, or influence.

Stereotyping The process of classifying people in terms of ready-made categories and assuming that the people in that category all have the same characteristics.

Stimulus Anything, internal or external to the person, that stimulates (goads, spurs, or stirs) the person to respond.

Style One's distinctive way of doing something (speaking, for example), based on one's choices (the words one selects, for example).

Symbol A sign that suggests several possible meanings. (See *Sign* and *Signal.*)

Symbol response A delayed, thinking (reflective instead of reflexive) reaction.

Synchronic linguistics The study of a language at a specific time.

Synchronic semantics The study of meaning at a specific time or period.

Syntax The study of sentence formation.

Taboo words Words that are forbidden to be spoken in "polite society"; profane words and obscene words that violate linguistic norms.

Transmission The production of message(s).

Unobtrusiveness The quality of not standing out, of not calling attention to itself.

Vague generalities The use of abstract and general words; a level of abstraction so high that it conveys little specific information.

Value judgments Messages that state a rating of something based on one's own personal scale of values; messages that render assessments.

Values Criteria (standards) used in judging ideas, behaviors, events, people, or things; guidelines about what is of worth and what is not of worth.

Verbal In words.

Visual (or visible) Something that can be seen.

Vocabulary A collection of words.

Vocal Related to, or produced by, the human voice.

Volume An attribute of voice related to degree of loudness.

Word A spoken symbol.

World view The organized structure of concepts, beliefs, values, and attitudes from which one views the world; the perspective from which one communicates (both in sending and receiving messages); the vantage point from which one responds to ideas, behavior, and people. (A synonym for *frame of reference.*)

INDEX